X Window Applications Programming

Second Edition

JOHNSON & REICHARD

MIS: PRESS

A Subsidiary of
Henry Holt and Co., Inc.

Second Edition—1992

ISBN Book 1-55828-178-9
ISBN Book/Disk 1-55828-180-9

Printed in the United States of America
10 9 8 7 6 5 4 3 2 1

TRADEMARKS

Acknowledgments

To Penny Johnson Reichard, for her patience, understanding and support when deadlines loomed and nerves were frazzled.

To Mike Wexler, who read through this manuscript thoroughly and made many helpful suggestions. Thanks, Mike, for all the help!

To Julie Swanson at *Computer User* magazine in Minneapolis-St. Paul.

To Steven Berkowitz, Pansy Sapp and all the other good folks at MIS:Press in New York City.

To David Burnette, our supportive editor at *UNIX Review* whose keen editing and suggestions helped us expand our working knowledge of the X Window System.

To all the readers of the first edition of *X Windows Applications Programming,* whose support and helpful suggestions made the second edition possible. If you want to comment on this book, just drop us a note via UUCP mail at kreichard@mcimail.com.

And finally, to Geisha, whose presence at the computer is irreplaceable.

Contents

SECTION IV: X TOOLKITS

Introduction

Welcome to the second edition of *X Window Applications Programming*! Whether you're a beginning X programmer or an experienced programmer wishing to catch up with Releases 4 and 5 of the X Window System, we hope you find this book useful and enlightening.

This book covers the basics of programming in the X Window System. It is the type of book we wanted, but couldn't find, when we first tackled applications written for the X Window System: a book that shows how to easily and painlessly start programming in X. When we started programming X applications, we grabbed and read every available book or article. Most of the material provided a reference to the X library, or Xlib, calls—and not much else. While those books are extremely valuable for advanced X programming, they didn't provide a suitable introduction to X, nor did they provide real-life examples of X programming. How, for example, to draw rubber-band lines (Chapter 10). How, even, to draw a line in blue on the display (Chapter 4). In short, the simple building blocks that lead to more detailed applications.

Throughout this book, we concentrate on showing you how to get things done, and get things done immediately. The X Window System is far too large and complex to deal with completely in one book. (That's why we wrote *Advanced X Window Applications Programming*, the logical successor to this tome.) This is not a pure reference work, but a tutorial describing the key features you will need to get started writing X Window System applications. The emphasis is always on the features necessary for creating real-life applications. We list those features at the end of each chapter, so can you go back and review them if needed.

The X Window System is a large and complex system. Much of that complexity comes from X attempting to deal with virtually every type of computer graphics display available. X also attempts to provide a complete graphics system—complete enough to create windowing interfaces `a la Macintosh, and complete enough to handle graphics-intensive page-design or computer-aided design (CAD) packages.

In some respects, not much has changed since 1989, when we first wrote *X Window Application Programming*. However, the X world has expanded past a small group of technically oriented programmers into a large and diverse group of programmers and users. X is now the windowing system of choice in the workstation and UNIX worlds, and is poised to grow strongly in the microcomputer and minicomputer worlds. Corporations as diverse as IBM, Apple, Sun, Quarterdeck, and Hewlett-Packard are committed to serving the growing X market.

That's because the X Window System helps solve what often seems like an intractable problem: How to provide a common interface across many different computers, running a number of operating systems, with a number of different displays. The computer industry is entering the era of *open systems*, where industry standards are paramount and proprietary architectures are out. X provides a graphical interface that runs on everything from IBM PCs to large mainframes and supercomputers. Cray supercomputers can display their output on DEC or Sun workstation displays. X is not tied to a single vendor—the perfect solution to the problems posed by open systems.

This book is intended for beginners at X, in business and academia, who are:

- Determining the feasibility of committing to the X Window System
- Porting company software to run under X
- Trying to provide a multivendor common look and feel for applications
- Trying to learn more about the basic philosophy behind X
- Beginning applications development under X

In this preface, we'll go over some basic X concepts and structures, as well as the X Window System's history. Don't worry if you aren't ready to jump into X programming after reading this preface; it's merely meant to get you acquainted with the X terminology and environment. Everything mentioned in this introduction will be explained in more detail in later chapters.

THE HISTORY OF X

To gain a conceptual understanding of the X Window System, it's helpful to look at X's history and note the initial goals of the X Window System designers.

In 1984, Massachusetts Institute of Technology (MIT) officials were faced with a problem common to the business- and academic-computing worlds: they were the owners of a motley set of incompatible workstations acquired through donation and purchase. The goal was building a network of graphical workstations that could be used as teaching aids. Faced with a crazy quilt of operating systems and hardware vendors, the decision was made to form Project Athena, an MIT development team working in association with DEC and IBM.

Project Athena's solution was to design a network that would run local applications while being able to call on remote sources—a network that ultimately led to the X Window System—roughly based on a Stanford University software environment called W. By linking together IBMs, DECs, and other disparate workstations through a graphical networking environment, the designers created the first operating environment that was truly hardware- and vendor-independent—the X Window System.

As Robert Scheifler and James Gettys wrote in their *X Window System: The Complete Reference to Xlib, X Protocol, ICCCM, XLFD*, the development team had the following goals when designing X:

- Do not add new functionality unless an implementation cannot complete a real application without it.
- It is as important to decide what a system is not, as to decide what it is. Do not serve all the world's needs, but make the system extensible so that additional needs can be met in an upwardly compatible fashion.
- The only thing worse than generalizing from one example is generating from no examples at all.
- If a problem is not completely understood, it is probably best to provide no solution at all.
- If you get 90 percent of the desired effect for 10 percent of the work, use the simpler solution.
- Isolate complexity as much as possible.
- Provide mechanism rather than policy. In particular, place user-interface policy in the client's hands.

Of these guidelines, the final one is the most applicable to our needs; we'll go into it further when we discuss X Window System philosophies.

The X Window System was a success. By 1986, news of X had spread to the point where the outside world was asking for access. In March 1988, MIT officially released Version 11 Release 2, even though an incomplete release numbered Release 1 appeared earlier in September 1987. The latest version is Release 5, issued in September 1991. (Most of this book covers releases 3 and 4, because most vendors have not upgraded to Release 5 at the time of this writing. Still, we cover selected topics in Release 5 that impact programmers. We've flagged features that were added in Releases 4 and 5, so those who must maintain applications on multiple platforms can tackle the necessary portability dilemmas.) X Window System development is now overseen by the fore-mentioned X Consortium, formed in January 1988.

WHY X NOW?

To a large extent, X Window is the right windowing system at the right time. In the past, hardware on the minicomputer level and down didn't have the horsepower to support such an powerful graphics networking system at an affordable price. With the rise of low-cost, powerful workstations and microcomputers, the X Window System thus becomes a most viable product.

In addition, there are several other reasons why X is a desirable development tool.

A Flexible Windowing System

The X Window System supplies the necessary tools to create a smooth and flexible user interface at a time when users are growing increasingly accustomed to window-style interfaces. Witness the enormous success of the Apple Macintosh and the increasing acceptance for Microsoft Windows on the microcomputer level, coupled with the popularity enjoyed by Sun Microsystems' OpenWindows and Digital Equipment Corporation's DECWindows. Research shows that windowing interfaces are easier to learn and use than character-based interfaces. While X is merely part of the trend toward windowing systems, it has more flexibility and greater potential than any of the fore-mentioned systems.

That's because, to a large extent, those systems are tied to a single hardware environment and a single vendor. As we kick off an era where linking computers of all sorts is a paramount concern for software designers and developers anywhere, those limitations hinder efforts at cross-vendor development. That's not true with the X Window System. X is operating-system independent and network transparent. By separating the window manager and the window server, it's possible to link together disparate makes of hardware without costly emulation cards and exotic networking schemes. Because the user interface is only making X calls, there's no reliance on any operating system.

Why? Because of the designers' original credo of providing mechanism, not policy; the software designer—and, to an extent, the user—has the final say on how exactly the interface will look. Through programming, the application itself defines the window interface and the look and feel of the application. Lawsuits aside, you could set up any kind of interface you want. Looking for icons and windows a la Macintosh? No problem. Looking for something that looks more like NeWS? Again, no problem. As far as X is concerned, the look and feel of the interface is relatively unimportant. X provides the mechanism upon which you can build many different styles of user interface. And many vendors have, from Sun with its OpenWindows to various producers of desktop managers, like IXI X.Desktop and Visix Looking Glass.

This especially becomes important when discussing the X Window System and the UNIX operating system. In the past, UNIX has been accused—and rightfully so—of having a terribly unfriendly and cryptic user interface. With the X Window System as an interface, UNIX applications can be made easier to use. In fact, the same argument can be applied to other operating systems that have been accused of being unfriendly, such as MS-DOS and VMS.

X, by being operating-system independent, encourages the portability of software. The standard X C library routines, called Xlib, are the same on every machine running X. That means your interface code ports directly from one machine to another, as all the X calls are the same. Because the user interface typically takes up 30 to 60 percent of the code, this makes your applications a lot more portable.

Shared Resources

The X Window System allows devices such as mice, keyboards, and graphics displays to be shared by several programs at the same time. Actually, as far as X is concerned, your entire workstation is a display—a display consists of a keyboard, a pointing device (usually a mouse), and one or more monitor screens. Multiple screens can work together, linked by the keyboard and the pointing device.

In addition, X allows greater resources to be shared among a network. A worker using a Sun workstation or a Macintosh can use X to access a supercomputer, with the computing results displayed on the Mac or Sun. Is this a return to the centralized computing of the 1950s and 1960s, with power centered in one powerful machine (in our example, the Cray) and users linked by less-powerful satellites? Conceptually, perhaps, but in the real world, no. X allows the effective use of networked resources. Simple economics dictates that not everyone is going to have the power of a minicomputer—or a mainframe, for that matter—sitting at their desk. Yet there are computational tasks, like weather-pattern projections or other scientific computing, that require very powerful computers. X allows the lesser tasks, like spreadsheet management or word processing, to be performed at the desktop level, while the computational-heavy tasks can be performed on the computer with the proper horsepower.

Uniformity Across Product Lines

As mentioned, the X Window System has been adapted to several different operating systems, including UNIX, MS-DOS, A/UX, Mac OS, and VMS. The X Window System is a standard application execution environment. Well-behaving applications written for one machine don't have to be rewritten for other machines.

The X Window System has been endorsed as a graphic windowing environment by several large computer corporations that formed the X Consortium. The consortium's membership includes full members Apple Computer, AT&T, Bull, Digital Equipment Corp., Hewlett-Packard, IBM, NCR, Sony, Sun Microsystems, and Xerox. In essence, X has been adopted by the major hardware manufacturers as a windowing system of choice.

WHAT IS X?

Now that we've told you why the X Window System is such a fabulous operating environment, we'll give you the conceptual nuts and bolts of the X Window System.

A Client/Server Axis

The X Window System architecture is based on a simple client/server relationship, where the display server is the program that controls and draws all output to the display monitors, tracks client input, and updates your windows accordingly, while clients are application programs that perform specific tasks. Because X is a networked environment, the client and server don't necessarily compute on the same system (although they certainly can and do in a number of situations).

Instead, the X Window System allows distributed processing. For instance, a Sun workstation can run an X server and call upon the processing power of a Cray supercomputer within the network, displaying the results of the Cray's computations on the Sun's monitor.

This is the first time—but not the last—where we find X terminology differing slightly from accepted computer-science terminology. In the microcomputer and minicomputer network worlds, a server is the hardware device running at the center of the network, distributing data and processing power to networked workstations and terminals. For our purposes, a server is a local software program that controls a display. Since other systems on the network have access to your display, the X server cannot be thought of as the same as file servers are thought of in a local-area network (LAN).

We're moving more and more to environments that stretch the definitions of client and server. We have file, printer, mail, terminal, database, and now, with X, graphics servers. Each server provides some form of specialized service to client applications. The confusing part about the X server is the common usage where the server is the big machine in the center of the network. The X server, or display, provides graphics services to applications.

Here, a display is a keyboard, pointing device (usually a mouse), and one or more screens, usually associated with a computer workstation. The display server keeps track of multiple input, allowing users to run several different clients (such as a database manager, word processor, and a graphics application). A display can be running multiple screens, linked together by the keyboard and mouse. But as long as a single user is limited to a single workstation, the multiple screens constitute a single display.

The server acts as the traffic cop between programs (called either clients or applications) running on local or remote systems, and the power of the local system. The server:

- Allows access to a display by other clients.
- Does two-dimensional drawing, freeing up the client from processing-intensive graphics.
- Keeps track of resources (such as windows, cursors, fonts and graphics context) that are shared between clients.
- Allows distributed processing, as mentioned above.
- Allows multitasking, if X is used in conjunction with a multitasking operating system. When used with UNIX, for instance, X allows you to call on UNIX's multitasking capabilities.

- Allows limited communications between cooperating applications, through the means of X properties, selections, and message-passing (covered in depth in *Advanced X Window Applications Programming*).

And, perhaps most importantly, the server tracks input from the display and informs the clients. In X, such inputs are called events. When you press down a key, that's an event; when you let it back up, that's another event. Similarly, when you manipulate your cursor with a mouse, that's still another event. These events are delivered to the applications through an event queue. We'll discuss events in greater detail in Chapter 6.

As mentioned above, clients are applications programs that can be run simultaneously. We use the terms applications and clients interchangeably throughout the book. (There are some specialized X clients, such as window and session managers that don't look much like applications, but all of our programs fit squarely on the application side of things.) A client can use several servers simultaneously, depending on the network configuration.

Unlike many systems, such as the Mac OS, the window manager is the client that oversees the sizing and placing of windows on your display. All X Window System installations should come equipped with at least one window manager, such as `twm`, the Tab Window Manager (and formerly, Tom's Window Manager). `twm` allows you to resize windows, arrange your window order, create more windows, and several other functions. In Chapter 2 we'll explain window managers in more depth.

HOW DOES X RELATE TO MOTIF AND OPEN LOOK?

As we said before, X provides the building blocks, allowing programmers and software designers to create their own interfaces.

The two most popular specifications for interfaces are Open Look (created by AT&T and Sun Microsystems) and Motif (pushed by the Open Software Foundation). Both have their admirers, and their admirers sometimes elevate discussions regarding the two interfaces into something akin to a religious war. Programmers shouldn't have to choose between the two, and they don't have to—thanks to the underlying X Window System.

Both encompass many things: specifications for a specific graphical interface, style guides for providing application consistency, programmer's toolkits and window managers. Both are based on the X Window System. If we dissect Open

Look and Motif, we see that the Motif toolkit is based on the Xt Intrinsics, while Open Look/XView is more closely tied to the X Library. Another Open Look toolkit, the Open Look Intrinsics Toolkit, or OLIT, is based on the Xt Intrinsics like Motif.

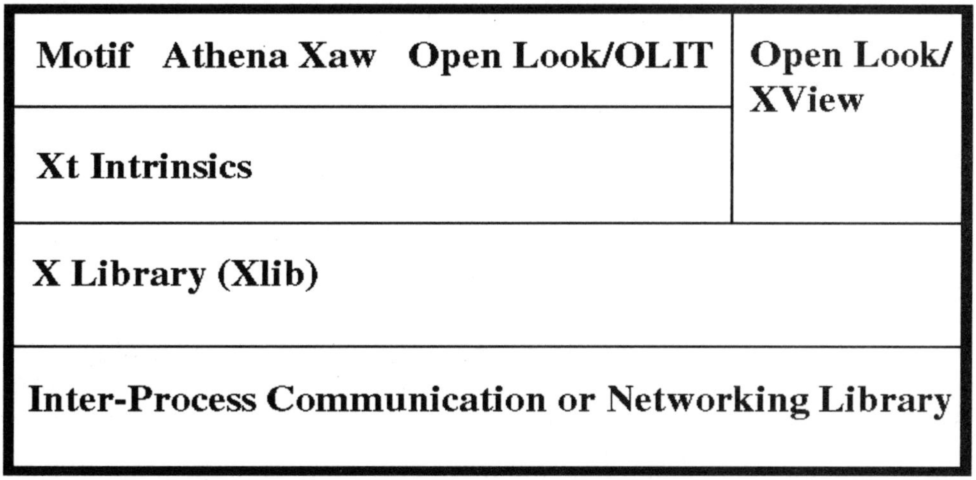

Figure 0.1. Xt-based Toolkits.

Contrary to popular opinion, you can easily run Motif programs on an Open Look system and vice versa, thanks to them both being based on X. You won't have the full look and feel of Motif without the Motif window manager (`mwm`), but you can still run Motif programs. And X programs based on Xlib will run under both the Motif and Open Look window managers. Before tackling either Motif or Open Look programming, we'd advise that you go through this book and master the basics of X before moving up a level. You'll find that even though the Motif and Open Look toolkits provide a great many features, serious applications require you to use the X library as well.

THE SUM OF ITS PARTS

In many ways X is the sum of its parts. By splitting X up into its components, we can return later and see how the components work together.

The generic X Window System as shipped by MIT consists of the Xlib graphics subroutine library, the X network protocol, an X toolkit, and several window managers (described earlier). The application programmer links the client program through Xlib, a library of graphics and window functions.

Xlib

Xlib contains about 400 routines that map to X protocol requests or provide utility functions. Xlib coverts the C language function calls, such as `XDrawLine` to draw a line, to the X protocol requests that implement the given function. These functions include creating, destroying, moving, and sizing windows; drawing lines and polygons (which will be explained in Chapter 3), setting background patterns, and tracking the mouse. It also allows you to access windows in a variety of ways, including overlapping and simultaneous output to multiple windows. It supports multiple fonts, common raster operations, line drawing, and both color and monochrome applications.

X Toolkits

X toolkits are program subroutine libraries that can make programming easier. These toolkits, from such vendors as Hewlett-Packard, AT&T/Sun, IBM/Project Athena, DEC, and Sony, vary slightly and are under constant revision, but there are a lot of similarities between the different implementations. Most toolboxes, for instance, include scroll bars, buttons, pop-up menus, window borders, and dialog boxes. Toolkits will be covered in greater detail in Section IV.

The X Network Protocol

The X network protocol defines data structures used to transmit requests between clients and servers. Technically speaking, the X network protocol is an asynchronous stream-based interprocess communication instead of being based on procedure calls or a kernel-call interface. The applications don't do the work here; the protocol is a function of Xlib. This structure speeds up information exchange.

If you're interested (and, quite frankly, there's no reason to be under most circumstances unless you're debugging), the protocol specification is supplied by the MIT X Consortium on tape (see Appendix E) and defined in *X Window System Protocol, Version 11*, by Robert Scheifler, which is contained as part of the X Window distribution tape. You may already have the document online if you're working on a UNIX system; it can be found on the directory tree under `doc/Protocol/spec`.

Currently the X network protocol is implemented only on DECnet, TCP/IP, and Token Ring, although future implementations with other networking schemes are planned. A few vendors of X terminals support the X protocol over a serial link, such as NCD's Xremote.

THIS BOOK'S APPROACH TO X

This book is organized into 20 chapters that introduce you to key concepts in X Window System programming. Since the best way to learn how to program something is to do it, each chapter includes working source-code examples. We've completely revised all the source code examples from the 1989 edition, bringing them all up to date. We've tested these sources on Releases 3, 4, and 5 of X (as we fully realize that, while the cutting edge is using Release 5—the latest and greatest as of this writing—it will be years until the commercial vendors of X update their systems, and even longer for most users to upgrade). Many users would prefer never to upgrade—subscribing to the philosophy, "If it works, don't fix it." We know what it's like to support software on multiple X platforms, and we've taken the portable approach throughout this book. In Section I, each chapter will describe a standalone program that implements the concepts described in the chapter. In Section II, we cover standards in the X world that your applications should follow. In Section III, each chapter will build on one program, a full-fledged X Window System application. (No, you won't have to program using an ever-present "Hello World" example—if you're really interested in a "Hello World" X programming example, we'll tell you where to find it in the bibliography of X Window System resources.) Section IV introduces the X toolkit sets, including the free Athena widget set and the Motif toolkit. These toolkits are under constant revision, so Section IV will introduce basic toolkit concepts and identify the major suppliers—after that you're on your own. The appendices deal with event types, sample X clients, ordering the X Window System, and an annotated bibliography of X Window System books and articles.

Be warned, however, that we expect you to have a working knowledge of the C programming language. Although there are X Window System implementations in other programming languages, all examples given herein are in C.

TYPOGRAPHICAL CONVENTIONS

In this book, the following typographical conventions have been used:

- C program code references (such as function names and file names) within a text paragraph will appear in a Courier 12-point typeface, as in the following example:

  The function `XDisplayName` will translate the `NULL` into the actual name used by X.

- Actual program examples and listings will appear in monospaced type.

Section I

LEARNING X PROGRAMMING

In this section, we start our programming tutorial with an explanation of the X Window System, followed by the very basics of what you'll need to know to create your own X Window applications. You'll learn how to:

- **Establish a connection to the server**.
- **Create windows**, which is what a windowing system is all about.
- **Draw using X**. After all, X is a graphical interface, and most graphical applications involve drawing.
- **Incorporate color into your X applications**. This includes a description of the X color database, which simplifies matters for the programmer.
- **Draw text and load fonts**. When discussing text, we'll also discuss how to call different fonts through X.
- **Approach events**. Events are how applications know if something happened to the display. You can't program in X without fully comprehending X events and event-driven programming.
- **Create and manipulate cursors for windows**.
- **Create bitmaps, icons, and pixmaps**.
- **Program rubber-band lines**. These are the cornerstone of any mouse-based drawing application.

Chapter 1

BUILDING A FIRST X PROGRAM

X Window System programming begins with an understanding of X's structure. X is a network-oriented window system that divides the workload into two parts: the *server* controls a display screen (or screens), and *clients* (or application programs) requesting services of the server, such as opening windows and drawing lines or text into the windows. All X applications, such as text editors, spreadsheets, and clock displays, are clients of the X server. The X server is normally a separate process. Clients communicate to the server through a connection, usually a network-type connection. The first step in any X program is connecting to the server.

The `XOpenDisplay` function opens up a network connection to the server. This connection could be a TCP/IP socket, a DECnet connection, or perhaps a shared memory link on a local machine, depending on the machine running the X server. (Don't worry about the mechanism—`XOpenDisplay` will set up the proper connection. This is part of the X Window System's much-vaunted portability.)

Connecting to an X server is one of the most confusing operations in X, and it's unfortunate that programmers, end users, and system integrators must begin their X experiences with this procedure. X servers are separate processes that own the screen, keyboard, and mouse. The server allows multiple applications to share the graphics hardware and manages the task of sending keyboard input to the proper applications. Before the X server can do anything for your application, you must establish a communications link to the server, using XOpenDisplay.

XOpenDisplay takes one parameter: the name of the display (server) you want to talk to. (Note that from the X programmer's perspective the terms display and X server are synonymous.) This name is a character string, formatted in a special way. A typical default display is the local machine and screen; if you're using a Sun SPARC workstation with one monitor, the typical default display will be the console screen with the Sun's keyboard and mouse. XOpenDisplay then returns a pointer to a Display structure, which contains information about the display. You can connect to an X server using the code below:

```
#include      <stdio.h>
#include      <X11/Xlib.h>

Display       *display;

display = XOpenDisplay( (char *) NULL );
```

Every C source file that calls the X library (or Xlib) routines should include the header file Xlib.h. By convention, this file will be located in a subdirectory X11, usually in /usr/include/X11 or /usr/local/include/X11 on machines running the UNIX operating system or close variants. (Some of the other header files in the X11 directory will be introduced later, as needed.)

Header File	***Use***
<X11/Xlib.h>	Standard Xlib definitions
<X11/X.h>	X constants, included by Xlib.h
<X11/Xcms.h>	Needed for device-independent color, new in R5
<X11/Xutil.h>	Structures and definitions for well-behaved applications
<X11/Xresource.h>	Defines types for resource-manager functions

Header File	***Use (cont.)***
`<X11/Xatom.h>`	Predefined Atom IDs
`<X11/cursorfont.h>`	IDs for cursors in standard cursor font
`<X11/keysymdef.h>`	Definition of KeySyms
`<X11/keysym.h>`	Defines types of KeySyms; includes `keysymdef.h`
`<X11/Xlibint.h>`	Defines for extended Xlib
`<X11/Xproto.h>`	Types and symbols for X protocol
`<X11/Xprotostr.h>`	Types and symbols for X protocol
`<X11/X10.h>`	Declarations for X10 compatibility functions

Almost all Xlib routines start with a capital X. The `XOpenDisplay` function takes a display name as a parameter and returns a pointer to a `Display` structure. This `Display` pointer will be used in almost every X function call thereafter, as it specifies to which display the X output should go. (Yes, we *are* implying that you can connect to more than one X server at the same time, but this is an advanced topic, so see Chapter 20 in *Advanced X Window Applications Programming*.)

We stated earlier that `XOpenDisplay` takes one parameter—the name of the X server, or display, to connect to. Yet, we passed the constant `NULL` instead of a valid name.

DEFAULT DISPLAY NAMES

The `NULL` parameter tells `XOpenDisplay` to use a preconfigured default display name—whatever that may be. In true UNIX fashion, you're responsible for the preconfiguration. This default name is stored in the `DISPLAY` environment variable, and, ideally, the `DISPLAY` environment variable holds a valid X server name.

Since X is a network-oriented windowing system, you could specify that you want your windows to appear on another display on another machine. For example, you may want to run a numerically intensive client program on a Cray-2 and display the output on a Hewlett-Packard workstation display.

This is very useful if you use `telnet` or `rlogin` to log in to another machine on the network. Even though you've logged in to another machine, you want any X applications you run to send their output to your display—the X server that's right in front of you. You'll often want to change the `DISPLAY` environment variable to make this happen.

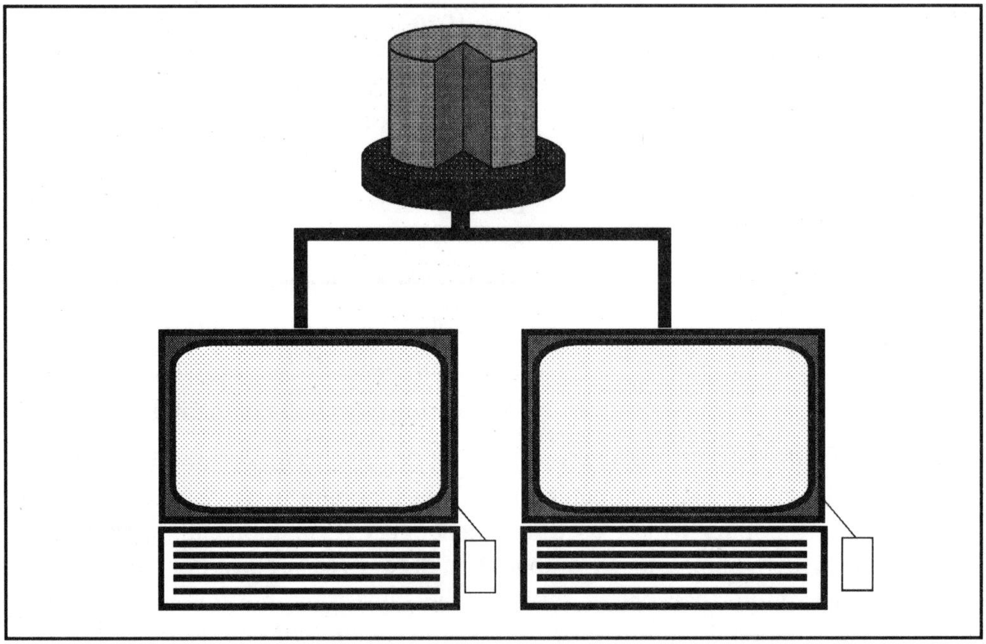

Figure 1.1. Two Computers Connected Over a Network, Running X.

BASIC FORMAT OF DISPLAY NAMES

The basic format of display names is fairly simple. The display name has four parts:

- A *hostname*, the network name of the machine on which the X server computes. For TCP/IP connections, you can also use the internet address, such as 192.6.1.44.
- A *special character*, usually a colon, specifying what network method should be used, such as DECnet or TCP/IP sockets. Two colons (::) means DECnet. One colon (:) usually means Ethernet. Sometimes, though, a special name (unix:0 or just :0.0) means to use UNIX domain sockets (or other high-speed local protocol) to connect to the X server.
- A *number* telling to which X server you want to connect, of the many that could be running on one host. X servers start counting at zero, so the first X server has a number of 0.
- A *screen number*. Remember that screens are usually physical monitors, and that one X server can control a number of monitors tied together with one

keyboard and pointing device, such as a mouse. This concept of multiple monitors, as we described above, can be very confusing. Some systems have two (or more) monitors for one keyboard and mouse. These twinheaded systems are often used for computer-aided design, or CAD. In this case, you'll need to tell `XOpenDisplay` on which of the many monitors—called *screens* in X jargon—you want your applications to appear. The screen number begins with a decimal point (or period), and then follows with the number. Remember to start counting at zero. If you have only one screen, then you can skip the screen number.

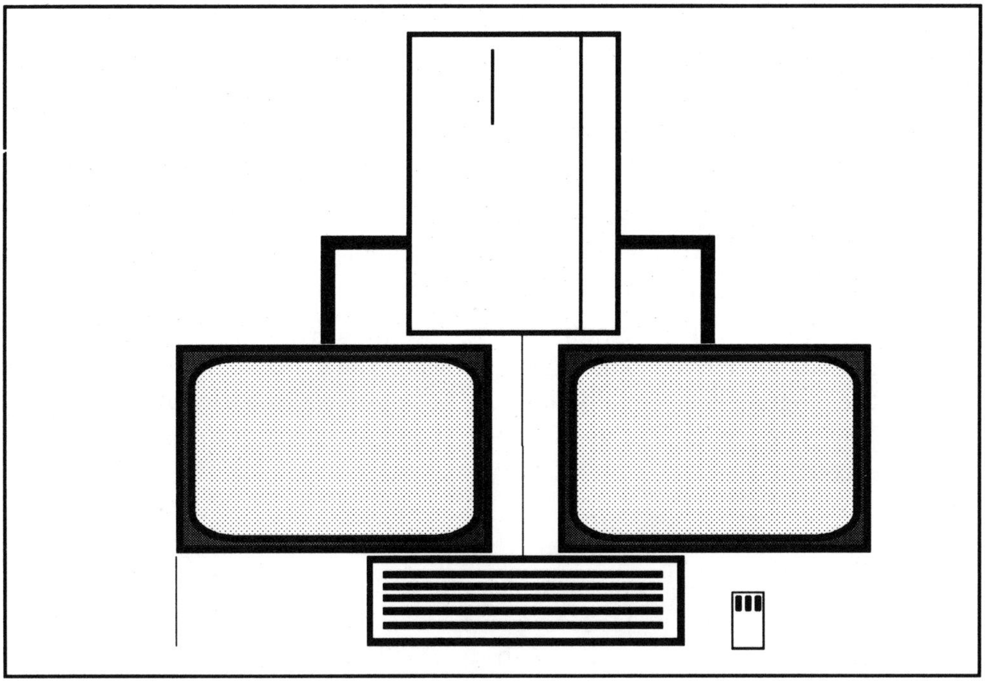

Figure 1.2. A Multiheaded X Server.

These rules seem complex, but you'll find that it simpler in practice. For instance, the first X server on a machine named `nokomis` would have an X display name of `nokomis:0.0`.

If the machine `nokomis` has two monitors for the X server, and you wanted your application's windows to appear on the second monitor, you'd use a display name of `nokomis:0.1`. If you're just using screen 0, you can use `nokomis:0`.

If your machine supports multiple users, and you are using the second X server, you would have a display name of `nokomis:1`.

X1 Release 5 uses `:0.0` as the default display name, while previous releases used `unix:0`.

THE DISPLAY ENVIRONMENT VARIABLE

You'll often set the `DISPLAY` environment yourself using a command, such as the C shell's `setenv`. If your command interpreter shell is `csh`, the following command will set the `DISPLAY` environment variable to the first X server on a machine with a hostname of `nokomis`:

```
setenv DISPLAY nokomis:0.0
```

The `DISPLAY` environment variable is extremely important. Without it, you'll need to pass the proper X server name every time you call `XOpenDisplay`, as well as passing the display name as a command-line parameter to every X application. (We cover this topic further in Chapter 11.)

For now, though, the default display should suffice. If `XOpenDisplay` returns a `NULL` pointer, no connection was made. You can assume something went wrong. The program is essentially finished, since no windows can run without first establishing a connection to an X server. You can check for success with the following code:

```
if ( display == (Display *) NULL )
        {
        fprintf( stderr,
              "ERROR: Cannot connect to X server [%s]\n",
              XDisplayName( (char *) NULL ) );
        exit( 1 );
        }
```

The function `XDisplayName` will translate the `NULL` into the actual name used by X, based on the value of the `DISPLAY` environment variable.

```
char    *display_name;
char    *ptr;

ptr = XDisplayName( display_name );
```

THE DEFAULT SCREEN

After establishing a display connection, you must determine on which screen your application is running. Some computers, such as the Sun 3 family, allow multiple screens for one X server. The `Display` pointer returned by `XOpenDisplay` contains this data, as well as other useful information. Screens are numbered, starting at zero. The `DefaultScreen` macro returns the screen number for the default screen. Since 99 percent of all X servers support just one screen, chances are this number is zero.

```
Display      *display;
int          screen;

screen = DefaultScreen( display );
```

THE ROOT WINDOW

Each X screen contains a root window covering the entire screen. You can think of the root window as a sort of screen background. When you want to change your screen background, using a program such as *xsetroot*, you're really changing the root window.

Finding the ID of the root window is necessary when opening any application windows. The macro `RootWindow` returns the root window ID for a given screen on a given display:

```
Display      *display;
int          screen;
Window       rootwindow;

rootwindow = RootWindow( display, screen );
```

A FUNCTION THAT OPENS A DISPLAY CONNECTION

We've created a function, `ConnectToServer`, that connects to an X server. (We'll use this function throughout the rest of the book.) `ConnectToServer` takes the display name of the X server and returns a `Display` pointer, the default screen number and the root window on the default screen. `ConnectToServer` returns a non-int type, so you'll need to predeclare `ConnectToServer` wherever this routine is used, with:

```
Display *ConnectToServer();
```

`ConnectToServer` is in the file `connect.c`:

```
/*
 *      connect.c
 *      Code to connect to an X server.
 *
 *      Written for X Window Applications
 *      Programming, 2nd Edition
 */

#include <stdio.h>
#include <X11/Xlib.h>

Display *ConnectToServer( display_name, screen, rootwindow )

char    display_name[];   /* name of display */
int     *screen;          /* RETURN: default screen */
Window  *rootwindow;      /* RETURN: root window */

/*
 *      Sets up a connection to an X server (called a
 *      Display), and then gets the default screen
 *      number and root window ID on that display
 *      and screen.
 *
 *      display_name names the X server to connect to.
 *
 *      If the display_name is NULL, then the value of
 *      the DISPLAY environment variable is used.
 *      XOpenDisplay does this automatically.
 */

{       /* ConnectToServer */
        Display *display;

        /*
         * Connect to X server
         */
        display  = XOpenDisplay( display_name );
```

```
        /*
         * Check for errors. We assume a failure
         * to connect is a fatal error.
         */
        if ( display == (Display *) NULL )
             {
             (void) fprintf( stderr,
                "Cannot connect to X server [%s]\n",
                XDisplayName( display_name ) );

             exit( 1 );
             }

        /*
         * Get the screen number
         */
        *screen = DefaultScreen( display );

        /*
         * Get the ID of this screen's root window
         */
        *rootwindow = RootWindow( display, *screen );

        return( display );

}       /* ConnectToServer */

/* end of file connect.c */
```

EXPLORING THE X ENVIRONMENT

Once you've established a connection to the X server, you should ask if it supplies color planes or only monochrome and the size of the display screen. If the display screen is 640 by 480 pixels (as on a Macintosh IIx) you don't want to create a window at pixel location 800, 800, because that location wouldn't be on the screen.

The number of bit planes (for color or grey-scale monitors) is returned by the macro `DefaultDepth`.

```
Display      *display;
int          screen;
int          depth;

depth = DefaultDepth( display, screen );
```

If the depth is `1`, you have a monochrome system (or at least a monochrome default visual—see Chapter 4 for more information on visuals). If the depth is greater than one, you may have a color system or a grey-scale system with a number of shades of grey. Unfortunately, the `DefaultDepth` macro doesn't distinguish between the two. Determining if you have color available is very important for good-looking applications. (We'll show how to determine if you have a color system in Chapter 4.)

The size of the screen is returned from two macros: `DisplayWidth` and `DisplayHeight`.

```
Display       *display;
int           screen;
int           width, height;

width     = DisplayWidth( display, screen );
height    = DisplayHeight( display, screen );
```

These macros return the size of the display in pixels (or picture elements), the number of dots on the screen in the vertical (`DisplayHeight`), and horizontal (`DisplayWidth`) directions.

You can check for the actual size of the monitor, in millimeters, by using the `DisplayHeightMM` and `DisplayWidthMM` macros.

```
Display       *display;
int           screen;
int           width_mm, height_mm;

width_mm      = DisplayWidthMM( display, screen );
height_mm     = DisplayHeightMM( display, screen );
```

Creating true WYSIWYG (or what-you-see-is-what-you-get) applications depends on this information. Unfortunately, the values returned by these macros are fraught with error. Usually these numbers are hard-coded so that you cannot tell the difference if the user has a 16-inch monitor or a 19-inch monitor.

Other useful information includes the vendor who wrote the X server and the vendor's X server version and release number. As of this writing, the most recent version of X is Version 11, Release 5. Many commercial servers are still at releases 3 or 4. (All of the code is this book was tested on releases 3, 4, and 5.)

```
Display       *display;

(void) printf( "%s version %d of the X Window System\n",
```

```
        ServerVendor( display ),
        VendorRelease( display ) );
```

The ServerVendor macro returns a string that usually contains a vendor name, such as `MIT X Consortium` or `Apple Computer, Inc.` Some X terminals, though, lie about their `ServerVendor` information to fool certain software. Don't depend on the accuracy of `ServerVendor`.

The `VendorRelease` macro is a number for the vendor's version of the server. This `VendorRelease` number has nothing to do with the X release number, such as R4 or R5. R4 and R5 refer to releases from the MIT X Consortium. Most UNIX vendors, for example, take the generic MIT release and customize it for their workstation platforms. Thus the `VendorRelease` number for Hewlett-Packard systems will follow HP's numbering scheme, while the VendorRelease number for Data General systems will follow DG's different numbering scheme. This number is mainly useful when providing bug reports to the vendor.

Other somewhat useful information is the X network protocol version numbers, obtained through this macro:

```
Display     *display;

(void) printf( "X protocol %d.%d\n",
        ProtocolVersion( display ),
        ProtocolRevision( display ) );
```

The `ProtocolVersion` macro should return the network protocol version (or major) number—in this case 11. The `ProtocolRevision` macro is less clear; it appears it should return the release number, but instead usually returns a `0`, since there's been no revision of the X network protocol (everyone "extends" the protocol, rather than revises it).

For the generic MIT X Consortium release, the `ProtocolVersion` returns `11`, the `ProtocolRevision` returns `0`, and the `VendorRelease` returns `5000` for X11 R5. In Release 4 from the MIT X Consortium, `VendorRelease` returns `4` (you apparently gain 4996 releases between R4 and R5). If your X server comes from a vendor (as opposed to the X Consortium), you might have a hard time figuring out if you are running X11 R3 or R4. `VendorRelease` is not a good way to try to determine what release of the X library you are using. (In fact, we found no good way to tell this from within an application at runtime, until Release 5, with `XlibSpecificationRelease`.

Starting with Chapter 2, we'll use a hard-coded symbol. This isn't the most elegant solution, but it works.)

New X releases add new rules and new functions, often making older functions obsolete. The upgrade from R3 to R4, for example, involved substantial incompatible changes. (You can still use the older, compatible functions, but you're advised against it.) In addition, most vendor releases correspond to an MIT X Consortium release, but not all do.

THE "COLORS" BLACK AND WHITE

Every X server preallocates at least two colors: black and white. These colors may not even look like the black and white we're all used to, but these colors are supposed to contrast, so you can write text in one color on a background of the other color and have the text be able to be seen by a human observer. You can create a monochrome application with a minimum of work, although using color is a much more complex procedure. We'll use black and white exclusively until we get to Chapter 4 and discuss color.

Different X servers allocate different spots in their color tables for black and white. This will become important in Chapter 9, where we cover icons and bitmaps. For now, we'll just print out the color numbers associated with black and white. The macros `BlackPixel` and `WhitePixel` return the default color indexes in the default colormap for black and white, respectively. These color indexes are unsigned long ints.

```
Display         *display;
int             screen;
unsigned long   black, white;

black = BlackPixel( display, screen );

white = WhitePixel( display, screen );
```

Many times these numbers will be `0` and `1` (or `1` and `0`, respectively), since black and white are usually the first two colors allocated. Some vendors, like Data General, use 0 for black and 255 for white (see the end of this chapter). There's nothing wrong with this, but you can't assume black and white will be assigned to any particular color index numbers.

CLOSING THE DISPLAY CONNECTION

When you are done with the connection to the X server (usually at the end of your program), it is a nice practice to close the connection gracefully. `XCloseDisplay` closes a connection to an X server. Once you call `XCloseDisplay`, the `Display` pointer is no longer valid.

```
Display      *display;

XCloseDisplay( display );
```

When your program terminates under most versions of UNIX, the operating system usually breaks all connections by closing all open file descriptors. This makes the call to `XCloseDisplay` technically unnecessary. Since X runs on more than one operating system and you don't know if this capability is built into the operating system (in theory, your applications shouldn't depend on a particular operating system), it's a good idea to call `XCloseDisplay`.

THE FIRST X PROGRAM CODE

The first X program presented here opens a connection to the X server and then reports some information about the server. The code is built up in two C program files: `chap1.c` and `connect.c`.

We split the code into two sections in order to isolate the functions. Throughout this book, we'll follow a similar structure. The various parts of any program will be separated into modules, with the full intent of reusing (or enhancing) some of the modules later. Also, each chapter will contain chapter-specific code that we won't be reusing.

The file `chap1.c` contains the meat of the first program. It contains two functions, `main` and `PrintXInfo`. `PrintXInfo` gets some information about the server and prints that information. We assume here that the program will be called from an *xterm* window (so that `printf` will work properly). *xterm* is a client application program running under X. It provides a shell terminal into the UNIX operating system (or whatever operating system your machine runs) to run standard terminal-oriented programs such as the *vi* editor or the C compiler. In this case, *xterm* provides `stdout` for our application to use.

Contents of the file `chap1.c`:

```
/*
 *      chap1.c
 *      Example program for Chapter 1.
 *      Opens a display connection and
 *      then prints out info about the X
 *      server and the hardware it runs on.
 *
 *      Written for X Window Applications
 *      Programming, 2nd Edition
 */

/*
 *      UNIX/Posix include files.
 */
#include <stdio.h> /* For NULL */

/*
 *      Just about all X programs
 *      need to include Xlib.h.
 */
#include <X11/Xlib.h>

main( argc, argv )

int     argc;
char    *argv[];

{       /* main */
        Display *display;
        Display *ConnectToServer(); /* connect.c */
        Window  rootwindow;
        int     screen;

        /*
         * Connect to default X server
         */
        display = ConnectToServer( (char *) NULL,
                &screen,
                &rootwindow );
```

```
        /*
         * Get and print information about the
         * X server we connected to.
         */
        PrintXInfo( display, screen );

        /*
         * Close connection to X server
         */
        XCloseDisplay( display );

}       /* main */

PrintXInfo( display, screen )

Display      *display;
int          screen;

/*
 *      PrintXInfo prints information to
 *      the starting terminal (usually an xterm),
 *      that is, stdout, about the current X
 *      Window display and screen.
 */

{       /* PrintXInfo */
        int  depth;

        /*
         * Print information on the server's
         * version. Don't always trust the
         * string returned by ServerVendor,
         * since some X servers cheat, pretending
         * to be something they're not.
         */

        (void) printf( "%s version %d of the %s\n",
             ServerVendor( display ),
             VendorRelease( display ),
             "X Window System" );
```

```
/*
 * Print information on the X protocol version.
 * In most cases, this will be 11.0.
 */
(void) printf( "X protocol %d.%d\n",
     ProtocolVersion( display ),
     ProtocolRevision( display ) );

/*
 * Get the number of "color" or grey-scale planes.
 * If only 1, then we have a monochrome system.
 * If > 1, we still may not be color, but instead
 * grey scale (or something similar).
 */
depth  = DefaultDepth( display, screen );

if ( depth == 1 )
     {
     (void) printf( "Color plane depth....%d (mono)\n",
        depth );
     }
else
     {
     (void) printf( "Color plane depth....%d\n",
        depth );
     }

/*
 * Get the size of the screen in pixels.
 */
(void) printf( "Display Width........%d pixels\n",
      DisplayWidth( display, screen ) );
(void) printf( "Display Height.......%d pixels\n",
      DisplayHeight( display, screen ) );

/*
 * Black and white are normally preallocated, but
 * sometimes use different numbers.
 */
(void) printf( "Black................%ld\n",
     BlackPixel( display, screen ) );

(void) printf( "White................%ld\n",
     WhitePixel( display, screen ) );
```

```
        /*
         * Get the name of the display, usually unix:0
         */
        (void) printf( "For the display [%s]\n",
             XDisplayName( display ) );

}       /* PrintXInfo */

/* end of file chap1.c */
```

COMPILING AND LINKING THE EXAMPLE PROGRAM

Compile and link the example program with a command like:

```
        cc -o chap1 chap1.c connect.c -lX11
```

You can also use the Makefile in Appendix A, and type:

```
make chap1
```

or

```
make all
```

to compile and link all the example programs. (You'll probably need to configure this Makefile first; look in Appendix A). We strongly suggest you get the Chapter 1 program running, so that you can determine any extra steps you'll need to compile and link X Window programs.

Every X program in this book requires you to link in the X library, usually a file called `libX11.a` in the `/usr/lib` directory, but your system may have this library in a nonstandard place. Using Sun's OpenWindows X product, you'll probably need to look in `$OPENWINHOME/lib`. The X include files, namely `Xlib.h`, should be stored in `/usr/include/X11` on a standard installation, and `$OPENWINHOME/include` with OpenWindows. You should also check that your `LD_LIBRARY_PATH` and `OPENWINHOME` environment variables are set up properly.

If you're using X11 Release 5 on systems that don't have an ANSI C compiler, you may need to define X_WCHAR to specify that your system doesn't define `wchar_t`.

This first program may seem overly simplistic, but we have a strong reason for starting with this method: You should test the X setup on your machine. If the compiler cannot find the X `include` files, for example, you'll have to deal with this problem before you can move on.

The other area of concern is finding the X library (`X11`) for the link phase. If you have problems in these regards, check with your system administrator. (That sounds like a cop-out, but each machine may have a different setup. In most cases, the `include` files are in `/usr/include/X11` and the library is in `/usr/lib` or `/usr/lib/X11`, if you are running X under the UNIX operating system.) On the Data General Aviion, the X libraries may be in `/usr/opt/X11/lib`, requiring a command like:

```
cc -o chap1 chap1.c connect.c -L/usr/opt/X11/lib -lX11
```

COMPILING ON 386 UNIX PLATFORMS

Popular 386/486 UNIX System V platforms often need special compile and link options. Esix System V R4 wants a command like:

```
cc -DSYSV -DSVR4_0 -Di386 -o chap1 chap1.c \
     connect.c -lX11 -lsocket -lnsl -lns
```

SCO Open Desktop wants a similar command:

```
cc -DSYSV -Di386 -DLAI_TCP -o chap1 chap1.c \
     connect.c -lX11 -ltlisock -lsocket -lnsl_s
```

Interactive 386/ix wants the `inet` library linked in:

```
cc -o chap1 chap1.c connect.c -lX11 -linet
```

If you must use special options, we strongly suggest you enter this option into the Makefile once, and avoid typing the complex command lines for every program.

RUNNING THE FIRST EXAMPLE PROGRAM

This first program makes sure you can compile and link X programs, as well as show if the X server is up and running. Here's some sample output of the first example program.

Sun SPARCStation-1, under SunOS 4.0.3c, running MIT X Consortium X11 R5:

MIT X Consortium version 5000 of the X Window System
X protocol 11.0

Color plane depth	8
Display Width	1152 pixels
Display Height	900 pixels
Black	1
White	0

For the display [:0.0]

Data General Aviion 410 under DG-UX 4.32 running Data General's X11 R4:

Data General Corporation version 440 of the X Window System
X protocol 11.0

Color plane depth	8
Display Width.	1280 pixels
Display Height	1024 pixels
Black	0
White	255

For the display [unix:0.0]
(Note that White is 255, not 1 as expected. Expect the unexpected with X.)

PC compatible running Hummingbird Exceed/Plus X Terminal Software running Hummingbird's X11 R4:

Hummingbird Communications Ltd. version 0 of the X Window System
X protocol 11.0

Color plane depth.	4
Display Width	800 pixels
Display Height	600 pixels
Black	0
White	1

For the display [mryuk:0.0]

SUMMARY

All X applications start by setting up a connection to the X server. This involves a basic call with `XOpenDisplay`. At this time, you'll want to ask the X server to provide basic information about itself, including version and release numbers, if color is supported, and the size of the screen.

XLIB FUNCTIONS AND MACROS INTRODUCED IN THIS CHAPTER

```
BlackPixel
DefaultDepth
DefaultScreen
DisplayHeight
DisplayHeightMM
DisplayWidth
DisplayWidthMM
ProtocolRevision
ProtocolVersion
RootWindow
ServerVendor
VendorRelease
WhitePixel
XCloseDisplay
XDisplayName
XOpenDisplay
```

Chapter 2

CREATING WINDOWS

Creating windows is what a windowing system is all about. And the X Window System primarily handles windows—rectangles on the screen that can be drawn into, can overlap, and can be stacked on top of one another.

Unfortunately, creating a window is an involved process under X. The reason for the complexity is X's stated goal of providing mechanism, not policy, for user-interface design. This usually translates to each X library function presenting a confusing array of options and parameters. To create a window, you must make a number of choices, from the simple—where should it go—to the complex things, such as the attributes of the window's border (thick, thin, or nonexistent; red, blue, or black; and so on).

Windows are data structures stored in the X server. The server handles clipping to window boundries and manages a display made up of multiple, overlapping windows.

Windows can have *child windows*, or *subwindows*. These window children are clipped to the boundries of their parent windows. In all other respects, they act as full-fledged windows. In fact all windows, except for the root window, are child windows. Your top-level application windows will be children of the root window.

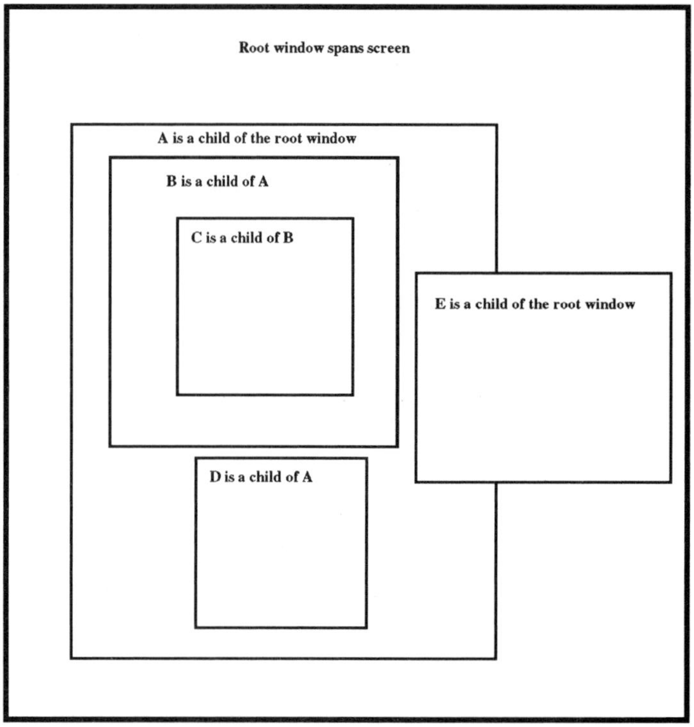

Figure 2.1. Windows and Child Windows.

In your applications, each window is identified by an ID of the `Window` type (usually an unsigned long 32-bit integer). Once this window identifier is returned from X, it is used to specify in which window you want to draw in later drawing calls. To get a window ID, you need to create a window or use the system-wide default root window.

THE ROOT WINDOW

Each X screen has a *root window*, which spans the entire screen. This is the highest-level ancestor of all other windows on a given screen. The macro `RootWindow`, introduced last chapter, returns the Window ID of this default window. You can use this window ID, to a limited extent, like any other window ID. You can draw into it or change its background. Normally, though, your applications won't mess with the screen background formed by the root window. Instead, you'll want to create your own windows to hold spreadsheet data and so forth.

CREATING WINDOWS

Creating or opening a window on the display forms a complex task. To hide most of the sticky details, we'll create a function, `OpenWindow`, to handle the details of creating a window and then placing it on the screen. By placing the details within the `OpenWindow` function, much of the complex specifics of window creation are isolated from the other code.

The X library provides two window-creation functions, `XCreateSimpleWindow` and `XCreateWindow`.

```
#include <X11/Xlib.h>

Display          *display;
Window           parent_window;
int              x, y;
unsigned int     width, height, border_width;
unsigned long    border_pixel, background_pixel;

window = XCreateSimpleWindow( display,
             parent_window,
             x, y, width, height,
             border_width,
             border_pixel,
             background_pixel );
```

`XCreateSimpleWindow` returns the window identifier (of type `Window`) or `None`, a constant defined as `0`, if the call was not successful (for example, if the X server is out of memory). The first parameter to `XCreateSimpleWindow` defines the target display (remember, X can run multiple displays on multiple machines). This pointer was returned by `XOpenDisplay`, which we covered in the last chapter.

The next parameter is the parent for the new window. If you are creating a subwindow for an application, then the parent is obvious. The first window your program creates, however, appears to have no parent (it is a top-level window). In this case, you use the root window as the parent. The macro `RootWindow` returns the Window ID for this window.

Next, `XCreateSimpleWindow` asks for the location of the window. All locations in X are given in pixels. For any rectangular shape (such as a window or a box), this pixel location is the upper-left corner. X also gives sizes in pixels, and most routines call for a width and height (in pixels) to specify a size. Note that, even though the values for width and height are unsigned ints, never use a size greater than 32,767 pixels. The screen may not be big enough for your request, so X may change it. In addition, the window manager, such as mwm (the Motif window manager), controls windows on the display. The window manager has the option of arbitrarily changing where your window will go. It's best to view all parameters sent to an X server as requests, which may or may not be honored.

In the X Window System, the origin 0,0 is located in the upper-left corner of the screen. The X coordinate gains in size going right, and the Y coordinate gains going down.

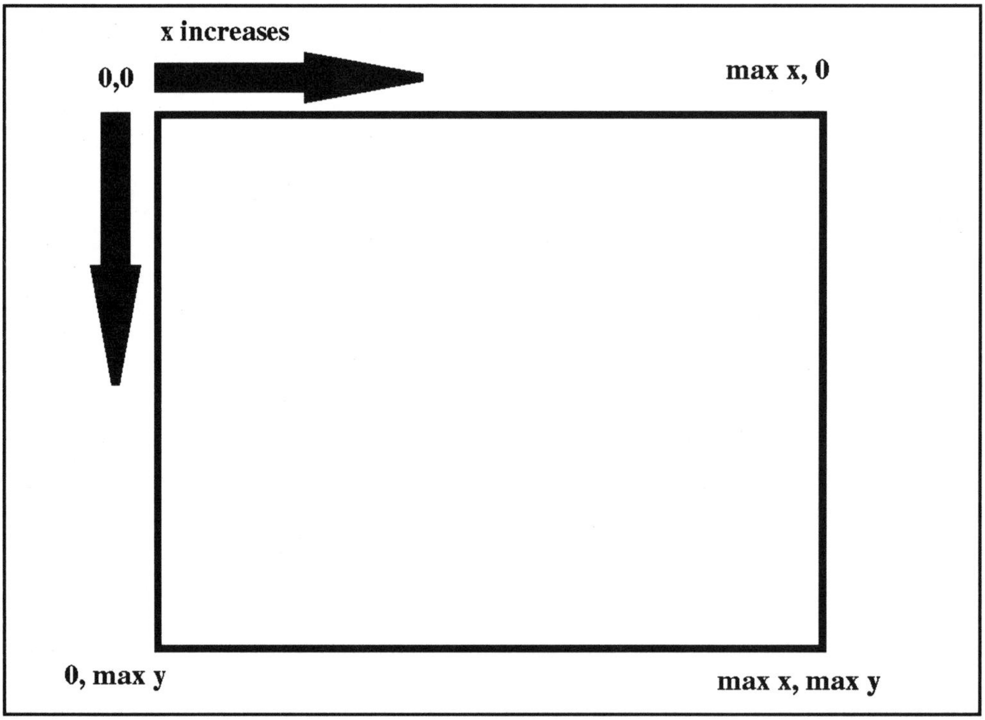

Figure 2.2. The X Window Coordinate System.

The border_width is the number of pixels wide that the window's border should be. If you're creating a child of the root window (that is, parent_window is the root window), window managers may override the border width.

The border_pixel is the color index of the border. The term *pixel* here is confusing, but it's used throughout X Window documentation. Here, pixel refers to an index number in a colormap, just like the black and white we covered last chapter.

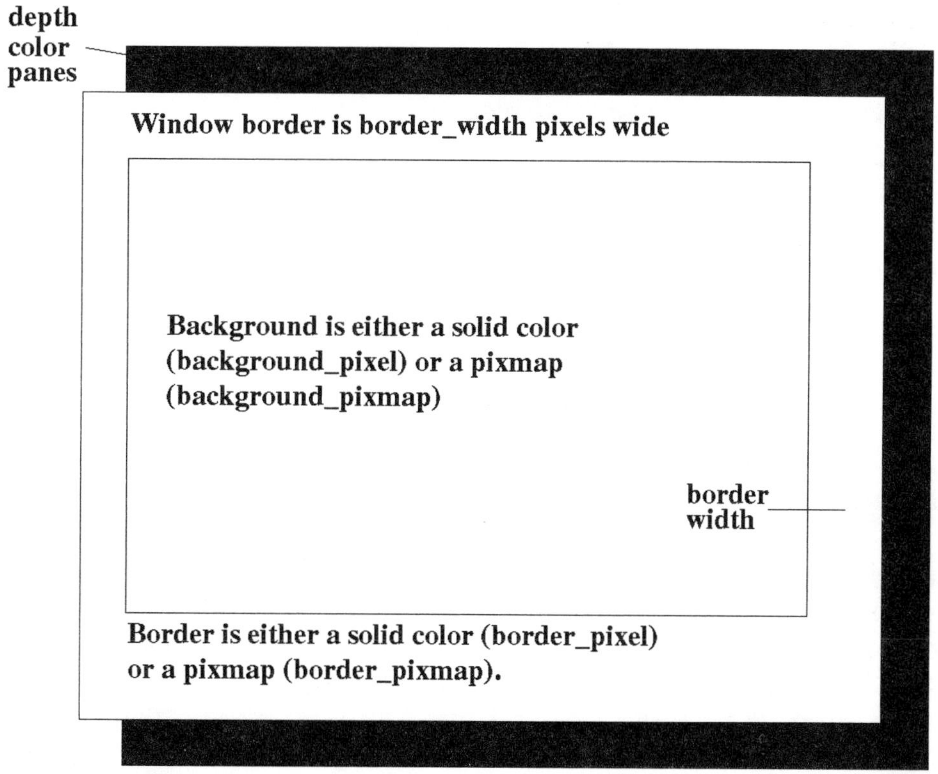

Figure 2.3. Anatomy of a Window.

Similarly, the `background_pixel` identifies the color of the window's background.

`XCreateSimpleWindow` takes the fewest parameters and is generally simpler than `XCreateWindow`. Any options not included in `XCreateSimpleWindow` are inherited from the `parent_window`. But `XCreateSimpleWindow` isn't adequate for most X applications. Instead, we'll use `XCreateWindow` exclusively.

```
#include <X11/Xlib.h>

Display               *display;
Window                parent_window;
int                   x, y;
unsigned int          width, height;
unsigned int          border_width;
int                   depth;
```

```
unsigned int          class;
Visual                *visual;
unsigned long         valuemask;
XSetWindowAttributes  *attributes;

window = XCreateWindow( display,
             parent_window,
             x, y, width, height,
             border_width,
             depth,
             class,
             visual,
             valuemask,
             attributes );
```

`XCreateWindow` is similar to `XCreateSimpleWindow`. Most of the parameters are the same, so we'll cover only the new ones.

The depth parameter specifies the number of color planes. It is a good idea to use the system default depth, by passing the constant `CopyFromParent`. `CopyFromParent` means to use the depth of `parent_window`. However, X servers don't support all possible depths, and you can easily generate an error if you don't pass a proper depth. `CopyFromParent` is safe.

The class can be the constant `InputOutput`, `InputOnly`, or `CopyFromParent`. Virtually all windows are `InputOutput` class (or type), meaning you can draw output and accept keyboard and mouse input. Transparent windows (often used for drawing rubber-band lines) are called `InputOnly` windows.

The visual describes an abstract model for graphics hardware capabilities, usually associated with color. There are many choices here, but for now we'll use `CopyFromParent`.

The next value is a mask value, specifying which values from the `XSetWindowAttributes` structure are actually used (the rest will take on default values). This mask is made up of *bit-flags*, where each bit indicates whether a certain field in the structure is filled or not. In most cases, you join the various bitmask constants for the fields you fill in by using `OR`.

Xlib makes frequent use of masks to specify which values in a complex structure are actually filled in. Unfortunately, sometimes the mask is part of the structure, and sometimes, as in the `XSetWindowAttributes` structure, the mask is not. The final parameter is then a pointer to the `XSetWindowAttributes` structure set up above.

The `XSetWindowAttributes` structure looks like:

```
typedef struct {
     Pixmap              background_pixmap;
     unsigned long       background_pixel;
     Pixmap              border_pixmap;
     unsigned long       border_pixel;
     int                 bit_gravity;
     int                 win_gravity;
     int                 backing_store; /* NotUseful,WhenMapped, Always */
     unsigned long       backing_planes;
     unsigned long       backing_pixel;
     Bool                save_under; /* should bits under be saved? */
     long                event_mask;
     long                do_not_propagate_mask;
     Bool                override_redirect;/* override window manager? */
     Colormap            colormap;
     Cursor              cursor;
     } XSetWindowAttributes;
```

The first step in creating an X window is setting up a few attributes. In this first example, we will concentrate on only a few—more will come later. A mask, described above, tells X which parts of the structure are used and which are unused, so you do not need values for all the structure's fields. The attributes are placed in an `XSetWindowAttributes` structure:

```
#include <X11/Xlib.h>
#include <X11/Xutil.h>

Display                 *display;
int                     screen;
XSetWindowAttributes    attributes;
unsigned long           attr_mask;

/*
 * Set up window attributes before creating window.
 */
attributes.event_mask  = ExposureMask;
attributes.border_pixel = BlackPixel( display, screen );
attributes.background_pixel = WhitePixel( display, screen );

/*
 * Set up attribute mask for the fields we
```

```
 * are actually using. OR together the
 * mask flag values. Don't confuse
 * CWBackPixel with CWBackingPixel!
 */
attr_mask = CWEventMask | CWBackPixel | CWBorderPixel;
```

Setting the `border_pixel` field tells X we want a black border for the window. As we stated in the last chapter, all X servers have at least two colors defined by macros: `BlackPixel` and `WhitePixel`. These do not have to be black and white, but should at least be different colors. The advantage of using the `BlackPixel` and `WhitePixel` macros is that they should have values on all X displays—monochrome, grey scale, or color—making the code portable between monochrome and color displays. In the above code section, the window border is set to `BlackPixel`, and the inside background of the window is set to `WhitePixel`.

THE EVENT MASK

We set an event mask of `ExposureMask` to ask for *`Expose` events*. `Expose` events are generated when an application needs to refresh part of one of its windows. (We'll cover `Expose` events below.) Your applications should always ask for `Expose` events at window-creation time, since *backing store* may cut down on the number of `Expose` events received by your application. This is normally good, but sometimes your application may never see the initial `Expose` event that tells the application to draw into its windows. Asking for `Expose` events in the `XCreateWindow` call solves this potential problem.

OVERRIDING WINDOW MANAGERS

The `override_redirect` field in the `XSetWindowAttributes` structure tells any window manager in use to leave this request alone. Leaving a window alone usually means not putting a title bar around the window. Overriding window managers is normally considered unfriendly. The `override_redirect` field is typically set to `True` for short-lived pop-up menus and other windows that will appear on the screen only for a short time. Don't use it for long-lived application windows.

X defines procedures (the mechanism) for how to implement many different types of user interfaces, but it explicitly does not define the policy of how those interfaces will look. Much of this policy is implemented in a window manager, such as the Open Look window manager, olwm. Users are free to run any window manager (or none at all) that they like. X11 itself comes from MIT with twm, the Tab (or Tom's) window manager.

Much of the latest work using X has been in the area of standardizing interfaces and window managers. Digital Equipment Corporation developed the DECwindows window manager. AT&T and Sun Microsystems have olwm. And the Open Software Foundation has mwm. All X programs should be set up to interact to some degree with any window manager.

The following code added to the section above will tell the window manager to leave your program's window alone. Normally this will result in a radically different display, and your window should appear more quickly when you run the example program below. We suggest you try the example program with the code below commented out and also with this code compiled in to see the differences. This will give you a good idea what window managers do. Note that, for well-behaved applications, you don't want to set the override_redirect field to True—just use this for pop-up menus.

```
attributes.override_redirect  = True;
attr_mask |= CWOverrideRedirect;
```

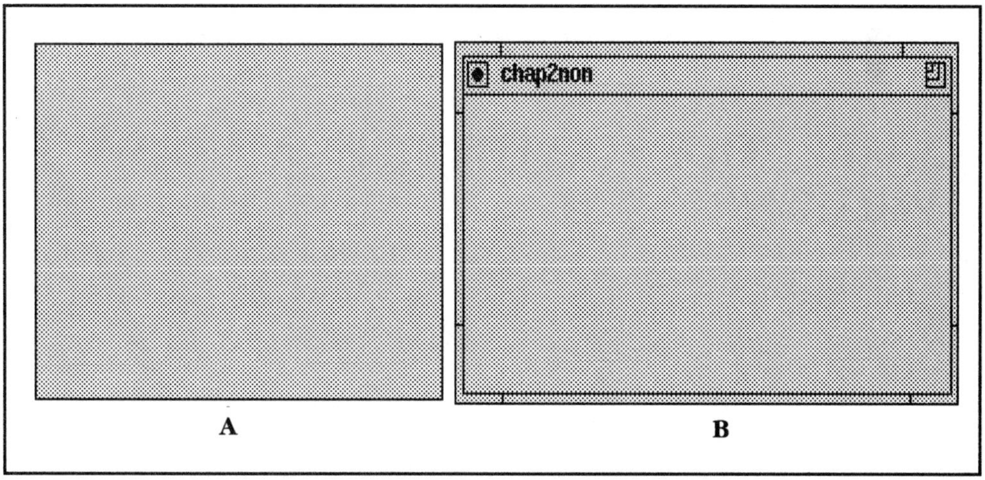

Figure 2.4. Overriding Window Managers. The Window A Overrides the Window Manager, While Not Overriding the Window Manager in B.

SETTING THE ATTRIBUTE MASKS

The attr_mask tells X which of the fields in the XSetWindowAttributes structure are actually used for the current request. For each field, there is a symbol defined that specifies that the field is set. In this case, the symbols are CWBackPixel, CWBorderPixel, and CWEventMask. By OR-ing these values together, we set the correct bit pattern in attr_mask. Don't confuse CWBackPixel, a flag for the background color of the window, with CWBackingPixel, a flag for a color value used in restoring planes.

Mask Bits	*Value*	*Mask Bits*	*Value*
CWBackPixmap	(1L<<0)	CWBackingPixel	(1L<<8)
CWBackPixel	(1L<<1)	CWOverrideRedirect	(1L<<9)
CWBorderPixmap	(1L<<2)	CWSaveUnder	(1L<<10)
CWBorderPixel	(1L<<3)	CWEventMask	(1L<<11)
CWBitGravity	(1L<<4)	CWDontPropagate	(1L<<12)
CWWinGravity	(1L<<5)	CWColormap	(1L<<13)
CWBackingStore	(1L<<6)	CWCursor	(1L<<14)
CWBackingPlanes	(1L<<7)		

The XSetWindowAttributes structure is then passed to X as part of the XCreateWindow call. Putting it all together, we get the function OpenWindow, from the file window.c, which creates a window.

SOURCE CODE FOR THE OPENWINDOW FUNCTION

```
#include <X11/Xlib.h>
#include <X11/Xutil.h>

#define        BORDER_WIDTH    2

Window OpenWindow( display, parent, x, y, width, height,
        bordercolor, backcolor, event_mask, visual )

Display       *display;       /* X server connection */
Window        parent;         /* parent window */
```

```
int             x, y;           /* location */
int             width, height;  /* size */
unsigned long   bordercolor;    /* border color */
unsigned long   backcolor;      /* background color */
unsigned long   event_mask;     /* Just Expose will do */
Visual          *visual;        /* normally CopyFromParent */

{       /* OpenWindow */
        Window                  window;
        XSetWindowAttributes  attributes;
        unsigned long         attr_mask;

        /*
         * Set up window attributes before
         * creating window. Don't confuse
         * CWBackPixel with CWBackingPixel!
         */
        attributes.event_mask = event_mask;
        attributes.border_pixel = bordercolor;
        attributes.background_pixel    = backcolor;
        attr_mask   = CWEventMask |
                CWBackPixel |  CWBorderPixel;

        /*
         * Override-Redirect windows make an end-run
         * around a window manager. Try the program
         * with the next two lines commented out,
         * and also with them compiled in. Normally,
         * well-behaved X applications only use
         * override-redirect windows for pop-up menus.
         * Don't abuse override-redirect windows and
         * don't have your application's main window
         * use override-redirect.
         */
        /*
        attributes.override_redirect    =True;
        attr_mask                       |=CWOverrideRedirect;
        */

        /*
         * Create the window.
         */
        window = XCreateWindow( display,
```

```
                parent,
                x, y, width, height,
                BORDER_WIDTH,
                CopyFromParent,      /* depth */
                InputOutput,         /* class */
                visual,
                attr_mask,
                &attributes );

        return( window );

}       /* OpenWindow */
```

We arbitrarily decide on a window border width of 2 pixels. You can change this if you want.

SENDING HINTS TO THE WINDOW MANAGER

After creating a window, the next step requires your application to send *hints* to the window manager about your window. The window manager, which enforces a user interface style, may accept or deny any hinted request—hence the hints. Most window managers will try to deliver what your application wants, but you can never be sure. If your application fights the window manager, the window manager wins.

SIZE HINTS

The first set of hints are called *size hints* to the window manager, if a window manager is running. The basic set of hints described here are simply the position and size of the new window. This may seem odd to send the same information again, just after calling `XCreateWindow` and passing a position and a size for the new window.

Window managers have the option of choosing a different position and size for you, so you are hinting that this is really the position and size you want. The `XSizeHints` structure contains the size hints.

```
typedef struct {
        long flags;          /* which fields in this struct are filled */
        int  x, y;           /* Obsolete */
        int  width, height;  /* Obsolete */
        int  min_width, min_height;
        int  max_width, max_height;
        int  width_inc, height_inc;
        struct {
             int x;       /* numerator */
             int y;       /* denominator */
             } min_aspect, max_aspect;
        int  base_width, base_height;     /* new in R4 */
        int  win_gravity;                 /* new in R4 */
        } XSizeHints;
```

The `min` and `max` aspects are ratios. The `width_inc` and `height_inc` are used to specify increments for sizing. Text-based programs, for example, want to have their windows resized in increments based on columns and rows of text, which depends on the font in use. The `base_width` and `base_height` are new in R4 and are the desired window size. Even though the x,y, width, and height fields are obsolete, fill them in anyway so that old window managers will work with your applications. Old window managers won't check the `base_width` and `base_height` fields.

As above, there is a mask: the `flags` field showing which values of the structure are being filled in. In this case, though, the flags are part of the `XSizeHints` structure, while the flags for the `XSetWindowAttributes` structure is not contained in the structure itself. The flags values are a set of mask values joined together with `OR`s.

Size Hints Mask Bits   Value

```
USPosition    (1L << 0)   /* user specified x, y */
USSize        (1L << 1)   /* user specified width, height */
PPosition     (1L << 2)   /* program specified position */
PSize         (1L << 3)   /* program specified size */
PMinSize      (1L << 4)   /* min size */
PMaxSize      (1L << 5)   /* max size */
PResizeInc    (1L << 6)   /* resize incremements */
PAspect       (1L << 7)   /* min and max aspect ratios */
PBaseSize     (1L << 8)   /* new in R4 */
PWinGravity   (1L << 9)   /* new in R4 */
```

Avoid the older flag, `PAllHints`, as new flags added after X11 Release 3 aren't part of it.

DETERMINING THE XLIB VERSION

5 Release

The X Library changes with each new version, and these changes introduce compatibility problems. Release 4, especially, added many new features over R3. The main problem is determining which X release you're compiling against. Until Release 5, there's no easy answer. Release 5 introduces a new symbol, `XlibSpecificationRelease`, defined in `Xlib.h`:

```
#define XlibSpecificationRelease    5
```

You can test against this symbol. If it doesn't exist, your X Library is at R4 or older. At R5 and, presumably, higher, you can check the value of `XlibSpecificationRelease` to see what release of Xlib you have. Unfortunately, most of the major, incompatible changes were introduced with R4. Because of this, we defined our own symbol—X11R4.

FILLING IN THE SIZE HINTS

The code below fills in an `XSizeHints` structure. Note that we have compilation conditional on whether you have a Release 4-based system or an older R3 or R2 system. Any system newer than R4, such as R5, should use the X11R4 definition. Any older system, such as Hewlett-Packard's X11 R3 under HP-UX 7.0, should *not* have the symbol X11R4 defined. Newer systems require the `base_width` and `base_height` fields to be filled in, yet these fields did not exist until Release 4. We set up the X11R4 definition in the Makefile in Appendix A. (The reason for the change is the rules for well-behaved X applications, the *Inter-Client Communications Conventions Manual*, or *ICCCM*. The *ICCCM 1.0* came out between R3 and R4, so the R4 version of the X Library is the first version to add the extra fields.)

```
int             x, y;
int             width, height;
XSizeHints      sizehints;

sizehints.x = x;                /* Obsolete */
sizehints.y = y;                /* Obsolete */
```

```
sizehints.height = height;     /* Obsolete */
sizehints.width = width;       /* Obsolete */
sizehints.min_height = height;
sizehints.min_width = width;

sizehints.flags = USPosition | USSize | PMinSize;

#ifdef X11R4    /* X11 Release 4 or higher, e.g., R5*/

sizehints.base_width  = width;
sizehints.base_height = height;
sizehints.flags |= PBaseSize;

#endif  /* X11R4 */
```

In this case, the `flags` field is special. The value `PPosition` means that the program chose the position and that the `x` and `y` fields are filled in. The value `USPosition` means that the user chose the position. Depending on the style of interface you want, it may be tempting to lie to the window manager here and always state that the user chose the position. Usually, though, the `USPosition` flag is set if the user passed a command-line parameter for the position, and the `PPosition` flag is set if the program is using a default value in lieu of a user-requested position. The `PSize` value provides similar information about the window's size: the width and height fields are filled in and these values were set by the program. `USSize` states that the user specified the size.

SETTING THE SIZE HINTS

Once the `XSizeHints` structure has some values, it is passed on to the window manager with the `XSetNormalHints` function. The *Normal* part of `XSetNormalHints` refers to the size of the window in its normal state, as opposed to iconic, withdrawn, or zoomed state. (The zoomed state is now obsolete.)

If you have a newer system, such as R4 or R5, you should use the `XSetWMNormalHints` function instead of `XSetNormalHints`. We again use the X11R4 symbol for conditional compilation.

```
Display         *display;
Window          window;
XSizeHints      sizehints;
```

```
#ifdef X11R4        /* X11 Release 4 or higher, e.g., R5*/

/*
 * XSetWMNormalHints is new in R4.
 * It replaces the old R3
 * XSetNormalHints routine.
 */
XSetWMNormalHints( display, window, &sizehints );

#else
/*
 * Use older, R2-R3 routine.
 */
XSetNormalHints( display, window, &sizehints );

#endif  /* pre-X11R4 */
```

ALLOCATING THE SIZE HINTS STRUCTURE

Since the `XSizeHints` structure gained a new field between Release 3 and Release 4, the designers of the X library added in a new function to dynamically allocate memory for an `XSizeHints` structure, `XAllocSizeHints`. The guarantee is that this function will allocate more space in the future, should the `XSizeHints` grow again. (In Release 5, the `XSizeHints` structure did not grow.)

```
XSizeHints   *sizehints_ptr;

sizehints_ptr = XAllocSizeHints();
```

Call `XFree` to free the memory when done.

```
char   *ptr;

XFree( ptr );
```

Or, in this case,

```
XFree( (char *) sizehints_ptr );
```

We didn't use `XAllocSizeHints`, since it is simpler to merely declare a variable to be of the `XSizeHints` type.

SOURCE CODE FOR SIZEHINT.C

The file `sizehint.c` forms a short module for setting a window's `XSizeHints`.

```
/*
 *      sizehint.c
 *      Code for sending the size hints to the
 *      window manager.
 *
 *      Written for X Window Applications
 *      Programming, 2nd Edition
 *
 *      Note: if you have an X11 Release 4-based
 *      system (or higher), you should define the
 *      symbol X11R4, as R4 added some new (preferred)
 *      functions for setting window hints.
 */

#include <X11/Xlib.h>
#include <X11/Xutil.h>

SetSizeHints( display, window, x, y, width, height )

Display       *display;
Window        window;
int           x, y, width, height;

{       /* SetSizeHints */
        XSizeHints  sizehints;

        /*
         * Get hint values
         */
        FillSizeHints( x, y, width, height,
             &sizehints );

#ifdef X11R4

        /*
         * XSetWMNormalHints is new in R4.
         * It replaces the old R3
```

```
         * XSetNormalHints routine.
         */
        XSetWMNormalHints( display,
             window,
             &sizehints );

#else
        /*
         * Use older, R2-R3 routine.
         */
        XSetNormalHints( display,
             window,
             &sizehints );

#endif

}       /* SetSizeHints */

FillSizeHints( x, y, width, height, sizehints )

int             x, y, width, height;
XSizeHints      *sizehints; /* RETURN */

/*
 *      Fills in an XSizeHints structure. Note that we
 *      lie and say that the user picked the size and
 *      location (USPosition and USSize). We could use
 *      PPosition and PSize, but it's easier to place
 *      your windows where you want.
 */

{       /* FillSizeHints */

        /*
         * Set size hints
         */
        sizehints->x  = x;           /* Obsolete */
        sizehints->y = y;       /* Obsolete */
        sizehints->height = height;/* Obsolete */
        sizehints->width = width;    /* Obsolete */
        sizehints->min_height = height;
        sizehints->min_width = width;
```

```
        sizehints->flags = USPosition | USSize | PMinSize;

#ifdef X11R4
        sizehints->base_width  = width;
        sizehints->base_height = height;
        sizehints->flags |= PBaseSize;
#endif /* X11R4 */

}       /* FillSizeHints */

/* end of file sizehint.c */
```

WM HINTS

The next set of hints are the *WM* (window manager) hints. These hints tell the window manager more about your application program. You can set up an icon for the window (which we cover in Chapter 9) and set the initial state; that is, whether the application should start iconic or not. The WM hints are stored in the `XWMhints` structure.

```
typedef struct {
    long      flags;          /* which fields are used */
    Bool      input;          /* Needs keyboard input? */
    int       initial_state;
    Pixmap    icon_pixmap;    /* pixmap to be used as icon */
    Window    icon_window;    /* window to be used with icon */
    int       icon_x, icon_y; /* initial position of icon */
    Pixmap    icon_mask;      /* pixmap mask for icon_pixmap */
    XID       window_group;   /* id of related window group */
              } XWMHints;
```

This structure may grow in the future, so you can use `XAllocWMHints` to allocate memory for it. Avoid using the older `AllHints` flag for this reason. Again, the flags field indicates which of the other fields are actually filled in. The flag constants include the following:

Name	***Value***
`InputHint`	`(1L << 0)`
`StateHint`	`(1L << 1)`
`IconPixmapHint`	`(1L << 2)`
`IconWindowHint`	`(1L << 3)`
`IconPositionHint`	`(1L << 4)`
`IconMaskHint`	`(1L << 5)`
`WindowGroupHint`	`(1L << 6)`

SOURCE CODE FOR THE FILE WMHINTS.C

The `SetWMHints` function in `wmhints.c` sets up the WM hints and fills in two fields in the `XWMHints` structure: the `initial_state` and `input` fields. The `initial_state` can be one of the following states:

State	***Value***	***Meaning***
WithdrawnState	0	Window is not visible.
NormalState	1	Window is visible.
IconicState	3	Window is replaced by an icon (if supported).

We pass the desired state to the `SetWMHints` function in the file `chap2.c`, below. You could start your program in `IconicState` or `NormalState` (the most common state).

4 Release

We set the input field to True so that the application receives keyboard input events. Prior to R4, setting this hint really didn't matter. But R4 and newer window managers require the `input` hint to be set to `True`. Remember to pass the `InputHint` flag, too.

```
/*
 *      wmhints.c
 *      Code for sending window hints to the window manager.
 *
 *      Written for X Window Applications
 *      Programming, 2nd Edition
 */
```

```
#include <X11/Xlib.h>
#include <X11/Xutil.h>

SetWMHints( display, window, initial_state )

Display      *display;
Window       window;
int          initial_state;

/*
 *      Sets the window manger or "WM" hints.
 *      The initial_state can be one of:
 *           WithdrawnState (0)
 *           NormalState (1)
 *           IconicState (3)
 */

{       /* SetWMHints */
        XWMHints wm_hints;

        /*
         * The flags field specifies which
         * parts of the structure are
         * filled in.
         */
        wm_hints.flags          = InputHint | StateHint;

        /*
         * This tells the window manager
         * whether we want the window to
         * start out in iconic or normal state.
         */
        wm_hints.initial_state = initial_state;

        /*

         * This tells the window manager
         * our application would like to
         * receive keyboard input, if the
         * application asks for keyboard
         * input.
         */
        wm_hints.input          = True;
```

```
        XSetWMHints( display,
              window,
              &wm_hints );

}       /* SetWMHints */

/* end of file wmhints.c */
```

ALLOCATING THE WM HINTS

Like the `XSizeHints` structure, `XWMHints` may grow in the future. You can use the X library function `XAllocWMHints` to dynamically allocate memory for an `XWMHints` structure:

```
XWMHints     *wmhints_ptr;

wmhints_ptr = XAllocWMHints();
```

Again, free the memory with `XFree` when done.

CLASS HINTS

The class hints provide clues to other applications as to what kind of class your application is. For example, the *emacs* text editor could share a class of TextEditor with the *xedit* editor. This would allow other X applications to ask if any text editor is currently running on a given X server. Electronic-mail programs, spreadsheets, and word processors are also common application classes (although there seems to be few attempts to really standardize on the class names and most applications use their own, private class names).

The forementioned rules for well-behaved X programs, the *ICCCM* (which we'll cover more in chapters 11 and 12), state that applications should register their class. (The size hints and WM hints are also required by these rules.)

The `XClassHint` structure contains two fields.

```
typedef struct {
        char    *res_name;
        char    *res_class;
        } XClassHint;
```

Usually you place the application's name (such as the contents of `argv[0]`) in the `res_name` field and a class name, such as *Examples* in the `res_class` field. The `res_class` usually starts with an upper-case letter.

SOURCE CODE FOR CLASSHNT.C

The file `classhnt.c`, below, contains a function, `SetClassHints`, to set the `XClassHint` hints for the window manager.

```
/*
 *      classhnt.c
 *      Code for sending class hints to
 *      the window manager.
 *
 *      Written for X Window Applications
 *      Programming, 2nd Edition
 */

#include <X11/Xlib.h>
#include <X11/Xutil.h>

SetClassHints( display, window, res_name, res_class )

Display      *display;
Window       window;
char         *res_name;
char         *res_class;

/*
 *       Sets the class hints (the WM_CLASS property)
 *       on the given window. res_name is usually
 *       argv[0] (the program's name) and res_class
 *       usually starts with an upper-case letter.
 */

{       /* SetClassHints */
        XClassHint  class_hints;

        class_hints.res_class = res_class;
        class_hints.res_name = res_name;

        XSetClassHint( display,
```

```
            window,
            &class_hints );

}       /* SetClassHints */

/* end of file classhnt.c */
```

ALLOCATING THE CLASS HINTS

The XClassHint structure, like the XSizeHints structure, may grow in the future, so you should use the function XAllocClassHint to dynamically allocate memory for an XClassHint structure. Remember to call XFree to free the memory when done.

```
XClassHint   *class_hints_ptr;

class_hints_ptr = XAllocClassHint();
```

WINDOW NAMES

Every window should have a name. In X, the XStoreName function sets a window's name to be a given text string.

```
Display      *display;
Window       window;
char         *name;

XStoreName( display, window, name );
```

The code in wmname.c, below, uses XStoreName to set a window's name.

```
/*
 *      wmname.c
 *      Code for setting a window name.
 *
 *      Written for X Window Applications
 *      Programming, 2nd Edition
 */

#include <X11/Xlib.h>
```

```
SetWindowName( display, window, name )

Display       *display;
Window        window;
char          name[];

{       /* SetWindowName */

        /*
         * Give the window a name, in case the window
         * manager provides title bars (most do). We use
         * the old, R3 method here, to avoid the complexities
         * of the XTextProperty structures, which were
         * introduced in X11 Release 4.
         */
        XStoreName( display, window, name );

}       /* SetWindowName */

/* end of file wmname.c */
```

X TEXT PROPERTIES

`XStoreName` is out of date. By accepting only eight-bit character data, `XStoreName` does not work well in places needing larger character sets, such as Asia. In Release 4 a new function, `XSetWMName`, was added. This function did not exist in Release 3, so you're stuck with a portability issue. (The upgrade from X11 R3 to R4 introduced a large number of compatibility issues. R4 is much more robust than R3, but application developers will probably have to support R3, R4, and R5 all for a long time. We sometimes need special compile-time options, but we've managed to create portable X applications without too much work.)

```
Display          *display;
Window           window;
XTextProperty    *text_property;

XSetWMName( display, window, text_property );
```

The window's name is stored in an `XTextProperty` structure.

CONVERTING TEXT STRINGS TO TEXT PROPERTIES

Your application probably starts with a window name stored in a text string. You must convert that string to an XTextProperty structure before calling XSetWMName.

```
typedef struct {
        unsigned char   *value;   /* property data */
        Atom            encoding;/* type of prop., e.g. STRING */
        int             format;   /* 8, 16, or 32 */
        unsigned long   nitems;   /* number of items in value */
        } XTextProperty;
```

The XStringListToTextProperty function converts a list of strings to an XTextProperty structure. XStringListToTextProperty returns a non-zero value on success and 0 on failure.

```
char                    **string_list;
int                     number_strings;
XTextProperty           *text_property;
int                     status;

status = XStringListToTextProperty( string_list,
             number_strings,
             text_property );
```

You can convert a text property back to a string list with XTextPropertyToStringList.

```
XTextProperty   *text_property;
char            ***string_list;     /* RETURN */
int             *number_strings;    /* RETURN */
int             status;

status = XTextPropertyToStringList ( text_property,
             string_list,
             number_strings )
```

XTextPropertyToStringList also returns a non-zero value on success and 0 on failure. Both of these functions are new in Release 4.

Use XFreeStringList to free the list of strings when done. XFreeStringList is called with:

```
char            **string_list;

XFreeStringList( string_list );
```

MAPPING THE WINDOW

After all this hinting, it's time to actually put the window on the screen. `XCreateWindow` "creates" a window, but actually having a window appear is a different matter. The `XMapWindow` function *maps* the window to the screen. (At this point, the window manager may intervene and change the placement of your window.) Until this time, the window was in a sort of never-never land—it existed but it never appeared on the screen. This two-step window creation process seems confusing, but it allows you to create a window, set all the hints for the window manager, and then (and only then) make the window appear.

```
Display         *display;
Window          window;

XMapWindow( display, window );
```

`XMapRaised` acts the same as `XMapWindow`, but it also raises the new window to the top, making it appear over other windows that may be in the way. In most cases `XMapWindow` will seem to act the same way, but `XMapRaised` is explicit about the placement. `XMapRaised` takes the same parameters as `XMapWindow`.

```
Display         *display;
Window          window;

XMapRaised( display, window );
```

You can later unmap a window, undoing the effects of `XMapWindow`, with the `XUnmapWindow` function, using the same parameters:

```
Display         *display;
Window          window;

XUnmapWindow( display, window ).
```

CLEARING WINDOWS

You can clear a window to its background color (or pixmap—whatever you set it up with), using `XClearWindow`.

```
Display       *display;
Window        window;

XClearWindow( display, window );
```

FLUSHING THE DISPLAY

To aid performance, Xlib keeps a cache of your output calls to the X server. Certain Xlib calls flush out this queue by sending all the requests to the X server as part of one communication block. Since all communication with the X server is over a network connection, and network connections place an overhead on each message passed, it is a good idea to queue up messages to send a number of requests with one communication packet.

There are times, though, when you want the X server to display all the output queued up so far. Use the `XFlush` function for this. `XFlush` takes one parameter, the display pointer. (The display pointer is used in almost every Xlib call.)

```
Display       *display;

XFlush( display );
```

Judicious use of `XFlush` can improve the look of applications and perceptions of speed. If you are drawing out a whole windowful of spreadsheet cells, call the Xlib drawing functions for the whole window and only then call `XFlush` to send out all the output at once, so it appears as if the whole window is updated at once. This generally looks better than drawing the window one cell at a time, even if the total time for the drawing is the same. If it looks to the user like all the items are drawn at the same time, the user's perception of speed is enhanced. This method also means there is less network traffic, which may be an issue in some systems.

DESTROYING THE WINDOW

Before exiting a program, it's a good idea to destroy all the windows used. The `XCloseDisplay` call normally destroys all windows, but it is a good idea to destroy any windows as soon as you are done with them. To do this, use the `XDestroyWindow` function:

```
Display       *display;
Window        window;

XDestroyWindow( display, window );
```

EXPOSING WINDOWS

Because windows in X can overlap, and most users run more than one X application at a time, it is very likely that another program's window will at some time overlap your program's window (or windows). If this overlapping window is moved away and no longer covers your window, the covered part of your window is considered *exposed*.

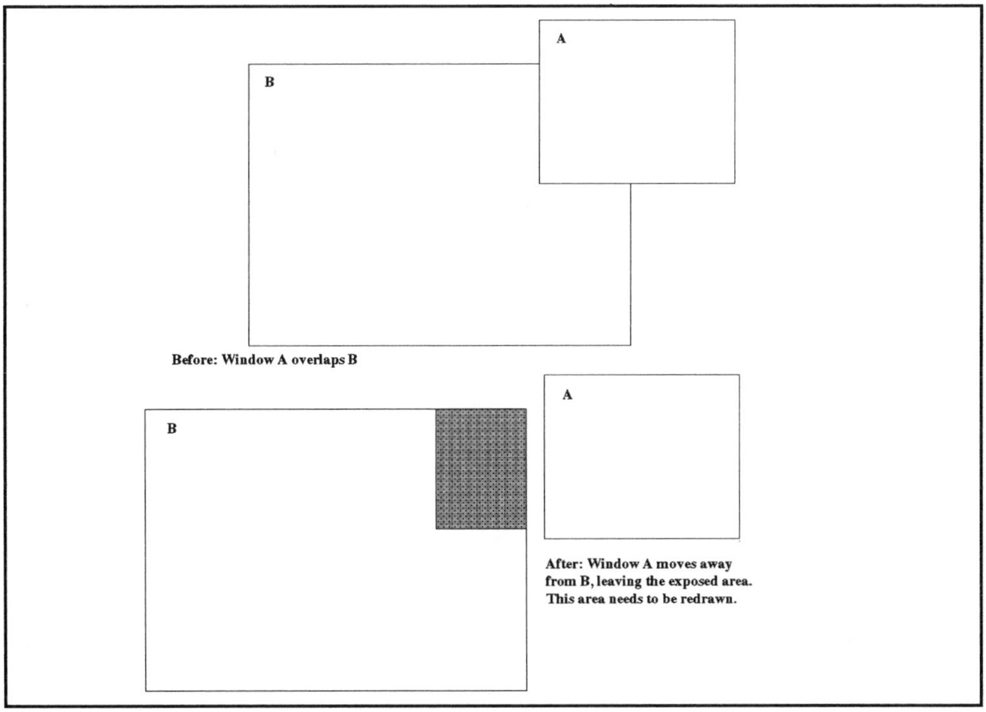

Figure 2.5. Generating Expose Events.

This exposed or damaged area must be redrawn. Among windowing systems, there's some debate over which side is responsible for redrawing the exposed area: the window server or the application program. The Amiga windowing system, for example, redraws the damaged area for you. This requires a lot of memory to save the data displayed by each window, especially on a 1,024 x 1,024-pixel screen with 8 color planes. In fact, the data in the window may be old and no longer worth saving.

The X Window System requires your application to redraw the exposed area. You can cut down on the number of `Expose` events by having your application ask for the X server to provide backing store on your windows, which means that the X server preserves any obscured areas. Not all X servers support backing store, and even those that do don't guarantee to provide backing store for all your windows all the time. (Low memory conditions usually make X servers give up backing store to use the precious memory for something considered more important.) Your application can ask for backing store by filling the `backing_store` field in the `XSetWindowAttributes` structure to one of the constants: `NotUseful`, `WhenMapped` or `Always`. `NotUseful` does *not* ask for backing store. Remember to also pass the `CWBackingStore` mask bit as part of the attribute mask (`attr_mask`, as covered earlier).

Even if you ask for backing store, your application can still expect to receive `Expose` events, if only to draw the window's contents for the first time. All X applications should expect—and handle—exposure events.

When an area becomes exposed, the X server will send your application an `Expose` event. When your program receives an `Expose` event, it should redraw the area that was previously covered up. Each of these events arrives with a rectangle (x,y, width, height) that identifies the exposed area.

All X applications that create windows are required to check for expose events and redraw the proper areas of their windows. Your applications can also check for other events, like keyboard or mouse events. We cover these (and many other) events in chapters 6 and 7.

ASKING FOR EXPOSE EVENTS

The first step is asking for expose events. We do this by filling in the `event_mask` field of the `XSetWindowAttributes` structure, like we did above, before calling `XCreateWindow`. Once you ask for a type of event, your application must ask the X library to deliver the event.

AWAITING EVENTS

There are two ways to check for incoming events: polling and blocking. In Chapter 6 we'll cover polling. For now, our example program will simply block until an event arrives from the X server.

The `XNextEvent` function blocks until an event arrives.

```
Display       *display;
XEvent        event;

XNextEvent( display, &event );
```

THE X EVENT UNION

The `XEvent` type is a union of all the possible base X window events.

```
typedef union _XEvent {
      int                          type;
      XAnyEvent                    xany;
      XKeyEvent                    xkey;
      XButtonEvent                 xbutton;
      XMotionEvent                 xmotion;
      XCrossingEvent               xcrossing;
      XFocusChangeEvent            xfocus;
      XExposeEvent                 xexpose;
      XGraphicsExposeEvent         xgraphicsexpose;
      XNoExposeEvent               xnoexpose;
      XVisibilityEvent             xvisibility;
      XCreateWindowEvent           xcreatewindow;
      XDestroyWindowEvent          xdestroywindow;
      XUnmapEvent                  xunmap;
      XMapEvent                    xmap;
      XMapRequestEvent             xmaprequest;
      XReparentEvent               xreparent;
      XConfigureEvent              xconfigure;
      XGravityEvent                xgravity;
      XResizeRequestEvent          xresizerequest;
      XConfigureRequestEvent       xconfigurerequest;
      XCirculateEvent              xcirculate;
      XCirculateRequestEvent       xcirculaterequest;
      XPropertyEvent               xproperty;
      XSelectionClearEvent         xselectionclear;
      XSelectionRequestEvent       xselectionrequest;
      XSelectionEvent              xselection;
      XColormapEvent               xcolormap;
      XClientMessageEvent          xclient;
      XMappingEvent                xmapping;
      XErrorEvent                  xerror;
      XKeymapEvent                 xkeymap;
      long                         pad[24];
      } XEvent;
```

The only field in which we're interested is the `xexpose` field.

THE EVENT LOOP

X applications typically use XNextEvent in an event loop. The application loops forever, checking for events, then reacting to the events. This concept of event-driven programming is a key for X applications (we'll show a number of fleshed-out event loops from Chapter 6 onward).

```
Display      *display;
XEvent       event;

while   ( 1 )
        {
        XNextEvent( display, &event );

        switch( event.type )
              {
              case Expose: /* the only type we know about now */
                    ...
                    break;
              case ...
              }
        }
```

DECODING EXPOSE EVENTS

When the type field in the XEvent union is set to Expose, you can use the xexpose portion of the union, an XExposeEvent structure.

```
typedef struct {
      int         type;
      unsigned    long serial;
      Bool        send_event;
      Display     *display;
      Window      window;
      int         x, y;
      int         width, height;
      int         count;
      } XExposeEvent;
```

The type field is already set to `Expose`. The window field contains the ID of the window in which the event occured. We're only creating one window this chapter, but real applications will have multiple windows. This makes the window field in the `XExposeEvent` structure important. Normally, if you have a variable of type `XEvent`, you access the window field in the `Expose` event with `event.xexpose.window`, and so on:

```
Window  window;
XEvent  event;

window = event.xexpose.window;
```

The x, y, width, and height fields store the size and location of the exposed area.

The count field is useful. `Expose` events are guaranteed to be generated in batches. That is, if a window moves about on the screen and this movement uncovers part of your application's window, all the `Expose` events for that movement will arrive in one batch. The count field counts down the events in the batch until 0, the last event in the batch.

This helps your application efficiently update the display. If you wait until all `Expose` events in a batch are completed, you could, for example, then update the smallest rectangle that encloses *all* the damaged area. (Or you could use an advanced X tool, regions.) Lazy applications could just redraw the entire window when this happens.

Updating the total exposed area just once would probably be more efficient than updating the exposed rectangle on each `Expose` event. Of course, this all depends on how expensive it is to redraw your window. A CAD package can expect to make a lot of calculations on every redraw, making the refresh operation fairly expensive in terms of CPU resources. The best refresh policy or method depends on your particular application. This may seem complex, but at least you have a choice.

In addition, we all know that some computers are more powerful than others. With X servers and X applications running over networks, finding the optimal refresh policy can be tough. Each client/server machine combination may result in a completely different optimal refresh policy. Some computers may be better at sending network communication than others (and some networks have more traffic than others). Some graphics systems draw faster than others.

Try different schemes for refreshing your application windows until you find a method that satisfies.

AN EXAMPLE PROGRAM TO CREATE A WINDOW AND ACQUIRE EVENTS

This chapter's example program shows how to create a window, map it to the screen and detect `Expose` events. When an `Expose` event arrives, the `chap2` program prints out the coordinates of the exposed area. Later programs will actually redraw window contents.

After 20 `Expose` events arrive, the `chap2` program quits. Most real applications will probably loop in an event-handling loop, at least until the user chooses to end the program.

SOURCE CODE FOR CHAP2.C

The file `chap2.c` contains the main function for the example program in Chapter 2.

```
/*
 *      chap2.c
 *      Example program for Chapter 2.
 *      Creates a window, shows Expose Events.
 *
 *      Written for X Window Applications
 *      Programming, 2nd Edition
 */

#include <stdio.h>
#include <X11/Xlib.h>
#include <X11/Xutil.h>

main( argc, argv )

int     argc;
char    *argv[];

{       /* main  */
        Display  *display;
        Display  *ConnectToServer(); /* connect.c */
        Window   rootwindow, window;
        Window   OpenWindow();       /* window.c */
        int      screen;
```

```
int      x, y, width, height;
Visual   *visual = CopyFromParent;
XEvent   event;
int      count;

/*
 * Connect to default X server
 */
display = ConnectToServer( (char *) NULL,
         &screen,
         &rootwindow );

/*
 * Create a window on the display
 */
x       = 10;
y       = 10;
width   = 300;
height  = 300;
window = OpenWindow( display,
         rootwindow,
         x, y, width, height,
         BlackPixel( display, screen ),
         WhitePixel( display, screen ),
         ExposureMask,  /* event mask */
         visual );

/*
 * Provide information to the window manager, if
 * one is in use. You do NOT want to fight the
 * window manager (it will win), so you always
 * want to provide the information it wants.
 */
SetStandardHints( display, window,
      argv[0], argv[0],
      x, y, width, height );

/*
 * Make the window actually appear
 */
XMapRaised( display, window );
XFlush( display );
```

```
/*
 * Loop until we get 20 Expose events.
 * You may have to put windows on top
 * on this window and move things
 * around for a while, until the 20 events
 * are in.
 */
count = 0;

while( count < 20 )
      {
      XNextEvent( display, &event );

      if ( event.type == Expose )
         {
         /*
          * Normally, you should redraw
          * part of your window when an
          * Expose event comes in. We'll
          * cover that in the next
          * chapter. For now, we'll just
          * print out the coordinates of
          * the exposed area.
          */
         count++;

         (void) printf( "For Expose event %d,",
            count );
         (void) printf( "the area is:\n" );

         (void) printf( "\tAt %d,%d,",
            event.xexpose.x,
            event.xexpose.y );

         (void) printf( " %d pixels wide, %d high\n",

            event.xexpose.width,
            event.xexpose.height );
         }

      }

/*
 * Close connection to X server
```

```
         */
        XCloseDisplay( display );

}       /* main */

/* end of file chap2.c */
```

SOURCE CODE FOR WINDOW.C

The file `window.c` contains the `OpenWindow` function described above, and a wrapper function to send hints to the window manager, `SetStandardHints`.

```
/*
 *      window.c
 *      Code for creating a window.
 *
 *      Written for X Window Applications
 *      Programming, 2nd Edition
 */

#include <X11/Xlib.h>
#include <X11/Xutil.h>

/*
 *      All our windows will have a 2-pixel wide border
 *      (which window managers like mwm and twm may override).
 *      You, of course, may want to change this, or pass the
 *      border-width as a parameter.
 */
#define      BORDER_WIDTH   2

/*
 *      Define application class.
 */
#define      APPL_CLASS     "Examples"

Window OpenWindow( display, parent, x, y, width, height,
        bordercolor, backcolor, event_mask, visual )

Display      *display;          /* X server connection */

Window       parent;            /* parent window */
int          x, y;              /* location */
```

```
int             width, height; /* size */
unsigned long   bordercolor;   /* window's border color */
unsigned long   backcolor;     /* window background color */
unsigned long   event_mask;    /* Just Expose will do */
Visual          *visual;       /* normally CopyFromParent */

{       /* OpenWindow */
        Window               window;
        XSetWindowAttributes attributes;
        unsigned long        attr_mask;

        /*
         * Set up window attributes before
         * creating window. Don't confuse
         * CWBackPixel with CWBackingPixel!
         */
        attributes.event_mask = event_mask;
        attributes.border_pixel = bordercolor;
        attributes.background_pixel = backcolor;
        attr_mask  = CWEventMask |
                CWBackPixel |  CWBorderPixel;

        /*
         * Override-Redirect windows make an end-run
         * around a window manager. Try the program
         * with the next two lines commented out,
         * and also with them compiled in. Normally,
         * well-behaved X applications only use
         * override-redirect windows for pop-up menus.
         * Don't abuse override-redirect windows and
         * don't have your application's main window
         * use override-redirect.
         */
        /*
        attributes.override_redirect  = True;
        attr_mask                    |= CWOverrideRedirect;
        */

        /*
         * Create the window.
         */
        window = XCreateWindow( display,
                parent,
```

```
                x, y, width, height,
                BORDER_WIDTH,
                CopyFromParent,      /* depth */
                InputOutput,         /* class */
                visual,
                attr_mask,
                &attributes );

             return( window );

        }    /* OpenWindow */

SetStandardHints( display, window, app_name, wind_name, x, y,
width, height )

Display      *display;
Window       window;
char         app_name[];     /* application name */
char         wind_name[];    /* window name */
int          x, y, width, height;

/*
 *      Convience wrapper function to call utility
 *      functions and set up the minimum necessary
 *      hints for the window manager. In section 2,
 *      we will expand on this.
 */

{       /* SetStandardHints */

        SetSizeHints( display, window,
             x, y, width, height );

        SetWindowName( display, window, wind_name );

        SetClassHints( display, window,
             app_name,       /* res_name */
             APPL_CLASS );   /* res_class */

        SetWMHints( display, window,
             NormalState );

}       /* SetStandardHints */

/* end of file window.c */
```

COMPILING AND LINKING THE CHAP2 PROGRAM

The chap2 program requires the following files:

```
chap2.c
classhnt.c
connect.c              (Chapter 1)
sizehint.c
window.c
wmname.c
wmhints.c
```

You can compile and link the chap2 program with a command like:

```
cc -o chap2 -DX11R4 chap2.c classhnt.c connect.c \
       sizehint.c window.c wmname.c wmhints.c -lX11
```

You can also use the Makefile in Appendix A and type:

```
make chap2
```

RUNNING THE EXAMPLE PROGRAM

The example program puts a window on the screen. After 20 Expose events, the program quits (using a primitive event loop). You can generate Expose events on the window by moving other windows on top of the sample window, then moving these windows off the sample window. The example program prints out the coordinates and size of the exposed areas.

All that work just to create a window! You'll find that windows form one of the most complex areas of the X library, just because there are so many options to choose from. The next chapter, which discusses drawing, should be a lot easier.

SUMMARY

Windows in the X Window System are arranged in a hierarchical fashion, existing either as a subwindow of the Root Window or an application's main window.

To open a window, it first must be created; you do this with XCreateSimpleWindow and XCreateWindow. At the same time, you give the window manager a set of parameters that defines the window's parent, location, border size/color, and background color.

After the window is created, you should send some information about the window, called hints, to the window manager (which may or may not be running). Then, the window should be mapped to the screen, where it actually appears.

All X programs should expect—and handle—`Expose` events, which tell your application to redraw "damaged" areas of its windows. (Damaged areas are created when an overlapping window is moved or eliminated.)

XLIB FUNCTIONS AND MACROS INTRODUCED IN THIS CHAPTER

```
XAllocClassHint
XAllocSizeHints
XAllocWMHints
XClearWindow
XCreateSimpleWindow
XCreateWindow
XDestroyWindow
XFlush
XFree
XFreeStringList
XMapWindow
XMapRaised
XNextEvent
XSetClassHint
XSetNormalHints
XSetWMHints
XSetWMName
XSetWMNormalHints
XStoreName
XStringListToTextProperty
XTextPropertyToStringList
XUnmapWindow
```

Chapter 3

DRAWING WITH X

Once a window is on the screen, the next step is putting something in the window. This chapter covers some common commands for drawing lines, rectangles, ovals, and the like. We also introduce a new data type, the GC, or graphics context.

After all the complexity involved with creating windows, drawing lines with X is rather simple. X defines a line as going from one pixel location (x1, y1) to another (x2, y2). `XDrawLine` draws such a line:

```
Display      *display;
Drawable     drawable;
GC           gc;
int          x1, y1;
int          x2, y2;

XDrawLine( display, drawable, gc,
        x1, y1, x2, y2 );
```

Note the new data type: the GC, or graphics context. We'll describe it in the next section.

A *drawable* is an X catch-all term for either windows and pixmaps (off-screen drawing areas). Most X drawing functions will draw into either a window or a pixmap. In most cases, though, your applications will draw into windows. (We cover pixmaps in Chapter 9.)

In X, the coordinate origin is in the upper-left corner of the window, and it grows by going to the right. The y coordinate grows going down. Depending on what graphics systems you're used to, the origin location may fool you for a while.

Rectangles are very similar, except that X treats all rectangular shapes as having a location (x, y) and a size (width, height). We've seen this consistent model of rectangles in the `XCreateWindow` function, as well as with `Expose` events. `XDrawRectangle` draws the outline of a rectangle:

```
Display         *display;
Drawable        drawable;
GC              gc;
int             x, y;
unsigned int    width, height;

XDrawRectangle( display, drawable, gc,
        x, y, width, height );
```

All measurements are in *pixels* (short for picture elements), which are dots on the screen. The size of these dots and the number of pixels on a screen will vary greatly—something that is one-inch (or one-centimeter, depending on how you measure) high on one monitor will undoubtedly be different on another vendor's screen.

THE GRAPHICS CONTEXT

Introduced above, the graphics context, or GC, is a catch-all data structure that contains almost everything needed to specify pen parameters for drawing. The GC contains the foreground and background colors, the width of the pen for drawing lines and whether lines should be dashed or solid.

```
typedef struct _XGC    {
      XExtData          *ext_data;
      GContext          gid;
      Bool              rects;
      Bool              dashes;
      unsigned long     dirty;
      XGCValues         values;
      } *GC;
```

Even though you see the fields in the GC structure here, don't mess with them. The X library maintains a complex cache of GC values, so always treat the structure as read-only. *Never* set values or directly access a GC structure; always use the graphic-context functions.

For now, the most important thing about the graphics context is that we must create one for the window before drawing.

GCs are tied to drawables. When creating a graphics context, you must specify for which window (or pixmap) it is created. (You can have more than one GC for a given window—we'll cover this in Chapter 10.)

CREATING THE GRAPHICS CONTEXT FOR A WINDOW

The function `XCreateGC` creates a new graphic context for a given window or pixmap. The following code creates a GC without filling in any of the common options.

```
Display            *display;
Drawable           drawable;
XGCValues          xgcvalues;
unsigned long      valuemask;
GC                 gc;

valuemask = 0L;    /* No options filled in */

gc = XCreateGC( display, drawable,
        valuemask, &xgcvalues );
```

Like the `XSizeHints` and `XSetWindowAttributes` structures, the valuemask is again a bitmask of the fields that are filled in; in this case, in the `XGCValues` structure.

THE GC VALUES STRUCTURE

The structure `XGCValues` can be filled in with values that deviate from the default. If so, the value mask needs to have certain bits set to tell the X server that the given values are being set. In this case (and in most cases), the GC can be created with just the straight defaults.

```
typedef struct {
    int             function;       /* e.g. GXxor */
    unsigned long   plane_mask;
    unsigned long   foreground;
    unsigned long   background;
    int             line_width;     /* line width (in pixels) */
    int             line_style;
    int             cap_style;
    int             join_style;
    int             fill_style;
    int             fill_rule;      /* EvenOddRule, WindingRule */
    int             arc_mode;       /* ArcChord, ArcPieSlice */
    Pixmap          tile;           /* tile pixmap for tiling ops */
    Pixmap          stipple;        /* 1 plane pixmap for stippling */
    int             ts_x_origin;    /* offset for tile or stipple ops */
    int             ts_y_origin;
    Font            font;           /* font for text */
    int             subwindow_mode;
    Bool            graphics_exposures;
    int             clip_x_origin;  /* origin for clipping */
    int             clip_y_origin;
    Pixmap          clip_mask;      /* only for bitmap clipping */
    int             dash_offset;    /* patterned/dashed line */
    char            dashes;
    } XGCValues;
```

If you fill in any fields in this structure, you need to set the valuemask to the bitwise OR of the proper bitmask constants.

Bitmask Name	***Value***
GCArcMode	(1L<<22)
GCBackground	(1L<<3)
GCCapStyle	(1L<<6)
GCClipMask	(1L<<19)
GCClipXOrigin	(1L<<17)
GCClipYOrigin	(1L<<18)
GCDashList	(1L<<21)
GCDashOffset	(1L<<20)
GCFillRule	(1L<<9)
GCFillStyle	(1L<<8)

Bitmask Name	***Value (cont.)***
`GCFont`	`(1L<<14)`
`GCForeground`	`(1L<<2)`
`GCFunction`	`(1L<<0)`
`GCGraphicsExposures`	`(1L<<16)`
`GCJoinStyle`	`(1L<<7)`
`GCLineStyle`	`(1L<<5)`
`GCLineWidth`	`(1L<<4)`
`GCPlaneMask`	`(1L<<1)`
`GCStipple`	`(1L<<11)`
`GCSubwindowMode`	`(1L<<15)`
`GCTile`	`(1L<<10)`
`GCTileStipXOrigin`	`(1L<<12)`
`GCTileStipYOrigin`	`(1L<<13)`

The most common use for a GC is to set colors for the foreground and background. The foreground color is the color in which the lines are drawn. The background color is often used as the background for drawing text (as will be shown in Chapter 5). Thus far, the only colors in use are `BlackPixel` and `WhitePixel`, which work on any X workstation, whether it is color or monochrome. Chapter 4 will show how to set other colors on color screens.

When you first create a GC, the following are default values:

XGCValues Field	***Default Value***
`arc_mode`	`ArcPieSlice`
`background`	`1`
`cap_style`	`CapButt`
`clip_mask`	`None`
`clip_x_origin`	`0`
`clip_y_origin`	`0`
`fill_style`	`FillSolid`
`fill_rule`	`EvenOddRule`
`font`	`implementation dependent`
`foreground`	`0`

XGCValues Field	*Default Value (cont.)*
function	GXcopy
graphics_exposures	True
join_style	JoinMiter
line_width	0 (use hardware accelerators, if any)
line_style	LineSolid
plane_mask	all planes (all 1s)
subwindow_mode	ClipByChildren

SOURCE CODE FOR GC.C

You can create a GC and set the foreground and background colors, all at the same time. We put together a function, `CreateGC`, to do just that, in the file `gc.c`.

```
/*
 *      gc.c
 *      Routine for creating a Graphics
 *      Context, or gc.
 *
 *      Written for X Window Applications
 *      Programming, 2nd Edition
 */

#include <stdio.h>
#include <X11/Xlib.h>
#include <X11/Xutil.h>

GC CreateGC( display, drawable, forecolor, backcolor )

Display          *display;
Drawable         drawable;
unsigned long    forecolor;
unsigned long    backcolor;

/*
 *      Creates a graphics context with the given
 *      foreground and background pixel values
 *      (colors).
 */
```

```
{       /* CreateGC */
        XGCValues   xgcvalues;
        GC          gc;

        xgcvalues.foreground = forecolor;
        xgcvalues.background = backcolor;

        gc = XCreateGC( display,
                drawable,
                ( GCForeground | GCBackground ),
                &xgcvalues );

        return( gc );

}       /* CreateGC */

/* end of file gc.c */
```

CHANGING A GRAPHICS CONTEXT

Once created, scads and scads of functions change the attributes of a GC. `XChangeGC` can change any of the parameters in the `XGCValues` structure. It takes a valuemask just like `XCreateGC`.

```
Display         *display;
GC              gc;
unsigned long   valuemask;
XGCValues       *xgcvalues;

XChangeGC( display, gc,
     valuemask, xgcvalues )
```

CHANGING THE FOREGROUND AND BACKGROUND COLORS

Since most changes to a GC are the foreground or background drawing colors, the X library has special functions for these tasks. The foreground and background colors are indexes into the current (for the GC) colormap. The values returned by `BlackPixel` and `WhitePixel` are valid for the default colormap. Unless you mess with colormaps, you're using the default colormap whether you know it or not.

```
Display         *display;
GC              gc;
unsigned long   foreground_color;
unsigned long   background_color;

XSetForeground( display, gc, foreground_color );

XSetBackground( display, gc, background_color );
```

QUERYING A GRAPHICS CONTEXT

You can retrieve current values from a graphics context with XGetGCValues. This routine is new in Release 4.

```
Display         *display;
GC              gc;
unsigned long  valuemask;    /* Which values to get */
XGCValues       xgcvalues;   /* RETURN */
int             status;

status = XGetGCValues( display, gc,
                valuemask, &xgcvalues );
```

DRAWING OVALS FROM ARCS

Lines and rectangles are easy; ovals, though, are a bit harder. X has no base functions for drawing circles, ellipses, or ovals. The only way to draw this kind of output is to roll something yourself. Probably the simplest way to do this is to draw an arc going all the way around a circular path, generating an oval shape.

In X, an arc is bounded by a rectangle, and the sweep of the arc is limited to the box formed by the rectangle. The arc begins at a start angle and draws an arc for a distance specified by a path angle. If that isn't confusing enough, the angle values are given in 64ths of a degree—meaning a full circular path is 360 degrees times 64—or 23,040. To make a arc go all the way around to form an oval, the start angle should be 0 (you should be able to start anywhere, but we've had the best luck with 0) and the path angle should be 360*64.

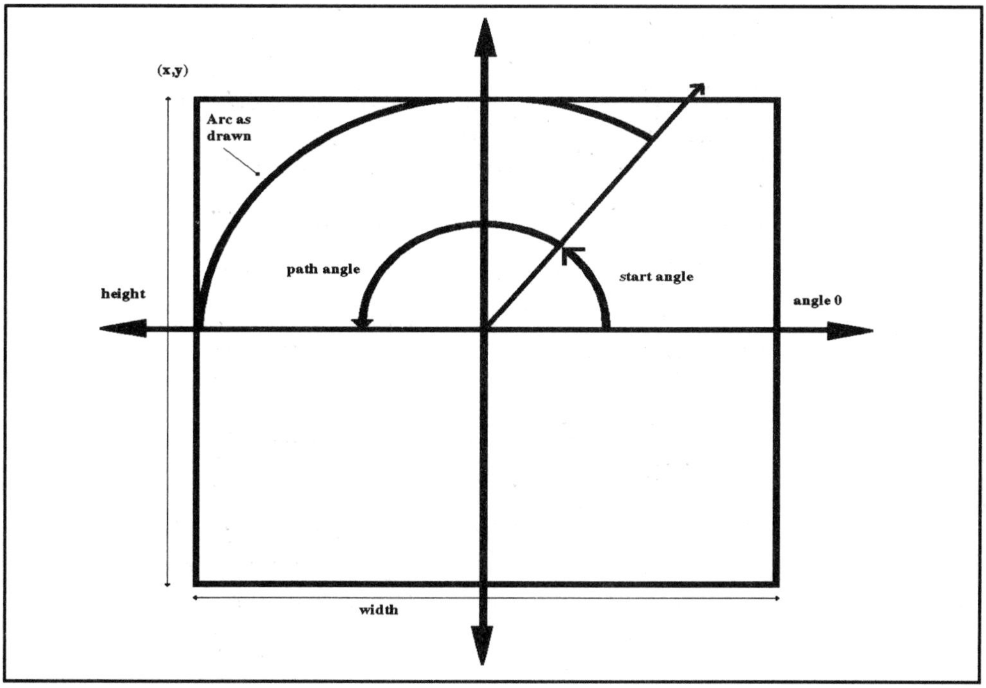

Figure 3.1. An Arc.

In the code below, these two constants are defined as `START_CIRCLE (0)` and `FULL_CIRCLE (360*64)`.

```
Display           *display;
Drawable          drawable;
GC                gc;
int               x, y;
unsigned int      width, height;
int               start_angle;    /* 0 for an oval */
int               path_angle;     /* 360*64 for an oval */

XDrawArc( display, drawable, gc,
        x, y, width, height,
        start_angle,
        path_angle );
```

To draw an oval, use:

```
XDrawArc( display, drawable, gc,
        x, y, width, height,
```

```
        START_CIRCLE,
        FULL_CIRCLE );
```

Note that the width and height must be positive numbers, or you can get in trouble, especially with shared-library X servers. You may want to test the width and height parameters each time you try to draw an arc or oval.

```
if ( width < 1 )
        {
        width = 1;
        }

if ( height < 1 )
        {
        height = 1;
        }
```

In the code example below, `oval.c`, the `DrawOval` routine takes care of the start and path angles and checks the width and height values. By hiding the internal details, you can now forget all about 64ths of a degree, by calling:

```
DrawOval( display, drawable, gc, x, y, width, height );
```

FILLING OVALS AND RECTANGLES

All of the above drawing commands simply draw the outline of an object. Many times, though, you want to fill in an object. X differentiates between drawing the outline and filling in an object. This may seem overly simple, but it is a way of keeping the Xlib function calls apart. An `XDrawSomething` routine draws an outline of a `Something` shape, while an `XFillSomething` fills in the object.

The calls to fill rectangles and ovals simply look like the above routines, but the `Draw` part is replaced by a `Fill` part:

```
Display         *display;
Drawable        drawable;
GC              gc;
int             x, y;
unsigned int    width, height;
int             start_angle;
int             path_angle;

XFillRectangle( display, drawable, gc,
        x, y, width, height );
```

```
XFillArc( display, drawable, gc,
        x, y, width, height,
        start_angle,
        path_angle );
```

SOURCE CODE FOR OVAL.C

The file `oval.c` contains routines for drawing and filling ovals, `DrawOval` and `FillOval`, respectively.

```
/*
 *      oval.c
 *      Routines for drawing and
 *      filling ovals under X.
 *
 *      Written for X Window Applications
 *      Programming, 2nd Edition
 */

#include <stdio.h>
#include <X11/Xlib.h>

/*
 *      Start circles at 0/64 degrees and
 *      go all the way around (360 degrees
 *      in 1/64 degree increments).
 */

#define START_CIRCLE   0
#define FULL_CIRCLE (360*64)

DrawOval( display, drawable, gc, x, y, width, height )

Display         *display;
Drawable        drawable;
GC              gc;
int             x, y;           /* location */
int             width, height; /* size */

{       /* DrawOval */

        /*
         * Never draw an "arc" with
```

```
         * a width/height < 1!!!
         */
        if ( width < 1 )
              {
              width = 1;
              }

        if ( height < 1 )
              {
              height = 1;
              }

        XDrawArc( display,
              drawable,
              gc,
              x, y, width, height,
              START_CIRCLE,
              FULL_CIRCLE );

}       /* DrawOval */

FillOval( display, drawable, gc, x, y, width, height )

Display         *display;
Drawable        drawable;
GC              gc;
int             x, y;           /* location */
int             width, height;  /* size */

{       /* FillOval */

        /*
         * Never draw an "arc" with
         * a width/height < 1!!!
         */
        if ( width < 1 )
              {
              width = 1;
              }

        if ( height < 1 )
              {
              height = 1;
              }
```

```
        XFillArc( display,
             drawable,
             gc,
             x, y, width, height,
             START_CIRCLE,
             FULL_CIRCLE );

}       /* FillOval */

/* end of file oval.c */
```

DRAWING MULTIPLE LINES, RECTANGLES, AND ARCS

Each drawing routine shown above requires at least one interaction with the X server, including clipping the output and setting up the graphics-context values. If you want to draw many lines (all with the same graphics context—meaning the same color and same size), there are a number of X routines to draw multiple objects. All the items though, must share the same drawable (usually a window) and the same graphics context. These multiple drawing functions are perfect for tasks like drawing real-time data-trending charts.

```
Display       *display;
Drawable      drawable;
GC            gc;
XArc          arcs[ ARBITRARY_SIZE ];
int           number_arcs;

XDrawArcs( display, drawable, gc,
        arcs, number_arcs );

XFillArcs( display, drawable, gc,
        arcs, number_arcs );
```

For `XDrawArcs` and `XFillArcs`, each arc is described in an array element in an array of `XArc` structures. The `XArc` structure looks like:

```
typedef struct {
        short           x, y;
        unsigned short  width, height;
        short           angle1, angle2;
        } XArc;
```

When drawing multiple arcs, you need to allocate an array of XArc structs, with as many elements as you plan on drawing. For example:

```
Display         *display;
Drawable        drawable;
GC              gc;
int             number_arcs;
XArc            arcs[ 42 ];

arcs[ 0 ].x       = 100;
arcs[ 0 ].y       = 100;
arcs[ 0 ].width   = 50;
arcs[ 0 ].height  = 50;
arcs[ 0 ].angle1  = 0;
arcs[ 0 ].angle2  = 360*64;
arcs[ 1 ].x       = 200;
arcs[ 1 ].y       = 200;
arcs[ 1 ].width   = 50;
arcs[ 1 ].height  = 50;
arcs[ 1 ].angle1  = 0;
arcs[ 1 ].angle2  = 360*64;

number_arcs = 2;

XDrawArcs( display, drawable, gc,
        arcs, number_arcs );
```

This draws two arcs on the screen. Like the multiple arc routines, the multiple rectangle routines also define a structure, this time called XRectangle:

```
typedef struct {
        short          x, y;
        unsigned short width, height;
        } XRectangle;
```

XDrawRectangles outlines multiple rectangles, while XFillRectangles fills multiple rectangles. Usually, you pass an array of the XRectangle structure, declared as large as you need.

```
Display         *display;
Drawable        drawable;
GC              gc;
XRectangle      rectangles[ ARBITRARY_SIZE ];
int             number_rectangles;
```

```
XDrawRectangles( dsplay, drawable, gc,
       rectangles, number_rectangles );

XFillRectangles( dsplay, drawable, gc,
       rectangles, number_rectangles );
```

Lines, too, have their own structure for a multiple line-drawing function, `XDrawLines`, called `XPoint`:

```
typedef struct {
       short x, y;
       } XPoint;
```

In this case, instead of the number of lines, you specify the number of points. All points are drawn connected, which is different from the above examples, where the shapes may well be unconnected.

```
Display            *display;
Drawable           drawable;
GC                 gc;
XPoint             points[ ARBITRARY_SIZE ];
int                number_points;
int                mode;

XDrawLines( display, drawable, gc,
       points, number_points, mode );
```

The mode can have one of two values: `CoordModeOrigin` or `CoordModePrevious`. `CoordModeOrigin` means that each point is specified relative to the drawable's origin (usually the window's origin). This is the way you would expect `XDrawLines` to act. `CoordModePrevious` specifies that each point x and y coordinates are relative to the last point in the `XPoint` array. The first point is relative to the origin of the drawable. This mode can be good for drawing lines in what is called *turtle geometry*: where the ending point of one line is the starting location for the next, and all movements are described as the motion from the last point (i.e., relative to the last point). These points can also be drawn as unconnected points, with the `XDrawPoints` function:

```
Display            *display;
Drawable           drawable;
GC                 gc;
XPoint             points[ ARBITRARY_SIZE ];
int                number_points;
int                mode;
```

```
XDrawPoints( display, drawable, gc,
        points, number_points, mode );
```

You can also draw just one point, of course, with XDrawPoint:

```
Display                 *display;
Drawable                drawable;
GC                      gc;
int                     x, y;

XDrawPoint( display, drawable, gc, x, y );
```

DRAWING TOO MANY LINES, RECTANGLES, OR ARCS

There are only so many requests that you can bundle together into one network packet and send off to the X server. Newer versions of the X library will break up very large requests, but older X libraries didn't break up big requests into packets.

Therefore, if you're sending giant packets to the X server with XDrawLines or one of the other multiple-item drawing functions, you may want to check on the largest size you can send out at once. XMaxRequestSize returns this size, in units of four bytes.

```
Display                 *display;
long                    max_req_size;

max_req_size = XMaxRequestSize(display)
```

Unfortunately, older versions of the X library didn't have XMaxRequestSize, which was introduced in R3.

WHEN TO DRAW

Your applications should never draw into their windows until the first Expose event arrives. That signifies that the window is mapped, on the screen and visible. Whenever Expose events arrive, your application should redraw the proper area of its windows. Always wait for the first Expose event before drawing, though, because your window may not be on the screen.

SOURCE CODE FOR CHAP3.C

The file `chap3.c` contains the `chap3` main function. It creates a window and maps the window to the screen. A `Redraw` function redraws some lines, ovals, and rectangles in the window when `Expose` events arrive. Note that we use the lazy method for handling `Expose` events: we redraw the entire window on every `Expose` event. Later example programs will use much smarter redraw methods.

The `chap3` program waits for 20 `Expose` events, then quits. Like the last chapter, real X applications would use a better event-handling loop, which we'll introduce starting in Chapter 6.

```
/*
 *      chap3.c
 *      Example program for Chapter 3. Draws lines,
 *      rectangles and ovals in a window.
 *
 *      Written for X Window Applications
 *      Programming, 2nd Edition
 */

#include <stdio.h>
#include <X11/Xlib.h>
#include <X11/Xutil.h>

main( argc, argv )

int     argc;
char    *argv[];

{       /* main */

        Display *display;
        Display *ConnectToServer(); /* connect.c */
        Window  rootwindow, window;
        Window  OpenWindow();       /* window.c */
        int     screen;
        int     x, y, width, height;
        Visual  *visual = CopyFromParent;
        GC      gc;
        GC      CreateGC();         /* gc.c */
        XEvent  event;
        int     count;
```

```
/*
 * Connect to default X server
 */
display = ConnectToServer( (char *) NULL,
        &screen,
        &rootwindow );

/*
 * Create a window on the display
 */
x      = 10;
y      = 10;
width  = 300;
height = 300;
window = OpenWindow( display,
        rootwindow,
        x, y, width, height,
        BlackPixel( display, screen ),
        WhitePixel( display, screen ),
        ExposureMask,
        visual );

/*
 * Provide information to the window manager.
 */
SetStandardHints( display, window,
     argv[0], argv[0],
     x, y, width, height );

/*
 * Create graphics context for drawing
 */
gc = CreateGC( display, window,
     BlackPixel( display, screen ),     /* fore */
     WhitePixel( display, screen ) );   /* back */

/*
 * Make the window actually appear
 */
XMapRaised( display, window );
XFlush( display );
```

```
        /*
         * Loop for 20 Expose events. Real programs
         * should go until done or the user quits.
         */
        count = 0;
        while( count < 20 )
                {
                XNextEvent( display, &event );

                if ( event.type == Expose )
                      {
                      Redraw( display, window, gc );
                      count++;
                      }

                }

        /*
         * Close connection to X server
         */
        XCloseDisplay( display );

}       /* main */

Redraw( display, window, gc )

Display       *display;
Window        window;
GC            gc;

/*
 *      Redraws contents of our window, by drawing
 *      and filling some simple shapes.
 */

{       /* Redraw */

        XDrawLine( display, window, gc,
              1, 1, 100, 100 );

        XDrawRectangle( display, window, gc,
                100, 100, 100, 100 );
```

```
        XFillRectangle( display, window, gc,
                200, 200, 100, 100 );

        DrawOval( display, window, gc,
                100, 100, 100, 100 );

        FillOval( display, window, gc,
                110, 110, 64, 64 );

        /*
         * Send all our requests over the network,
         * so that the drawing is visible.
         */
        XFlush( display );
}       /* Redraw */

/* end of file chap3.c */
```

COMPILING AND LINKING THE CHAP3 PROGRAM

The `chap3` program requires the following files:

`chap3.c`	
`classhnt.c`	(Chapter 2)
`connect.c`	(Chapter 1)
`gc.c`	
`oval.c`	
`sizehint.c`	(Chapter 2)
`window.c`	(Chapter 2)
`wmname.c`	(Chapter 2)
`wmhints.c`	(Chapter 2)

You can compile and link the `chap3` program with a command like:

```
cc -o chap3 -DX11R4 chap3.c classhnt.c connect.c \
        gc.c oval.c sizehint.c window.c wmname.c \
        wmhints.c -lX11
```

You can also use the Makefile in Appendix A and type:

```
make chap3
```

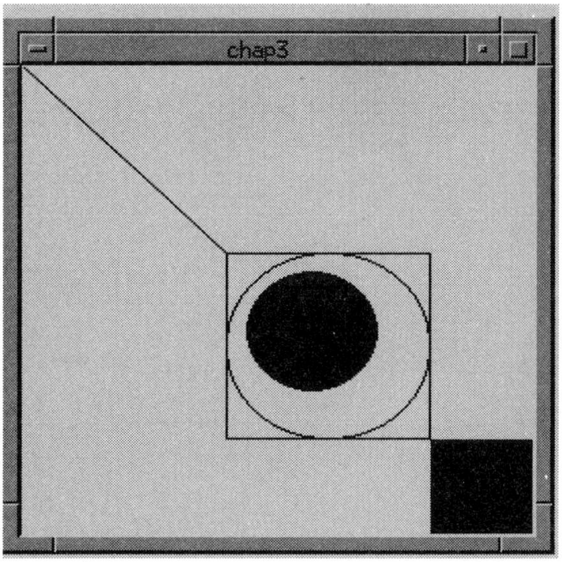

Figure 3.2. The Chap3 Program.

In the next chapter, we'll provide the same program, only drawing in color.

SUMMARY

X has a number of routines to draw into a window. In fact, most window-drawing functions can also draw into an arbitrary off-screen drawing area area called a Pixmap (used for icons). Lines and rectangles seem to be the basic X drawing functions. The X library provides no oval and circle functions, so you must come up with a means to draw them on your own, such as by drawing an arc about a whole circle. For performance reasons, X has multiple-drawing functions, such as XDrawLines, to cut down the network traffic and speed drawing when you want to draw a whole number of lines (with the same color, same pen size, and same GC).

XLIB FUNCTIONS AND MACROS INTRODUCED IN THIS CHAPTER

XChangeGC

XCreateGC

XDrawArc

XDrawArcs

XDrawLine

XDrawLines

XDrawPoint

XDrawPoints

XDrawRectangle

XDrawRectangles

XFillArc

XFillArcs

XFillRectangle

XFillRectangles

XGetGCValues

XMaxRequestSize

XSetBackground

XSetForeground

Chapter 4

COLOR

Drawing in color is fun. It can make selections clearer and highlight key areas of an interface. Unfortunately, color also is one of the most nonstandard aspects of graphic workstations. It seems that each graphic workstation uses a different means for specifying color. Some have color tables, some have color planes, and all seem to be different.

X, attempting to be device-independent, has to deal with all the many color implementations. Perhaps because of this, color in X appears overly complex. The seemingly simple task of drawing a line in blue leads to all sorts of contortions in initializing colors and finding visuals. This chapter aims at avoiding as much of the complexity as possible, while concentrating on the most common uses for color, such as drawing items using various colors. It suggests that using default color values helps make your code very portable while using the fewest workstation resources. The goal here is to draw graphic items in color, without all the mess. This chapter does not describe the entire X color model in depth, because it just isn't needed for most applications, quite frankly, and it is far too easy for the programmer to get bogged down in excruciating detail work that doesn't yield tangible improvements.

Color is probably the hardest area to grasp when trying to understand X. This chapter concentrates on the basic skills of drawing lines in red, green, or medium slate blue. After finishing this chapter, you may want to look up the X reference material from the X server vendor for your workstation, should you really desire more complexity than is presented here.

THE PORTABILITY AND USEFULNESS OF COLOR APPLICATIONS

As stated above, color is fun. But, it is not fun for those who only own monochrome systems. Before requiring color for your application, think carefully whether the color is actually needed. Adding even low-end color to a workstation typically adds $1,000 to $2,000 to the cost of the hardware, and much more if you want the ultimate in color workstations. Therefore, many installations have only monochrome or grey-scale systems. By requiring color, you will be precluding many potential users from ever using your software.

In addition, a significant number of people are partially or fully color blind. Others have a hard time differentiating between various hues—especially variations on blue. When designing a user interface, you must keep all these factors in mind.

Color, of course, can certainly add meaning to displays of data. Color, for example, can highlight dangerous areas in red in a factory-floor application. When all is said and done, color interfaces usually look better than monochrome. So, using color is a tradeoff: your interfaces look better in color, but the potential audience for an application may not be able to appreciate a color interface or may not have the computer hardware to do so.

When designing the interface, following a few guidelines will certainly help in this tradeoff:

- Design the original interface in monochrome (black and white). That way, you can still produce a monochrome version. One worthwhile piece of advice (from Apple Computer's *Inside Macintosh* series) is to color the black bits only. That way the interface will still work in black-and-white. In the previous examples, checking the macro `DefaultDepth` for a value of one means the program is running on a monochrome screen, under a monochrome default visual.

- Avoid going hog-wild with colors. Unless you are attempting realistic image visualization, stick to about eight colors only. The very popular 386 and 486 systems normally support only 16 colors, so you quickly run out of available colors as each X application grabs two or three. Again, too many colors will confuse the user. (Although if you are ray-tracing 3D views, you will want to use all the colors available on your screen.)
- Design your code to be as portable as possible. Stick to the most common areas of color handling in X. This means you won't take full advantage of everyone's display (especially if they are Silicon Graphics workstations). But your applications will be more likely to work, and work well, on different types of hardware. One of the prime advantages of the X Window System is that it runs on many different workstations by many different vendors.

Most of these different workstations are built on an RGB color model: red, green, and blue phosphors within each pixel are combined to form the different hues on the screen. Electron beams excite the phosphors, which provides the color. Simultaneously exciting all phosphors produces a white pixel; when all are unexcited, you're left with a black pixel.

Color displays use multiple bits within a pixel, or a dot on the screen, to further specify colors. These bits are also known as *planes*, and the most common color display contains between four and eight planes. You have access to many colors, even though a limited number of them are actually on the display at one time.

In contrast, monochrome displays only have one plane, and the phosphor is either on or off. Gray scales are simulated by making the red, green, and blue values equal.

At the other end of the spectrum, we're starting to see more and more workstations with up to 24 planes. These are high-performance systems; you can see many more colors at a time at a greater resolution, but the tradeoff is the overwhelming complexity of administering these screens. And, of course, these monitors are rather costly.

VISUALS

Obviously there needs to be a way for the base system to tell X its type. This is done through the *visual class*, a means for abstracting hardware differences. X provides six visual classes: `GrayScale`, `PseudoColor`, `DirectColor`, `StaticGray`, `StaticColor`, and `TrueColor`. The static visual classes (along with `TrueColor`) are read-only, while the others are read/write. By having read/write classes, this normally means that you can manipulate aspects about the visual class through your application programs and create your own colors.

If you want to get technical, you could write sections of your code that would handle each visual class differently, to get the most performance out of each system. This means, however, you would essentially be duplicating your graphics code six times over with a very limited payback.

Instead, it would be a lot easier to follow certain conventons and try to use the system defaults wherever possible, thereby making your applications work on any display monitor running X. We find that most color X servers support multiple visuals of all six types on the same screen anyway, but generally `PseudoColor` visuals are the easiest to write code for. (X colors never seem to look right, so the `PseudoColor` name fits.) In the code examples below, we'll work with `PseudoColor` visuals, as they are the most common. Most of these techniques work for all visuals.

Visuals apply to screens, so a multiscreen display could support quite a lot of visuals.

By the way, you can check what visuals your X server supports by using the *xdpyinfo* program. *Xdpyinfo* reports what the X server supports, including visuals:

```
name of display:    :0.0
version number:    11.0
vendor string:    MIT X Consortium
vendor release number:    5000
maximum request size:  262140 bytes
motion buffer size:  256
bitmap unit, bit order, padding:    32, MSBFirst, 32
image byte order:    MSBFirst
number of supported pixmap formats:    2
supported pixmap formats:
       depth 1, bits_per_pixel 1, scanline_pad 32
       depth 8, bits_per_pixel 8, scanline_pad 32
keycode range:    minimum 8, maximum 132
focus:  window 0x1c0000d, revert to PointerRoot
number of extensions:    4
       SHAPE
       MIT-SHM
       Multi-Buffering
       MIT-SUNDRY-NONSTANDARD
default screen number:    0
number of screens:    1
```

```
screen #0:
  dimensions:    1152x900 pixels (325x254 millimeters)
  resolution:    90x90 dots per inch
  depths (2):    1, 8
  root window id:    0x29
  depth of root window:    8 planes
  number of colormaps:    minimum 1, maximum 1
  default colormap:    0x27
  default number of colormap cells:    256
  preallocated pixels:    black 1, white 0
  options:    backing-store YES, save-unders YES
  current input event mask:    0xd0001d
    KeyPressMask    ButtonPressMask    ButtonReleaseMask
    EnterWindowMask    SubstructureRedirectMask  PropertyChangeMask
    ColormapChangeMask
  number of visuals:    6
  default visual id:  0x20
  visual:
    visual id:    0x20
    class:    PseudoColor
    depth:    8 planes
    size of colormap:    256 entries
    red, green, blue masks:    0x0, 0x0, 0x0
    significant bits in color specification:    8 bits
  visual:
    visual id:    0x21
    class:    DirectColor
    depth:    8 planes
    size of colormap:    8 entries
    red, green, blue masks:    0x7, 0x38, 0xc0
    significant bits in color specification:    8 bits
  visual:
    visual id:    0x22
    class:    GrayScale
    depth:    8 planes
    size of colormap:    256 entries
    red, green, blue masks:    0x0, 0x0, 0x0
    significant bits in color specification:    8 bits
  visual:
    visual id:    0x23
    class:    StaticGray
    depth:    8 planes
    size of colormap:    256 entries
```

```
    red, green, blue masks:    0x0, 0x0, 0x0
    significant bits in color specification:    8 bits
  visual:
    visual id:    0x24
    class:    StaticColor
    depth:    8 planes
    size of colormap:    256 entries
    red, green, blue masks:    0x7, 0x38, 0xc0
    significant bits in color specification:    8 bits
  visual:
    visual id:    0x25
    class:    TrueColor
    depth:    8 planes
    size of colormap:    8 entries
    red, green, blue masks:    0x7, 0x38, 0xc0
    significant bits in color specification:    8 bits
  number of mono multibuffer types:    6
    visual id, max buffers, depth:    0x20, 0, 8
    visual id, max buffers, depth:    0x21, 0, 8
    visual id, max buffers, depth:    0x22, 0, 8
    visual id, max buffers, depth:    0x23, 0, 8
    visual id, max buffers, depth:    0x24, 0, 8
    visual id, max buffers, depth:    0x25, 0, 8
  number of stereo multibuffer types:    0
```

Note that the system described above supports all six X visual types on the same screen. Most X color systems do this.

COLOR OVERVIEW

Most of the rest of this chapter describes six steps for using color in X applications.

1. The first step, of course, is to connect to an X server.
2. Find the desired visual; in our case, a `PseudoColor` visual. If the X server's default visual is a `PseudoColor` visual, use that. We advise to always use the defaults, if possible. If not, we need to climb through the visual tree, finding a `PseudoColor` visual.
3. Next, create a window, using the visual we found in the step above, instead of the constant `CopyFromParent` that we've been using.

4. If you don't use the default visual, you must create a colormap. Otherwise, you may be able to use the default colormap. If this colormap has enough free color entries, you can use the default. If not, you still have to create your own.
5. Whatever colormap you end up with, you'll then need to allocate colors from the colormap. We suggest using the English color names, like `Red` and `LimeGreen`, from the RGB color database.
6. Finally, we create a graphics context for our window and set the GC to draw in some of the colors we've allocated in the previous step.

GOING TECHNICOLOR, OR WHY THE DEFAULTS ARE USEFUL

For the best-looking applications, use the default visual and colormap, if at all possible. The default colormap is shared among most X applications, so it fills up quickly on a 16-color system. Most workstation hardware supports only one colormap at a time. If you create your own colormap, though, chances are the window manager will swap in your colormap when the mouse pointer is in your application's windows, and swap out the colormap when the pointer is in the rest of the other X client windows.

This colormap swapping will result in what are refered to as *technicolor* effects: the colors in either your window or the rest of the screen will go "blooey." These technicolor effects don't look good and tend to annoy users. Unless you really need the colors, don't create your own colormap. If at all possible, use the default visual and colormap. If you write an application that analyzes Magellan space probe data, you'll probably need every available color. But, if you're writing a graphical electronic-mail program, you probably don't (unless you're mailing 24-bit image data, of course).

In the code below, we'll try to use the default visual and colormap, if possible.

FINDING A PSEUDOCOLOR VISUAL

We've already covered connecting to X servers, so, the first step is to find a `PseudoColor` visual—preferably the default visual.

Up to now, we've used the constant `CopyFromParent` as our visual pointer when creating windows. What we're looking for now is a visual pointer with a class of `PseudoColor`:

```
typedef struct {
        XExtData        *ext_data;
        VisualID        visualid;
        int             class;
        unsigned long  red_mask, green_mask, blue_mask;
        int             bits_per_rgb;
        int             map_entries;
        } Visual;
```

Normally, you treat a visual pointer as a read-only structure and don't mess with its values.

THE DEFAULT VISUAL

The default visual just may have what we need—a class of `PseudoColor`. Most X color systems, in fact, make a `PseudoColor` visual the default. And a lot of free X software assumes this. Assuming anything about X (except that it's complicated) is not a good idea. Of course, vendors who make their X systems provide a different default visual just to be different aren't helping the situation any, even if they are technically correct. The bottom line is that you should verify that the default visual is a `PseudoColor` visual. Don't assume anything.

You can find the default visual with the macro `DefaultVisual`:

```
Display         *display;
int             screen;
Visual          *visual;

visual = DefaultVisual( display, screen );

if ( visual->class == PseudoColor )
        {
        /* we can use the default visual... */
        }
```

CLIMBING THE VISUAL TREE

If the default visual doesn't have the class you want, in this case `PseudoColor`, you need to climb through the list, or tree, of visuals that the X server supports, trying to find the type you want.

XMatchVisualInfo searches the list of supported visuals and finds one that provides the desired class and depth (number of color planes):

```
Display        *display;
int            screen;
int            desired_depth;
int            desired_class;
XVisualInfo    visual_info;    /* RETURN */
int            status;

status = XMatchVisualInfo( display, screen,
            desired_depth, desired_class,
            &visual_info);
```

XMatchVisualInfo returns a nonzero value on success, and fills in an XVisualInfo structure with information about the visual it found. On failure, XMatchVisualInfo returns 0.

In our case, the desired class would be PseudoColor. But we haven't any idea what the desired depth would be. Most X color systems provide 8 color planes (or 256 colors), but there are a lot of 386/486-based systems upgraded to UNIX from DOS that support VGA graphics with only 4 color planes. Still other systems provide 16-bit or 24-bit color. Yet, our programs should work fine on all these systems.

If you don't know a desired depth as well as the class, you cannot use XMatchVisualInfo. Instead, we find XGetVisualInfo works better:

```
Display          *display;
long             visual_info_mask;
int              number_visuals;
XVisualInfo      *visual_array;
XVisualInfo      visual_info_template;

visual_info_template.class  = PseudoColor;
visual_info_template.screen = screen;

visual_info_mask = VisualClassMask | VisualScreenMask;

visual_array = XGetVisualInfo( display,
               visual_info_mask,
               &visual_info_template,
               &number_visuals );
```

XGetVisualInfo takes a template of what we're looking for, as well as a mask that specifies which fields in the template are filled in, and then returns an array of information on all the supported visuals that match the template.

In our case, we want a PseudoColor visual on the current screen. XGetVisualInfo then returns information on all the matching supported visuals. Since we're not asking for very much, we may get a lot of entries back. You could, then, go through the returned XVisualInfo array and find the visual that best matches your needs. In the code below, though, we take the lazy approach and use the first returned PseudoColor visual, since we really won't use that many colors.

Both XGetVisualInfo and XMatchVisualInfo provide XVisualInfo structures that describe the visuals found:

```
typedef struct {
        Visual          *visual;
        VisualID        visualid;
        int             screen;
        unsigned int    depth;
        int             class;
        unsigned long   red_mask;
        unsigned long   green_mask;
        unsigned long   blue_mask;
        int             colormap_size;
        int             bits_per_rgb;
        } XVisualInfo;
```

Included in this structure is a pointer to the actual visual information. Use this pointer as the visual when creating a window.

XGetVisualInfo requires a now-familiar bitmask that tells the routine which fields in the XVisualInfo template are filled in. The constants for these bitmasks are:

Mask Bits	*Value*	*Mask Bits*	*Value*
VisualNoMask	0x0	VisualGreenMaskMask	0x20
VisualIDMask	0x1	VisualBlueMaskMask	0x40
VisualScreenMask	0x2	VisualColormapSizeMask	0x80
VisualDepthMask	0x4	VisualBitsPerRGBMask	0x100
VisualClassMask	0x8	VisualAllMask	0x1FF
VisualRedMaskMask	0x10		

When done with the `VisualInfo` array, free it with `XFree`:

```
XVisualInfo  *visual_array;

XFree( visual_array );
```

We've put together a function, `SetUpVisual`, which finds a PseudoColor visual. First, `SetUpVisual` checks to see if the screen's default visual will work. If so, the routine is done. If not, `SetUpVisual` calls `XGetVisualInfo` to find a `PseudoColor` visual on the current screen. We've placed `SetUpVisual` in the file `visual.c`.

SOURCE CODE FOR VISUAL.C

```
/*
 *      visual.c
 *      Routine for grabbing a PseudoColor visual.
 *
 *      Written for X Window Applications
 *      Programming, 2nd Edition
 */

#include <stdio.h>
#include <X11/Xlib.h>
#include <X11/Xutil.h>

SetUpVisual( display, screen, visual, depth )

Display      *display;
int          screen;
Visual       **visual; /* RETURN: pointer to visual found */
int          *depth;   /* RETURN: depth of visual */

/*
 *      SetUpVisual finds a PseudoColor visual
 *      on the given screen. If possible, uses the
 *      default visual, to avoid technicolor effects
 *      on the screen as you move the mouse around.
 */

{       /* SetUpVisual */
        int         number_visuals;
```

```
XVisualInfo    *visual_array;
XVisualInfo    visual_info_template;
int            status = False;

if ( DefaultVisual( display, screen )->class
      == PseudoColor )
      {
      *visual = DefaultVisual( display, screen );
      *depth = DefaultDepth( display, screen );
      status = True;
      }
else
      {
      /*
       * We are looking for a PseudoColor
       * visual on the current screen.
       */
      visual_info_template.class  = PseudoColor;
      visual_info_template.screen = screen;

      visual_array = XGetVisualInfo( display,
            VisualClassMask | VisualScreenMask,
            &visual_info_template,
            &number_visuals );

      /*
       * Did we find one?
       */
      if ( ( number_visuals > 0 ) &&
         ( visual_array != NULL ) )
         {
         /*
          * Choose the first PseudoColor visual
          */
         *visual = visual_array[0].visual;
         *depth  = visual_array[0].depth;
         XFree( visual_array );
         status  = True;
         }
      else
         {
         *visual = CopyFromParent;
         status  = False;
```

```
                }
            }

        return( status );

}       /* SetUpVisual */

/* end of file visual.c */
```

We use the visual returned by `SetUpVisual` in creating a window (using the `OpenWindow` function described in Chapter 2). Once we create the window, we need to create a colormap (or use the default).

THE DEFAULT X WINDOW COLORMAP

The X Window System uses a colormap to define the colors available to an application program. The X server associates every window with a colormap. This colormap provides an indirect method for defining colors that appear on the screen. You need a colormap to specify the colors you want to appear. In most cases, the standard colormap for a given workstation screen should be used, as long as you used the default visual for a given screen. The easiest way to get a colormap of your own is to use the default colormap:

```
Display         *display;
int             screen;
Visual          *visual;
Colormap        colormap;
int             depth;

visual = DefaultVisual( display, screen );

if ( visual->class == PseudoColor )
        {
        colormap = DefaultColomap( display, screen );

        depth = DefaultDepth( display, screen );
        }
```

In the above example, if the depth is 1, then you have a monochrome system, making the colormap pretty useless. It is a good idea (and a most portable idea) to use the default colormap. Some workstations have a hardware read-only colormap that you cannot modify. Other workstations have limited memory resources. Don't forget that color normally takes up a lot of RAM. If at all possible, try to use the default system colormap; this also avoids the technicolor effects described above.

CREATING A COLORMAP

Unfortunately, you may need to create a colormap. `XCreateColormap` creates a colormap using the given visual:

```
Display       *display;
Window        window;
Visual        *visual;
int           amount_alloc;
Colormap      colormap;

amount_alloc = AllocNone;

colormap = XCreateColormap( display, window,
                visual, amount_alloc );

if ( colormap != None )
        {
        /* we have success... */
        }
```

The window ID passed to `XCreateColormap` is just used to get the screen on which the window resides. You'll find a lot of X library functions do this.

The allocation should be one of the constants `AllocNone` or `AllocAll`. We normally find that you want to allocate zero colormap entries when you create the colormap—at least with `PseudoColor` visuals. Instead, colormap entries are allocated later (which we'll cover below). If you're using a `StaticGray`, `StaticColor`, or `TrueColor` visual, the allocation *must* be `AllocNone`, or you'll generate an error.

`AllocAll` means all colormap entries are allocated at once.

Once the colormap is created, you need to associate the colormap with a given window, using `XSetWindowColormap`:

```
Display       *display;
Window        window;
```

```
Colormap     colormap;

XSetWindowColormap( display, window, colormap );
```

Never call `XInstallColormap` or `XUninstallColormap` (unless you're writing a window manager). On old Release 2 and 3 systems, sometimes users would avoid running a window manager, so applications had to install their colormaps manually. Now (ever since Release 4), installing colormaps is officially the province of the window manager. The `XSetColormap` function should be enough to get the window manager to install your colormap when necessary.

Once we've found the proper visual, we use the function `SetUpColormap` in the file `colormap.c` to either create a colormap or use the screen's default colormap.

SOURCE CODE FOR COLORMAP.C

```
/*
 *      colormap.c
 *      Colormap function.
 *
 *      Written for X Window Applications
 *      Programming, 2nd Edition
 */

#include <stdio.h>
#include <X11/Xlib.h>
#include <X11/Xutil.h>

SetUpColormap( display, screen, window, visual, colormap )

Display         *display;
int             screen;
Window          window;
Visual          *visual;
Colormap        *colormap;

/*
 *      SetUpColormap creates an X colormap using
 *      the given screen and visual. Uses the default
 *      colormap, if possible, to avoid technicolor
```

```
 *      effects on the screen as the mouse is moved
 *      around.
 */

{        /* SetUpColormap */
         int     status = False;

        if ( visual == DefaultVisual( display, screen ) )
             {
             *colormap = DefaultColormap( display, screen );

             status    = True;
             }
        else
             {
             /*
              * Create a colormap using the
              * visual found in SetUpVisual.
              */
             *colormap = XCreateColormap( display,
                           window,
                           visual,
                           AllocNone );

             /*
              * Check for failure.
              */
             if ( *colormap != None )
                {
                XSetWindowColormap( display, window,
                   *colormap );

                status = True;
                }
             else
                {
                /*
                 * At least have a
                 * colormap anyway.
                 */
                *colormap = DefaultColormap( display,
                      screen );
                }
```

```
            }

        return( status );

}       /* SetUpColormap */

/* end of file colormap.c */
```

FREEING COLORMAPS

When done with a colormap, you should call `XFreeColormap` to release the resources. Colormaps are precious commodities on most workstations, so if you don't need one anymore, free it:

```
Display      *display;
Colormap     colormap;

XFreeColormap( display, colormap );
```

DRAWING A LINE IN BLUE

Once you have a colormap, three things set up a user drawing a line in blue (or wheat or lime green or whatever). When learning a new graphics system, if you can learn how to draw a line in blue, you're 80 percent finished. This first step is always the hardest, and the rest comes much easier.

First, you need to find a match in the X server's color database for the name of your color. Second, you need to allocate (or find) a color cell in your colormap for the color. Third, you need to set the foreground color in a graphics context to the color in which you want to draw.

ENGLISH COLOR NAMES AND THE RGB DATABASE

Each X server maintains an RGB (that's red, green, blue) color database. This database has English color names with associated RGB values. The entry for blue, for example, has:

```
  0   0 255           blue
```

Other blue entries include:

```
240 248 255          alice blue
 25  25 112          midnight blue
  0   0 128          navy blue
100 149 237          cornflower blue
 72  61 139          dark slate blue
106  90 205          slate blue
123 104 238          medium slate blue
132 112 255          light slate blue
  0   0 205          medium blue
 65 105 225          royal blue
 30 144 255          dodger blue
  0 191 255          deep sky blue
135 206 235          sky blue
135 206 250          light sky blue
 70 130 180          steel blue
176 196 222          light steel blue
173 216 230          light blue
176 224 230          powder blue
 95 158 160          cadet blue
138  43 226          blue violet
  0   0 255          blue1
  0   0 238          blue2
  0   0 205          blue3
  0   0 139          blue4
```

On standard X systems, this RGB database is stored in `/usr/lib/X11/rgb.txt`. (Actually, this database is compiled to a data file, `/usr/lib/X11/rgb`, for speed. The `rgb.txt` file is the source text that you can read.) This database grew enormously between Release 3 (with 66 entries) and R4 (with over 600 entries). You'll must be careful about what names you use, as many of the more obscure names, like `gainsboro`, aren't listed in older (pre-R4) RGB databases.

The nice thing about the RGB database is that you can look up a color, such as `Red` or `LimeGreen`, on every X display and get back an RGB value for that color. `XLookupColor` does this:

```
Display      *display;
Colormap     colormap
XColor       exactcolor, hardwarecolor;
char         *colorname = "blue";
int          status;
```

```
status = XLookupColor( display, colormap,
            colorname,
            &exactcolor,
            &hardwarecolor );
```

XLookupColor tries to find a match between the text name of the color, stored in colorname, and an entry in the system color database. If there is a match, XLookupColor will return a nonzero value.

When naming these colors, do not put any spaces in the names. Also, case does not matter, as MediumSlateBlue and MEDIUMSLATEBLUE should resolve to the same color. (Most people find MediumSlateBlue easier to read, though.)

The exactcolor returns the RGB components from the color database, exactly as they are in the RGB database. The exactcolor is of the XColor structure type, defined as:

```
typedef struct
       {
       unsigned long  pixel;
       unsigned short red;
       unsigned short green;
       unsigned short blue;
       char           flags;
       char           pad;
       } XColor;
```

In this case, it is the red, green, and blue fields that are the most important. These values specify the red, green, and blue components of a given color. The values go from 0 (none) to 65,535 (max), or from 0,0,0 (black) to 65535,65535,65535 (white). The X server scales these values to numbers acceptable to your graphics hardware.

The flags field tells which of the red, green, and blue fields are used, and is a bitmask of DoRed, DoGreen, and DoBlue.

The hardwarecolor returns the RGB components of the closest hardware match for the asked-for color. Sometimes this match may not be the best (especially with a pink that doesn't seem too pink). But the RGB database is the default, it is widely available on most X servers, and the MIT X Consortium has asked that aesthetic-minded users come up with better color matches for various color systems—with few people volunteering for the work. (Releases 4 and 5 have dramatically better color definitions than R3 and before.)

After a color name has been looked up in the system color database, a particular color cell must be found or allocated in the application's colormap. Here, we use the hardwarecolor, with the function XAllocColor, to either find an existing color cell in the colormap or allocate a new cell for our color. Read-only color cells can be shared among applications, which makes sense, because there's no reason for each application to allocate a separate cell for the same red color. XAllocColor allocates a read-only color cell:

```
Display       *display;
Colormap      colormap
XColor        hardwarecolor;
int           status;

status = XAllocColor( display, colormap,
                  &hardwareCclor );
```

If XAllocColor returns a nonzero value, then the call was successful. Once the call is successful, you have a pixel value (in the XColor structure) that is an entry into the colormap where the new color is located. Previously, we only used only two standard pixel values, WhitePixel and BlackPixel. Now the colored pixel value can be used in the same way.

SETTING A GRAPHICS CONTEXT TO DRAW WITH A COLOR

The function XSetForeground, just like in the last chapter, will set a graphics context to use the given foreground color pixel value—in this case the result of the XAllocColor call. The drawing calls introduced last chapter can be used to draw lines in red, green, or NavyBlue:

```
Display       *display;
GC            gc;
XColor        hardwarecolor;

XSetForeground( display, gc,
                hardwarecolor.pixel );
```

You can combine XLookupColor and XAllocColor in one X library call. XAllocNamedColor will look up the English color name and allocate a colormap cell for the color:

```
Display          *display;
Colormap         colormap;
```

```
char            *colorname;
XColor          hardwarecolor, exactcolor;
unsigned long   color;
int             status;

status = XAllocNamedColor( display, colormap,
             colorname,
             &hardwarecolor,
             &exactcolor );

if ( status != 0 )
       {
       color = hardwarecolor.pixel;
       }
```

Note the strangely reversed order on the `hardwarecolor` and `exactcolor`.

That's all there is to starting out with color in X. It may be all you need for your applications.

SOURCE CODE FOR COLOR.C

The file `color.c` contains the utility function `AllocNamedColor`, which uses `XAllocNamedColor` to allocate a cell in a colormap for the given color name. We pass a default color, usually black or white, to `AllocNamedColor`, so that there is a fallback. (Your applications could, for example, fall back to monochrome in the worst-case scenario.)

```
/*
 *      color.c
 *      Color cell routine for X.
 *
 *      Written for X Window Applications
 *      Programming, 2nd Edition
 */

#include <stdio.h>
#include <X11/Xlib.h>
#include <X11/Xutil.h>

unsigned long AllocNamedColor( display, colormap,
       colorname, default_color )
```

```
Display          *display;
Colormap         colormap;
char             colorname[];
unsigned long    default_color;

/*
 *      Allocates a read-only (sharable) color cell in
 *      the given colormap, using the RGB database to
 *      convert the color name to an RGB value.
 */

{       /* AllocNamedColor */
        XColor          hardwarecolor, exactcolor;
        unsigned long   color;
        int             status;

        status = XAllocNamedColor( display, colormap,
                        colorname,
                        &hardwarecolor,
                        &exactcolor );

        if ( status != 0 )
                {
                color = hardwarecolor.pixel;
                }
        else
                {
                color = default_color;
                }

        return( color );

}       /* AllocNamedColor */

/* end of file color.c */
```

A NOTE ON THE TERM PIXEL

The designers of X use *pixel* to mean a dot on a screen (what IBM used to call pels, for picture elements). They also use *pixel* to refer to an index into a colormap, like the colors we allocated above. This tends to befuddle the matter.

A color pixel is an unsigned long value, much like the value returned by `BlackPixel`. This is an index into a colormap.

A pixel on the screen is a dot. Typical screens have `DisplayWidth * DisplayHeight` pixels available to draw into.

AN EXAMPLE PROGRAM TO DRAW A LINE IN BLUE

We've put together an example program that allocates color cells and draws using those colors. Most of the program is just an extension of the last chapter's program. The file `chap4.c` contains the main function.

SOURCE CODE FOR CHAP4.C

```
/*
 *      chap4.c
 *      Example program for Chapter 4. Introduces color
 *      and drawing in color.
 *
 *      Written for X Window Applications
 *      Programming, 2nd Edition
 */

#include <stdio.h>
#include <X11/Xlib.h>
#include <X11/Xutil.h>

/*
 *      Global colors
 */
unsigned long   black, white, red;
unsigned long   green, blue, magenta;

main( argc, argv )

int     argc;
char    *argv[];
```

```
/* main */
Display        *display;
Display        *ConnectToServer();/* connect.c */
Window         rootwindow, window;
Window         OpenWindow(); /* window.c */
int            screen;
int            x, y, width, height;
Visual         *visual = CopyFromParent;
GC             gc;
GC             CreateGC();          /* gc.c */
XEvent         event;
int            count, depth, status;
Colormap       colormap;
unsigned long  AllocNamedColor();   /* color.c */

/*
 * Connect to default X server
 */
display = ConnectToServer( (char *) NULL,
          &screen,
          &rootwindow );

/*
 * Find a PseudoColor visual for our window
 */
status = SetUpVisual( display, screen,
         &visual,
         &depth );

if ( status != True )
     {
     (void) fprintf( stderr,
        "Error in finding a PseudoColor visual.\n" );
     XCloseDisplay( display );
     exit( 1 );
     }

/*
 * Create a window on the display
 */
x       = 10;
y       = 10;
width   = 300;
```

```
height = 300;
window = OpenWindow( display,
        rootwindow,
        x, y, width, height,
        BlackPixel( display, screen ),
        WhitePixel( display, screen ),
        ExposureMask,
        visual );

/*
 * Provide information to the window manager.
 */
SetStandardHints( display, window,
     argv[0], argv[0],
     x, y, width, height );

/*
 * Set up a Colormap, AFTER we've created the window.
 */
status = SetUpColormap( display, screen, window,
        visual, &colormap );

if ( status != True )
     {
     (void) fprintf( stderr,
        "Error: Could not create a Colormap.\n" );
     XCloseDisplay( display );
     exit( 1 );
     }

/*
 * Set up colors in the Colormap
 */
black   = AllocNamedColor( display, colormap,
        "black", BlackPixel( display, screen ) );

white   = AllocNamedColor( display, colormap,
        "white", WhitePixel( display, screen ) );

red     = AllocNamedColor( display, colormap,
        "red", black );

blue    = AllocNamedColor( display, colormap,
        "blue", black );
```

```
        green   = AllocNamedColor( display, colormap,
                  "green", black );

        magenta = AllocNamedColor( display, colormap,
                  "magenta", black );

        /*
         * Create graphics context for drawing
         */
        gc = CreateGC( display, window,
             black,       /* foreground */
             white ); /* background */

        /*
         * Make the window actually appear
         */
        XMapRaised( display, window );
        XFlush( display );

        /*
         * Loop for 20 Expose events. Real programs
         * should go until done or the user quits.
         */
        count = 0;
        while( count < 20 )
             {
             XNextEvent( display, &event );

             if ( event.type == Expose )
                {
                Redraw( display, window, gc );
                count++;
                }
             }

        /*
         * Close connection to X server
         */
        XCloseDisplay( display );

}       /* main */

Redraw( display, window, gc )
```

```
Display       *display;
Window        window;
GC            gc;

/*
 *      Redraws contents of our window, by drawing
 *      lines, rectangles and ovals in color.
 */

{       /* Redraw */

        XSetForeground( display, gc, blue );

        XDrawLine( display, window, gc,
              1, 1, 100, 100 );

        XSetForeground( display, gc, red  );
        XDrawRectangle( display, window, gc,
                100, 100, 100, 100 );

        XSetForeground( display, gc, green );
        XFillRectangle( display, window, gc,
                200, 200, 100, 100 );

        XSetForeground( display, gc, black );
        DrawOval( display, window, gc,
                100, 100, 100, 100 );

        XSetForeground( display, gc, magenta );
        FillOval( display, window, gc,
                110, 110, 64, 64 );

        /*
         * Send all our requests over the network,
         * so that the drawing is visible.
         */
        XFlush( display );

}       /* Redraw */

/* end of file chap4.c */
```

COMPILING AND LINKING THE CHAP4 PROGRAM

The `chap4` program requires the following files:

`chap4.c`	
`classhnt.c`	(Chapter 2)
`color.c`	
`colormap.c`	
`connect.c`	(Chapter 1)
`gc.c`	(Chapter 3)
`oval.c`	(Chapter 3)
`sizehint.c`	(Chapter 2)
`visual.c`	
`window.c`	(Chapter 2)
`wmname.c`	(Chapter 2)
`wmhints.c`	(Chapter 2)

You can compile and link the `chap4` program with a command like:

```
cc -o chap4 -DX11R4 chap4.c classhnt.c color.c \
        colormap.c connect.c gc.c oval.c sizehint.c \
        visual.c window.c wmname.c wmhints.c -lX11
```

You can also use the Makefile in Appendix A and type:

```
make chap4
```

RUNNING THE CHAP4 PROGRAM

The `chap4` program acts just like the `chap3` program, except that we now use color. After 20 `Expose` events, the `chap4` program quits. Again, you'll see a line, rectangles, and ovals in the window, which is redrawn on `Expose` events.

X11 RELEASE 5 DEVICE-INDEPENDENT COLOR

All the color functions described so far provide for inexact colors, but this is enough for most X applications. Some applications, though, especially in prepress and publishing work, demand exact coloration.

X bases colors on RGB (Red, Green, Blue) definitions, and these RGB values permeate the X protocol. RGB values, unfortunately, don't look the same on every monitor. While most of us don't care how exact our reds are, exact colors are very important for electronic-publishing packages and for users interested in scientific visualization. Because of these problems, X11 Release 5 introduces a device-independent way to specify exact colors. (The color database and English color names already provide a device-independent way to ask for a color like red, but this red may look different on every monitor—it still should look somewhat like red, though.)

X11 Release 5 supports the following ways to define color:

- RGB (the same old way)
- RGB Intensity
- CIE XYZ
- CIE xyY
- CIE uvY
- CIE Luv
- CIE Lab
- Tektronix HVC

These methods for specifying colors are far too advanced for an introductary book. In fact, unless TekHVC or CIE means something to you, you may want to skip ahead to the end of the chapter. We won't get into the science of color, but we will get you started with the `Xcms` (X Color Management System) routines.

The X color management routines provide a way for your application to specify an exact color and then have the X library translate that color into an RGB value for a particular screen. Under the hood, with the `Xcms` routines, you're really allocating straight RGB values. These routines act entirely on the client side of X and just translate your desired color into an appropriate RGB value. Sounds simple, doesn't it? It isn't.

The first caveat: to properly translate an exact color specification to an appropriate RGB value for your screen, you'll need some form of hardware device to exactly cailbrate your monitor. Once calibrated, information on the screen must be accessible to your applications. The latest rules for well-behaved X applications, the *Inter-Client Communications Conventions Manual 1.1*, describes a means to store such device color-characterization data, called an XDCCC, so that X applications can access it. This information includes the *device gamut*, the colors are displayable on your screen so that your applications (normally under the hood with the `Xcms` routines) can modify color specifications to fit within the screen's capability—called the *gamut compression*.

This XDCCC information is used to translate CIE XYZ color triplets to RGB values on the screen. (The CIE 1931 standard is used to describe perceivable colors.) The CIE XYZ format is used by all the `Xcms` routines to translate to RGB. All other color formats, such as TekHVC, are mapped to CIE XYZ format before the translation to RGB. (You can look in Chapter 13 of Foley and van Dam's *Computer Graphics* for more on CIE color.)

THE X COLOR MANAGEMENT ROUTINES

The first thing you'll notice about the `Xcms` routines is how closely they match the regular X color routines. `XcmsLookupColor` corresponds to `XLookupColor` and `XcmsAllocNamedColor` corresponds to `XAllocNamedColor`.

`XcmsLookupColor` acts much like `XLookupColor` in that it converts a color "name" string to two `XcmsColor` structures, both an exact value and the closest value supported by the hardware:

```
#include  <X11/Xcms.h>

Display             *display;
Colormap            colormap;
char                *colorname = "rgbi:0.5/0.3/0.7";
XcmsColor           hardwarecolor, exactcolor;
unsigned long       color;
int                 status;
XcmsColorFormat     format = XcmsUndefinedFormat;

status = XcmsLookupColor( display, colormap,
                colorname,
                &exactcolor,
```

```
                &hardwarecolor,
                format );

if ( status != XcmsFailure )
        {
        /* success... */
        }
```

All the Xcms routines need the include file Xcms.h. XcmsLookupColor returns a status of XcmsFailure on errors, XcmsSuccess on success, and XcmsSuccessWithCompression to indicate that, while the routine succeeded, it had to convert the color specification using gamut compression.

The color name must be in a special Xcms syntax described below. The format is the type of color space in which the color name is defined. You can use the constant XcmsUndefinedFormat to signify that you don't know the format for the color name. That's a handy value, since your application won't always know what way the color name was formatted.

The allowed formats are:

XcmsUndefinedFormat
XcmsCIEXYZFormat
XcmsCIEuvYFormat
XcmsCIExyYFormat
XcmsCIELabFormat
XcmsCIELuvFormat
XcmsTekHVCFormat
XcmsRGBiFormat
XcmsRGBFormat.

The XcmsColorFormat data type is normally an unsigned int:

```
typedef unsigned int XcmsColorFormat;
```

Both the hardwarecolor and the exactcolor are returned in XcmsColor structures, a union of structures for all the supported color spaces:

```
typedef struct {
        union {
              XcmsRGB          RGB;
              XcmsRGBi         RGBi;
              XcmsCIEXYZ       CIEXYZ;
              XcmsCIEuvY       CIEuvY;
```

```
        XcmsCIExyY        CIExyY;
        XcmsCIELab        CIELab;
        XcmsCIELuv        CIELuv;
        XcmsTekHVC        TekHVC;
        XcmsPad          Pad;
        } spec;
    unsigned long        pixel;
    XcmsColorFormat      format;  /* which format */
    } XcmsColor;
```

Each element in the spec union is a structure for a given type of color formatting:

```
typedef struct {
        unsigned short  red;
        unsigned short  green;
        unsigned short  blue;
} XcmsRGB;
```

The RGB values are scaled from 0x0000 to 0xFFFF:

```
typedef struct {
        XcmsFloat     red;     /* 0.0 - 1.0 */
        XcmsFloat     green;   /* 0.0 - 1.0 */
        XcmsFloat     blue;    /* 0.0 - 1.0 */
} XcmsRGBi;
```

The XcmsFloat data type is normally a double:

```
typedef double XcmsFloat;

typedef struct {
        XcmsFloat     X;
        XcmsFloat     Y;
        XcmsFloat     Z;
} XcmsCIEXYZ;

typedef struct {
        XcmsFloat     u_prime; /* 0.0 - 1.0 */
        XcmsFloat     v_prime; /* 0.0 - 1.0 */
        XcmsFloat     Y;       /* 0.0 - 1.0 */
} XcmsCIEuvY;

typedef struct {
        XcmsFloat     x;       /* 0.0 - 1.0 */
        XcmsFloat     y;       /* 0.0 - 1.0 */
        XcmsFloat     Y;       /* 0.0 - 1.0 */
```

```
} XcmsCIExyY;

typedef struct {
        XcmsFloat       L_star;  /* 0.0 - 100.0 */
        XcmsFloat       a_star;
        XcmsFloat       b_star;
} XcmsCIELab;

typedef struct {
        XcmsFloat       L_star;  /* 0.0 - 100.0 */
        XcmsFloat       u_star;
        XcmsFloat       v_star;
} XcmsCIELuv;

typedef struct {
        XcmsFloat       H;       /* 0.0 - 360.0 */
        XcmsFloat       V;       /* 0.0 - 100.0 */
        XcmsFloat       C;       /* 0.0 - 100.0 */
} XcmsTekHVC;

typedef struct {
        XcmsFloat       pad0;
        XcmsFloat       pad1;
        XcmsFloat       pad2;
        XcmsFloat       pad3;
} XcmsPad;
```

`XcmsPad` is for padding.

XCMS COLOR NAMES

The `Xcms` routines expect color names to be in a certain format:

Type	***Color Format***
`XcmsCIEXYZFormat`	CIEXYZ:*X/Y/Z*
`XcmsCIEuvYFormat`	CIEuvY:*u/v/Y*
`XcmsCIExyYFormat`	CIExyY:*x/y/Y*
`XcmsCIELabFormat`	CIELab:*L/a/b*
`XcmsCIELuvFormat`	CIELuv:*L/u/v*
`XcmsRGBFormat`	rgb:*r*/g/*b*
`XcmsRGBiFormat`	rgbi:*ri/gi/bi*
`XcmsTekHVCFormat`	TekHVC:*H/V/C*

For example, "CIEXYZ:0.234/0.32/0.288" and "rgbi:0.5/0.3/0.7" are validly formatted `Xcms` color names.

All the numbers except for *r/b/g* are floating point numbers. The RGB numbers are hex values. These RGB values can also be in the old format of *#rgb*. The RGB intensity numbers go from 0.0 to 1.0 (full intensity).

Once you've converted an `Xcms` color name into an `XcmsColor` structure, you can then allocate a color cell with `XcmsAllocColor`:

```
Display          *display;
Colormap         colormap;
XcmsColor        cmscolor;
unsigned long    color;
int              status;

status = XcmsAllocColor( display, colormap,
                &cmscolor,
                XcmsUndefinedFormat );

if ( status != XcmsFailure )
        {
        color = cmscolor.pixel;
        }
```

`XcmsAllocNamedColor` combines `XcmsLookupColor` with `XcmsAllocColor`:

```
Display             *display;
Colormap            colormap;
XcmsColor           cmscolor;
unsigned long       color;
int                 status;
XcmsColor           hardwarecolor, exactcolor;
char                *colorname = "rgbi:0.5/0.3/0.7";
XcmsColorFormat     format = XcmsUndefinedFormat;

status = XcmsAllocNamedColor( display, colormap,
                colorname,
                &hardwarecolor,
                &exactcolor,
                format );
```

Note that early R5 documentation on `XcmsAllocNamedColor` is incorrect. The `format` parameter really does go at the end.

SOURCE CODE FOR COLORCMS.C

The file `colorcms.c` mirrors `color.c`. Both have a function to allocate a named color, but `colorcms.c` uses `XcmsAllocNamedColor` rather than `XAllocNamedColor`:

```
/*
 *      colorcms.c
 *      Device-independent color cell routine for X.
 *
 *      Written for X Window Applications
 *      Programming, 2nd Edition
 */

#include <stdio.h>
#include <X11/Xlib.h>
#include <X11/Xutil.h>
#include <X11/Xcms.h>

unsigned long CmsAllocNamedColor( display, colormap,
        colorname, default_color )

Display         *display;
Colormap        colormap;
char            colorname[];
unsigned long   default_color;

/*
 *      Allocates a read-only (sharable) color cell in
 *      the given colormap, using the X Color
 *      Management System routines to convert an
 *      arbitrary color name to an RGB value.
 */

{       /* CmsAllocNamedColor */
        XcmsColor     hardwarecolor, exactcolor;
        unsigned long color;
        int           status;

        status = XcmsAllocNamedColor( display,
                colormap,
                colorname,
                &hardwarecolor,
```

```
                &exactcolor,
                XcmsUndefinedFormat );

        if ( status != XcmsFailure )
             {
             color = hardwarecolor.pixel;
             }
        else
             {
             printf("XcmsFailure on [%s]\n", colorname );
             color = default_color;
             }

        return( color );

}       /* CmsAllocNamedColor */

/* end of file colorcms.c */
```

That's just the tip of the iceberg for device-independent color in X. A sample program, `chap4cms`, allows you to test out CIE, Tek, and RGB color names with `XcmsAllocNamedColor`:

SOURCE CODE FOR CHAP4CMS.C

```
/*
 *      chap4cms.c
 *      Example program for Chapter 4. Introduces
 *      device-independent color and drawing in color.
 *
 *      Written for X Window Applications
 *      Programming, 2nd Edition
 */

#include <stdio.h>
#include <X11/Xlib.h>
#include <X11/Xutil.h>

/*

 *      Global colors
 */
```

```
#define MAX_COLORS  10

unsigned long   colors[ MAX_COLORS + 1];
int             color_count;

main( argc, argv )

int     argc;
char    *argv[];

{       /* main */
        Display         *display;
        Display         *ConnectToServer();/* connect.c */
        Window          rootwindow, window;
        Window          OpenWindow();    /* window.c */
        int             screen;
        int             x, y, width, height;
        Visual          *visual = CopyFromParent;
        GC              gc;
        GC              CreateGC();      /* gc.c */
        XEvent          event;
        int             count, depth, status;
        Colormap        colormap;
        unsigned long   CmsAllocNamedColor(); /* colorcms.c */
        int             max;

        /*
         * Connect to default X server
         */
        display = ConnectToServer( (char *) NULL,
                &screen,
                &rootwindow );

        /*
         * Find a PseudoColor visual for our window
         */
        status = SetUpVisual( display, screen,
                &visual,
                &depth );

        if ( status != True )
              {
              (void) fprintf( stderr,
                 "Error in finding PseudoColor visual.\n" );
```

```
        XCloseDisplay( display );
        exit( 1 );
        }

/*
 * Create a window on the display
 */
x      = 10;
y      = 10;
width  = 300;
height = 300;
window = OpenWindow( display,
          rootwindow,
          x, y, width, height,
          BlackPixel( display, screen ),
          WhitePixel( display, screen ),
          ExposureMask,
          visual );

/*
 * Provide information to the window manager.
 */
SetStandardHints( display, window,
        argv[0], argv[0],
        x, y, width, height );

/*
 * Set up a Colormap, AFTER we've created the window.
 */
status = SetUpColormap( display, screen, window,
          visual, &colormap );

if ( status != True )
        {
        (void) fprintf( stderr,
           "Error: Could not create a Colormap.\n" );
        XCloseDisplay( display );
        exit( 1 );
        }

/*
 * Set up colors in the Colormap
 */
```

```
max = argc - 1;

if ( max > MAX_COLORS )
      {
      max = MAX_COLORS;
      }

for( color_count = 0; color_count < max;
      color_count++ )
      {
      colors[color_count] =
         CmsAllocNamedColor( display,
               colormap,
               argv[color_count+1],
               BlackPixel( display, screen ) );
      }

/*
 * Create graphics context for drawing
 */
gc = CreateGC( display, window,
      colors[0],     /* foreground */
      colors[1] );   /* background */

/*
 * Make the window actually appear
 */
XMapRaised( display, window );
XFlush( display );

/*
 * Loop for 20 Expose events. Real programs
 * should go until done or the user quits.
 */
count = 0;
while( count < 20 )
      {
      XNextEvent( display, &event );

      if ( event.type == Expose )
         {
         Redraw( display, window, gc );
         count++;
```

```
                }
            }

        /*
         * Close connection to X server
         */
        XCloseDisplay( display );

}       /* main */

Redraw( display, window, gc )

Display *display;
Window  window;

GC      gc;

/*
 *      Redraws contents of our window, by drawing
 *      lines, rectangles and ovals in color.
 */

{       /* Redraw */
        int   i;

        i = 0;
        XSetForeground( display, gc, colors[i] );

        XDrawLine( display, window, gc,
             1, 1, 100, 100 );

        if ( i < color_count )
             {
             i++;
             }

        XSetForeground( display, gc, colors[i] );

        XDrawRectangle( display, window, gc,
                100, 100, 100, 100 );

        if ( i < color_count )
```

```
            {
            i++;
            }

        XSetForeground( display, gc, colors[i] );

        XFillRectangle( display, window, gc,
                200, 200, 100, 100 );

        if ( i < color_count )
            {
            i++;
            }

        XSetForeground( display, gc, colors[i] );

        DrawOval( display, window, gc,
                100, 100, 100, 100 );

        if ( i < color_count )
            {
            i++;
            }

        XSetForeground( display, gc, colors[i] );

        FillOval( display, window, gc,
                110, 110, 64, 64 );

        /*
         * Send all our requests over the network,
         * so that the drawing is visible.
         */
        XFlush( display );

}       /* Redraw */

/* end of file chap4.c */
```

COMPILING AND LINKING THE CHAP4CMS PROGRAM

The `chap4cms` program requires the following files:

chap4cms.c	
classhnt.c	(Chapter 2)
colorcms.c	
colormap.c	
connect.c	(Chapter 1)
gc.c	(Chapter 3)
oval.c	(Chapter 3)
sizehint.c	(Chapter 2)
visual.c	
window.c	(Chapter 2)
wmname.c	(Chapter 2)
wmhints.c	(Chapter 2)

You can compile and link the `chap4cms` program with a command like:

```
cc -o chap4cms -DX11R4 chap4cms.c classhnt.c colorcms.c \
       colormap.c connect.c gc.c oval.c sizehint.c \
       visual.c window.c wmname.c wmhints.c -lX11
```

You can also use the Makefile in Appendix A and type:

```
make chap4cms
```

RUNNING THE CHAP4CMS PROGRAM

The `chap4cms` programs acts just like the `chap4` program, above, except that we now need to pass five color names, using the `Xcms` color name syntax. After 20 `Expose` events, the `chap4cms` program quits. You must have X11 Release 5 to compile and run this program.

Here's a few sample command lines to try out. Some of these numbers are derived from the X11 Release 5 documentation. You can look in the R5 documentation for more information.

```
chap4cms rgbi:0.5/0.3/1.0 rgb:ff/ff/00 rgb:00/ff/ff \
        CIEXYZ:0.2344/0.32/0.288

chap4cms CIEXYZ:0.11111/0.77777/0.233333 \
        CIEXYZ:0.2344/0.5/0.8777 CIEXYZ:0.2344/0.6/0.777

chap4cms TekHVC:0.0/20.0/0.0 TekHVC:0.0/40.0/0.0 \
        TekHVC:0.0/60.0/0.0 TekHVC:0.0/70.0/0.0 \
        TekHVC:0.0/90.0/0.0

chap4cms CIEXYZ:0.08443233/0.06011398/0.01840693 \
        CIEXYZ:0.06713718/0.03366278/0.31293880 \
        CIEXYZ:0.22601070/0.28905571/0.47233452 \
        CIEXYZ:0.34672401/0.54832153/0.44658871

chap4cms CIExyY:0.399960/0.506334/0.887844 \
        CIELuv:95.4938/0.061521/1.295631 \
        CIELab:52.6524/0.728736/0.688501
```

XCMSDB

R5 also adds a new standard X program, `xcmsdb`. `xcmsdb` loads and queries screen-color characterization data properties. These properties are stored on the root window for the screen and describe the exact color calibration of the screen.

You can use `xcmsdb` to set up the data used by the `Xcms` routines to convert colors to and from the CIEXYZ format.

SUMMARY

This introduction to X color has explicitly been made brief to concentrate on the essential details (it gets worse should you choose to delve into color with X in more depth). If at all possible, try to use the default visual and colormap and design your applications to work in monochrome or color.

The visual class abstracts hardware differences through six visual classes: `GrayScale`, `PseudoColor`, `DirectColor`, `StaticGray`, `StaticColor`, and `TrueColor`. The static visual classes (along with `TrueColor`) are read-only, while the others are read/write. By having read/write classes, you can manipulate aspects about the visual class through your application programs and create your own colors.

Using the default colormap, the first step for drawing in color is to find a match for the color name in the system-wide color data base with `XLookupColor`. Then, allocate a color cell (or find a matching cell) with the function `XAllocColor`. `XAllocNamedColor` does both functions in one. Finally, set a graphics context so that its foreground color is the color you want. Draw using this graphics context.

Release 5 introduces a new way to allocate color, using the device independent color management system, or `Xcms`. If you need exact color, you'll need these routines.

XLIB FUNCTIONS AND MACROS INTRODUCED IN THIS CHAPTER

```
DefaultColormap
DefaultVisual
XAllocColor
XAllocNamedColor
XcmsAllocColor
XcmsAllocNamedColor
XcmsLookupColor
XCreateColormap
XFreeColormap
XGetVisualInfo
XLookupColor
XMatchVisualInfo
XSetWindowColormap
```

Chapter 5

TEXT AND FONTS

The most common operation in a windowing system is drawing text. In fact, almost every application program, big or small, relies on text in one way or another. Therefore, it's mandatory for you to know how X treats text and how to use attractive text to your advantage.

FONTS

Designing attractive interfaces is a key to successful applications. The starting point for this design is deciding how you treat the text within the design. That means, in most cases, choosing the right typeface for your application.

Typography is an ancient art; over the centuries typographers have developed literally thousands of different kinds of typefaces. You won't need all of these different typefaces, of course; a few will suffice.

You gain access to these different typefaces by loading *fonts*. A complete set of characters of one size of one typeface—including uppercase and lowercase letters, punctuation marks, and numerals—is called a *font*. All fonts in X are bitmaps; each character has a specific bitpattern within the font. Each face, style, and size correspond to at least one font—Times at 25 pixels high and Times at 12 pixels high are two different fonts. This is different than Adobe's Postscript-defined fonts: Postscript describes fonts by outline, which can be resized depending on the dimensions defined by the application and later filled in. The X11 Release 5 font server offers the ability to scale fonts, and many font servers support outline scalable fonts. This font server serves fonts to the X server. Your X applications, though, still treat these fonts as bitmaps, once scaled to the proper size.

Different fonts and typefaces have different characteristics:

- Fonts are either *serif* or *sans serif*. Serif characters have a smaller line that finishes off a large stroke, such as the strokes at the top and bottom of the letter *I*. Sans serif fonts do not have these finishing strokes. This text, for instance, is set in a serif face, while the headlines are set in a sans serif face.
- A font can be *proportional-spaced* or *fixed-width*. A fixed-width font allows the same width for each character: for instance, an *m* takes up as much space as an *i*. A fixed-width font emulates a typewriter. A proportional-spaced font emulates typeset material, such as the letters on this page, in which the proportions between letters are not equal.
- Some fonts are better suited to some tasks than others. The serif font used in this text has been found to be easier to read than most sans serif faces. The more elaborate serif fonts are more suited to special effects or headlines, as are all bold faces. You want to make your text as easy to read as possible; know which fonts to use for emphasis and know which fonts to use for readability.
- Not all X servers support all fonts. You have to carefully design your applications to have a set of fallback fonts, in case the desired fonts are not available. Sun's OpenWindows, for example, provides a set of Open Look fonts that are not commonly available on other platforms. Watch out.
- Additionally, in X, a font has another set of attributes: single-byte (8-bit) fonts and two-byte (16-bit) fonts. The single-byte fonts can handle up 256 characters, while the two-byte fonts can handle up 65,536 characters. Text in Japanese, Chinese, or Korean, for example, requires many more characters than 256. But, unless you're creating an application intended for Asian users, you won't need to worry about two-byte fonts.

5 Release

X11 Release 5 introduces a whole set of *wide character* and *multi-byte* internationalization routines, designed to make your applications port better to more countries. These new functions require a working knowledge of ANSI (or ISO) C *setlocale* conventions. We consider these topics too advanced for a beginning Xlib book, but recommend that you look up the R5 documentation on internationalization (often abbreviated *i18n* because there are 18 letters between the *i* and the *n* in internationalization).

LOADING FONTS

Before a font can be used by your program, it must be loaded into the X server. The X server then shares the font among all programs that want to use a particular font. When all references to a font are over, the X server may free up the memory and data structures associated with the font. Thus, loading a font does not load the font into your application program—the font is loaded into the server. To load a font, use `XLoadQueryFont`:

```
Display         *display;
XFontStruct     *font_struct;
char            *font_name;

font_struct = XLoadQueryFont( display, font_name );

if ( font_struct == (XFontStruct *) NULL )
        {
        /*
         * An error occurred. Don't
         * try to use the font.
         */
else
        {
        /* font loaded OK... */
        }
```

`XLoadQueryFont` returns a pointer to an `XFontStruct` structure. This structure contains a host of information about the font; the most useful information is used to tell how large the font is. If you do not care about the size of the font, you can use the function `XLoadFont` to just get a font ID. (With `XLoadQueryFont`, the font ID is stored in the fid field of the `XFontStruct` struct, or `font_struct->fid`.) The font ID allows you to draw text, but does not have enough information to get the font's size, should you need to make this kind of calculation. We find you almost always need to determine the size of any fonts loaded, so we always use `XLoadQueryFont`:

```
Display      *display;
char         *font_name;
Font         font_id;

font_id = XLoadFont( display, font_name );
```

Normally, you will want to use the function `XLoadQueryFont`, as `XLoadFont` generates an X error if the font cannot be loaded.

SOURCE CODE FOR LOADFONT.C

The function `LoadFont`, below, loads in a font of a given name and returns a pointer to an `XFontStruct`. `LoadFont` takes a font name and a fallback font name, in case the first font fails to load. If both fail to load, `LoadFont` quits the application. (You should be able to come up with a better error-handling method, but it serves our needs at this time.)

```
/*
 *      loadfont.c
 *      Contains utility function
 *      LoadFont.
 *
 *      Written for X Window Applications
 *      Programming, 2nd Edition
 */

#include  <stdio.h>
#include  <X11/Xlib.h>

XFontStruct *LoadFont( display, font_name,
        fallback_font_name )

Display *display;
char    font_name[];           /* name of font to load */
char    fallback_font_name[]; /* backup font name */

/*
 *      LoadFont loads in an X font into an XFontStruct
```

```
 *      and returns a pointer to that structure. If the
 *      font font_name cannot be loaded, LoadFont
 *      then tries to load in the fallback_font_name font.
 *      If THAT fails, too, then LoadFont will terminate
 *      your program. We're sure you can come up with
 *      a better error-handling routine.
 */

{       /* LoadFont */
        XFontStruct *font_struct;

        font_struct = XLoadQueryFont( display,
                      font_name );

        if ( font_struct == (XFontStruct *) NULL )
                {
                /*
                 * Try to load in
                 * fallback font
                 */
                 font_struct = XLoadQueryFont( display,
                      fallback_font_name );

             if ( font_struct == (XFontStruct *) NULL )
                  {
                  (void) fprintf( stderr,
                     "Error loading fonts [%s] [%s]\n",
                     font_name,
                     fallback_font_name );

                  XCloseDisplay( display );
                  exit( 1 );
                  }
             }

        return( font_struct );

}       /* LoadFont */

/* end of file loadfont.c */
```

SETTING UP THE GRAPHICS CONTEXT

To draw with a newly loaded font, you need to set a graphics context to use that font when drawing. To do this, use the function XSetFont:

```
Display      *display;
XFontStruct  *font_struct;
GC           gc;

XSetFont( display, gc,
             font_struct->fid );
```

XSetFont takes the font ID, the number returned by XLoadFont, or the number in the fid (font id) field of an XFontStruct structure. When you draw with the given graphics context, the text will be drawn in the new font.

DRAWING TEXT

Once you have set up a graphics context with a font, you can start to draw text. X has two main functions for drawing text: XDrawString and XDrawImageString. XDrawString only draws the foreground bits of a character, while XDrawImageString draws the foreground in the GC's foreground color and the background in the GC's background color. In the diagram below, XDrawImageString displays all the letters of the string. XDrawString, however, does not overwrite the background bits of the string:

```
Display      *display;
Drawable     drawable;
GC           gc;
int          x, y;
char         *string;
int          string_length;

string_length = strlen( string );

XDrawImageString( display, drawable, gc, x, y,
             string, string_length );

XDrawString( display, drawable, gc, x, y,
             string, string_length );
```

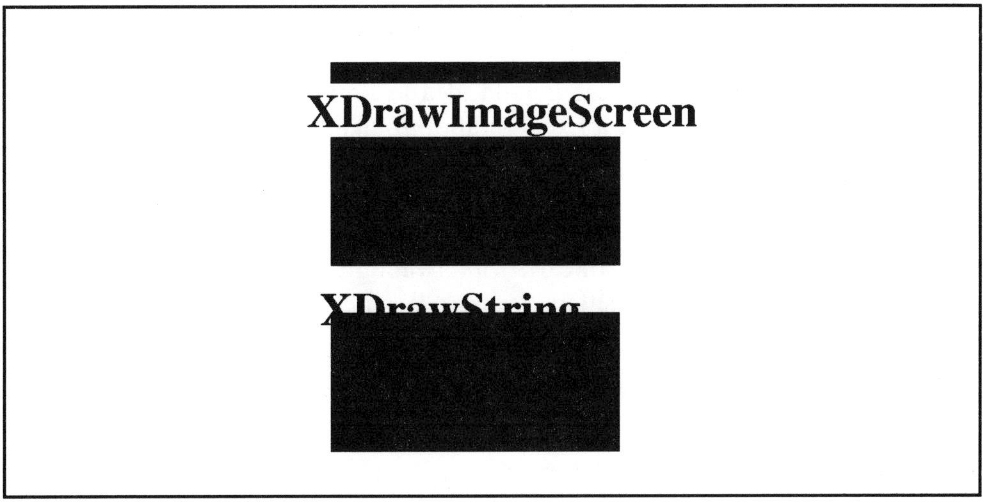

Figure 5.1. XDrawString and XDrawImageString.

All string drawing routines require you to pass the length of the string. The Xlib call will assume that there are at least as many characters in the string as you tell it. In other words, don't lie to the X server.

WHERE THE TEXT IS DRAWN

X draws text starting at an x, y pixel location. The *x* coordinate location is at the beginning (far left) of the text string. The *y* coordinate location starts at the text baseline. Letters that drop below the baseline, such as *p*, *q*, and *j*, drop below the y coordinate location given to `XDrawString`. Letters will go above the y position and may also drop below the position.

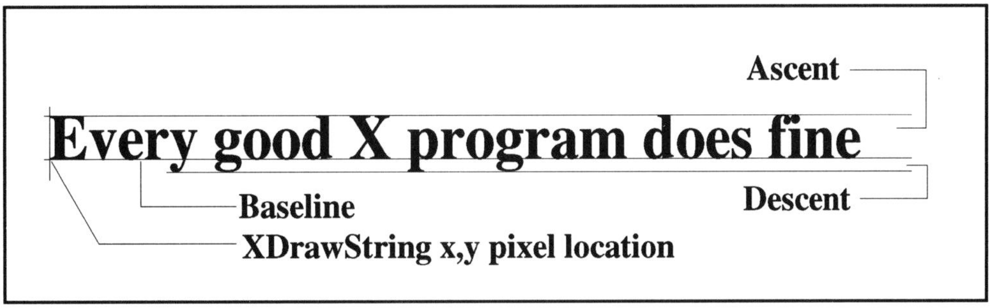

Figure 5.2. X Text Baseline.

FINDING OUT HOW LARGE A FONT IS

To help position a text string, it is a good idea to figure out how large the string will appear in a given font. For a fixed-width font, like *9x15*, the width of any text string is the number of characters times the width of one character:

```
        width = strlen(  string ) * width_of_one_character;
```

For proportional-width fonts, like *variable*, though, this is not the case. In a proportional-width font, some letters, such as *W* and *M*, are far wider than other letters, such as *i*, *l*, and *t*.

In all cases, to find out the width of a text string in a given font, use the `XTextWidth` function:

```
XFontStruct      *font_struct;
char             *string;
int              string_length;
int              width;

string_length = strlen( string );

width = XTextWidth( font_struct, string, string_length );
```

The height of a character string is a bit different. In most cases, you want the possible height necessary for one line of text, with both descending and ascending characters, rather the just the height of the string. Why? Most checks on a font height are for spacing lines of text vertically. Line 1 should not write over line 2, and so on.

To get the possible height of a font, you can access elements of the `XFontStruct`:

```
XFontStruct      *font_struct;
int              height;

height = font_struct->ascent +
                 font_struct->descent;
```

The `XFontStruct` in its entirety (from the include file `X11/Xlib.h`), looks like:

```
typedef struct {
    XExtData     *ext_data;          /* Place for X extension data */
    Font         fid;                /* Font ID for the font */
```

```
    unsigned     direction;          /* "hint" for direction the font is drawn */
    unsigned     min_char_or_byte2; /* first character */
    unsigned     max_char_or_byte2; /* last character  */
    unsigned     min_byte1;          /* first row of chars that exists */
    unsigned     max_byte1;          /* last row of chars that exists  */
    Bool         all_chars_exist;    /* flag if all chars have non-zero size */
    unsigned     default_char;       /* char to print for an undefined char */
    int          n_properties;       /* how many properties there are */
    XFontProp    *properties;        /* pointer to array of additional props */
    XCharStruct  min_bounds;         /* minimum bounds over all chars  */
    XCharStruct  max_bounds;         /* minimum bounds over all chars  */
    XCharStruct  *per_char;          /* first_char to last_char information */
    int          ascent;             /* extent above baseline for spacing */
    int          descent;            /* descent below baseline for spacing */
    } XFontStruct;
```

Most of these fields will be of little use, though, except for the `fid`, `ascent`, and `descent`.

SOURCE CODE FOR FONTHT.C

The function `FontHeight`, below, returns the height of a line of text in a given font, by adding the `ascent` and `descent` fields in the `XFontStruct`. This could easily be a macro.

```
/*
 *      fontht.c
 *      Determines height of text in
 *      a given font.
 */

#include  <X11/Xlib.h>

FontHeight( font_struct )

XFontStruct  *font_struct;

{       /* FontHeight */
        int  height;

        height = font_struct->ascent +
                 font_struct->descent;
```

```
        return( height );

}       /* FontHeight */

/* end of file fontht.c */
```

FREEING FONTS

When you are through with a font, tell the X server that you are done with it. This way, the X server can make most efficient use of the limited resources available in the workstation, such as memory. Two functions free up the font, `XFreeFont` and `XUnloadFont`:

```
Display       *display;
XFontStruct   *font_struct;

XFreeFont(  display, font_struct );

Display       *display;
Font          font_id;

XUnloadFont( display, font_id );
```

Use `XFreeFont` if you originally loaded the font into an `XFontStruct` structure (with `XLoadQueryFont`). Use `XUnloadFont` if you originally loaded the font and just used the font ID (with `XLoadFont`).

As a general rule, always try to free up resources in the X server when done.

TIPS ON USING FONTS

When people inexperienced with design principles suddenly have access to many different fonts, they usually go hog-wild in their use of different faces. The end result, unfortunately, is a very unattractive design, more representing a ransom note made up of disparate letter clips from different newspapers and magazines. Aesthetically speaking, therefore, it is a good idea to avoid the use of many fonts. If the output looks like a ransom note, it probably won't look professional, unless you do this by choice and are aiming at a certain effect, such as laughter, from your users. For best results, generally stick to one font per window and two fonts maximum. Aim for an integrated look and feel to your software. Try to stick to standard fonts, the most likely fonts to be available on the greatest number of systems. Use a special larger font for emphasis. When you need multiple fonts, you can often use an italic or bold version or a different size of the same font.

FINDING THE AVAILABLE FONTS

A standard X application program called `xlsfonts` lists the available fonts on a workstation. Running `xlsfonts` on a Release 4 or higher X server will result in pages and pages of text output. Release 5 adds a font server with many more possible fonts.

Here's some sample output:

```
-adobe-courier-medium-o-normal—8-80-75-75-m-50-iso8859-1
-adobe-courier-medium-r-normal—10-100-75-75-m-60-iso8859-1
-adobe-courier-medium-r-normal—11-80-100-100-m-60-iso8859-1
-adobe-courier-medium-r-normal—12-120-75-75-m-70-iso8859-1
-adobe-courier-medium-r-normal—14-100-100-100-m-90-iso8859-1
-adobe-times-medium-r-normal—24-240-75-75-p-124-iso8859-1
-bitstream-charter-medium-r-normal—14-100-100-100-p-78-
iso8859-1
9x15
8x13
fixed
cursor
variable
olglyph-10
```

The list above names just a few of the fonts that should be available (the list was taken from the generic MIT X11 R5). Each X installation has its own set of available fonts. The fonts listed above should be available on most systems, but don't assume so. We have found that while most systems have the font files, not all systems have correctly set up all these fonts. Usually the problem is with the font path, that is, directories where the X server is told to check for fonts. The font path is often set up incorrectly, so the X server will not access all the fonts.

Another problem is not setting up font *aliases* correctly (you'll need to talk to the person who installed X on your workstation to check this one out). The *variable* font, for example, is normally an alias for another (usually Helvetica) font. The long font names are based on an X standard called the X Logical Font Description Conventions, or XLFD. A document describing the XLFD is included with the X Window System from the MIT X Consortium.

DECODING LONG FONT NAMES

When you run a program like `xlsfonts`, you'll see that most of the X font names are extremely long and complex, such as:

```
-adobe-courier-bold-r-normal—11-80-100-100-m-60-iso8859-1
```

The actual format of these names makes sense and is described in the XLFD. Most names begin with a leading hyphen and then a font foundry (e.g., company) name, such as Adobe:

-*adobe*-courier-bold-r-normal—11-80-100-100-m-60-iso8859-1

These names need to be registered with the X Consortium and you'll notice that a number of font vendors, such as Adobe and Bitstream, have donated fonts for X. Next comes the font family name field, such as Courier:

-adobe-*courier*-bold-r-normal—11-80-100-100-m-60-iso8859-1

The weight follows, usually bold or medium:

-adobe-courier-*bold*-r-normal—11-80-100-100-m-60-iso8859-1

Then comes the slant field, a code that signifies the slant. The slant is one of the following codes:

Code	***Meaning***
`i`	italic
`o`	oblique
`r`	roman
`ri`	reverse italic
`ro`	reverse oblique
`ot`	other

-adobe-courier-bold-*r*-normal—11-80-100-100-m-60-iso8859-1

The set-width name describes the width of the letters. Some examples are condensed, semicondensed, narrow, normal, and double wide:

-adobe-courier-bold-r-*normal*—11-80-100-100-m-60-iso8859-1

After the set-width name comes space for any extra information necessary to identify the font, such as *sans* (for sans serif). This space is not used in our example, nor for most fonts.

Now we start seeing the font's size. The pixel size field indicates the size in dots on the screen; in our case, 11. Zero indicates a scalable font.

`-adobe-courier-bold-r-normal—`*`11`*`-80-100-100-m-60-iso8859-1`

The point size field describes the size in terms of points (1/72nd of an inch). This field is 10 times the point size. The 80 means our font is an 8-point font:

`-adobe-courier-bold-r-normal—11-`*`80`*`-100-100-m-60-iso8859-1`

After the point size follows the dots-per-inch in the X and Y directions. Our example is 100x100 dots per inch (most are either 75 or 100 dpi):

`-adobe-courier-bold-r-normal—11-80-`*`100-100`*`-m-60-iso8859-1`

The spacing field determines if a font is monospaced or proportional:

Spacing	***Meaning***
`p`	proportional
`m`	monospaced
`c`	char cell/monospaced, e.g., suitable for using with xterm

`-adobe-courier-bold-r-normal—11-80-100-100-`*`m`*`-60-iso8859-1`

The average width field provides an average size on tenths of pixels, or 6 pixels, in our example:

`-adobe-courier-bold-r-normal—11-80-100-100-m-`*`60`*`-iso8859-1`

Finally, the charset registry and encoding fields tell what kind of character set we have. Most are ISO 8859-1 (Latin-1, a superset of ASCII).

`-adobe-courier-bold-r-normal—11-80-100-100-m-60-`*`iso8859`*`-1`

A program called `xfontsel` can help you choose fonts using the long font name format.

The X11 Release 5 font server makes many more fonts available, often to all the machines on a network. This is great, but adds yet another area where users can incorrectly configure their system—and they probably will never know about it. The lesson here is that your applications cannot depend on any X fonts. Your applications require some form of fallback strategy in case needed fonts aren't available.

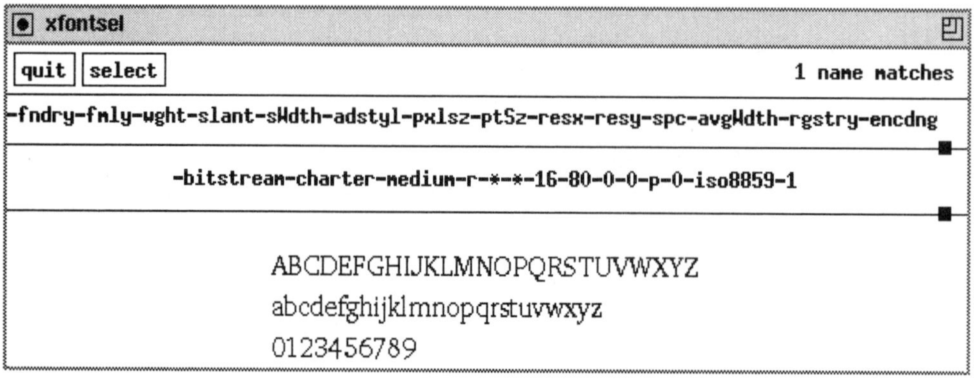

Figure 5.3. The xfontsel Program.

Some common fonts that seem to be universal are *fixed*, *8x13*, a fixed-width font where each character fits a 8-by-13 pixel cell, *9x15* and *variable*, a proportional-width font that looks vaguely like Helvetica.

An X application called *xfd* (X font displayer) will display the characters in a font. Normally, if *xfd* cannot find the font, then your program will not, either. The command below will create a window and display the characters in the font named *variable*:

```
% xfd -fn variable
```

LIMITED X SERVER RESOURCES

Some servers, especially for X terminals, simply won't have the resources (mainly RAM) to load a lot of different fonts.

X terminals exist mainly to provide an inexpensive hardware entry point to the X Window System. An X terminal acts much like an ASCII terminal, using another computer for the processing power and the terminal's smarts just for the display—only the X terminals have a lot more smarts than traditional ASCII terminals. Due to cost constraints, though, most X terminals have a limited amount of RAM. Fonts, like any other X resource, use up RAM. In an X terminal environment, using the least amount of resources is a good idea.

The best advice on the question of fonts is to let the user decide which fonts to use—after all, the customer knows best. If you allow the user to specify the font to use through a command-line argument (covered in more depth in Chapter 11), then it is the user's problem to pick the right font from the user's available fonts. Typically, the command-line option is `-font fontname` (or `-fn fontname`) where `fontname` is the actual name of an X font.

Letting the user decide the font is especially useful because X runs on many different types of hardware. A color Sun SPARC workstation, for example, comes with either a 16-inch or 19-inch color monitor—both at the same pixel resolution. This means that the dots are much smaller on the 16-inch monitor. The standard X default font, *8x13*, looks tiny on a 16-inch monitor and more acceptable on the 19-inch screen. Users with the smaller screen may opt to use a larger font, such as *9x15*, just to be able to read the text. An Apple Macintosh IIx, on the other hand, has a standard 640-by-480 pixel resolution. On this screen, users typically want to use the smallest fonts available, due to the smaller screen resolution.

AN EXAMPLE PROGRAM TO DRAW TEXT

The `chap5` example program, below, creates a window and then displays some shapes and text in the window. It shows the two main X text routines, `XDrawString` and `XDrawImageString`. The output of `XDrawString` appears only where a shape is not, since `XDrawString` only draws the foreground bits of a character. `XDrawImageString`, on the other hand, draws both the foreground and background bits, so its output is always visible (unless you have the foreground and background pixels set to the same value).

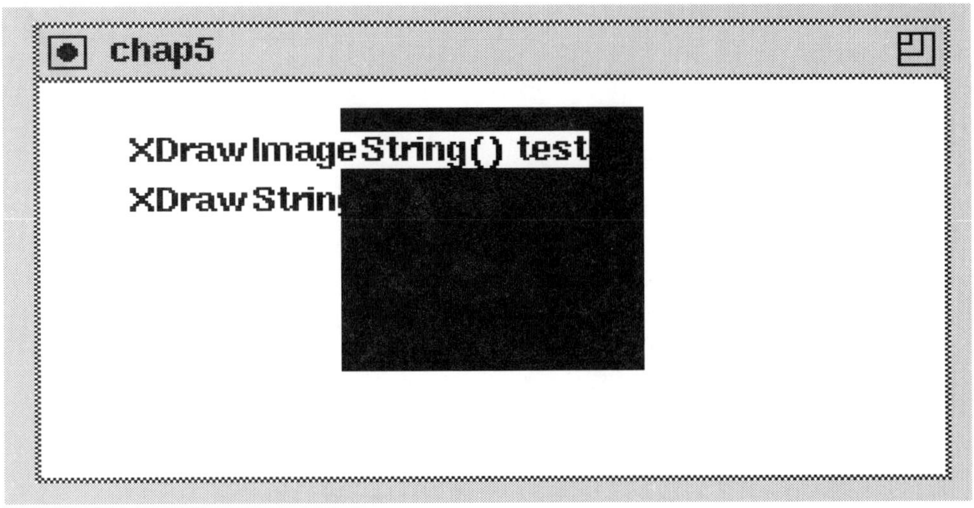

Figure 5.4. The Chap5 Program in Action.

SOURCE CODE FOR CHAP5.C

```
/*
 *      chap5.c
 *      Example program for Chapter 5.
 *
 *      Written for X Window Applications
 *      Programming, 2nd Edition
 */

#include <stdio.h>
#include <X11/Xlib.h>
#include <X11/Xutil.h>

/*
 *      Use the program xlsfonts to find a font name that
 *      your server supports. Then, after you get this program
 *      working, try a different font. The "fixed" font is a
 *      common font that we'll use as a fallback font, in case
 *      the system cannot load the original font (FONT_NAME).
 *      You'll find the most font problems when working on
 *      another machine or X terminal.
 */
#define FONT_NAME               "variable"
#define FALLBACK_FONT_NAME      "fixed"

main( argc, argv )

int     argc;
char    *argv[];

{       /* main */
        Display     *display;
        Display     *ConnectToServer();     /* connect.c */
        Window      rootwindow, window;
        Window      OpenWindow();           /* window.c */
        int         screen;
        int         x, y, width, height;
        Visual      *visual = CopyFromParent;
        GC          gc;
        GC          CreateGC();       /* gc.c */
        XEvent      event;
```

```
int          count;
XFontStruct *font_struct;
XFontStruct *LoadFont();            /* loadfont.c */

/*
 * Connect to default X server
 */
display = ConnectToServer( (char *) NULL,
        &screen,
        &rootwindow );

/*
 * Create a window on the display
 */
x      = 10;
y      = 10;
width  = 300;
height = 150;
window = OpenWindow( display,
        rootwindow,
        x, y, width, height,
        BlackPixel( display, screen ),
        WhitePixel( display, screen ),
        ExposureMask,
        visual );

/*
 * Provide information to the window manager.
 */
SetStandardHints( display, window,
     argv[0], argv[0],
     x, y, width, height );

/*
 * Create graphics context for drawing
 */
gc = CreateGC( display, window,
     BlackPixel( display, screen ),
     WhitePixel( display, screen ) );

/*
 * Load a font
```

```
         */
        font_struct = LoadFont( display,
                        FONT_NAME,
                        FALLBACK_FONT_NAME );

        /*
         * Now, set the GC to draw with this font.
         */
        XSetFont( display, gc,
                font_struct->fid );

        /*
         * Make the window actually appear
         */
        XMapRaised( display, window );
        XFlush( display );

        /*
         * Loop for 20 Expose events. Real programs
         * should go until done or the user quits.
         */
        count = 0;
        while( count < 20 )
                {
                XNextEvent( display, &event );

                if ( event.type == Expose )
                    {
                    Redraw( display, window, gc, font_struct );
                    count++;
                    }
                }

        /*
         * Free the font, now that we're done with it.
         */
        XFreeFont( display, font_struct );
        XCloseDisplay( display );

}       /* main */
```

```
Redraw( display, window, gc, font_struct )

Display      *display;
Window       window;
GC           gc;
XFontStruct  *font_struct;

/*
 *      Redraws contents of our window, by
 *      drawing text on a rectangle. Note that
 *      we need the XFontStruct pointer to get the
 *      height of the font (and also the width of
 *      text in the font, too, but we're not
 *      covering that here).
 */

{       /* Redraw */
        char string[400];
        int  y;

        XFillRectangle( display, window, gc,
                100, 10, 100, 100 );

        y = 30; /* draw at 30 pixels down from origin */

        (void) strcpy( string, "XDrawImageString() test" );

        XDrawImageString( display, window, gc,
              30, y,
              string, strlen( string ) );

        /*
         * Make next string be one "line" of text
         * lower than the string above.
         */
        y += FontHeight( font_struct ) + 5;

        (void) strcpy( string, "XDrawString() test" );

        XDrawString( display, window, gc,
              30, y,
              string, strlen( string ) );
```

```
        /*
         * Send all our requests over the network,
         * so that the drawing is visible.
         */
        XFlush( display );

}       /* Redraw */

/* end of file chap5.c */
```

COMPILING AND LINKING THE CHAP5 PROGRAM

The `chap5` program requires the following files.

`chap5.c`	
`classhnt.c`	(Chapter 2)
`connect.c`	(Chapter 1)
`fontht.c`	
`gc.c`	(Chapter 3)
`loadfont.c`	
`sizehint.c`	(Chapter 2)
`window.c`	(Chapter 2)
`wmname.c`	(Chapter 2)
`wmhints.c`	(Chapter 2)

You can compile and link the `chap5` program with a command like:

```
cc -o chap5 -DX11R4 chap5.c classhnt.c connect.c fontht.c \
       gc.c loadfont.c sizehint.c window.c wmname.c \
       wmhints.c -lX11
```

You can also use the Makefile in Appendix A and type:

```
make chap5
```

SUMMARY

The X Window System has the ability to use many different typefaces, sizes, and styles. X calls these text fonts. X fonts are bitmap images of each character in the font.

Before using a font, load it into the X server with `XLoadQueryFont` or `XLoadFont`. When finished with the font, free it with `XFreeFont` or `XUnloadFont` (if you used `XLoadQueryFont` or `XLoadFont`, respectively).

To draw with a font in a given window, set the graphics context for the window to use the font, with `XSetFont`.

`XDrawString` will draw a character string to a given pixel position in a given window on the display. `XDrawImageString` does the same, but it also draws in a background for the characters.

Unless you are writing a ransom note, avoid abusing fonts. Fonts and typefaces can make your use interface cleaner, easier to read, and exciting. Fonts can also make your interface look downright unprofessional and boring.

XLIB FUNCTIONS AND MACROS INTRODUCED IN THIS CHAPTER

```
XDrawImageString
XDrawString
XFreeFont
XLoadFont
XLoadQueryFont
XSetFont
XTextWidth
XUnloadFont
```

Chapter 6

EVENTS AND EVENT-DRIVEN PROGRAMMING

This chapter discusses events in X. X events are messages generated by the X server or other applications, sent to your program. We've seen the `Expose` event already in Chapter 2. This chapter goes on to cover the most important events.

The X server generates an event when the user presses a key on the keyboard. The server generates an event when a mouse button is pressed. (Another event happens when the mouse button is released.) An event occurs when a window-manager program works with the user to change the size of a window on the screen. And an event happens when one program sends an event to another program.

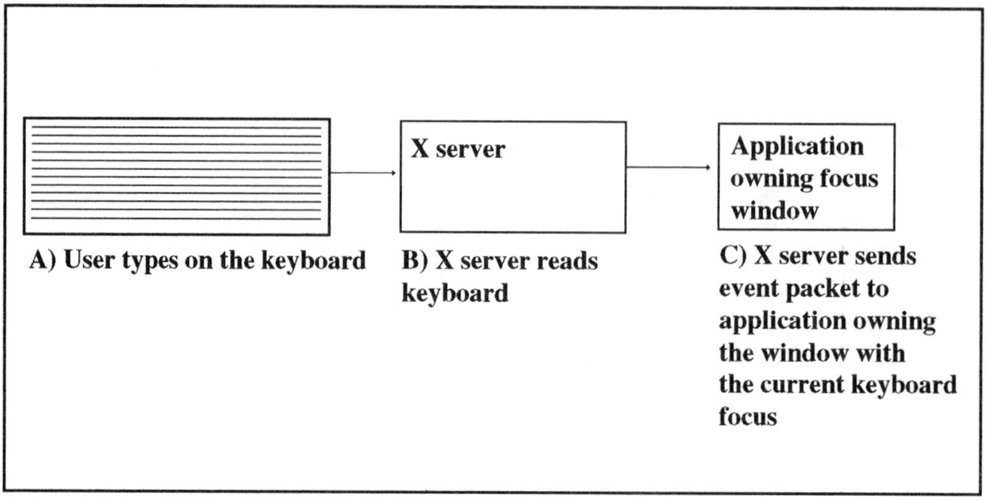

Figure 6.1. Generating an Event.

Events tell your application programs exactly what is happening on the display screen. More technically, an event is a fixed-size packet of information sent to your program by the X server. X provides many different types of events, and each one interprets the contents of the data packet differently. X uses these events to such an extent that your programs will become driven by these events.

EVENT-DRIVEN PROGRAMMING

Event-driven programs are literally driven—or controlled—by incoming events from the system, but in this case the system is the X server. Event-driven programs are not like traditional batch programs. A batch program, such as a program to strip out all the control characters from a text file, takes in user input only at the beginning, usually to get the names of the input and output files. The batch program then chugs away on the input and produces the output. The program is in total control of itself.

In an event-driven program, however, the program cedes control to the user. The user drives the actions of the program through a series of many events. The program is really still in control, but it gives the user the feeling that the user is running the show. The big difference with event-driven programming is that events can come in at any time and in any order. This places the meat of most event-driven programs in a central loop that takes each event as it comes in and responds to that event in some way.

It is very important when designing the event-driven user interface to provide some feedback for each user-initiated event. The user needs to know that your program received the event and is doing something. Highlighting a choice or beeping the speaker are common ways to provide the feedback. This feedback must appear as soon as possible, even if the action to be taken on the event will take a long time. You need to let the user know that the event is received and understood—otherwise the user will probably try the event again and again, pounding on the same key until a response is seen.

Typical event-driven programs have an initialization section in the beginning, then an event loop, and finally a section to perform any necessary clean-ups at the end. Programmers experienced with Microsoft Windows, IBM Presentation Manager, or the Apple Macintosh will feel right at home with event-driven programming.

THE X EVENT MODEL

Events in X are generated from windows, which means an X program without any windows normally has a difficult time receiving events from the X server. The X server provides each connection (i.e., each application program) an event queue. This is a first-in first-out list of all events generated for the program's windows. Application programs read events from this queue and respond to them in some way. A word-processor application, for example, receives keypress events and then displays each character pressed in the word processor's window (or windows).

Keys pressed on the keyboard go to whatever window currently has the keyboard focus. This window is normally the window where the mouse pointer is located. Moving the mouse pointer into a window will *focus* the keyboard to that window. In X, this model is called *focus follows mouse*. X, though, in providing the mechanism without the policy, allows this feature to be changed. Window managers may focus the keyboard on a window that does not have the mouse pointer inside. Usually this is done by the *click to type* model, in which the user clicks the mouse in a window, making that window the *active* window, the window with the keyboard focus. Application programs may also grab control of the keyboard or grab control of individual keys. Grabbing control of individual keys is particularly dangerous.

A program that provides a consistent help system may want to grab control of a key labeled *Help*, for example. But a program that takes over the *e* key would make most word-processing tasks nearly impossible.

ASKING FOR EVENTS

When learning X, you will come across a number of statements that clearly show the design goals of X's creators. One such statement is: In X, your program will only receive the type of events that you ask for. This is another example of X providing the underlying mechanism without any user-interface policy. In this case, the statement is not completely true, but it does pan out in general.

In general, your program will only receive events it asked for with a few exceptions. This statement is also a subtle way of blaming yourself for any problems. (Keep repeating "Remember, you only get what you asked for.")

X provides two main ways to ask for certain types of events. We covered the first method in Chapter 2 on windows. The `XCreateWindow` call takes an `XSetWindowAttributes` structure, a structure with an `event_mask` field. Filling this field with flags for the type of events your window wants and passing the proper bitmask will result in those events coming to the window. The second method is to use the function `XSelectInput` after a window is created:

```
Display         *display;
Window          window;
unsigned long   event_mask;

XSelectInput( display, window, event_mask );
```

`XSelectInput` tells X that you are interested in receiving certain types of events for a given window. That can mean a given window and all its child windows that are beneath it in the window hierarchy.

Unless explicitly commanded otherwise, X events normally propagate up through the hierarchy of windows. An event will go to the lowest-level window in the hierarchy that asked for it. If this lowest-level child window does not handle events, the event will propagate up one level to the child's immediate parent window to see if the parent will handle the event, and so on all the way up to the root window. If the event propagates all the way up to the root window, though, chances are it will not be dealt with.

You can call `XSelectInput` on only the parent (highest level) window for your application and still receive all events (all the events asked for) for your program's child windows if those child windows did not have an `XSelectInput` call made on them or did not pass an event mask to the `XCreateWindow` function. You could also call `XSelectInput` on all child windows as well. Each application may dictate a different scheme for catching events.

We solve this hassle by explicitly asking for events on every window created with the OpenWindow function (see Chapter 2). We find it's best to have each window ask for the events it wants. This tends to be less confusing.

THE EVENT MASK

As part of the XSelectInput call, or in the event_mask field of the XSetWindowAttributes structure, you must pass an event mask. This mask has certain bits set that tell the X server which events your program is interested in receiving. In a familiar fashion, you OR these mask bits together to create the full mask, such as:

```
unsigned long   event_mask;

event_mask = ButtonPressMask | KeyPressMask;
```

This asks for just keyboard and mouse button-press events. When your program starts looking for more events, the above expression can get rather complicated. Because this event mask may be used in more than one place (for some special event-checking functions shown below), you may, for consistency's sake, want to place the event mask in a globally accessible format. Using the C preprocessor's define command ensures that any changes to the event mask will propagate throughout your program. This is the method used by the example programs below.

```
#define EVENT_MASK (ButtonPressMask    | \
             KeyPressMask       | \
             ExposureMask       | \
             StructureNotifyMask)
```

There are event masks to ask for just about every event type (a few types arrive whether you want them or not).

Mask Defined	***Asks for Event Type***
Button1MotionMask	MotionNotify
Button2MotionMask	MotionNotify
Button3MotionMask	MotionNotify
Button4MotionMask	MotionNotify

Mask Defined	*Asks for Event Type (cont.)*
Button5MotionMask	MotionNotify
ButtonMotionMask	MotionNotify (any button)
ButtonPressMask	ButtonPress
ButtonReleaseMask	ButtonRelease
ColormapChangeMask	ColormapNotify
EnterWindowMask	EnterNotify
ExposureMask	Expose
FocusChangeMask	FocusIn, FocusOut
KeymapStateMask	KeymapNotify
KeyPressMask	KeyPress
KeyReleaseMask	KeyRelease
LeaveWindowMask	LeaveNotify
NoEventMask	None
OwnerGrabButtonMask	None
PointerMotionHintMask	None
PointerMotionMask	MotionNotify
PropertyChangeMask	PropertyNotify
ResizeRedirectMask	ResizeRequest
StructureNotifyMask	CirculateNotify, ConfigureNotify, DestroyNotify, GravityNotify, MapNotify, ReparentNotify, UnmapNotify
SubstructureNotifyMask	CirculateNotify, ConfigureNotify, CreateNotify, DestroyNotify, GravityNotify, MapNotify, ReparentNotify, UnmapNotify
SubstructureRedirectMask	CirculateRequest, ConfigureRequest, MapRequest
VisibilityChangeMask	VisibilityNotify

`XSelectInput` and `XCreateWindow` tell the X server that your program is interested in receiving certain types of events. Next, your program must actively pick up those events in which it is interested.

RECEIVING EVENTS FROM THE X SERVER

There are two main methods for picking up events from the X server: block your program awaiting an event or poll the server to check if any events are available. If your program performs background processing, you will have no choice—your program cannot block awaiting events from X. In most cases, your program can simply wait until X sends in an event. Blocking in this manner is a lot friendlier to your host computer and local-area network—polling takes up a lot of CPU resources.

The main blocking event function is `XNextEvent`, which we introduced in Chapter 2. `XNextEvent` checks to see if any events are in the program's event queue. If so, it returns the first event in line. If not, it waits until an event appears in the queue:

```
Display       *display;
XEvent        event;

XNextEvent( display, &event );
```

Other block-on-input event calls include `XWindowEvent`, `XMaskEvent`, and `XPeekEvent`. `XWindowEvent` returns the next event for a given window that matches a given event mask. `XMaskEvent` returns the next event for a given application that matches a given event mask. `XPeekEvent` "peeks" at the next event in the event queue, but does not remove that event; it allows an application to look ahead into the event queue:

```
Display          *display;
Window           window;
XEvent           event;
unsigned long    event_mask;

XWindowEvent( display, window, event_mask, &event );

XMaskEvent( display, event_mask, &event );

XPeekEvent( display, &event );
```

In general, use XNextEvent, unless you are looking for a particular type of event (XMaskEvent) or an event for just one window (XWindowEvent). XNextEvent or XPeekEvent can be used with the nonblocking function XPending (see below) to check ahead for a set of incoming events (such as Expose events).

POLLING FOR EVENTS

The other method of X event checking is polling for events—checking to see if an event is available, but not blocking waiting for one. As stated above, most programs can wait for events. They therefore should wait for events, as polling is very expensive, takes up a lot of CPU time, and creates a lot of network traffic. If your application needs to perform work in the background or if it handles more than one X server (such as a program to allow users to "chat" with other users on different displays), then you probably need to poll for incoming events (or use select, if you're running under UNIX, see below).

You can check if events are pending in the event queue with the function XPending, which returns the number of events remaining in the event queue:

```
Display        *display;
int            number_events;

number_events = XPending( display );
```

XPending does not check for specific types of events, so that even if XPending returns that a number of events wait in the queue, a call for a specific event (using XMaskEvent, for example) may still cause your program to wait. In addition, XPending only checks your program's internal queue. While XPending may return 0, meaning no events remaining in the queue, the X server may have queued up events for your application. Periodically call the XFlush function to get these events placed into your program's internal queue. XFlush flushes out the application's internal buffer of X commands and takes in any input waiting in the X server. (XFlush was introduced in Chapter 2.)

Other polling routines correspond to the above waiting event routines. These polling routines return a value of True if such an event is available, and False if no such event is available. You will notice the correspondence in that the only difference in some of the function names is that the word Check is added. For example, XCheckWindowEvent acts like XWindowEvent, but XCheckWindowEvent does not wait until an event comes in. It will return right away with either an event (returning `True`) or no event (returning `False`).

`XCheckWindowEvent` returns `True` if an event is pending for the given window and matches the given event mask. `XCheckMaskEvent` returns `True` if an event is pending that matches the given event mask. `XCheckTypedEvent` returns `True` if an event of a given type awaits in the event queue. Note that some event mask values may return more than one type of event. `XCheckTypedWindowEvent` returns `True` if an event in the queue has the given type and is for the given window:

```
Display         *display;
Window          window;
XEvent          event;
int             type;
int             status;
unsigned long   event_mask;

status = XCheckWindowEvent( display, window,
                event_mask, &event );

status = XCheckMaskEvent( display, event_mask,
                &event );

status = XCheckTypedEvent( display, type,
                &event );

status = XCheckTypedWindowEvent( display, window,
                type, &event );
```

These `XCheck`*`Something`*`Event` routines can be used in an `if` statement, as below, to check if any events have arrived:

```
Display         *display;
Window          window;
XEvent          event;
unsigned long   event_mask;

if ( XCheckWindowEvent( display, window,
            event_mask, &event ) == True )
            {
            /* handle the event here */
            }
```

FRIENDLIER POLLING WITH SELECT

If your system has the function `select`, as most UNIX systems do, you can use `select` to block until an event comes in either from the X server or from another input source, such as a pipe or other file descriptor. You can set a time-out with `select` so that your application does not wait forever. If you use `select`, however, you'll need to get a file descriptor for the connection to the X server. The macro `ConnectionNumber` returns this value:

```
Display       *display;
int           file_descriptor;

file_descriptor = ConnectionNumber( display );
```

`ConnectionNumber` returns the file descriptor for the X server connection on most versions of UNIX. If you're running under another operating system, what `ConnectionNumber` returns is undefined.

EVENT TYPES

The `XEvent` type is a C language union—a union of C structures. Each type of event has its own structure—its own interpretation of the `XEvent` data. The actual `XEvent` union is rather long:

```
typedef union _XEvent {
        int                     type;
        XAnyEvent               xany;
        XKeyEvent               xkey;
        XButtonEvent            xbutton;
        XMotionEvent            xmotion;
        XCrossingEvent          xcrossing;
        XFocusChangeEvent       xfocus;
        XExposeEvent            xexpose;
        XGraphicsExposeEvent    xgraphicsexpose;
        XNoExposeEvent          xnoexpose;
        XVisibilityEvent        xvisibility;
        XCreateWindowEvent      xcreatewindow;
        XDestroyWindowEvent     xdestroywindow;
        XUnmapEvent             xunmap;
        XMapEvent               xmap;
        XMapRequestEvent        xmaprequest;
```

```
XReparentEvent          xreparent;
XConfigureEvent         xconfigure;
XGravityEvent           xgravity;
XResizeRequestEvent     xresizerequest;
XConfigureRequestEvent  xconfigurerequest;
XCirculateEvent         xcirculate;
XCirculateRequestEvent  xcirculaterequest;
XPropertyEvent          xproperty;
XSelectionClearEvent    xselectionclear;
XSelectionRequestEvent  xselectionrequest;
XSelectionEvent         xselection;
XColormapEvent          xcolormap;
XClientMessageEvent     xclient;
XMappingEvent           xmapping;
XErrorEvent             xerror;
XKeymapEvent            xkeymap;
long                    pad[24];
} XEvent;
```

The first element of the `XEvent` union is the type. The type field tells, surprisingly enough, what type of event of event has been received. Each bit in the event mask corresponds to at least one type of event (with a few exceptions):

```
switch( event.type )
    {
    /* ... */
    }
```

Each type of event has its own structure, part of the `XEvent` union. All structures share a common part, which is held in the `XAnyEvent` structure:

```
typedef struct {
    int             type;
    unsigned long   serial; /* # last request processed by server */
    Bool            send_event; /* true if from XSendEvent */
    Display         *display;
    Window          window;
    } XAnyEvent;
```

Appendix B, "X Event Types and Structures," contains a full list of the X event types and structures. Code to handle events follows the template below:

```
Display     *display;
XEvent      event;
```

```
XNextEvent( display, &event );

switch( event.type )
        {
        case Expose:   ...
        case MapNotify:   ...
        case ButtonPress: ...
        case KeyPress: ...
        case ConfigureNotify: ...
        ...
        }
```

MOUSE BUTTON EVENTS

X, like most recent computer graphics packages, requires a mouse for efficient use. (Anywhere the word mouse is used, you could replace it with trackball, joystick, or whatever other pointing device your system has.) Most X software seems to assume a three-button mouse (users of Hewlett-Packard or Apple products, for example, emulate the extra mouse buttons with some interesting contortions). X itself defines up to five mouse buttons, but most software only assumes a left, middle, and right mouse button.

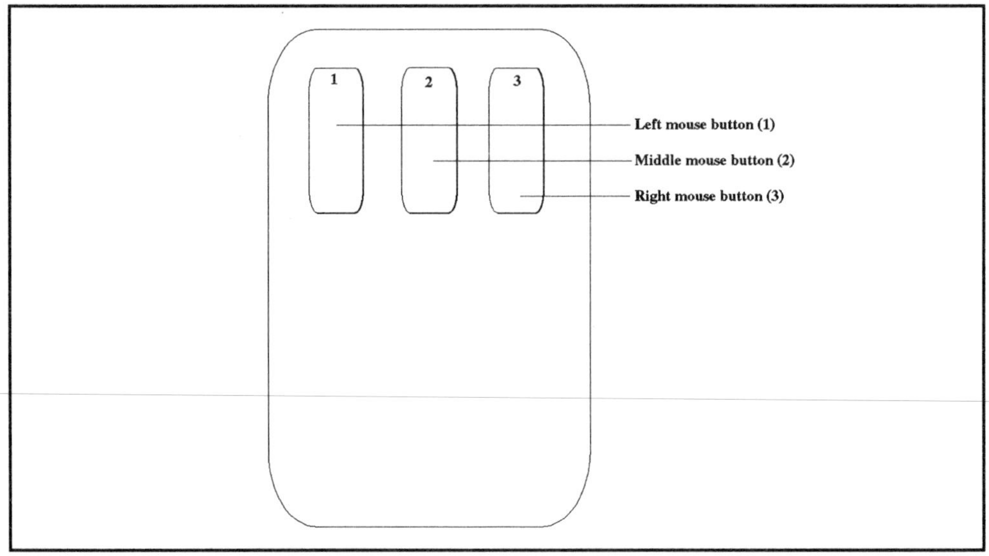

Figure 6.2. The X Mouse Buttons.

X mouse-button events are generated when:

- The user presses down a particular mouse button
- The user releases the button
- The user moves the mouse pointer
- The user moves the mouse pointer while holding down a mouse button within an active window or within the child of an active window

Depending on the style of user interface you want to develop, you may want to check for one or more of these events. Unless you really need to, though, try to skip the mouse movement events—each pixel of motion generates a `MotionNotify` event, and on a 1,024 x 1,024-pixel monitor, that can mean a lot of events coming in quickly. These events bog down your program's performance.

The masks to request mouse pointer events include:

Mask	***Meaning***
`ButtonMotionMask`	The mouse is moved while a button is pressed
`Button1MotionMask`	The mouse is moved while button 1 is pressed
`Button2MotionMask`	The mouse is moved while button 2 is pressed
`Button3MotionMask`	The mouse is moved while button 3 is pressed
`Button4MotionMask`	The mouse is moved while button 4 is pressed
`Button5MotionMask`	The mouse is moved while button 5 is pressed
`ButtonPressMask`	A mouse pointer button is pressed down
`ButtonReleaseMask`	A mouse pointer button that was pressed down was released
`PointerMotionMask`	The mouse pointer was moved (which happens very often)
`PointerMotionHintMask`	Special mask that asks X to compress a number of mouse movements into one event

The events your program will receive will be:

Event	***Meaning***
`ButtonPress`	For button pressings
`ButtonRelease`	For releasing buttons that were pressed
`MotionNotify`	For any of the motion masks

The key to these mouse events includes finding out in which window the event took place, determining the x, y location of the event, and determining which mouse buttons were pressed at the time of the event.

```
typedef struct {
        int           type;         /* ButtonPress or ButtonRelease */
        unsigned long serial;
        Bool          send_event;
        Display       *display;
        Window        window;
        Window        root;
        Window        subwindow;
        Time          time;         /* milliseconds */
        int           x, y;         /* pointer x, y coords in window */
        int           x_root, y_root;

        unsigned int state;         /* key or button mask */
        unsigned int button;
        Bool          same_screen; /
        } XButtonEvent;

typedef XButtonEvent  XButtonPressedEvent;
typedef XButtonEvent  XButtonReleasedEvent;

typedef struct {
        int           type;         /* MotionNotify */
        unsigned long serial;
        Bool          send_event;
        Display       *display;
        Window        window;
        Window        root;
        Window        subwindow;
        Time          time;         /* milliseconds */
        int           x, y;         /* pointer x, y coords in window */
        int           x_root, y_root;
        unsigned int state;         /* key or button mask */
        char          is_hint;
        Bool          same_screen;/
        } XMotionEvent;

typedef XMotionEvent  XPointerMovedEvent;
```

The answer to the first step is found in the `XEvent` union. The window in which the event took place is found in the `window` field for button events:

```
Window        window;
XEvent        event;

window = event.xbutton.window;
```

Or, for motion events:

```
window = event.xmotion.window;
```

Next, the x, y location is in the x and y fields:

```
int     x, y;

x  = event.xbutton.x;
x  = event.xbutton.y;
```

Or,

```
x  = event.xmotion.x;
y  = event.xmotion.y;
```

Finding out which button was pressed or released is a bit more complicated. In a `ButtonPress` event, the `state` field will normally be `0` if no other modifer keys are pressed. The `button` field will contain which button caused the event: `Button1`, `Button2`, `Button3`, `Button4`, or `Button5`.

For a `ButtonRelease` event, the `state` field and the `button` field will contain the state just before the event (e.g., containing the button that was pressed and then released).

For a MotionNotify event, only the state field will be available.

MODIFIER KEYS

This `state` field tells not only the state of the mouse pointer buttons, but also the state of any modifier keys, such as the Shift, Caps (Shift) Lock, Control, or Meta keys. X does not consider the Num Lock key a modifier. Instead, your applications must handle Num Lock on their own—and many vendors, such as Data General, treat the Num Lock key in nonstandard ways. (There is a proposal to standardize this, though.)

Most of these modifier keys are self-explanatory, save for the Meta key. The Meta key is a key that typically performs an alternate function and is often labeled as the *Alt* key. Most Meta keys are located next to the Spacebar on the keyboard.

On the Sun SPARCStation, it is the left diamond-shaped key next to the Spacebar and not the key next to it labeled Alt. On a Sun 3, the Meta keys are the Left or Right keys. On the HP 9000 Series 800, the Extend Char key performs this function, and on the Apple Mac IIx, it is the command key (labeled with an apple outline and a pretzel shape). The Data General Aviion and SCO Open Desktop both use the Alt key as the Meta key. You can use the standard X client program *xev* (see below) to find out the special mappings on your keyboard.

To check for these keys, check for certain bits in the state field, using the following masks:

Mask	***Meaning***
`Button1Mask`	The first mouse button was down
`Button2Mask`	The second mouse button was down
`Button3Mask`	The third mouse button was down
`Button4Mask`	The fourth mouse button was down (usually not available)
`Button5Mask`	The fifth mouse button was down (usually not available)
`ShiftMask`	A shift key was down
`ControlMask`	Control key was down
`LockMask`	Caps lock was down
`Mod1Mask`	Typical Meta key was down
`Mod2Mask`	Second Meta key
`Mod3Mask`	Another Meta key often not found on the keyboard
`Mod4Mask`	Another Meta key often not found on the keyboard
`Mod5Mask`	Another Meta key often not found on the keyboard

Sample code to check this would look like:

```
XEvent  event;

if ( event.xbutton.state & Button1Mask )
        {
        /* Button 1 is down */
        }
```

For user-interface design, a quick `ButtonPress` then `ButtonRelease` is usually refered to as a button *click*. When checking for these events, it is a good idea to provide some user feedback when the first event comes in—the `ButtonPress`. This is so the user doesn't repeatedly press the mouse button (or hold it down for a long time) under the mistaken impression that the application didn't notice the `ButtonPress`. The fact that many X connections are over a network introduces a potential time lag between the arrival of the `ButtonPress` and `ButtonRelease`.

KEYBOARD EVENTS

Like the mouse-button events, you can check when a keyboard key is pressed and when it is released. Most software, though, needs only to worry about when a key is pressed. If you wait for a key to be released, then you run the same dangers described above in the mouse-button section.

Each X workstation from each vendor uses a different keyboard. X abstracted various keyboard keys using the concept of a KeySym. KeySyms allow your program to map various propietary keyboard schemes into portable code.

The basic task of a KeySym is to convert a machine-specific key code into a generic letter, such as the letter *A*. X also allows for the ability of some keyboards to program a given key to send a string of characters—sort of a keyboard macro. X does this by having each normal QWERTY key send back an ASCII character string, even if the string is only one letter long, such as *A*.

The Xlib function `XLookupString` converts a `KeyPress` event into the ASCII character string pressed on the keyboard, basing this on the keyboard mapping. With `XLookupString`, you must pass a character buffer, one large enough to hold most returned strings, as well as the length of your buffer. We've found a buffer wide enough for one-character plus a terminating `NULL` works fine. If you think this length is too small, make it larger:

```
XKeyEvent        event;
char             keybuffer[20];
XComposeStatus   composestatus;
KeySym           keysym;
int              length, max_bytes;

max_bytes = 1;

length = XLookupString( &event,
             keybuffer,
             max_bytes,
             &keysym,
             &composestatus );

keybuffer[1] = '\0'; /* terminate */

(void) printf( "KeyPress <%s> key\n", keybuffer );
```

We've also found that some versions of the X library, especially on 386 UNIX platforms, fail to terminate the key buffer, no matter how long it is. So we've adopted the approach of asking for only one character, then terminating the buffer ourselves.

Length is the number of characters returned by `XLookupString`. It can be `0` (for no ASCII string bound to the given key) or `1` (for most keys, such as the *g* key), or > `1` if a key has been bound to a character string, which almost never happens.

You can use returned KeySym to check for keys like the F1 function key, the Help key, or the Page-Down key. How to do this will be described in the next chapter.

The `composestatus` is not implemented on all revisions of X11. For most applications, you can ignore the `XComposeStatus` value.

ENTER/LEAVE WINDOW EVENTS

In X, any keys typed at the keyboard usually go to the window where the mouse pointer sits. Moving the mouse pointer to another window often changes the keyboard focus to the new window. (This focus change generates other events, `FocusIn` and `FocusOut`.)

Whenever the mouse pointer leaves a window, the X server generates a `LeaveNotify` event for the window the mouse just left and an `EnterNotify` for the window the mouse pointer enters. If the keyboard focus changes (which normally occurs with the mouse-pointer motion, but doesn't have to), your applications get a `FocusOut` event on the window that lost the keyboard focus and a `FocusIn` event on the window that is the new focus of the keyboard.

Some X client programs, like *xterm*, may fill in the text cursor on a `FocusIn` and convert the cursor to an outline on a `FocusOut`. This provides an added visual cue to the user for which window "owns" the keyboard—that is, which window will get keyboard input when the user types.

That part sounds easy, but X adds a twist: the X server will generate `EnterNotify/LeaveNotify` and `FocusIn/FocusOut` events on windows that are virtually crossed. When the keyboard focus (or the mouse pointer) is moved from one window to another across the screen, some of the windows in between are virtually crossed. Rather than designing a virtual event-handler routine, it is easier to simply treat each `EnterNotify/LeaveNotify` and `FocusIn/FocusOut` event in good faith.

You ask for `EnterNotify/LeaveNotify` events with an `EnterWindowMask` and a `LeaveWindowMask`, respectively, as a parameter to `XSelectInput` or in `XCreateWindow`. Focus change events are selected with the `FocusChangeMask`.

The only relevant portion of the `XEvent` union is the window on which the event was generated. For `EnterNotify/LeaveNotify` events, this looks like:

```
Window        window;
XEvent        event;

window = event.xcrossing.window;
```

And for focus events:

```
window = event.xfocus.window;
```

CONFIGURENOTIFY EVENTS

`ConfigureNotify` events occur when your window's configuration, such as its size or position, changes. Select this event with `StructureNotifyMask`:

```
typedef struct {
       int                  type;       /* ConfigureNotify */
       unsigned long        serial;
       Bool                 send_event;
       Display              *display;
       Window               event;
       Window               window;
       int                  x, y;
       int                  width, height;
       int                  border_width;
       Window               above;
       Bool                 override_redirect;
       } XConfigureEvent;
```

If the window's size or position has changed, the x, y, width, and height fields have the new values. Most window managers allow users to resize and move windows about the screen. By watching for `ConfigureNotify` events, your application can keep track of changes to its windows. Note that you should normally ignore the x, y fields. (Most window managers will reparent your application windows, so the x and y values will be local. Check out the *ICCCM* for more information.)

MAPNOTIFY EVENTS

MapNotify events occur when a window is mapped. XMapWindow and XMapRaised ask the X server to map a window, but a window manager may intervene, so your application has no idea how long it takes to actually map the window to the screen. Asking for MapNotify events with the StructureNotifyMask can tell at least when the window is actually mapped, although checking for Expose events should work fine:

```
typedef struct {
        int             type; /* MapNotify */
        unsigned long   serial;
        Bool            send_event;
        Display         *display;
        Window          event;
        Window          window;
        Bool            override_redirect; /* boolean, is override set */
        } XMapEvent;
```

AN EXAMPLE PROGRAM TO CHECK EVENTS

The chap6 program, below, asks for ButtonPress, ConfigureNotify, Expose, KeyPress, and MapNotify events with the following event mask:

```
ButtonPressMask | KeyPressMask | ExposureMask | StructureNotifyMask
```

As each event arrives (via XNextEvent), the program prints the relevent fields of the XEvent structure. Press *q* to quit.

SOURCE CODE FOR CHAP6.C

The file chap6.c contains the main function for the chap6 program:

```
/*
 *      chap6.c
 *      Example program for Chapter 6.
 *
 *      Written for X Window Applications
 *      Programming, 2nd Edition
 */
```

```
#include <stdio.h>
#include <X11/Xlib.h>
#include <X11/Xutil.h>

#define FONT_NAME          "variable"
#define FALLBACK_FONT_NAME  "fixed"

/*
 *      Globals for black and white colors
 */

unsigned long   black, white;

/*
 *      Global strings for button IDs
 */

static char     *ButtonIds[]=
                   {
                   "No Button",
                   "Button1",
                   "Button2",
                   "Button3",
                   "Button4",
                   "Button5"
                   };

/*
 *      Set up event mask.
 */

#define EVENT_MASK (ButtonPressMask    | \
             KeyPressMask        | \
             ExposureMask        | \
             StructureNotifyMask)

main( argc, argv )

int     argc;
char    *argv[];

{       /* main */
        Display     *display;
        Display     *ConnectToServer();    /* connect.c */
```

```
Window      rootwindow, window;
Window      OpenWindow();           /* window.c */
int         screen;
int         x, y, width, height;
Visual      *visual = CopyFromParent;
GC          gc;
GC          CreateGC();             /* gc.c */
XEvent      event;
int         done;
XFontStruct *font_struct;
XFontStruct *LoadFont();            /* loadfont.c */

/*
 * Connect to default X server
 */
display = ConnectToServer( (char *) NULL,
        &screen,
        &rootwindow );

/*
 * Set up "colors" we'll use
 */
black = BlackPixel( display, screen );
white = WhitePixel( display, screen );

/*
 * Create a window on the display
 */
x      = 10;
y      = 10;
width  = 300;
height = 200;
window = OpenWindow( display,
        rootwindow,
        x, y, width, height,
        black, white,
        EVENT_MASK,
        visual );

/*
 * Provide information to the window manager.
 */
```

```
SetStandardHints( display, window,
     argv[0], argv[0],
     x, y, width, height );

/*
 * Create graphics context for drawing
 */
gc = CreateGC( display, window, black, white );

/*
 * Load a font
 */
font_struct = LoadFont( display,
              FONT_NAME,
              FALLBACK_FONT_NAME );

/*
 * Now, set the GC to draw with this font.
 */
XSetFont( display, gc,
     font_struct->fid );

/*
 * Make the window actually appear
 */
XMapRaised( display, window );
XFlush( display );

/*
 * Loop for 20 Expose events. Real programs
 * should go until done or the user quits.
 */
done = False;
while( !done )
     {
     XNextEvent( display, &event );

     switch( event.type )
        {
        case Expose:
           (void) printf( "Expose event <%d,%d>",
              event.xexpose.x,
              event.xexpose.y );
```

```
        (void) printf( " by <%d,%d> #%d\n",
            event.xexpose.width,
            event.xexpose.height,
            event.xexpose.count );

        if ( event.xexpose.count == 0 )
            {
            (void) printf(
              "\tLast Expose event.\n" );
            }
        break;
    case MapNotify:
        (void) printf(
          "MapNotify: Window was mapped.\n" );
        break;
    case ButtonPress:
        (void) printf(
            "ButtonPress: %s at <%d,%d>\n",
            ButtonIds[event.xbutton.button],
            event.xbutton.x,
            event.xbutton.y );
        AppendKeyStateMessage(
            event.xbutton.state );
        break;
    case KeyPress:
        done = HandleKeyPress( &event );
        break;

    case ConfigureNotify:
        (void) printf(
            "Window configuration changed\n");

        (void) printf( "<%d,%d> by <%d,%d>\n",
            event.xconfigure.x,
            event.xconfigure.y,
            event.xconfigure.width,
            event.xconfigure.height );
        break;
    }

/*
 * In this simple text program, we redraw on every
 * event. Normally, you only need to redraw
```

```
                 * on Expose events.
                 */
                Redraw( display, window, gc );
                }

        /*
         * Free the font, now that we're done with it.
         */
        XFreeFont( display, font_struct );
        XCloseDisplay( display );

}       /* main */

Redraw( display, window, gc )

Display         *display;
Window          window;
GC              gc;

{       /* Redraw */

        DrawString( display, window, gc,
                30, 30, "Chapter 6: Press q to quit." );

        /*
         * Send all our requests over the network,
         * so that the drawing is visible.
         */
        XFlush( display );

}       /* Redraw */

HandleKeyPress( event )

XKeyEvent       *event;

/*
 *      Displays information about a KeyPress event.
 *      Note that HandleKeyPress is passed a pointer
 *      to an XKeyEvent structure, even though the event
 *      was originally placed in an XEvent union. X
 *      overlays the various structure types into a union
 *      of structures. By using the XKeyEvent, we can access
```

```
 *      the keyboard elements more easily.
 *
 *      Returns True if the user typed in a "q" (to quit),
 *      False otherwise.
 */

{       /* HandleKeyPress */
        int             done = False;
        char            keybuffer[20];
        XComposeStatus  composestatus;
        KeySym          keysym;

        XLookupString( event,
              keybuffer,
              1,
              &keysym,
              &composestatus );

        keybuffer[1] = '\0'; /* terminate */

        (void) printf( "KeyPress <%s> key\n", keybuffer );

        AppendKeyStateMessage( event->state );

        /*
         * Quit if a "q" is hit.
         */
        if ( keybuffer[0] == 'q' )
              {
              done = True;
              }

        return( done );

}       /* HandleKeyPress */

/* end of file chap6.c */
```

SOURCE CODE FOR APPEND.C

The file `append.c` appends to a string describing a key or button press, especially the modifier key (such as `Shift` or `Control` modifiers) state:

```
/*
 *      append.c
 *      Routine to convert a Key/Button
 *      state to a string, used by chapter 6.
 *
 *      Written for X Window Applications
 *      Programming, 2nd Edition
 */

#include <stdio.h>
#include <X11/Xlib.h>
#include <X11/Xutil.h>

AppendKeyStateMessage( state )

unsigned int state;

/*
 *      Appends a message based on the current state of
 *      the shift keys, etc.
 */

{       /* AppendKeyStateMessage */
        char  string[400];

        (void) strcpy( string, "    " );    /* initialize */

        if ( state & Button1Mask )
              {
              (void) strcat( string, "Button1 " );
              }

        if ( state & Button2Mask )
              {
              (void) strcat( string, "Button2 " );
              }

        if ( state & Button3Mask )
              {
              (void) strcat( string, "Button3 " );
              }

        if ( state & Button4Mask )
```

```
          {
          (void) strcat( string, "Button4 " );
          }

     if ( state & Button5Mask )
          {
          (void) strcat( string, "Button5 " );
          }

     if ( state & ShiftMask )
          {
          (void) strcat( string, "Shift " );
          }

     if ( state & LockMask )
          {
          (void) strcat( string, "Lock " );
          }

     if ( state & ControlMask )
          {
          (void) strcat( string, "Control " );
          }

     if ( state & Mod1Mask )
          {
          (void) strcat( string, "Mod1 " );
          }

     if ( state & Mod2Mask )
          {
          (void) strcat( string, "Mod2 " );
          }

     if ( state & Mod3Mask )
          {
          (void) strcat( string, "Mod3 " );
          }

     if ( state & Mod4Mask )
          {
          (void) strcat( string, "Mod4 " );
          }
```

```
        if ( state & Mod5Mask )
              {
              (void) strcat( string, "Mod5 " );
              }

        /*
         * Only append message if we've
         * added any information.
         */
        if ( strlen( string ) > 4 )
              {
              (void) printf( "%s\n", string );
              }

}       /* AppendKeyStateMessage */

/* end of file append.c */
```

SOURCE CODE FOR DRAWSTR.C

The file `drawstr.c` contains a convenience function for calling `XDrawImageString`:

```
/*
 *      drawstr.c
 *      DrawString utility function.
 *
 *      Written for X Window Applications
 *      Programming, 2nd Edition
 */

#include <X11/Xlib.h>

DrawString( display, window, gc, x, y, string )

Display      *display;
Window       window;
GC           gc;
int          x, y;
char         string[];
```

```
/*
 *      Draws a text string using XDrawImageString.
 */

{       /* DrawString */

        XDrawImageString( display, window, gc,
             x, y, string, strlen( string ) );

}       /* DrawString */

/* end of file drawstr.c */
```

COMPILING AND LINKING THE CHAP6 PROGRAM

The chap6 program requires the following files.

append.c	
chap6.c	
classhnt.c	(Chapter 2)
connect.c	(Chapter 1)
drawstr.c	
gc.c	(Chapter 3)
loadfont.c	(Chapter 5)
sizehint.c	(Chapter 2)
window.c	(Chapter 2)
wmname.c	(Chapter 2)
wmhints.c	(Chapter 2)

You can compile and link the chap6 program with a command such as:

```
cc -o chap6 -DX11R4 append.c chap6.c classhnt.c connect.c \
       drawstr.c gc.c loadfont.c sizehint.c window.c wmname.c \
       wmhints.c -lX11
```

You can also use the Makefile in Appendix A and type:

```
make chap6
```

RUNNING THE CHAP6 PROGRAM

The `chap6` program creates a window that looks like:

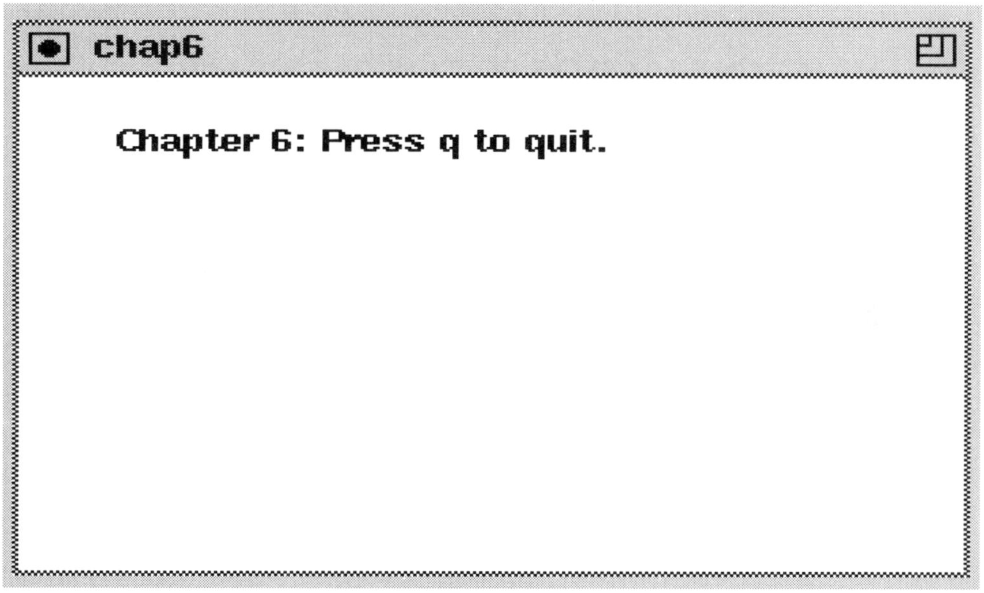

Figure 6.3. The Chap6 Program in Action.

The text output of the `chap6` program will look something like the following, depending on what keys you press. Press *q* to quit. Notice the two window configuration events as the window manager intercepts the window mapping (and places a title bar above our window).

```
Window configuration changed
<10,10> by <300,200>
Window configuration changed
<10,31> by <300,200>
MapNotify: Window was mapped.
Expose event <0,0> by <300,200> #0
        Last Expose event.
ButtonPress: Button1 at <145,122>
ButtonPress: Button2 at <145,122>
ButtonPress: Button3 at <145,122>
KeyPress <g> key
KeyPress <G> key
```

```
   Shift
KeyPress <d> key
   Mod1
KeyPress <q> key
```

FINDING OUT ABOUT THE X EVENT MODEL WITH THE XEV PROGRAM

After running these examples, you should have a good idea how events in X work. The standard X client program, *xev*, can also help discover the look and feel for X events. The *xev* program places a window on the screen and then prints out any events that happen in that window, much like our example program (but more extensive). Not all X packages come with *xev*, but most do.

SUMMARY

X uses events to tell your application program that something happened. This includes keyboard-generated events, such as keypresses; mouse-generated events, such as moving the mouse pointer; and window-generated events, such as moving your window to the top of the heap, exposing contents that were previously hidden.

X only sends your application events of the event types you ask for (except for a few types that X bluntly states you ask for no matter what). Your application asks for events during the `XCreateWindow` call or with the `XSelectInput` function. When calling `XSelectInput` or filling in the `XSetWindowAttributes` structure for `XCreateWindow`, you pass a value whose bit-pattern contains the set of masks for the events you want. These masks are defined in the X include header files with descriptive names like `KeyPressMask`. We recommend asking for events at window creation time within the call to `XCreateWindow`.

To actually receive events from the X server, your application can poll the server or wait for the server to send an event. In most cases, waiting for an event with `XNextEvent` is just fine and is nicest to the system's resources.

Once your application acquires an event, the program needs to determine the event's type and react to the event.

The example program showed the use of event-checking routines.

XLIB FUNCTIONS AND MACROS INTRODUCED IN THIS CHAPTER

```
ConnectionNumber
XCheckMaskEvent
XCheckTypedEvent
XCheckTypedWindowEvent
XCheckWindowEvent
XClearWindow
XLookupString
XMaskEvent
XPeekEvent
XPending
XSelectInput
XWindowEvent
```

Chapter 7

KEYBOARD EVENTS

Almost every computer manufacturer uses a different keyboard. Some manufacturers even sell a number of different keyboards for their own products. Sun, for example, sells a Type 4 keyboard, which is radically different from its old Sun 3 keyboards, as well as a PC/AT-style keyboard.

Most of these keyboards will have special keys, including arrow keys, a numeric keypad, function keys, and PageUp and PageDown keys. Users tend to like being able to use their UpArrow key, among others, but the problem is how to do this in a generic way that will work on all (or virtually all) keyboards.

The designers of X were faced with the same problem. To solve this, they came up with concept of KeySyms, which we introduced last chapter. KeySyms form a set of generic symbols for various keys, like `XK_Up` for the UpArrow key. Most KeySym names begin with `XK_` and end with a description of the key, such as `XK_Begin` for a Begin (or Home) key. Each KeySym is really an arbitrary number with a C preprocessor define statement to give it a symbolic name (defined in the X include file `keysymdef.h`).

Every time the X server is ported to another machine, the porting process includes having the server translate the native keyboard format into these KeySyms. Therefore, using the KeySyms to identify these special keys will help make your code portable to other X workstations. And, since portability is the primary benefit of X, using KeySyms is a good idea.

When a `KeyPress` event arrives, the `XKeyEvent` part of the `XEvent` union is filled in:

```
typedef struct {
        int             type;  /* KeyPress or KeyRelease */
        unsigned long   serial;
        Bool            send_event;
        Display         *display;
        Window          window;
        Window          root;
        Window          subwindow;
        Time            time;  /* milliseconds */
        int             x, y;  /* pointer x, y coords in window */
        int             x_root, y_root;
        unsigned int    state; /* key or button mask */
        unsigned int    keycode;
        Bool            same_screen;/
        } XKeyEvent;

typedef XKeyEvent      XKeyPressedEvent;
typedef XKeyEvent      XKeyReleasedEvent;
```

The keycode field contains a vendor-dependent number for the key on the keyboard. Use the function `XLookupString` to convert the nonportable keycode to the portable KeySym associated with the key pressed:

```
XKeyEvent       event;
char            keybuffer[20];
XComposeStatus  composestatus;
KeySym          keysym;
int             length, max_bytes;

max_bytes = 1;

length = XLookupString( &event,
            keybuffer,
            max_bytes,
```

```
            &keysym,
            &composestatus );

keybuffer[1] = '\0'; /* terminate */

if ( length > 0 )
        {
        (void) printf( "KeyPress <%s> key\n", keybuffer );
        }
```

The `keybuffer` is a character array where ASCII keys will be put. If the user types an `e`, then the `keybuffer` will contain the NULL-terminated string "e".

The `max_bytes` tells X how many characters it can put into the `keybuffer`—you are responsible for allocating the storage for the `keybuffer`.

The value in the `composestatus` is not implemented in many versions of X11, so it is best to ignore this value.

For most ASCII-printable characters (the QWERTY keys on the keyboard), simply checking if `keybuffer[ 0 ]` is an ASCII-printable character or checking if the KeySym value is an ASCII-printable character will be fine. This avoids a lot of KeySym processing for the most common keys hit. `XLookupString` returns the number of bytes placed into the keybuffer, so check to be sure it is at least greater than 0. Otherwise, the keybuffer's contents are undefined.

For the function keys and the other special keys on the keyboard, you'll have to check the KeySym itself. The KeySyms are defined in the X header file `keysymdef.h`. (X header files are normally in the directory `/usr/include/X11`; if not, check with your system administrator.) One look in that file will show how many possible KeySyms there are. Worry only about the ones that make sense for a particular application; skip the rest.

The method used for handling the `KeyPress` events in the function `DecodeKeyPress` is as follows: first, verify that the event is a `KeyPress` or `KeyRelease` event. If your X server uses shared libraries, a call to `XLookupString` with a nonkey event can actually crash the X server. We consider this a bug, and it's probably been fixed by now, but many systems in the field may still experience this. Always verify the event type before calling `XLookupString`.

After verifying, we call `XLookupString` to get a KeySym for the event and any ASCII string associated with the event.

DECODING KEY EVENTS

The function `DecodeKeyPress` decodes an `XKeyEvent` generated by `KeyPress` or `KeyRelease` events:

```
DecodeKeyPress( event, keysym, string )

XKeyEvent     *event;
KeySym        *keysym;
char          string[];

{       /* DecodeKeyPress */
        XComposeStatus composestatus;
        int          length;

        *keysym = 0x0;
        string[0] = '\0';

        if ( ( event->type != KeyPress ) &&
             ( event->type != KeyRelease ) )
             {
             return( False );
             }

        /*
         * Convert event to a string
         */
        length = XLookupString( event,
                    string,
                    1,
                    keysym,
                    &composestatus );

        if ( length > 0 )
             {
             string[1] = '\0'; /* terminate */
             }
        else
             {
             string[0] = '\0';
             }
```

```
        return( IsMetaQ( event, string ) );

}       /* DecodeKeyPress */
```

When running the example program below and examining the file `keysymdef.h`, you will notice a lot of the function keys are defined to have double meanings. Most keyboards label function keys starting with F1 for the first function key, F2 for the second, and so on. Sun Microsystems keyboards, though, have function keys labeled F1 to F*n* across the top of the keyboard, as well as right and left function keys along the sides of the keyboard, labeled R1 to R*n* and L1 to L*n* (where *n* is the max number of function keys). Since many of the designers and early users of the X Window System use Sun workstations, these KeySyms became a part of X. Most other keyboards do not have the left and right function keys, though, but do have a large number of regular function keys. Because of this, `keysymdef.h` defines `XK_R1`, the first right function key for example, to be the same as `XK_F21`, the twenty-first regular function key.

To make matters worse, the Sun SPARCstation Type 4 keyboard has a keypad with the right function key labels as well as IBM PC-style keypad labels, such as Page Up, Page Down, Home, and End. Unfortunately, users may want to use the R9 key as the Page Up key—since the key does have that label—and there goes portability, at least with X11 R5 from the MIT X Consortium. Below, some of the special Sun Type 4 mappings are listed, along with the KeySyms that match the labels on the keys. If you want to handle this nonportable key processing, the `XK_Prior` KeySym (often called the PageUp key) and the `XK_R9` key should be treated the same. After running the example program below and trying out all the keys available, you might find some subtle incompatibilities on your keyboard.

In general, though, the KeySym concept aids portability and hides most of the details of specific keyboards.

Here are the common KeySyms:

Name	***Key on Keyboard***
`XK_Home`	Home
`XK_Left`	LeftArrow
`XK_Up`	UpArrow
`XK_Right`	RightArrow
`XK_Down`	DownArrow
`XK_Prior`	Prior, Previous, or PageUp
`XK_Next`	Next or PageDown

Name	*Key on Keyboard (cont.)*
XK_Begin	Begin, Beginning of Line
XK_End	End, End of Line
XK_Tab	Horizontal Tab
XK_Return	Return, Enter
XK_Scroll_Lock	Scroll Lock
XK_Escape	Escape, Esc
XK_BackSpace	Back Space
XK_Delete	Delete (rub out)
XK_Insert	Insert (HPs have XK_InsertChar and XK_InsertLine)
XK_Help	Help
XK_Num_Lock	NumLock
XK_KP_Enter	Enter key on keypad
XK_KP_F1..XK_KP_F4	PF1 to PF4 on keypad
XK_KP_0..XK_KP_9	Keypad digits
XK_A..XK_Z	A..Z
XK_a..XK_z	A..Z
XK_0..XK_9	0..9
XK_F1..XK_F10	F1 to F10 function keys
XK_L1..XK_L10	left function keys, or XK_F11..XK_F20
XK_R1..XK_R15	right function keys, or XK_F21..XK_F35

Note the duplication between normal, left, and right function keys.

SUN TYPE 4 KEYPAD CODES

The Sun Type-4 keyboard sports on odd keypad. Each key contains many markings. The KeySyms returned by XLookupString from MIT's X11 R5 aren't always what you expect. Other vendor's keyboards may have similar problems.

Key Markings/Number	*Right Func*	*X KeySym*	*Shifted KeySym*
Home/7	R7	XK_R7	XK_KP_7
UpArrow/8	R8	XK_Up	XK_KP_8

Key Markings/Number	*Right Func*	*X KeySym*	*Shifted KeySym (cont.)*
PgUp/9	R9	XK_R9	XK_KP_9
LeftArrow/4	R10	XK_Left	XK_KP_4
5	R11	XK_R11	XK_KP_5
RightArrow/6	R12	XK_Right	XK_KP_6
End/1	R13	XK_R13	XK_KP_1
DownArrow/2	R14	XK_Down	XK_KP_2
PgDn/3	R15	XK_R15	XK_KP_3
Ins/0		XK_Insert	XK_KP_0
Del/.		XK_Delete	XK_KP_Decimal
Enter		XK_KP_Enter	XK_KP_Enter
+		XK_KP_Add	XK_KP_Add
=	R4	XK_KP_R4	XK_KP_Equal
/	R5	XK_KP_R5	XK_KP_Divide
*	R6	XK_KP_R6	XK_KP_Multiply
-		XK_KP_Subtract	XK_KP_Subtract
Pause	R1	XK_R1	XK_Pause
PrSc	R2	XK_R2	XK_R2
Scroll Lock/Break	R3	XK_R3	XK_R3
Num Lock		XK_Num_Lock	XK_Num_Lock

CONVERTING FUNCTION KEYS TO STRINGS

The function `XKeySymToString` converts a KeySym, like `XK_Begin`, to a string, like "Begin". This is useful in verifying that a given key on the keyboard actually generates the KeySym you're expecting:

```
char         *ptr;
KeySym       keysym;

ptr = XKeysymToString( keysym );
```

The function `HandleKeyPress` checks for Meta keys and converts a KeySym into a string for function keys and the like. The routine merely prints out the keys pressed:

```
HandleKeyPress( event, keysym, keybuffer )

XKeyEvent     *event;
KeySym        keysym;
char          keybuffer[];

{       /* HandleKeyPress */

        /*
         * Check for META keys.
         */
        if ( ( event->state & Mod1Mask ) ||  /* META Keys */
             ( event->state & Mod2Mask ) )
             {
             (void) printf( "META-%s hit\n", keybuffer );
             }
        else
             {
             /*
              * Check if our keysym is a standard ASCII
              * character. Programmers in other countries
              * will want to change the next few lines.
              */
             if ( ( isascii(keysym) ) && ( !iscntrl(keysym) ) )
                {
                (void) printf( "KeyPress <%s> key\n",
                   keybuffer );
                }
             else
                {
                (void) printf( "KeyPress <%s>\n",
                   XKeysymToString( keysym ) );
                }
             }

        AppendKeyStateMessage( event->state );

}       /* HandleKeyPress */
```

META KEYS

In many menu-based interfaces, users can choose items in a menu though keyboard shortcuts. A common shortcut is allowing the user to hold down a Meta (or *Alt*) key and press a standard keyboard key. Alt-Q, for example, often means quit.

These Meta-key menu shortcuts are often preferred by expert users, the power users who use a given application program day in and day out. The only problem is that different keyboards, of course, use different keys for the Meta key. (And some keyboards have more than one Meta key—each with a different meaning.) As stated in the last chapter, on many IBM-compatible keyboards, the Meta key is labeled *Alt*. Macintoshes use a pretzel-shaped symbol and call it the command key. The Sun SPARCStation has an *Alt* key, but under X11 R5 from MIT, the SPARC Meta key is right next to the *Alt* key—the diamond-shaped key. On a Sun 3, the Meta key is simply labeled *Left*. Hewlett-Packard keyboards use the left *Extend Char* key.

In most cases, the Meta key is located near the bottom left of the keyboard, in the vicinity of the spacebar. Like the KeySyms, X abstracts all these keys into the Meta key. X also allows for up to five different Meta keys to be available on the keyboard.

To detect when the first Meta key is held down, check the `state` field of the `XKeyEvent` structure to see if the `Mod1Mask` bit is a 1. This `state` field also contains information on the status of the Control and Shift keys. Few keyboards really have (or use) more than one Meta key, so in most cases, checking `Mod1Mask` and perhaps `Mod2Mask` should do the trick:

```
XEvent  event;

if ( ( event->state & Mod1Mask ) ||
        ( event->state & Mod2Mask ) )
        {
        /* Meta key held down with, possibly, another key... */
        }
```

As shown in the last chapter, you can compare other masks against the `state` field, to see which keys are held down at the same time a `KeyPress` event comes in, including:

Mask	***Meaning***
`Button1Mask`	The first mouse button was down
`Button2Mask`	The second mouse button was down
`Button3Mask`	The third mouse button was down
`Button4Mask`	The fourth mouse button was down (usually not available)
`Button5Mask`	The fifth mouse button was down (usually not available)
`ShiftMask`	A Shift key was down
`ControlMask`	Control key was down
`LockMask`	Caps Lock was down
`Mod1Mask`	Typical Meta key was down
`Mod2Mask`	Second Meta key
`Mod3Mask`	Another Meta key often not found on the keyboard
`Mod4Mask`	Another Meta key often not found on the keyboard
`Mod5Mask`	Another Meta key often not found on the keyboard

DETECTING META KEYS

The following code detects whether an event is a key press or release and whether the Alt (Meta) key is pressed:

```
IsMetaKey( event )

XEvent        *event;

{       /* IsMetaKey */

        if ( ( event->type == KeyPress ) ||
             ( event->type == KeyRelease ) )
             {
             if ( ( event->xkey.state & Mod1Mask ) ||
                  ( event->xkey.state & Mod2Mask ) )
                  {
                  return( True );
                  }
             }

        return( False );

}       /* IsMetaKey */
```

USING ALT-Q TO QUIT

Many programs, especially on the Macintosh and on machines running DOS, use Alt-Q to quit. The following code will detect an Alt-Q (or Meta-Q) key combination:

```
IsMetaQ( event, string )

XKeyEvent          *event;
char               string[];

/*
 *      Returns True if the key event is
 *      for a Meta (or Alt) Q.
 */

{       /* IsMetaQ */
        int   status = False;

        if ( IsMetaKey( event ) == True )
              {
              if ( ( string[0] == 'Q' ) ||
                 ( string[0] == 'q' ) )
                 {
                 status = True;
                 }
              }

        return( status );

}       /* IsMetaQ */
```

SOURCE CODE FOR KEY.C

We combine these various functions (`DecodeKeyPress`, `IsMetaKey`, and `IsMetaQ`) in the file `key.c` contains the functions:

```
/*
 *      key.c
 *      Routine to decode a KeyPress event.
 */
```

```
#include <X11/Xlib.h>
#include <X11/Xutil.h>

DecodeKeyPress( event, keysym, string )

XKeyEvent     *event;
KeySym        *keysym;
char          string[];

/*
 *      DecodeKeyPress decodes a KeyPress event and
 *      returns a keysym and a string (if the key event
 *      was on a normal key, like the "A" key).
 */

{       /* DecodeKeyPress */
        XComposeStatus composestatus;
        int           length;

        *keysym = 0x0;
        string[0] = '\0';

        if ( ( event->type != KeyPress ) &&
             ( event->type != KeyRelease ) )
             {
             return( False );
             }

        /*
         * Convert event to a string
         */
        length = XLookupString( event,
                        string,
                        1,
                        keysym,
                        &composestatus );

        if ( length > 0 )
             {
             string[1] = '\0'; /* terminate */
             }
        else
             {
```

```
                string[0] = '\0';
                }

        return( IsMetaQ( event, string ) );

}       /* DecodeKeyPress */

IsMetaKey( event )

XEvent          *event;

/*
 *      Checks to see if:
 *              a) the event is a key event.
 *              b) The Meta-1 or Meta-2 key is pressed down.
 */

{       /* IsMetaKey */
        if ( ( event->type == KeyPress ) ||
              ( event->type == KeyRelease ) )
                {
                if ( ( event->xkey.state & Mod1Mask ) ||
                   ( event->xkey.state & Mod2Mask ) )
                   {
                   return( True );
                   }
                }

        return( False );

}       /* IsMetaKey */

IsMetaQ( event, string )

XKeyEvent       *event;
char            string[];

/*
 *      Returns True if the key event is
 *      for a Meta (or Alt) Q.
 */
```

```
{       /* IsMetaQ */
        int   status = False;

        if ( IsMetaKey( event ) == True )
              {
              if ( ( string[0] == 'Q' ) ||
                  ( string[0] == 'q' ) )
                  {
                  status = True;
                  }
              }

        return( status );

}       /* IsMetaQ */

/* end of file key.c */
```

MOUSE BUTTONS

X11 assumes that most workstations have a mouse or other pointing device, called a *pointer* in X terminology, and that each mouse has three buttons, although up to five buttons are allowed. Some vendors, like Hewlett-Packard and Apple, use a mouse with fewer than three buttons. In those cases, the missing mouse buttons are usually simulated by other means. With Hewlett-Packard's two-button mouse, the middle mouse button is simulated by pressing both mouse buttons at the same time. With a Macintosh's one-button mouse, two other mouse buttons are simulated with special keys on the keyboard, depending on the type of keyboard. Well-behaved X applications should not depend on mice with three buttons, but many existing packages do.

When designing user interfaces, it is a good idea to consider what types of machines will be running the software. To be the most generic, assume only one mouse button or treat all mouse buttons the same. If your company has standardized on a given workstation vendor or mouse style, this won't be a problem.

To determine which mouse button was pressed on a `ButtonPress` event, check the `button` field, as we described last chapter. (The `state` field can also be checked as shown above.) `ButtonRelease` events work the same way, but signify that a button previously pressed has been released.

WHEN THE KEYBOARD MAPPING CHANGES

X allows applications to dynamically change the keyboard mapping. Many X applications require certain keys, and your keyboard may not have these keys available. Again, these X applications would not be considered well-behaved, but many of us simply don't have a choice when we try to get X software running. The `xmodmap` program provides the mean to make most of these key changes.

When the keyboard mapping has been changed for whatever reason, X will send out a `MappingNotify` event. Your application will receive this event regardless of any event mask setting in the call to `XSelectInput` or `XCreateWindow`, as you get `MappingNotify` events no matter what.

Do not confuse a `MappingNotify` event with a `MapNotify` event. The first refers to a keyboard-mapping change, and the second to a window being mapped to the screen.

When a `MappingNotify` event comes in, call the function `XRefreshKeyboardMapping` to update the internal mapping information (within your application program) for the keyboard:

```
XEvent        event;
Display       *display;

...

XNextEvent( display, &event );

switch( event.type )
       {
       case MappingNotify:
             XRefreshKeyboardMapping( &event );
             break;
       ...
       }
```

AN EXAMPLE PROGRAM TO READ KEY AND MOUSE EVENTS

The `chap7` example program for this chapter creates a window and reads in events on that window, much like last chapter's program. The `chap7` program, however, provides more information on key and mouse events. Type Alt-Q (or Meta-Q, whichever terminology you prefer), to quit.

Sample output from the `chap7` program follows:

```
Window configuration changed
<10,10> by <300,200>

Window configuration changed
<10,31> by <300,200>
MapNotify: Window was mapped
Expose event <0,0> by <300,200> #0
       Last Expose event in sequence
Pointer Enters window.
KeyPress <Shift_L>
KeyPress <A> key
   Shift
KeyPress <Return>
KeyPress <BackSpace>
KeyPress <Delete>
KeyPress <F3>
KeyPress <F29>
KeyPress <Help>
KeyPress <Meta_L>
META-q hit
   Mod1
```

SOURCE CODE FOR CHAP7.C

```
/*
 *      chap7.c
 *      Example program for Chapter 7.
 *
 *      Written for X Window Applications
 *      Programming, 2nd Edition
 */

#include <stdio.h>
#include <ctype.h>
#include <X11/Xlib.h>
#include <X11/Xutil.h>
```

```
#define FONT_NAME         "variable"
#define FALLBACK_FONT_NAME  "fixed"

/*
 *      Globals for black and white colors
 */
unsigned long   black, white;
*
 *      Globals for button IDs
 */
static char  *ButtonIds[]=
                   {
                   "No Button",
                   "Button1",
                   "Button2",
                   "Button3",
                   "Button4",
                   "Button5"
                   };

/*
 *      Set up event mask.
 */

#define EVENT_MASK (ButtonPressMask | \
             ButtonReleaseMask            | \
             EnterWindowMask              | \
             LeaveWindowMask              | \
             KeyPressMask                 | \
             ExposureMask                 | \
             StructureNotifyMask)

main( argc, argv )

int     argc;
char    *argv[];

{       /* main */
        Display     *display;
        Display     *ConnectToServer();
        Window      rootwindow, window;
        Window      OpenWindow();
```

```
int          screen;
int          x, y, width, height;
Visual       *visual = CopyFromParent;
GC           gc;
GC           CreateGC();
XEvent       event;
int          done;
XFontStruct *font_struct;
XFontStruct *LoadFont();
KeySym       keysym;
char         string[400];

/*
 * Connect to default X server
 */
display = ConnectToServer( (char *) NULL,
        &screen,
        &rootwindow );

/*
 * Set up "colors" we'll use
 */
black = BlackPixel( display, screen );
white = WhitePixel( display, screen );

/*
 * Create a window on the display
 */
x      = 10;
y      = 10;
width  = 300;
height = 200;
window = OpenWindow( display,
        rootwindow,
        x, y, width, height,
        black, white,
        EVENT_MASK,
        visual );

/*
 * Provide information to the window manager.
 */
SetStandardHints( display, window,
```

```
        argv[0], argv[0],
        x, y, width, height );

/*
 * Create graphics context for drawing
 */
gc = CreateGC( display, window, black, white );

/*
 * Load a font
 */
font_struct = LoadFont( display,
                FONT_NAME,
                FALLBACK_FONT_NAME );

/*
 * Now, set the GC to draw with this font.
 */
XSetFont( display, gc,
        font_struct->fid );

/*
 * Make the window actually appear
 */
XMapRaised( display, window );
XFlush( display );

/*
 * Loop on events. Quit when the user types
 * a Meta-Q.
 */
done = False;

while( !done )
        {
        XNextEvent( display, &event );

        switch( event.type )
            {
            case Expose:
                (void) printf( "Expose event <%d,%d>",
```

```
            event.xexpose.x,
            event.xexpose.y );

         (void) printf( " by <%d,%d> #%d\n",
            event.xexpose.width,
            event.xexpose.height,
            event.xexpose.count );

         if ( event.xexpose.count == 0 )
            {
            (void) printf(
             "\tLast Expose event in batch\n");
            }
         break;
      case MapNotify:
         (void) printf(
            "MapNotify: Window was mapped\n" );
         break;
      case ButtonPress:
         (void) printf(
            "ButtonPress: %s at <%d,%d>\n",
            ButtonIds[event.xbutton.button],
            event.xbutton.x,
            event.xbutton.y );
         AppendKeyStateMessage(
            event.xbutton.state );
         break;
      case EnterNotify: /* new in chap7 */
         (void) printf(
            "Pointer Enters window.\n" );
         break;
      case LeaveNotify: /* new in chap7 */
         (void) printf(
            "Pointer Leaves window.\n" );
         break;
      case ButtonRelease: /* new in chap7 */
         (void) printf(
            "ButtonRelease: %s at <%d,%d>\n",
            ButtonIds[event.xbutton.button],
            event.xbutton.x,
            event.xbutton.y );
         AppendKeyStateMessage(
            event.xbutton.state );
         break;
```

```
            case KeyPress:
               done = DecodeKeyPress( &event, &keysym,
                     string );

               HandleKeyPress( &event,
                     keysym, string );
               break;

            case ConfigureNotify:
               (void) printf(
                  "Window configuration changed\n");

               (void) printf( "<%d,%d> by <%d,%d>\n",
                  event.xconfigure.x,
                  event.xconfigure.y,
                  event.xconfigure.width,
                  event.xconfigure.height );
               break;
            case MappingNotify: /* new in chap7 */
               (void) printf(
                  "MappingNotify event\n" );
               XRefreshKeyboardMapping( &event );
               break;
            }

         /*
          * In this simple text program, we redraw on every
          * event. Normally, you only need to redraw
          * on Expose events.
          */
         Redraw( display, window, gc );
         }

      /*
       * Free the font, now that we're done with it.
       */
      XFreeFont( display, font_struct );
      XCloseDisplay( display );

}     /* main */

Redraw( display, window, gc )
```

```
Display         *display;
Window          window;
GC              gc;

{       /* Redraw */

        DrawString( display, window, gc,
              30, 30, "Chapter 7: Press Meta-Q to quit." );

        /*
         * Send all our requests over the network,
         * so that the drawing is visible.
         */
        XFlush( display );

}       /* Redraw */

HandleKeyPress( event, keysym, keybuffer )

XKeyEvent       *event;
KeySym          keysym;
char            keybuffer[];

/*
 *      Displays information about a KeyPress event.
 *      Note that HandleKeyPress is passed a pointer
 *      to an XKeyEvent structure, even though the event
 *      was originally placed in an XEvent union. X
 *      overlays the various structure types into a union
 *      of structures. By using the XKeyEvent, we can access
 *      the keyboard elements more easily.
 */

{       /* HandleKeyPress */

        /*
         * Check for META keys.  Many programs use keyboard
         * shortcuts for menu choices.
         * Such code would go here.
         *
         */
        if ( ( event->state & Mod1Mask ) ||  /* META Keys */
              ( event->state & Mod2Mask ) )
```

```
            {
            (void) printf( "META-%s hit\n", keybuffer );
            }
        else
            {
            /*
             * Check if our keysym is a standard ASCII
             * character. Programmers in other countries
             * will want to change the next few lines.
             */
            if ( ( isascii(keysym) ) && ( !iscntrl(keysym) ) )
                {
                (void) printf( "KeyPress <%s> key\n",
                    keybuffer );
                }
            else
                {
                (void) printf( "KeyPress <%s>\n",
                    XKeysymToString( keysym ) );
                }
            }

        AppendKeyStateMessage( event->state );

}       /* HandleKeyPress */

/* end of file chap7.c */
```

COMPILING AND LINKING THE CHAP7 PROGRAM

The `chap7` program requires the following files:

`append.c`	(Chapter 6)
`chap7.c`	
`classhnt.c`	(Chapter 2)
`connect.c`	(Chapter 1)
`drawstr.c`	(Chapter 6)
`gc.c`	(Chapter 3)

```
key.c
loadfont.c              (Chapter 5)
sizehint.c              (Chapter 2)
window.c                (Chapter 2)
wmname.c                (Chapter 2)
wmhints.c               (Chapter 2)
```

You can compile and link the `chap7` program with a command like:

```
cc -o chap7 -DX11R4 append.c chap7.c classhnt.c connect.c \
    drawstr.c gc.c key.c loadfont.c sizehint.c window.c wmname.c \
    wmhints.c -lX11
```

You can also use the Makefile in Appendix A and type:

```
make chap7
```

SUMMARY

X generalizes keyboard event processing using the concept of KeySyms. KeySyms provide a symbolic way of identifying the various special keys on the keyboard, independent of the actual make and model of keyboard in use. Using KeySyms can help make your code portable to multiple platforms and help avoid issues specific to any one keyboard.

Because many KeySyms are defined in `keysymdef.h`, and because most of the keys pressed will be QWERTY-type alphanumeric keys, you probably want to check for a `KeyPress` event of those types of keys first. This will optimize performance for the most common case. After checking for the standard keys, then check for the special keyboard keys, such as the Prior (or PageUp) key and the Help key.

You'll also want to check for Meta keys, usually used in conjunction with other keys (such as an Alt-A combination) to extend the keyboard's capabilities.

Also, different vendors provide different pointing devices; most X applications assume the user has three mouse buttons, while X allows up to five. Unless there are special circumstances—for instance, if you're porting or designing an application that will be run only on workstations from a single vendor—it's best to assume the user only has access to one pointer button.

XLIB FUNCTIONS AND MACROS INTRODUCED IN THIS CHAPTER

`XKeysymToString`

`XRefreshKeyboardMapping`

Chapter 8

CURSORS

X supports many different cursor shapes, such as the ubiquitous left-pointing arrow, the watch (letting you know the system is busy) and the pointing hand. X follows the clever notion that cursors are characters in a font. Since each character in a font is really a symbolic picture, why can't a cursor be the same thing? This may seem weird, but the designers of X spent a lot of time optimizing text output. At one level, text characters are merely bitmap images, or *glyphs*, that need to be drawn in sequence very quickly. Even in a graphical environment, 80 percent of what you display is still text. Why not take advantage of the optimized text output routines to draw cursors?

Actually, cursors are two characters in a font. The first character is the outline of the cursor; the second character of the pair is the mask, which defines the shape of the *cursor*. A whole font, the font named cursor, contains a standard set of X cursors. If you don't like the shapes in the cursor font, you can still create your own (see below), but it is easiest to use the standard.

To get a good look at the available cursors in the cursor font, use the X program that displays fonts, `xfd`. Simply type:

```
% xfd -font cursor
```

at the command prompt (on a UNIX workstation) and the `xfd` client program will pop up a window with the cursor shapes and their masks.

To use one of the cursor font cursors for your application's window, the cursor must first be created. Use `XCreateFontCursor` to create a cursor from the standard cursor font:

```
#include  <X11/cursorfont.h>

Display       *display;
int           cursor_number;
Cursor        cursor;

/*
 * Use gumby cursor, our favorite.
 */
cursor_number = XC_Gumby;

cursor = XCreateFontCursor( display,
                cursor_number );

if ( cursor != (Cursor) None )
       {
       /* we have success... */
       }
```

`XCreateFontCursor` returns a Cursor ID of the new cursor. The include file `cursorfont.h` contains 77 different cursor names, each of which corresponds to an even-numbered character in the cursor font (the odd-numbered characters are the masks).

Cursor	***Number***
XC_XCursor	0
XC_arrow	2
XC_based_arrow_down	4
XC_based_arrow_up	6
XC_boat	8

Cursor	*Number (cont.)*
`XC_bogosity`	10
`XC_bottom_left_corner`	12
`XC_bottom_right_corner`	14
`XC_bottom_side`	16
`XC_bottom_tee`	18
`XC_box_spiral`	20
`XC_center_ptr`	22
`XC_circle`	24
`XC_clock`	26
`XC_coffee_mug`	28
`XC_cross`	30
`XC_cross_reverse`	32
`XC_crosshair`	34
`XC_diamond_cross`	36
`XC_dot`	38
`XC_dotbox`	40
`XC_double_arrow`	42
`XC_draft_large`	44
`XC_draft_small`	46
`XC_draped_box`	48
`XC_exchange`	50
`XC_fleur`	52
`XC_gobbler`	54
`XC_gumby`	56
`XC_hand1`	58
`XC_hand2`	60
`XC_heart`	62
`XC_icon`	64
`XC_iron_cross`	66
`XC_left_ptr`	68
`XC_left_side`	70

Cursor	*Number (cont.)*
XC_left_tee	72
XC_leftbutton	74
XC_ll_angle	76
XC_lr_angle	78
XC_man	80
XC_middlebutton	82
XC_mouse	84
XC_pencil	86
XC_pirate	88
XC_plus	90
XC_question_arrow	92
XC_right_ptr	94
XC_right_side	96
XC_right_tee	98
XC_rightbutton	100
XC_rtl_logo	102
XC_sailboat	104
XC_sb_down_arrow	106
XC_sb_h_double_arrow	108
XC_sb_left_arrow	110
XC_sb_right_arrow	112
XC_sb_up_arrow	114
XC_sb_v_double_arrow	116
XC_shuttle	118
XC_sizing	120
XC_spider	122
XC_spraycan	124
XC_star	126
XC_target	128
XC_tcross	130
XC_top_left_arrow	132

Cursor	*Number (cont.)*
XC_top_left_corner	134
XC_top_right_corner	136
XC_top_side	138
XC_top_tee	140
XC_trek	142
XC_ul_angle	144
XC_umbrella	146
XC_ur_angle	148
XC_watch	150
XC_xterm	152

SPECIFYING A CURSOR DURING WINDOW CREATION

In X, each window can be associated with a cursor shape. Whenever the mouse pointer is in the window, the pointer shape is set to the shape of the cursor defined for that window. (This is done automatically by the X server.) If you do not define a cursor, the cursor will be inherited from the parent window. The root window's default cursor is a big X. If you do not define a cursor for your window, it will inherit the big X cursor.

You can set the cursor you want for a window when you first create the window with the `XCreateWindow` function.

The cursor is part of the `XSetWindowAttributes` structure:

```
XSetWindowAttributes  attributes;
Cursor                cursor;
unsigned long         attr_mask;

/* Create cursor first... */

/* Fill cursor ID into attributes struct */
attributes.cursor = cursor;
attr_mask |= CWCursor;

/* call XCreateWindow... */
```

You can also define a cursor for an already-created window with the XDefineCursor function:

```
Display       *display;
Window        window;
Cursor        cursor;

XDefineCursor( display, window, cursor );
```

You can undo the cursor definition with the XUndefineCursor function:

```
Display       *display;
Window        window;

XUndefineCursor( display, window );
```

Calling XUndefineCursor means the window will now use the cursor of its parent.

CREATING YOUR OWN CURSORS

You can create your own cursors out of bitmaps (single-plane pixmaps, which we'll cover in more depth next chapter) or other fonts, one font character or bitmap for the cursor mask and one font character of bitmap for the cursor itself. Each cursor created in this manner needs a *hot spot*, the point that is considered the x, y location of the cursor. With an arrow cursor, for example, you want the hot spot to be at the tip of the arrow. With a watch cursor, a good hot spot is the center of the watch. You can also specify the color of the cursor foreground and background, should you desire a colored cursor.

Use XCreatePixmapCursor to create a cursor from two pixmaps:

```
Display         *display;
Pixmap          cursor_pixmap, mask_pixmap;
XColor          foreground_color;
XColor          background_color;
unsigned int    hot_x, hot_y;        /* "hot" spot */
Cursor          cursor;

cursor = XCreatePixmapCursor( display,
                cursor_pixmap,
                mask_pixmap,
                &foreground_color,
```

```
                &background_color,
                hot_x, hot_y );
```

Normally, cursors fit in a 16 x 16-pixel cell. You can make larger cursors, although not all systems support this. Both the cursor and the mask pixmaps must have a depth of one plane. The colors are `XColor` structures defined in Chapter 4.

To create a cursor from a character—called a glyph, as we mentioned above—in a font, use the `XCreateGlyphCursor` function:

```
Display         *display;
Font            cursor_font_id, mask_font_id;
XColor          foreground_color;
XColor          background_color;
unsigned int    cursor_char, mask_char;
Cursor          cursor;

cursor = XCreateGlyphCursor( display,
                cursor_font_id,
                mask_font_id,
                cursor_char, mask_char,
                &foreground_color,
                &background_color );
```

In this case, the hot spot is formed by the origins of the characters. These origins are placed at the same position in the new cursor.

The values for `cursor_char` and `mask_char` define the characters in the respective fonts used for creating the cursor. More information on loading fonts can be found in Chapter 5 on text.

FREEING UP CURSOR RESOURCES

Cursors do take up RAM in the X server, so it is a good idea to free them up when you are finished with the cursor. Use `XFreeCursor`:

```
Display *display;
Cursor  cursor;

if ( cursor != (Cursor) None )
        {
        XFreeCursor( display, cursor );
        }
```

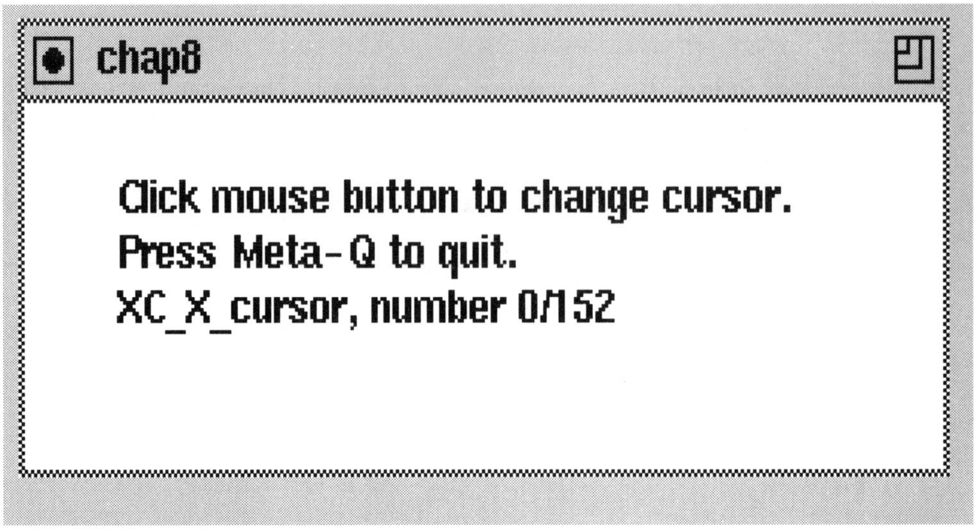

Figure 8.1. The Chap8 Program.

BUSY CURSORS

When your application does processing that may take a long time, you can display a "busy" cursor in your applications windows. Most busy cursors have clock, stopwatch, or hourglass shapes.

The busy cursor helps let users know the application is busy doing something. We strongly advise providing this kind of feedback to users, so that they have a better idea what is going on. This is all part of event-driven programming, in which users control applications and not vice versa.

One way to implement a busy cursor would be to create a clock-shaped cursor (such as `XC_watch` in the cursor font) and then call `XDefineCursor` to set this cursor on all your application windows. This means, though, that your application must remember all the original window cursors, so they can be restored when the busy task finishes.

Another technique involves creating an `InputOnly` (transparent) window covering your entire application (all your application windows). Set the cursor for this `InputOnly` window to the busy clock shape. Then, when the busy task is finished, merely unmap or destroy the busy `InputOnly` window.

A PROGRAM TO DISPLAY THE CURSOR FONT

We've created a program, `chap8`, to view the various cursors in the cursor font. Each click of the mouse in the `chap8` window switches to the next cursor from the cursor font. Typing Alt-Q quits the program.

SOURCE CODE FOR CHAP8.C

The main workings of the `chap8` program lie in the file `chap8.c`:

```
/*
 *      chap8.c
 *      Example program for Chapter 8.
 *
 *      Written for X Window Applications
 *      Programming, 2nd Edition
 */

#include <stdio.h>
#include <X11/Xlib.h>
#include <X11/Xutil.h>
#include <X11/cursorfont.h>

#define FONT_NAME          "variable"
#define FALLBACK_FONT_NAME  "fixed"

/*
 *      Globals for black and white colors
 */
unsigned long   black, white;

/*
 *      Global String names for cursors.
 *      The index into this table is
 *      1/2 the cursor number.
 */
static char *cursor_names[] =
                {
                "XC_X_cursor",
```

```
"XC_arrow",
"XC_based_arrow_down",
"XC_based_arrow_up",
"XC_boat",
"XC_bogosity",
"XC_bottom_left_corner",
"XC_bottom_right_corner",
"XC_bottom_side",
"XC_bottom_tee",
"XC_box_spiral",
"XC_center_ptr",
"XC_circle",
"XC_clock",
"XC_coffee_mug",
"XC_cross",
"XC_cross_reverse",
"XC_crosshair",
"XC_diamond_cross",
"XC_dot",
"XC_dotbox",
"XC_double_arrow",
"XC_draft_large",
"XC_draft_small",
"XC_draped_box",
"XC_exchange",
"XC_fleur",
"XC_gobbler",
"XC_gumby",
"XC_hand1",
"XC_hand2",
"XC_heart",
"XC_icon",
"XC_iron_cross",
"XC_left_ptr",
"XC_left_side",
"XC_left_tee",
"XC_leftbutton",
"XC_ll_angle",
"XC_lr_angle",
"XC_man",
"XC_middlebutton",
"XC_mouse",
"XC_pencil",
```

```
                    "XC_pirate",
                    "XC_plus",
                    "XC_question_arrow",
                    "XC_right_ptr",
                    "XC_right_side",
                    "XC_right_tee",
                    "XC_rightbutton",
                    "XC_rtl_logo",
                    "XC_sailboat",
                    "XC_sb_down_arrow",
                    "XC_sb_h_double_arrow",
                    "XC_sb_left_arrow",
                    "XC_sb_right_arrow",
                    "XC_sb_up_arrow",
                    "XC_sb_v_double_arrow",
                    "XC_shuttle",
                    "XC_sizing",
                    "XC_spider",
                    "XC_spraycan",
                    "XC_star",
                    "XC_target",
                    "XC_tcross",
                    "XC_top_left_arrow",
                    "XC_top_left_corner",
                    "XC_top_right_corner",
                    "XC_top_side",
                    "XC_top_tee",
                    "XC_trek",
                    "XC_ul_angle",
                    "XC_umbrella",
                    "XC_ur_angle",
                    "XC_watch",
                    "XC_xterm"
                    };

/*
 *      Set up event mask.
 */
#define EVENT_MASK (ButtonPressMask    | \
             KeyPressMask        | \
             ExposureMask)

main( argc, argv )
```

```
int     argc;
char    *argv[];

{       /* main */
        Display      *display;
        Display      *ConnectToServer();
        Window       rootwindow, window;
        Window       OpenWindow();
        int          screen;
        int          x, y, width, height;
        Visual       *visual = CopyFromParent;
        GC           gc;
        GC           CreateGC();
        XEvent       event;
        int          done;
        XFontStruct  *font_struct;
        XFontStruct  *LoadFont();
        char         string[400];
        int          cursor_number = XC_X_cursor;
        Cursor       cursor;
        KeySym       keysym;

        /*
         * Connect to default X server
         */
        display = ConnectToServer( (char *) NULL,
                &screen,
                &rootwindow );

        /*
         * Set up "colors" we'll use
         */
        black = BlackPixel( display, screen );
        white = WhitePixel( display, screen );

        /*
         * Create a window on the display
         */
        x      = 10;
        y      = 10;
        width  = 300;
        height = 100;
        window = OpenWindow( display,
```

```
        rootwindow,
        x, y, width, height,
        black, white,
        EVENT_MASK,
        visual );

/*
 * Provide information to the window manager.
 */
SetStandardHints( display, window,
     argv[0], argv[0],
     x, y, width, height );

/*
 * Create graphics context for drawing
 */
gc = CreateGC( display, window, black, white );

/*
 * Load a font
 */
font_struct = LoadFont( display,
              FONT_NAME,
              FALLBACK_FONT_NAME );

/*
 * Now, set the GC to draw with this font.
 */
XSetFont( display, gc,
     font_struct->fid );

/*
 * Create an initial cursor
 */
cursor = XCreateFontCursor( display,
        cursor_number );

if ( cursor != (Cursor) None )
     {
     /*
      * Set window to use new cursor
      */
     XDefineCursor( display,
```

```
                window,
                cursor );
            }

    /*
     * Make the window actually appear
     */
    XMapRaised( display, window );
    XFlush( display );

    /*
     * Loop on events. Quit when the user types
     * a Meta-Q.
     */
    done = False;

    while( !done )
          {
          XNextEvent( display, &event );

          switch( event.type )
             {
             case Expose:
                if ( event.xexpose.count == 0 )
                   {
                   Redraw( display, window, gc,
                      font_struct,
                      cursor_number );
                   }
                break;
             case ButtonPress:
                cursor_number += 2;

                if ( cursor_number > XC_xterm )
                   {
                   cursor_number = 0;
                   }

                /*
                 * Free old cursor
                 */
                if ( cursor != (Cursor) None )
                   {
```

```
                XFreeCursor( display, cursor );
                }

             /*
              * Create new cursor
              */
             cursor = XCreateFontCursor( display,
                   cursor_number );

             if ( cursor != (Cursor) None )
                {
                /*
                 * Set window to use new cursor
                 */
                XDefineCursor( display,
                   window,
                   cursor );
                }

             /*
              * Clear out window to
              * clean up old message.
              */
             XClearWindow( display, window );

             Redraw( display, window, gc,
                font_struct,
                cursor_number );
             break;
          case KeyPress:
             done = DecodeKeyPress( &event, &keysym,
                   string );
             break;
          case MappingNotify:
             XRefreshKeyboardMapping( &event );
             break;
          }
       }

   /*
    * Free the font, now that we're done with it.
    */
   XFreeFont( display, font_struct );
```

```
        XCloseDisplay( display );

}       /* main */

Redraw( display, window, gc, font_struct, cursor_number )

Display      *display;
Window       window;
GC           gc;
XFontStruct  *font_struct;
int          cursor_number;

{       /* Redraw */
        int  x, y, height;
        char string[100], name[100];

        /*
         * Determine height of one line
         */
        height = FontHeight( font_struct ) + 1;

        y = 30;
        x = 30;

        DrawString( display, window, gc,
             x, y, "Click mouse button to change cursor." );

        y += height;

        DrawString( display, window, gc,
             x, y, "Press Meta-Q to quit." );

        y += height;

        /*
         * Get Cursor name
         */
        GetCursorName( cursor_number, name );

        (void) sprintf( string, "%s, number %d/%d",
             name,
             cursor_number,
```

```
                XC_num_glyphs - 2 );

        DrawString( display, window, gc,
                x, y, string );

        /*
         * Send all our requests over the network,
         * so that the drawing is visible.
         */
        XFlush( display );

}       /* Redraw */

GetCursorName( cursor_number, name )

int     cursor_number;
char    name[];

/*
 *      Converts a cursor number into a
 *      name, from the standard cursor
 *      font.
 */

{       /* GetCursorName */
        int   cursor_index;

        /*
         * The index into our name table is
         * one-half the cursor number.
         */
        cursor_index = cursor_number / 2;

        if ( cursor_index < 0 )
              {
              cursor_index = 0;
              }

        if ( cursor_index > ( XC_num_glyphs - 2 ) )
              {
              cursor_index = XC_num_glyphs - 2;
              }
```

```
        (void) strcpy( name, cursor_names[cursor_index] );
}       /* GetCursorName */

/* end of file chap8.c */
```

COMPILING AND LINKING THE CHAP8 PROGRAM

The `chap8` program requires the following files:

`chap8.c`	
`classhnt.c`	(Chapter 2)
`connect.c`	(Chapter 1)
`drawstr.c`	(Chapter 6)
`fontht.c`	(Chapter 5)
`gc.c`	(Chapter 3)
`key.c`	(Chapter 7)
`loadfont.c`	(Chapter 5)
`sizehint.c`	(Chapter 2)
`window.c`	(Chapter 2)
`wmname.c`	(Chapter 2)
`wmhints.c`	(Chapter 2)

You can compile and link the `chap8` program with a command like:

```
cc -o chap8 -DX11R4 chap8.c classhnt.c connect.c drawstr.c \
      fontht.c gc.c key.c loadfont.c sizehint.c window.c wmname.c \
      wmhints.c -lX11
```

You can also use the Makefile in Appendix A and type:

```
make chap8
```

SUMMARY

With X, cursors are not special drawings, but are merely two characters in a font. The first character is the outline of the cursor, the second character of the pair is the mask, which defines the shape of the cursor. A whole font, the font named *cursor*, contains a standard set of X cursors.

In X, each window can be associated with a cursor shape. Whenever the mouse pointer is in the window, the pointer shape is set to the shape of the cursor defined for that window.

You can create your own cursors out of bitmaps or other fonts. Make sure that you assign a hot spot to the cursor. You can also specify the color of the cursor foreground and background, should you desired a colored cursor.

XLIB FUNCTIONS AND MACROS INTRODUCED IN THIS CHAPTER

`XCreateFontCursor`
`XCreateGlyphCursor`
`XCreatePixmapCursor`
`XDefineCursor`
`XFreeCursor`
`XUndefineCursor`

Chapter 9

BITMAPS AND ICONS: OFF-SCREEN DRAWING WITH PIXMAPS

All of our drawing so far has gone into windows on the display. But sometimes you want to draw into an off-screen area, later copying part (or all) of that area to a window on the screen. The X Window Systems provides *pixmaps* for this purpose. Pixmaps work well for bitmap image files, icons, and backing store for complex drawings.

Pixmaps are X Window off-screen drawing areas. Pixmaps reside in the X server, and you can draw into them just like drawing into windows. Pixmaps have a width and height, but no x,y location on the screen. And pixmaps have depth, or color planes, just like windows.

You can create pixmaps with XCreatePixmap:

```
Display         *display;
Drawable        drawable;
unsigned int    width, height, depth;
Pixmap          pixmap;

pixmap = XCreatePixmap( display, drawable,
             width, height, depth);
```

The `drawable` parameter is used to determine on which screen to place the pixmap.

When you create a pixmap, you specify the desired depth. A large pixmap at a large depth obviously uses a lot of X server memory. A depth of one generates a monochrome pixmap, also called a *bitmap*. Bitmaps are very important, especially since program icons are bitmaps.

PIXMAPS AND WINDOWS

Pixmaps and windows are both drawables, so most drawing routines work on both windows and pixmaps. You can draw into pixmaps just like drawing into windows, but since pixmaps are off-screen, you won't see the results of the drawing.

Remember to create a separate graphics context for drawing into the pixmap. This won't always be the same as the GC you create for drawing into windows. To see the results of drawing, you copy data from the pixmap to a window. Two functions copy data from a pixmap to a window (or to another pixmap for that matter), `XCopyArea` and `XCopyPlane`:

```
Display          *display;
Drawable         src_drawable;    /* Source */
Drawable         dest_drawable;   /* Destination */
GC               gc;
int              src_x, src_y;    /* Source location */
unsigned int     width, height;
int              dest_x, dest_y; /* Destination location */
unsigned long    which_plane;

XCopyArea ( display,
        src_drawable, dest_drawable, gc,
        src_x, src_y, width, height,
        dest_x, dest_y );

which_plane = 0x01;

XCopyPlane( display,
        src_drawable, dest_drawable, gc,
        src_x, src_y, width, height,
        dest_x, dest_y,
        which_plane );
```

`XCopyArea` copies a rectangular area—all the dots, or pixels—from one drawable to another. These drawables can be pixmaps or windows. Watch out, though, as both drawables must have the same depth and the same root window (that is, be on the same screen).

`XCopyPlane` copies one bit-plane of one drawable to another (usually a pixmap to a window, but not always). The bit plane to copy, `which_plane`, is normally `0x01`, which copies the first (and only) plane of a one-plane bitmap to another drawable. The nice thing about `XCopyPlane` is that the two drawables, the source and destination, don't need to have the same depth. In fact, we use `XCopyPlane` quite a lot for copying a bitmap (a single-plane pixmap) to a window.

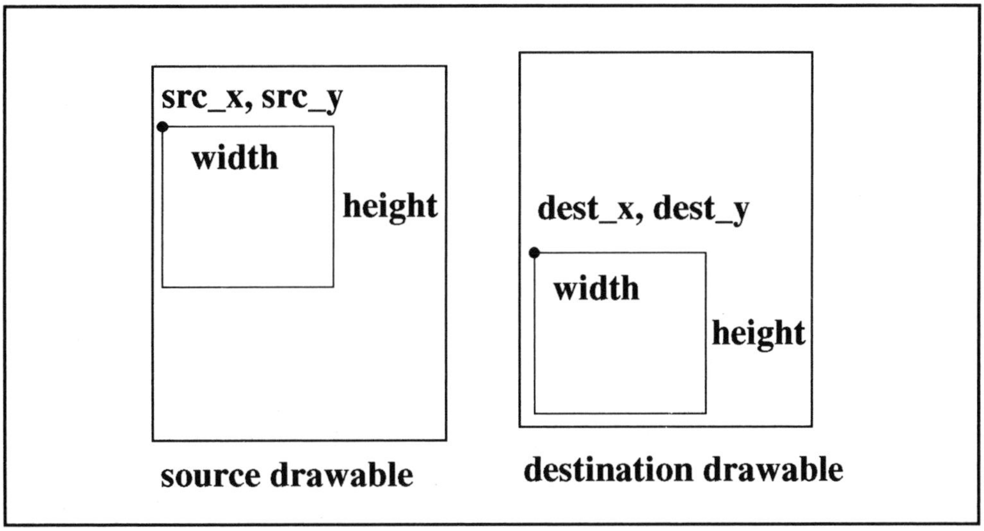

Figure 9.1. Copying Between Drawables.

When using `XCopyPlane` or `XCopyArea`, always make sure that the rectangle of the source x, y, width, and height are in the source drawable.

USING A PIXMAP AS BACKING STORE FOR A WINDOW

Using `XCopyArea`, you could create a pixmap just the size and depth of your application's window. Then you could use the pixmap as backing store for the window. That is, draw all output twice to *both* the pixmap *and* the window. That way the pixmap is always a copy of the window.

When Expose events arrive, use XCopyArea to copy parts of the pixmap to the window (use the x, y, width, and height fields of the XExposeEvent structure as the source and destination x, y and width, height to pass to XCopyArea).

This is great in concept, because it frees your code from having to worry about Expose events. But this can use a lot of memory if your application window is large. Your application also has the problem of figuring out what to do if the window is enlarged or shrunk.

CLEARING PIXMAPS

When pixmaps are created, their contents are undefined. With Release 3, most pixmaps were cleared to nulls, so that they were effectively created blank. MIT R4 (and beyond), though, does not clear pixmap memory on creation. Other vendors' X servers may or may not clear a pixmap on creation. Always clear any pixmaps you create.

You clear pixmaps by filling a rectangle with whatever color you want. Pixmaps have no concept of a window background color, and you cannot call XClearWindow on a pixmap.

SOURCE CODE FOR PIXMAP.C

The file pixmap.c contains two routines to help update a window from a backing bitmap (single-plane pixmap):

```
/*
 *      pixmap.c
 *      Routine to update a window from a pixmap.
 */

#include  <X11/Xlib.h>

UpdateWindowFromBitmap( display, window, gc, bitmap, event,
        max_width, max_height )

Display       *display;
Window        window;                      /* window to update */
GC            gc;
Pixmap        bitmap;                      /* Image to use */
XExposeEvent  *event;                      /* area to update */
int           max_width, max_height;       /* size of pixmap */
```

```
/*
 *      This routine assumes that the window and the bitmap
 *      share the same size, or close to the same size.
 */

{       /* UpdateWindowFromBitmap */

        CopyPlane( display, bitmap, window, gc,
             event->x, event->y,
             event->width, event->height,
             max_width, max_height );

}       /* UpdateWindowFromBitmap */

CopyPlane( display, src_draw, dest_draw, gc, x, y, width,
        height, max_width, max_height )

Display      *display;
Drawable     src_draw, dest_draw;
GC           gc;
int          x, y, width, height;
int          max_width, max_height;

{       /* CopyPlane */

        /*
         * Make sure we update a
         * valid area.
         */
        if ( ( ( width + x ) <= max_width ) &&
             ( ( height + y ) <= max_height ) &&
             ( x < max_width ) && ( y < max_height ) )
             {
             XCopyPlane( display,
                src_draw,    /* source */
                dest_draw,   /* dest */
                gc,
                x, y,        /* source X, Y */
                width,
                height,
                x, y,        /* dest X, Y */
                0x01 );      /* just one plane */
             }

}       /* CopyPlane */

/* end of file pixmap.c */
```

PIXMAPS USE X SERVER RESOURCES

Pixmaps tend to use a lot of memory in the X server, so whenever you are done with a pixmap, free it using XFreePixmap:

```
Display        *display;
Pixmap         pixmap;

XFreePixmap( display, pixmap );
```

BITMAPS

X places a lot of emphasis on single-plane pixmaps, also called *bitmaps*. Bitmaps are used as icons and to create cursors. X fonts are described in terms of bitmaps. X even defines a portable means of storing bitmaps to disk. The X bitmap file format is an ASCII text format, used to avoid byte-ordering problems on many different architectures. This format doesn't store the pixmap per se, but instead stores the raw data used to generate the bitmap.

The odd thing about the X bitmap file format is that the format actually creates snippets of valid C code. (This is a monochrome format. A color format, called XPM for X PixMap, is proposed, but has yet to be adopted as an X standard.)

A TEST ICON

The file icon.xbm is used as a sample icon in the chap9 program. It is also an example of the X ASCII bitmap file format. Notice that it really is a C code fragment.

```
#define icon_width 32
#define icon_height 32
static char icon_bits[] = {
   0x00, 0x00, 0x00, 0x00, 0x00, 0x00, 0x00, 0x00, 0x10, 0x04, 0x00, 0x00,
   0x10, 0x04, 0x00, 0x00, 0x20, 0xc2, 0x89, 0x08, 0x20, 0x22, 0x8a, 0x08,
   0x40, 0x21, 0x92, 0x04, 0x80, 0x20, 0x92, 0x04, 0x80, 0x20, 0x52, 0x05,
   0x80, 0x20, 0x22, 0x02, 0x80, 0xc0, 0x21, 0x02, 0x00, 0x00, 0x00, 0x00,
   0x00, 0x00, 0x00, 0x00, 0xc0, 0x00, 0x00, 0x03, 0xc0, 0x01, 0x80, 0x03,
   0x80, 0x03, 0xc0, 0x01, 0x00, 0x0f, 0xf0, 0x00, 0x00, 0x1c, 0x38, 0x00,
```

```
0x00, 0x38, 0x1c, 0x00, 0x00, 0x70, 0x0e, 0x00, 0x00, 0xe0, 0x07, 0x00,
0x00, 0xc0, 0x03, 0x00, 0x00, 0xe0, 0x07, 0x00, 0x00, 0x70, 0x0e, 0x00,
0x00, 0x38, 0x1c, 0x00, 0x00, 0x1c, 0x38, 0x00, 0x00, 0x0f, 0xf0, 0x00,
0x80, 0x03, 0xc0, 0x01, 0xc0, 0x01, 0x80, 0x03, 0xe0, 0x00, 0x00, 0x07,
0x00, 0x00, 0x00, 0x00, 0x00, 0x00, 0x00, 0x00};
```

SAVING BITMAPS TO FILES

You can save a bitmap to an ASCII file in the format described above using the `XWriteBitmapFile` function:

```
Display      *display;
char         filename[];
Pixmap       bitmap;
int          width, height;
int          status, hot_x, hot_y;

hot_x = -1;  /* no hotspot */
hot_y = -1;

status = XWriteBitmapFile( display,
                 filename,
                 bitmap,
                 width, height,
                 hot_x, hot_y );

if ( status == BitmapSuccess )
        {
        /* Success... */
        }
```

If the status returned is not `BitmapSuccess`, you have not saved the bitmap to a file. A status of `BitmapNoMemory` means that the routine failed in some way. The hotspots are for cursors, so if you have an icon (or other non-cursor bitmap), simply set the x and y hotspots to -1.

READING IN BITMAP FILES

You can read in an ASCII bitmap file from disk with `XReadBitmapFile`:

```
Display      *display;
Window       window;
```

```
char           filename[];
int            width, height; /* RETURNED size */
int            x_hotspot, y_hotspot;
int            status;
Pixmap         pixmap;

status = XReadBitmapFile( display,
                   window,
                   filename,
                   &width, &height,
                   &pixmap,
                   &x_hotspot, &y_hotspot );
if ( status == BitmapSuccess )
       {
       /* Success... */
       }
```

XReadBitmapFile returns BitmapSuccess on success and BitmapOpenFailed, BitmapFileInvalid, or BitmapNoMemory on errors.

SOURCE CODE FOR BITMAP.C

The file bitmap.c contains two convenience routines, LoadBitmap and SaveBitmap:

```
/*
 *      bitmap.c
 *      Routines to load and save bitmap
 *      files.
 */

#include  <X11/Xlib.h>
#include  <X11/Xutil.h>

Pixmap LoadBitmap( display, window, filename,
       width, height )

Display        *display;
Window         window;
char           filename[];
int            *width, *height;  /* RETURNED size */

{      /* LoadBitmap */
       int      x_hotspot, y_hotspot;
       int      status;
       Pixmap   pixmap;
```

```
        status = XReadBitmapFile( display,
                window,
                filename,
                width, height,
                &pixmap,
                &x_hotspot, &y_hotspot );

        if ( status != BitmapSuccess )
             {
             pixmap = (Pixmap) None;
             }

        return( pixmap );

}       /* LoadBitmap */

SaveBitmap( display, filename, bitmap, width, height )

Display         *display;
char            filename[];
Pixmap          bitmap;
int             width, height;

{       /* SaveBitmap */
        int   status;

        status = XWriteBitmapFile( display,
                filename,
                bitmap,
                width, height,
                -1, -1 );    /* no hotspot */

        return( status );

}       /* SaveBitmap */

/* end of file bitmap.c */
```

USING THE X BITMAP FILE FORMAT IN C PROGRAMS

Since the X bitmap file format is really made up of C code fragments, you can include such a file in a C program with `#include` or simply use a text editor to stick the code into a C file. You can then call two X functions to create pixmaps from that raw data. `XCreatePixmapFromBitmapData` creates a pixmap (one to multiplane) from the raw bitmap data. XCreateBitmapFromData creates a single-plane pixmap from the raw data:

```
Display          *display;
Drawable         drawable;
char             *data;
unsigned int     width, height;
unsigned long    foreground, background;
unsigned int     depth;
Pixmap           bitmap, pixmap;

bitmap = XCreateBitmapFromData( display, drawable,
             data, width, height );

pixmap = XCreatePixmapFromBitmapData( display, drawable,
        data, width, height,
        foreground, background, depth);
```

DRAWING INTO BITMAPS

You need to clear all pixmaps at creation time. Bitmaps, as single-plane pixmaps, use special values for colors. Because bitmaps are monochrome, all 1 bits within a bitmap indicate the foreground color and all 0 bits indicate the background color. The GC used with XCopyArea and XCopyPlane specify the actual colors.

To clear a bitmap, use a foreground color of `0L`:

```
Display         *display;
Pixmap          bitmap;
GC              gc;
unsigned int width, height;

pix_gc = CreateGC( display, bitmap, 0L, 0L );

/*
 * Clear the pixmap
 */
XFillRectangle( display, bitmap, pix_gc,
        0, 0, width, height );
```

When drawing into a bitmap, though, you normally want to use a color of `1L` to set 1s into the bitmap:

```
XSetForeground( display, pix_gc, 1L );
```

ICONS

Most window managers support icons for application windows. Users iconize windows, turning them into small icons on the screen. Icons especially help on smaller-monitor screens. These icons can be created with the bitmap program and converted to a single-plane X pixmap using one of the functions above or `XReadBitmapFile`.

Because icons are the domain of the window manager, the manager may desire icons to be a certain size and shape. Officially, your program should keep a selection of potential icons at various sizes or be able to generate icons at various supported sizes on cue.

Instead of having your programs keep a range of icons in various sizes and shapes—hoping one will be accepted by the window manager—it is simpler to just try out one icon. If the window manager doesn't accept the icon, you lose. If your program keeps a range of icons in various shapes and sizes, you still lose if you don't have the correct size. Anyway, window managers are not always in use, and window managers are not required to accept any icons from your program. So, there is no real reason to worry unduly about the icon sizes and shapes—it really isn't worth the effort or added complexity for your programs, unless you really like icons.

The sample icon above uses a 32x32 size. That size seems to be accepted by most window managers, including `mwm`, the Motif window manager, and `olwm`, the Open Look window manager (two common managers).

Once the icon is created as a pixmap, it is passed to the window manager through the `XSetWMHints` (for X Set Window Manager Hints) Xlib function, as we documented in Chapter 2. If `XSetWMHints` was already called, you can use `XGetWMHints` to retrieve the current `WM` hints values and then add in the `IconPixmapHint`:

```
Display       *display;
Window        window;
Pixmap        icon;
XWMHints      *wmhints;

/*
 * Get old hints values,
 * because we want to add
 * to what is already there.
 */
wmhints = XGetWMHints( display, window );
```

```
if ( wmhints == (XWMHints *) NULL )
        {
        wmhints = (XWMHints *) malloc( sizeof(XWMHints) );

        if ( wmhints == (XWMHints *) NULL )
              {
              return( False );
              }

        wmhints->flags = 0;
        }

/*
 * Set up our icon
 */
wmhints->flags |= IconPixmapHint;

wmhints->icon_pixmap = icon;

XSetWMHints( display, window, wmhints );

XFree( wmhints );
```

ICON NAMES

Icons can also have names. These names are usually displayed along with the icon bitmap when your program is iconized. Not all window managers support icon names so you don't have a lot of choice in the matter, but because most window managers do support both icons and icon names, it's a good idea to set an icon name for your application's windows. XSetIconName sets a window's icon name:

```
Display       *display;
Window        window;
char          *iconname;

XSetIconName( display, window, iconname )
```

4 Release

XSetIconName supports only standard 8-bit text, so in Release 4, XSetWMIconName joined the X library. XSetWMIconName supercedes XSetIconName:

```
Display             *display;
Window              window;
XTextProperty       *text_property;

XSetWMIconName (display, window, text_property)
```

We use `XSetIconName` even though it's obsolete, because `XSetWMIconName` doesn't exist on R3 and older systems. This is yet another X compatibility problem.

Icon names should be short, because there isn't normally a lot of room to display the icon. Most X applications just use the program name in `argv[0]`, such as *xterm*. Your window's title can be a lot longer than the icon name.

SOURCE CODE FOR ICON.C

The file `icon.c` contains two utility functions to load in a bitmap file, convert that file to a single-plane pixmap, and then set that pixmap as a window's icon. `LoadIcon` loads up a bitmap and then calls `SetWindowIcon`, which sets a window's icon and icon name:

```
/*
 *      icon.c
 *      Routine for setting a window's icon.
 */

#include  <stdio.h>
#include  <X11/Xlib.h>
#include  <X11/Xutil.h>

LoadIcon( display, window, filename, iconname )

Display       *display;
Window        window;
char          filename[];
char          iconname[];

/*
 *      Loads a bitmap from a file, then
 *      sets that bitmap as the window's
 *      icon.
 */

{       /* LoadIcon */
        Pixmap  icon;
```

```
        Pixmap   LoadBitmap();
        int      icon_width, icon_height;

        icon = LoadBitmap( display, window,
                           filename,
                          &icon_width, &icon_height );

        if ( icon != (Pixmap) None )
              {
              (void) SetWindowIcon( display, window,
                 icon, iconname );
              }
}       /* LoadIcon */

SetWindowIcon( display, window, icon, iconname )

Display       *display;
Window        window;
Pixmap        icon;
char          iconname[]; /* name of iconic window */

/*
 *      Tells the window manager about
 *      our icon. See window.c for more
 *      on the WM Hints.
 */

{       /* SetWindowIcon */
        XWMHints *wmhints;

        /*
         * Get old hints values,
         * because we want to add
         * to what is there.
         */
        wmhints = XGetWMHints( display, window );

        if ( wmhints == (XWMHints *) NULL )
              {
              wmhints = (XWMHints *) malloc( sizeof(XWMHints) );

              if ( wmhints == (XWMHints *) NULL )
                 {
                 return( False );
                 }

              wmhints->flags = 0;
              }
```

```
        /*
         * Set up our icon
         */
        wmhints->flags |= IconPixmapHint;

        wmhints->icon_pixmap = icon;

        XSetWMHints( display, window, wmhints );

        XFree( wmhints );

        /*
         * Use older, R3 routine to set icon
         * name for compatibility. Look up
         * XSetWMIconName on newer X systems.
         */
        XSetIconName( display, window, iconname );

        return( True );

}       /* SetWindowIcon */

/* end of file icon.c */
```

SOURCE CODE FOR CHAP9.C

The `chap9` program creates a window and a window icon and then draws dots in the window whenever the user clicks a mouse button in the window. The dots are written to a backing pixmap, so that the window can be redrawn on `Expose` events. We'll use the backing pixmap technique to support the bitmap editor we create in Section 3.

```
/*
 *      chap9.c
 *      Example program for Chapter 9.
 *
 *      Written for X Window Applications
 *      Programming, 2nd Edition
 */

#include <stdio.h>
#include <X11/Xlib.h>
#include <X11/Xutil.h>
```

```
/*
 *      Globals for black and white colors
 */
unsigned long   black, white;

/*
 *      Set up event mask.
 */
#define EVENT_MASK (ButtonPressMask        | \
                    KeyPressMask           | \
                    ExposureMask)

/*
 *      Name of bitmap file we'll use for an icon.
 *      You can create this bitmap file with the
 *      standard X program named bitmap.
 */
#define ICON_FILENAME "icon.xbm"

main( argc, argv )

int     argc;
char    *argv[];

{       /* main */
        Display *display;
        Display *ConnectToServer();
        Window  rootwindow, window;
        Window  OpenWindow();
        int     screen;
        int     x, y, width, height;
        Visual  *visual = CopyFromParent;
        GC      gc, pix_gc;
        GC      CreateGC();
        XEvent  event;
        int     done;
        Pixmap  bitmap;
        char    string[20];
        KeySym  keysym;

        /*
         * Print a help message
         */
        (void) printf( "Button clicks in the window will\n" );
        (void) printf( "draw dots. Meta-Q will quit.\n" );
```

```
/*
 * Connect to default X server
 */
display =   ConnectToServer( (char *) NULL,
            &screen,
            &rootwindow );

/*
 * Set up "colors" we'll use
 */
black = BlackPixel( display, screen );
white = WhitePixel( display, screen );

/*
 * Create a window on the display
 */
x      = 10;
y      = 10;
width  = 300;
height = 100;
window =    OpenWindow( display,
            rootwindow,
            x, y, width, height,
            black, white,
            EVENT_MASK,
            visual );

/*
 * Provide information to the window manager.
 */
SetStandardHints( display, window,
     argv[0], argv[0],
     x, y, width, height );

/*
 * Load up bitmap file and
 * turn it into an icon.
 */
LoadIcon( display, window,
     ICON_FILENAME, argv[0] );

/*
 * Create graphics context for drawing
 */
gc = CreateGC( display, window, black, white );
```

```
/*
 * Create a large pixmap to draw into,
 * the same size as our window.
 */
bitmap = XCreatePixmap( display, rootwindow,
        width, height,
        1 );      /* depth of 1, so a bitmap */

if ( bitmap == (Pixmap) None )
      {
      (void) fprintf( stderr,
         "Error creating pixmap.\n" );
      XCloseDisplay( display );
      exit( 1 );
      }

/*
 * Create a GC for the pixmap
 */
pix_gc = CreateGC( display, bitmap, 0L, 0L );

/*
 * Clear the pixmap
 */
XFillRectangle( display, bitmap, pix_gc,
      0, 0, width, height );

XSetForeground( display, pix_gc, 1L );

/*
 * Make the window actually appear
 */
XMapRaised( display, window );
XFlush( display );

/*
 * Loop on events. Quit when the user types
 * a Meta-Q.
 */
done = False;

while( !done )
      {
      XNextEvent( display, &event );
```

```
            switch( event.type )
               {
               case Expose:
                  /*
                   * Update contents of window
                   * from our "backing" pixmap.
                   */
                  UpdateWindowFromBitmap( display,
                     window, gc, bitmap,
                     &event,
                     width, height );
                  XFlush( display );
                  break;
               case ButtonPress:
                  /*
                   * Draw a dot for each button
                   * press. Draw to BOTH window
                   * and pixmap.
                   */
                  XDrawPoint( display, window, gc,
                     event.xbutton.x,
                     event.xbutton.y );

                  XDrawPoint( display, bitmap, pix_gc,
                     event.xbutton.x,
                     event.xbutton.y );
                  XFlush( display );
                  break;
               case KeyPress:
                  done = DecodeKeyPress( &event,
                        &keysym, string );
                  break;
               case MappingNotify:
                  XRefreshKeyboardMapping( &event );
                  break;
               }
            }

        XCloseDisplay( display );

}       /* main */

/* end of file chap9.c */
```

COMPILING AND LINKING THE CHAP9 PROGRAM

The chap9 program requires the following files.

bitmap.c	
chap9.c	
classhnt.c	(Chapter 2)
connect.c	(Chapter 1)
gc.c	(Chapter 3)
icon.c	
key.c	(Chapter 7)
pixmap.c	
sizehint.c	(Chapter 2)
window.c	(Chapter 2)
wmname.c	(Chapter 2)
wmhints.c	(Chapter 2)

You can compile and link the chap9 program with a command like:

```
cc -o chap9 -DX11R4 bitmap.c chap9.c classhnt.c connect.c gc.c \
        icon.c key.c pixmap.c sizehint.c window.c wmname.c \
        wmhints.c -lX11
```

You can also use the Makefile in Appendix A and type:

```
make chap9
```

RUNNING THE CHAP9 PROGRAM

Move the mouse into the chap9 window and click the mouse buttons to draw dots into both the window and the backing pixmap. When Expose events arrive, the chap9 program redraws the dots by copying the contents of the backing pixmap to the window. If you iconize the window, note the icon. Press Alt-Q to quit.

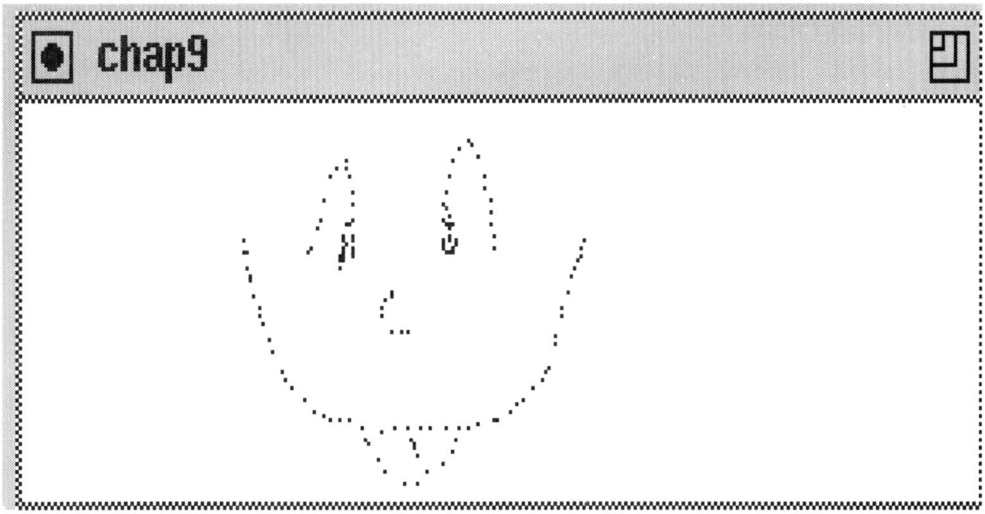

Figure 9.2. The Chap9 Program.

SUMMARY

Pixmaps are X Window off-screen drawing areas. Pixmaps reside in the X server, and you can draw into them just like drawing into windows. Pixmaps have a width and height, but no x,y location on the screen. And pixmaps have depth, or color planes, just like windows.

Pixmaps and windows are both drawables, so most drawing routines work on both windows and pixmaps. You can draw into pixmaps just like drawing into windows, but since pixmaps are off-screen, you won't see the results of the drawing. To see the results of drawing, you copy data from the pixmap to a window. Two functions copy data from a pixmap to a window (or to another pixmap for that matter): `XCopyArea` and `XCopyPlane`.

Using `XCopyArea`, you could create a pixmap just the size and depth of your application's window. Then you could use the pixmap as backing store for the window. When `Expose` events arrive, use `XCopyArea` to copy parts of the pixmap to the window (use the x, y, width and height fields of the `XExposeEvent` structure as the source and destination x, y and width, height to pass to `XCopyArea`).

When pixmaps are created, their contents are undefined. With Release 3, most pixmaps were cleared to nulls, so that they were effectively created blank. MIT R4 (and beyond), though, does not clear pixmap memory on creation. Other vendors' X servers may—or may not—clear a pixmap on creation. Always clear any pixmaps you create.

X places a lot of emphasis on single-plane pixmaps, also called bitmaps. Bitmaps are used as icons and to create cursors. X fonts are described in terms of bitmaps. X even defines a portable means of storing bitmaps to disk. The X bitmap file format is an ASCII text format, used to avoid byte-ordering problems on many different architectures. This format doesn't store the pixmap per se, but instead stores the raw data used to generate the bitmap.

XLIB FUNCTIONS AND MACROS INTRODUCED IN THIS CHAPTER

```
XCopyArea
XCopyPlane
XCreatePixmap
XFreePixmap
XGetWMHints
XReadBitmapFile
XSetIconName
XSetWMIconName
XWriteBitmapFile
```

Chapter 10

RUBBER-BAND LINES

Almost every graphics drawing package uses rubber-band lines, rectangles, and ovals. Rubber-band lines provide feedback when users draw lines using a mouse. The term *rubber-band* is used because the lines look like there is a rubber band connecting the starting and current ending points. As the user moves the mouse, the ending point constantly shifts. The rubber-band effect provides feedback. If the line were locked in now, it would look like Figure 10.1.

The easiest way to create this rubber-band effect in X is to create a special graphics context for rubber-banding. Each GC, or graphics context, has a *graphics function* field that determines its mode for drawing.

The term *function* here is a misnomer. It doesn't mean an Xlib C function, but actually the name of the mode, or operation, identifier stored in the `function` field of the GC. Using the term function for both Xlib C language functions and a drawing mode is a bit confusing, but that is the official X terminology. Once this graphics context is created, the drawing function (mode) should be changed so that is draws in exclusive-or (or xor) mode.

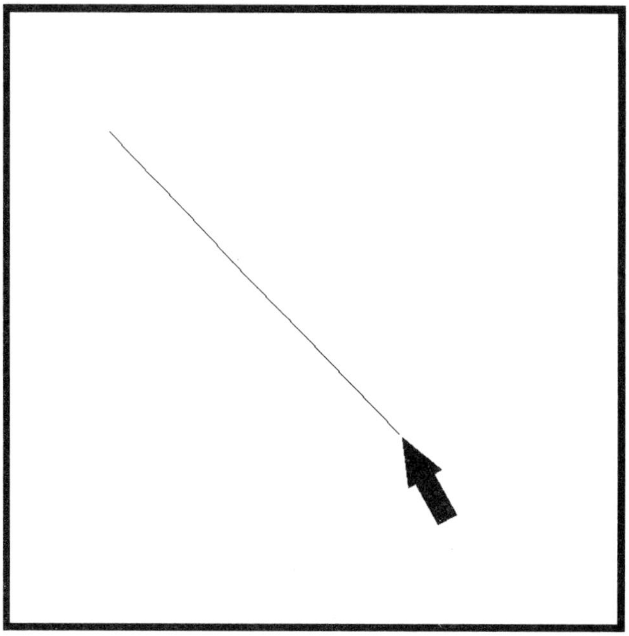

Figure 10.1. A Rubber-band Line.

RASTER OPERATION FUNCTIONS

X provides 16 drawing modes, often called *raster operations* (or *raster ops*), which control the output of a drawing operation, based on the bits you want to draw and the bits already on the screen in the area in which you want to draw. The xor mode takes advantage of a neat feature of exclusive-or: if you apply an exclusive-or operation when drawing once, you can restore the original picture (erasing the new items) by redrawing the same items again, again applying an exclusive-or operation when drawing. This allows for rubber-band lines.

Each raster op follows the same approach. There is a set of pixels you want to draw, called the *source*. And there is a set of pixels already on the screen, called the *destination*, in the area in which you want to draw. X applies the GC raster function to the source and the destination dots to produce the result, which is then drawn to the screen. (This sounds a lot more complicated than it really is.)

The default GC raster function is called `GXcopy`, and it operates like you would expect most graphics operations to operate: `GXcopy` ignores the destination bits. `GXcopy` takes the source pixels and splats them across the destination, wiping out the destination pixels underneath the source. If you draw a black line on top of a blank white background, you see the black line.

`GXcopy` is the default value for a GC's function field when you first create the graphics context. The opposite of `GXcopy` is an operation that leaves the destination area alone. Normally, this operation is called not drawing in the first place, but in X it is called `GXnoop` (for no-operation).

`GXnoop` is like not drawing. But you get the added benefit of sending an X packet over the network to the X server and forcing the X server to interpret the packet. Unless you are porting the X server to run on a new hardware platform and want to test the server, you will probably never use `GXnoop`.

Aside from `GXcopy`, the most commonly-used GC graphics function is `GXxor`, the exclusive-or mode introduced in this chapter. `GXxor` is used mainly for drawing rubber-band lines, boxes, and ovals. (Note the spelling of `GXxor`. There is also a `GXor` and a `GXnor`.)

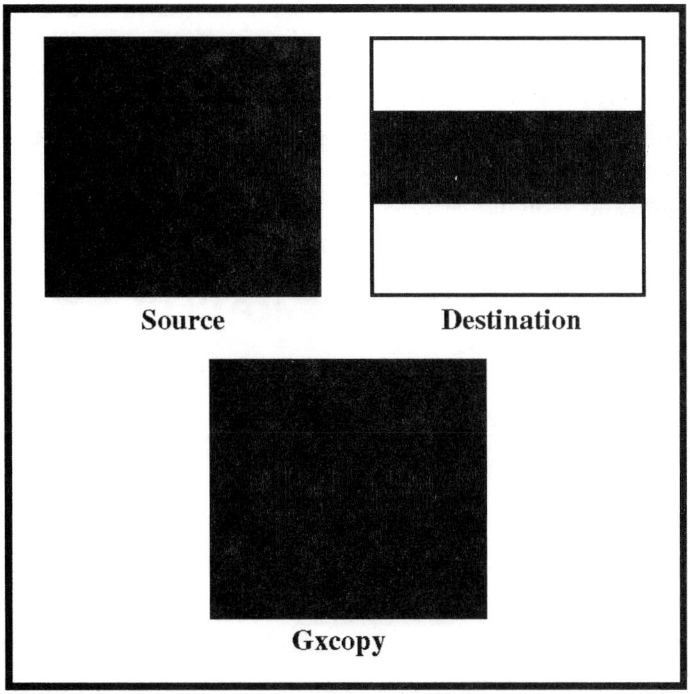

Figure 10.2. GXcopy.

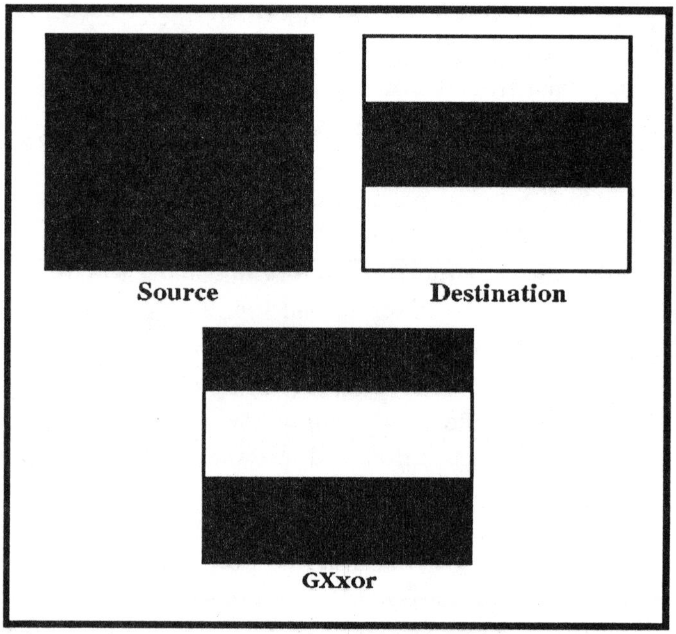

Figure 10.3. GXxor.

The rest of the GC graphics functions are self-explanatory, as they seem to cover every possible variation you could ever conceive. Most users will find them, for the most part, superfluous.

SUMMARY OF THE GC GRAPHICS FUNCTIONS

The GC function names are defined in the include file `X.h` (usually included automatically from the file `Xlib.h`).

GC Function Name	***What It Does***	***Value in X.h (in hexidecimal)***
`GXand`	ANDS source and destination bits	0x1
`GXandInverted`	Inverts source (NOT source), then ANDS with destination bits	0x4
`GXandReverse`	ANDS source with inverted destination bits ((NOT dest) AND source)	0x2

(cont.)

GC Function Name	***What It Does***	***Value in X.h (in hexidecimal)***
`GXclear`	Clears out area (not portable!)	0x0
`GXcopy`	Places down source, wipes out destination bits (default)	0x3
`GXcopyInverted`	Inverts the source (NOT source), wipes out destination bits	0xC
`GXequiv`	Inverts the source (NOT source), then XORS with destination bits ((NOT source) XOR dest)	0x9
`GXinvert`	Inverts the destination bits (NOT dest)	0xA
`GXnand`	Inverts the source (NOT source), inverts the destination (NOT dest), then ors the two ((NOT source) OR (NOT dest))	0xE
`GXnoop`	Leaves the destination bits alone	0x5
`GXnor`	Inverts the source (NOT source), Inverts the destination (NOT dest) and ands the two together((NOT source) AND (NOT dest))	0x8
`GXor`	Ors the source and the destination bits (source OR dest)	0x7
`GXorInverted`	Inverts the source (NOT source), then ors with the destination bits ((NOT source) OR dest)	0xD
`GXorReverse`	Ors the source with the inverted destination bits (source OR (NOT dest))	0xB
`GXset`	Sets all the bits in the drawing area (not portable!)	0xF
`GXxor`	Exclusive-ors the source and the destination bits (used for rubber-band lines)	0x6

Be careful when using the GC functions `GXclear` and `GXset`, as these functions do not necessarily work the same way on every machine. They depend on the use of 1 and 0 for the values of `BlackPixel` and `WhitePixel`—and these values do not hold true on all X servers, as we've seen. In general, it is best to avoid these modes if possible. In general, the only modes most people will ever use are `GXcopy` and `GXxor`. And, you'll use `GXcopy` 99 percent of the time.

RUBBER-BAND LINES

If drawn twice, a line drawn in exclusive-or mode will disappear, leaving the original drawing intact. The basic method for drawing rubber-band lines is:

1. Create a new GC for the rubber-band effect, in addition to the regular GC used for drawing normal items in the window.
2. Set the new GC's (graphics) function field to `xor` mode (GXxor), with the `XSetFunction` Xlib function.
3. Select an x,y coordinate location as an anchor point (the first point selected for the line). The goal is now to have the user select the second anchor point (the other end point for the line).
4. Draw an initial line in `xor` mode (using the new GC) saving the line coordinates.
5. Each time the pointer (mouse) moves, redraw the old line, using the `xor` GC. This makes the old line disappear. Adjust the coordinates to the new mouse position, and then draw the line to the new location, again in `xor` mode. Save these line coordinates.
6. When the user selects the line's end point, redraw the line, using the `xor` GC, to erase it. Then, draw the line using the normal drawing GC (and not the `GXxor` GC), so that it appears on the display in its permanent likeness.

The `chap10` example program does just that. The first step, though, is to create a special graphics context for drawing in xor mode.

CREATING AN XOR GC

Creating an xor graphics context is the same as creating any graphics context, as in the file `gc.c` from Chapter 3. There are three exceptions, though, when filling the `XGCValues` structure:

- Set the foreground color to the exclusive or of the desired foreground and background colors:

```
xgcvalues.foreground = forecolor ^ backcolor;
```

- Set the background to `0`:
  `xgcvalues.background = 0;`
- Set the function field to `GXxor`:
  `xgcvalues.function  = GXxor;`

Pass the proper flags to `XCreateGC`: `GCBackground`, `GCForeground` and `GCFunction`. The function `CreateXorGC`, in `xor.c`, below, does just that.

SOURCE CODE FOR XOR.C

```
/*
 *      xor.c
 *      Routine for creating a Graphics
 *      Context, or gc to be used for
 *      Xor-mode drawing.
 *
 *      Written for X Window Applications
 *      Programming, 2nd Edition
 */

#include <stdio.h>
#include <X11/Xlib.h>
#include <X11/Xutil.h>

GC CreateXorGC( display, drawable, forecolor, backcolor )

Display         *display;
Drawable        drawable;
unsigned long   forecolor;
unsigned long   backcolor;

/*
 *      Creates a graphics context with the given
 *      foreground and background pixel values
 *      (colors).
 */

{       /* CreateXorGC */
        XGCValues  xgcvalues;
        GC         gc;
```

```
        xgcvalues.foreground = forecolor ^ backcolor;
        xgcvalues.background = 0;
        xgcvalues.function   = GXxor;

        gc = XCreateGC( display,
             drawable,
             ( GCForeground | GCBackground | GCFunction ),
             &xgcvalues );

        return( gc );

}       /* CreateXorGC */

/* end of file xor.c */
```

Once the rubber-band GC is set up, use the normal drawing functions, such as `XDrawLine`, `XDrawRectangle`, and `XDrawArc` (from Chapter 3). Be sure to pass the new rubber-band xor GC as the GC parameter when drawing rubber-band lines.

One warning for using the `GXxor` GC function—if other drawing takes place between the time the line is first drawn in xor mode and the time the line is redrawn (to clear it out), the original picture may not be restored. This method of using `GXxor` depends on the original picture not changing between calls. Normally, no other program will be drawing to your windows, so this shouldn't be a problem. If you intend to draw using `GXxor` over other windows, you should be aware of this. Window managers typically allow you to move windows about the screen. These window managers often use `GXxor` to draw a ghost outline of the window showing its size and shape so you can better place it. These window managers need to stop all other graphics output while this takes place, or the screen will tend to appear "messy." All graphics output from other programs can be held up by grabbing the X server exclusively for your program during this time.

RUBBER-BAND RECTANGLES AND OVALS

Drawing rubber-band rectangles and ovals is much the same as drawing rubber-band lines. Ovals need a bounding rectangle, which ends up at a lower position than the starting position, so the first point must have X and Y coordinate values less than the second point's X and Y coordinate values. If you move the mouse pointer up after selecting the first point, the example program will stop drawing rubber-band ovals until the mouse is moved to a point lower than the starting location. This code had to be added to the example program.

Ovals, since they are made by the function `XDrawArc`, also take longer to draw than rubber-band lines or rectangles. Try replacing `XDrawArc` with `XDrawRectangle` or `XDrawLine` in the function `DrawItem` in the file `chap10.c`, later in this chapter, and you will see just how long the drawing of ovals takes.

MORE NOTES WHEN USING RASTER FUNCTIONS

Note that a number of GC raster ops gave different results when run on a color system than when run on a monochrome system. The GC functions `GXcopyInverted`, `GXequiv`, `GXinvert`, `GXnand`, `GXnor`, `GXorInverted`, and `GXorReverse` all output some variety of green or tan on a color system (depending on what color cells are already allocated). There's a great difference between an X server with eight color planes and an X server with one color plane. When inverting colored pixels, you normally get other colored pixels (black and white are colors in X). When inverting on a monochrome system, the only choices are black and white. The problem with applying mathematical operations, such as xor, on color numbers is that the operation may result in a number that is not defined in your colormap, or that is defined but won't be visible on the window's background. Using any raster op other than `GXcopy` may result in a confusing display.

Before using any GC modes other than `GXcopy` or `GXxor`, test them and experiment to find the mode you want. We suspect you'll find `GXxor` and `GXcopy` sufficient for almost everything.

SOURCE CODE FOR CHAP10.C

We're gradually building a mouse-based bitmap editor. The `chap10` program allows you to draw items into a window using rubber-band lines, rectangles, or ovals. Move the mouse to a starting location then press a mouse button. Drag the mouse while holding the button, and watch the rubber-band shape in the window expand or contract as you move the mouse. When drawing rectangles or ovals, nothing will be drawn if you move the mouse up after selecting the starting point, because of the X library limitation on drawing negative rectangles or ovals. Note that with clever dynamic manipulation of the starting location and the size, you could draw the rectangles or ovals in any direction.

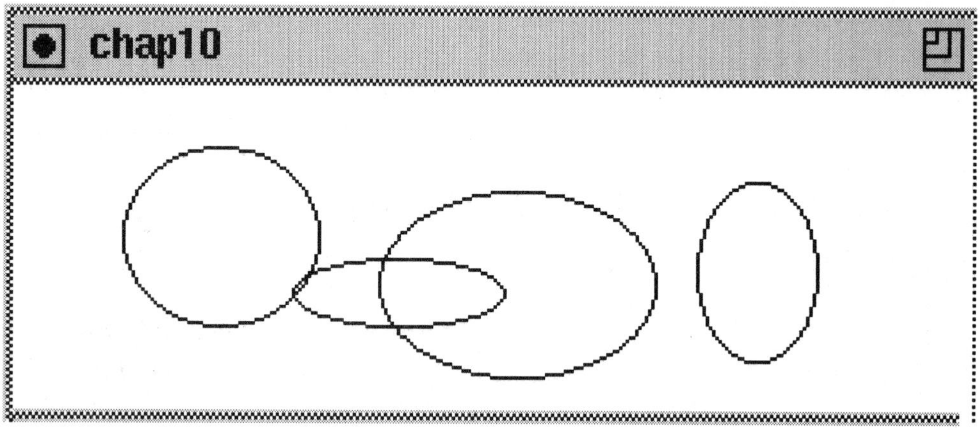

Figure 10.4. The chap10 Program.

```
/*
 *      chap10.c
 *      Example program for Chapter 10.
 *
 *      Written for X Window Applications
 *      Programming, 2nd Edition
 */

#include <stdio.h>
#include <X11/Xlib.h>
#include <X11/Xutil.h>

/*
 *      Globals for black and white colors
 */
unsigned long   black, white;

/*
 *      Globals for drawing points
 */
```

```
int     start_x = (-1);
int     start_y = (-1);
int     last_x  = (-1);
int     last_y  = (-1);

/*
 *      Set up event mask.
 */
#define EVENT_MASK (ButtonPressMask    | \
           ButtonReleaseMask  | \
           ButtonMotionMask   | \
           KeyPressMask       | \
           ExposureMask)

/*
 *      Name of bitmap file we'll use for an icon.
 *      You can create this bitmap file with the
 *      standard X program named bitmap.
 */
#define ICON_FILENAME "icon.xbm"

main( argc, argv )

int     argc;
char    *argv[];

{       /* main */
        Display *display;
        Display *ConnectToServer();
        Window  rootwindow, window;
        Window  OpenWindow();
        int     screen;
        int     x, y, width, height;
        Visual  *visual = CopyFromParent;
        GC      gc, pix_gc, xor_gc;
        GC      CreateGC(), CreateXorGC();
        XEvent  event;
        int     done;
        Pixmap  bitmap;
        Pixmap  LoadBitmap();
        char    string[20];
        KeySym  keysym;
```

```
/*
 * Print a help message
 */
(void) printf( "Holding a mouse button down and\n" );
(void) printf( "dragging will draw a shape.\n" );
(void) printf( "Meta-Q will quit.\n" );

/*
 * Connect to default X server
 */
display =   ConnectToServer( (char *) NULL,
            &screen,
            &rootwindow );

/*
 * Set up "colors" we'll use
 */
black = BlackPixel( display, screen );
white = WhitePixel( display, screen );

/*
 * Create a window on the display
 */
x       = 10;
y       = 10;
width   = 300;
height  = 100;
window = OpenWindow( display,
         rootwindow,
         x, y, width, height,
         black, white,
         EVENT_MASK,
         visual );

/*
 * Provide information to the window manager.
 */
SetStandardHints( display, window,
     argv[0], argv[0],
     x, y, width, height );

/*
 * Load up bitmap file and
```

```
     * turn it into an icon.
     */
    LoadIcon( display, window,
          ICON_FILENAME, argv[0] );

    /*
     * Create graphics context for drawing
     */
    gc = CreateGC( display, window, black, white );

    xor_gc = CreateXorGC( display, window, black, white );

    /*
     * Create a large pixmap to draw into,
     * the same size as our window.
     */
    bitmap = XCreatePixmap( display, rootwindow,
             width, height,
             1 );      /* depth of 1, so a bitmap */

    if ( bitmap == (Pixmap) None )
          {
          (void) fprintf( stderr,
             "Error creating pixmap.\n" );
          XCloseDisplay( display );
          exit( 1 );
          }

    /*
     * Create a GC for the pixmap. Note we
     * use 0L to draw "blank" dots in the
     * 1-plane pixmap (bitmap).
     */
    pix_gc = CreateGC( display, bitmap, 0L, 0L );

    /*
     * Clear the pixmap
     */
    XFillRectangle( display, bitmap, pix_gc,
          0, 0, width, height );

    /*
     * Draw 1's into the
```

```
     * 1-plane pixmap.
     */
    XSetForeground( display, pix_gc, 1L );

    /*
     * Make the window actually appear
     */
    XMapRaised( display, window );
    XFlush( display );

    /*
     * Loop on events. Quit when the user types
     * a Meta-Q.
     */
    done = False;

    while( !done )
          {
          XNextEvent( display, &event );

          switch( event.type )
             {
             case Expose:
                /*
                 * Update contents of window
                 * from our "backing" pixmap.
                 */
                UpdateWindowFromBitmap( display,
                   window, gc, bitmap,
                   &event,
                   width, height );
                XFlush( display );
                break;
             case ButtonPress:
                /*
                 * Save current point as
                 * starting location for
                 * drawing.
                 */
                start_x = event.xbutton.x;
                start_y = event.xbutton.y;
```

```
        last_x  = start_x;
        last_y  = start_y;

        /*
         * Draw item in Xor mode
         */
        DrawItem( display, window,
           xor_gc,
           start_x, start_y,
           last_x, last_y );

        XFlush( display );
        break;
     case ButtonRelease:
        /*
         * Clear out Xor drawing
         */
        DrawItem( display, window,
           xor_gc,
           start_x, start_y,
           last_x, last_y );

        /*
         * Draw item for real.
         */
        DrawItem( display, window,
           gc,
           start_x, start_y,
           last_x, last_y );

        /*
         * Draw item into backing pixmap.
         */
        DrawItem( display, bitmap,
           pix_gc,
           start_x, start_y,
           last_x, last_y );

        /*
         * Reset drawing points.
         */
        start_x = (-1);
```

```
        start_y = (-1);
        last_x  = (-1);
        last_y  = (-1);
        break;
     case MotionNotify:
        /*
         * These events are generated
         * when a mouse button is
         * held down, because we
         * used the ButtonMotionMask
         * event mask.
         */

        /*
         * Draw item in Xor mode
         * to clear.
         */
        DrawItem( display, window,
           xor_gc,
           start_x, start_y,
           last_x, last_y );

        /*
         * Set up new points
         */
        last_x = event.xmotion.x;
        last_y = event.xmotion.y;

        /*
         * Draw again with new point
         */
        DrawItem( display, window,
           xor_gc,
           start_x, start_y,
           last_x, last_y );

        break;
     case KeyPress:
        done = DecodeKeyPress( &event,
              &keysym, string );

        break;
     case MappingNotify:
```

```
                    XRefreshKeyboardMapping( &event );
                    break;
                 }

              /*
                * Send drawing commands out over network.
               */
              XFlush( display );
              }

        XCloseDisplay( display );

}       /* main */

DrawItem( display, drawable, gc, x1, y1, x2, y2 )

Display      *display;
Drawable     drawable;
GC           gc;
int          x1, y1;     /* starting point */
int          x2, y2;     /* ending point */

/*
 *      Draws an "item" (a line or a rectangle or
 *      whatever). With this function, we can
 *      easily switch to drawing a rectangle, for
 *      example.
 */

{       /* DrawItem */
        int  width, height;

        /*
         * Uncomment the drawing item you want.
         * Comment out the rest.
         */

        /*
        XDrawLine( display, drawable, gc,
             x1, y1, x2, y2 );
        */
```

```
        /*
         * NEVER allow ovals to have a
         * negative width or height!
         */
        width = x2 - x1;

        if ( width < 0 )
              {
              width = 0;
              }

        height = y2 - y1;

        if ( height < 0 )
              {
              height = 0;
              }

        DrawOval( display, drawable, gc,
              x1, y1, width, height );

        /*
        XDrawRectangle( display, drawable, gc,
              x1, y1, width, height );
        */
}       /* DrawItem */

/* end of file chap10.c */
```

COMPILING AND LINKING THE CHAP10 PROGRAM

The `chap10` program requires the following files:

`bitmap.c`	(Chapter 9)
`chap10.c`	
`classhnt.c`	(Chapter 2)
`connect.c`	(Chapter 1)
`gc.c`	(Chapter 3)

`icon.c`	(Chapter 9)
`key.c`	(Chapter 7)
`pixmap.c`	(Chapter 9)
`sizehint.c`	(Chapter 2)
`window.c`	(Chapter 2)
`wmname.c`	(Chapter 2)
`wmhints.c`	(Chapter 2)
`xor.c`	

You can compile and link the `chap10` program with a command like:

```
cc -o chap10 -DX11R4 bitmap.c chap10.c classhnt.c connect.c gc.c \
       icon.c key.c pixmap.c sizehint.c window.c wmname.c \
       wmhints.c xor.c -lX11
```

You can also use the Makefile in Appendix A and type:

```
make chap10
```

SUMMARY

Rubber-band lines are the cornerstone of any mouse-based drawing application. To create rubber-band lines in the X Window System, you need to create a special graphics context (GC), which then lets you access the 16 drawing modes (or raster operations) provided under X.

Each raster operation has the same structure: the source (a desired set of pixels) and the destination (a set of pixels already on the screen) are joined by the GC raster function to the source and the destination to produce the result, which is then drawn to the screen. The default GC raster function is called `GXcopy`, and it is the function you'll use most often.

The process for creating rubber-band lines can be summarized in these six steps:

1. Create a new GC for the rubber-band effect. When creating this GC, set the foreground color to the exclusive-or of the desired foreground and background colors. Set the background to `0` and set the function field to `GXxor`. Then, pass the proper flags to `XCreateGC`: `GCBackground`, `GCForeground`, and `GCFunction`.

2. Set the new GC's (graphics) function field to xor mode `(GXxor)` with the `XSetFunction` Xlib function.
3. Select an x,y coordinate location as an anchor point. The user selects the second anchor point.
4. Draw an initial line in xor mode (using the new GC), saving the line coordinates.
5. Each time the pointer (mouse) moves, redraw the old line, using the xor GC. This makes the old line disappear. Adjust the coordinates to the new mouse position and then draw the line to the new location, again in xor mode. Save these line coordinates.
6. When the user selects the line's end point, redraw the line, using the xor GC, to erase it. Then, draw the line using the normal drawing GC (and not the `GXxor` GC), so that it appears on the display in its permanent likeness.

XLIB FUNCTIONS AND MACROS INTRODUCED IN THIS CHAPTER

`XSetFunction`

Section II

FOLLOWING THE RULES FOR WELL-BEHAVED X PROGRAMS

In this section, we extend our programming tutorial by covering some of the standards that X applications are expected to follow. Most of these standards are described in a document called the *Inter-Client Communications Conventions Manual*, or *ICCCM*. In this section, you'll learn:

- The command-line parameters that X programs are expected to follow, including the following:

Command Line	***Meaning***
`-help`	Print help message.
`-display`	Use the display name following for the X server.
`-geometry`	Accept user location and/or size for the window.
`-font`	Use the font name that follows, instead of the default.
`-iconic`	Begin in iconic state.
`-name`	
`-title`	Use the text following as the window's title, rather than the default.

- More information that your programs are expected to send to the window manager, and how to encapsulate the steps necessary for creating a well-behaved top-level window.
- Error-handling utilities to prevent X errors from terminating your programs.

Chapter 11

COMMON COMMAND-LINE PARAMETERS

X programs tend to accept a number of standard command-line arguments to set up various parameters of the program, like the color in which it should draw, the font it should use, and where it should place its window. Users expect applications to accept these commands, so it's a good idea to support them. These commands typically start with a dash and then the value to set, such as:

```
-display display_name
```

to specify on which display (X server) the program should open its windows. Remember, the network transparency built into X allows a program to be run on one machine and display its output on another.

Some command-line arguments may be abbreviated, such as `-fn` for `-font`. A list of some standard arguments appear below.

Command Line	***Meaning***
`-h`	
`-help`	Print help message
`-display`	Use the display name following for the X server.
`-geom`	
`-geometry`	Accept user location and/or size for the window
`-fn`	
`-font`	Use the font name that follows, instead of the default
`-iconic`	Begin in iconic state
`-name`	Look up resources for customizing; also default window title
`-title`	Use the text following as the window's title, rather than the default

These commands are very important. Almost every X application follows the standard, and these commands allow users a means to customize the startup of a program. Because X is network-oriented, it is extremely important to allow the display-name parameter—for example, to specify the X server.

The meaning of the help option should be obvious. We covered the display name in Chapter 1, but didn't introduce the command-line parameter. The geometry specifies a window's size and location. We'll cover the iconic option in Chapter 12, along with the window title option.

The following options are used to set the colors of windows:

Command Line	***Meaning***
`-background`	
`-bg`	Set background color
`-bd`	
`-bordercolor`	Set border color
`-fg`	
`-foreground`	Set foreground color

You will need to choose which, if any, of these options your programs will support. Some of the options just don't make sense for a desktop-publishing program or an industrial-control application, for example. But most X applications should support at least the first list, and most of the second. The color-setting options are important as the same color combinations may work on some monitors but be unreadable on others.

CHECKING COMMAND-LINE ARGUMENTS

The function `FindParameter`, below, checks the command-line parameters for a given `look_for` string, returning the value of the parameter. For example, if `look_for` is "-display", then `FindParameter` would return the display name parameter, if it were present in the command-line parameters, `argv`.

`FindParameter` returns a character pointer, so you'll need to predeclare it:

```
char    *FindParameter();
```

We'll use the `FindParameter` function to look for display and font names, as well as the window's geometry in the following program.

SOURCE CODE FOR ARGS.C

```
/*
 *      args.c
 *      Utility routine for searching
 *      command-line parameters.
 *
 *      Written for X Window Applications
 *      Programming, 2nd Edition
 */

#include <stdio.h>

char *FindParameter( argc, argv, look_for )

int     argc;
char    *argv[];
char    look_for[]; /* search string */

/*
 *      Searches the command-line parameters for a
 *      a match with the search string look_for.
 *      If found, then returns the next command-line
 *      parameter, or the current command-line
```

```
 *      parameter, if there are no more parameters.
 *      Returns NULL if nothing is found.
 */

{       /* FindParameter */
        int   count, length;

        length = strlen( look_for );

        count = 1;  /* skip argv[0] */

        while( count < argc )
              {
              if ( strncmp( look_for, argv[count], length ) == 0 )
                 {
                 count++;

                 if ( count < argc )
                    {
                    return( argv[count] );
                    }
                 else
                    {
                    return( argv[count-1] );
                    }
                 }
              count++;
              }

        return( (char *) NULL );

}       /* FindParameter */

/* end of file args.c */
```

DISPLAY NAMES

The X standard for display names is:

```
host:server.screen
```

where `host` is the machine's host name. The `server` is a number specifying the server (if multiple servers are running on one machine). The `screen` is a number specifying the screen, provided the server supports more than one screen. The default UNIX server is:

```
:0.0
```

which uses the current hostname for the initial part of the display name, or:

```
unix:0.0
```

or, just

```
unix:0
```

If you call `XOpenDisplay` with a `NULL` display name parameter, chances are `:0.0` will be the server name used.

SEARCHING FOR DISPLAY NAMES

The file `display.c` contains two useful utility functions. `FindDisplayName` searches the command-line parameters for a `-display` option and returns the display name, if found, or `NULL`, signifying that the default display name should be used (stored in the `DISPLAY` environment variable).

`OpenDisplay` acts like `ConnectToServer`, which we introduced in Chapter 1 (in `connect.c`), except `OpenDisplay` searches the command-line parameters for a display name, while `ConnectToServer` requires an explicit display name. `OpenDisplay` calls `FindDisplayName` to do the searching. Together, these functions take care of the `-display` option, as well as connecting to an X server. `OpenDisplay` returns a pointer to a `Display` type, so remember to predeclare the return type of this function:

```
Display      *OpenDisplay();
```

SOURCE CODE FOR DISPLAY.C

```
/*
 *      display.c
 *      Routines to open a connection to an X Server,
 *      based on a display name in the command-line
 *      parameters, e.g., "-display display_name"
 *
 *      Written for X Window Applications
 *      Programming, 2nd Edition
 */
```

```
#include <stdio.h>
#include <X11/Xlib.h>

FindDisplayName( argc, argv, display_name )

int     argc;
char    *argv[];
char    display_name[];       /* RETURN */

/*
 *      Searches the command-line parameters for a
 *      display name. If a "-display" option is
 *      found, then the command-line parameter
 *      following the "-display" is copied to
 *      display_name. This routine assumes that
 *      the display name will follow the "-display"
 *      option. Note that we are really only
 *      looking for "-disp" to allow users to
 *      type in a shorthand for "-display".
 */

{       /* FindDisplayName */
        char  *FindParameter();
        char  *ptr;

        ptr = FindParameter( argc, argv, "-disp" );

        if ( ptr != (char *) NULL )
              {
              (void) strcpy( display_name, ptr );

              return( True );
              }
        else
              {
              display_name[0] = '\0';

              return( False );
              }

}       /* FindDisplayName */

Display *OpenDisplay( argc, argv, screen, rootwindow )
```

```
int         argc;
char        *argv[];        /* command-line parameters */
int         *screen;        /* RETURN: default screen number */
Window      *rootwindow;    /* RETURN: root window ID */

/*
 *      Sets up a connection to an X server (called a
 *      Display), and then gets the default screen
 *      number and root window ID on that display.
 *      The display may be named in the command-line
 *      parameters, argv, with the "-display" option.
 *      If so, this routine expects a display name to
 *      follow the "-display".
 */

{       /* OpenDisplay */
        char    display_name[200];
        Display *display;
        Display *ConnectToServer();

        /*
         * Find display name. Will put a NULL in
         * display_name if not found.
         */
        (void) FindDisplayName( argc, argv, display_name );

        /*
         * Connect to X server. Note
         * that ConnectToServer will
         * call exit on errors.
         */
        display = ConnectToServer( display_name,
                    screen,
                    rootwindow );

        return( display );

}       /* OpenDisplay */

/* end of file display.c */
```

X GEOMETRY

X defines geometry as:

```
[=][Width x Height ][{+/-}XOffset{+/-}YOffset]
```

This geometry typically specifies the size and location of an application's main window, also called the top-level window. Note that the use of the leading equal sign (=) is now considered obsolete and officially discouraged.

The best way to figure out these geometries is though examples. Typical geometries include:

```
-geometry 100x200+5+5
```

For a 100-by-200-pixel window, place the window at coordinates +5, +5, from the upper-left corner (origin) of the window:

```
-geometry 100x200
```

Just make the window 100 pixels wide by 200 pixels high:

```
-geometry 100x200-35+5
```

Position the 100-by-200-pixel window with the right edge of the window in 35 pixels from the right edge of the screen, and down 5 pixels from the top of the screen. A negative `YOffset` value would mean that the window's lower edge should be positioned relative to the lower edge of the screen rather than the upper edge.

If your program takes in a geometry specification as a character string, you can use the function `XParseGeometry` to parse out the x, y, width, and height values from the string:

```
#include  <X11/Xutil.h>

char          *geometry;
int           x, y, width, height;
int           status;

status = XParseGeometry( geometry,
               &x, &y, &width, &height );
```

The return from `XParseGeometry`, the geometry status tells what values, if any, were discovered in the geometry string. The geometry status contains a bitmask of the values discovered:

```
XValue
YValue
WidthValue
HeightValue
XNegative
YNegative
```

`XParseGeometry` returns a geometry status value (an integer) that contains bit patterns for which, if any, of the values x, y, width, or height were set in the geometry string. The status value can be checked against the bit patterns `XValue` (the x value was set), `YValue` (the y value was set), `WidthValue` (the width value was set), `HeightValue` (the height value was set), `XNegative` (x is negative, specified from the right side of the screen, rather than the left), and `YNegative` (y is negative, with the window's bottom edge specified relative to the bottom of the screen).

The function `ParseGeometry` calls `XParseGeometry` to determine what size and location a window should have. Pass the default size and location in the x, y, width, and height parameters. The maximum values are the screen size—the values returned by `DisplayHeight` and `DisplayWidth`. The screen size is needed to calculate the negative x and y offsets:

```
ParseGeometry( geometry, max_width, max_height,
       x, y, width, height )

char         geometry[];
int          max_width, max_height;       /* screen size */
int          *x, *y, *width, *height;

{       /* ParseGeometry */
        int  status;
        int  x1, y1, width1, height1;

        status = XParseGeometry( geometry,
                   &x1, &y1, &width1, &height1 );

        if ( status & XValue )
             {
             *x = x1;
             }

        if ( status & YValue )
             {
             *y = y1;
             }
```

```
        if ( status & WidthValue )
              {
              *width = width1;
              }

        if ( status & HeightValue )
              {
              *height = height1;
              }

        if ( status & XNegative )
              {
              *x = max_width - *width + *x;
              }

        if ( status & YNegative )
              {
              *y = max_height - *height + *y;
              }

}       /* ParseGeometry */
```

SOURCE CODE FOR GEOMETRY.C

The file `geometry.c` contains all the functions necessary to check the command-line parameters for a `-geometry` option and then to parse that option:

```
/*
 *      geometry.c
 *      Routines to find and parse a geometry string.
 *      geometry strings are used to specify the
 *      size and location of a window, from the
 *      command-line.
 *
 *      Written for X Window Applications
 *      Programming, 2nd Edition
 */

#include <stdio.h>
#include <X11/Xlib.h>
#include <X11/Xutil.h>
```

```
FindGeometry( argc, argv, geometry )

int     argc;
char    *argv[];
char    geometry[]; /* RETURN */

/*
 *      Searches the command-line parameters for a
 *      window geometry option. If the "-geometry"
 *      option is found, then the command-line
 *      parameter following the "-geometry" is
 *      copied to a string. This string is then
 *      parsed to pull out an x,y location and
 *      a width, height size, if these are
 *      part of the geometry string.
 *      Note that we are really only
 *      looking for "-geom" to allow users to
 *      type in a shorthand for "-geometry".
 */

{       /* FindGeometry */
        char    *FindParameter();
        char    *ptr;

        ptr = FindParameter( argc, argv, "-geom" );

        if ( ptr != (char *) NULL )
              {
              (void) strcpy( geometry, ptr );

              return( True );
              }
        else
              {
              geometry[0] = '\0';

              return( False );
              }

}       /* FindGeometry */

ParseGeometry( geometry, max_width, max_height, x, y, width, height )
```

```
char     geometry[];
int      max_width, max_height;  /* screen size */
int      *x, *y, *width, *height;

{        /* ParseGeometry */
         int   status;
         int   x1, y1, width1, height1;

         status = XParseGeometry( geometry,
                  &x1, &y1, &width1, &height1 );

         if ( status & XValue )
               {
               *x = x1;
               }

         if ( status & YValue )
               {
               *y = y1;
               }

         if ( status & WidthValue )
               {
               *width = width1;
               }

         if ( status & HeightValue )
               {
               *height = height1;
               }

         if ( status & XNegative )
               {
               *x = max_width - *width + *x;
               }

         if ( status & YNegative )
               {
               *y = max_height - *height + *y;
               }

}        /* ParseGeometry */
```

```
CheckGeometry( argc, argv, max_width, max_height, x, y, width, height )

int     argc;
char    *argv[];
int     max_width, max_height;  /* screen size */
int     *x, *y, *width, *height;

{       /* CheckGeometry */
        char  geometry[200];

        if ( FindGeometry( argc, argv, geometry ) == True )
              {
              ParseGeometry( geometry,
                 max_width, max_height,
                 x, y, width, height );
              }

}       /* CheckGeometry */

/* end of file geometry.c */
```

FONT NAMES

As we stated in Chapter 5, some fonts look good on certain displays and bad on others. A very small font, such as *8x13,* looks better on a low-resolution monitor, like a 640x480 VGA display. The monitor size also impacts which fonts look good, since two monitors at the same pixel resolution may have different-sized dots. For example, Sun 16-inch and 19-inch monitors both have a 1152x900 resolution, but the 16-inch monitor has a much finer pixel size. In addition, your favorite fonts may not be available on all X servers, particularly limited-memory X terminals. It's best to allow your users to choose fonts if they want to, using the `-font` (and `-fn`) command-line parameters.

The function `LoadFontName`, below, searches the command-line parameters for a `-font` or `-fn` option, and then tries to load in that font. If there is no command-line font option, then `LoadFontName` uses a fallback font. `LoadFontName` returns a pointer to an `XFontStruct`:

```
XFontStruct  *LoadFontName();
```

SOURCE CODE FOR FONTNAME.C

The file `fontname.c` contains the function `LoadFontName`:

```
/*
 *      fontname.c
 *      Routines to check for a user-requested
 *      name and load that font.
 *
 *      Written for X Window Applications
 *      Programming, 2nd Edition
 */

#include <stdio.h>
#include <X11/Xlib.h>

XFontStruct *LoadFontName( display, argc, argv,
        font_name, fallback_font_name )

Display         *display;
int             argc;
char            *argv[];
char            font_name[];        /* RETURN */
char            fallback_font_name[];

/*
 *      Searches the command-line parameters for a
 *      font name. If a "-font" or "-fn" option is
 *      found, then the command-line parameter
 *      following the "-font" is copied to
 *      font_name. Then, the actual font is
 *      loaded. Returns a pointer to the font
 *      structure, or NULL on errors.
 */

{       /* LoadFontName */
        char            *FindParameter();
        char            *ptr;
        XFontStruct     *LoadFont();
        XFontStruct     *font_struct;

        ptr = FindParameter( argc, argv, "-font" );
```

```
        if ( ptr != (char *) NULL )
              {
              (void) strcpy( font_name, ptr );
              }
        else
              {
              /*
               * Look for "-fn"
               */
              ptr = FindParameter( argc, argv, "-fn" );

              if ( ptr != (char *) NULL )
                 {
                 (void) strcpy( font_name, ptr );
                 }
              }

        font_struct = LoadFont( display,
                 font_name, fallback_font_name );

        return( font_struct );

}       /* LoadFontName */

/* end of file fontname.c */
```

PROVIDING A HELP MESSAGE

The `-help` option (or just `-h`) is a standard for not only X Window applications, but also for many of the less-cryptic UNIX applications. If the user types:

```
programname -help
```

then your application should respond with a brief help message, usually a list of the accepted command-line parameters.

The function `CheckForHelp`, below, checks the command-line parameters for a `-h` or `-help` option. If one is found, `CheckForHelp` calls `PrintUsageMessage` to print out a help message. Both functions take an extra message parameter, so applications can extend the help message. The code is straightforward in the file `usage.c`:

SOURCE CODE FOR USAGE.C

```
/*
 *      usage.c
 *      Routine to display a usage message to the
 *      user on stdout.
 */

#include <stdio.h>

#ifndef True
#define True 1
#endif

#ifndef False
#define False   0
#endif

CheckForHelp( argc, argv, extra_message )

int     argc;
char    *argv[];
char    extra_message[];

/*
 *      Checks if the user passed a "-help"
 *      command-line parameter. If so, it
 *      prints out a help message and
 *      returns True. If not, it returns
 *      False.
 */

{       /* CheckForHelp */
        char     *FindParameter();
        char     *ptr;

        ptr = FindParameter( argc, argv, "-help" );

        if ( ptr != (char *) NULL )
             {
             PrintUsageMessage( extra_message );
```

```
                return( True );
                }

        return( False );

}       /* CheckForHelp */

PrintUsageMessage( extra_message )

char    extra_message[];

{       /* PrintUsageMessage */

        (void) fprintf( stderr,
                "\nThe allowable command line options are:\n" );
        (void) fprintf( stderr,
                "\t-display displayname \n" );
        (void) fprintf( stderr,
                "\t\tConnect to X server <displayname>\n" );
        (void) fprintf( stderr,
                "\t-geometry geometryspec \n" );
        (void) fprintf( stderr,
                "\t\tSpecify window location and size\n" );
        (void) fprintf( stderr,
                "\t-font fontname \n" );
        (void) fprintf( stderr,
                "\t\tLoad up font <fontname>\n" );
        (void) fprintf( stderr,
                "\t-title windowtitle\n" );
        (void) fprintf( stderr,
                "\t\tUse the name for the window title\n" );
        (void) fprintf( stderr,
                "\t-name windowtitle\n" );
        (void) fprintf( stderr,
                "\t\tSame as -title\n" );
        (void) fprintf( stderr,
                "\t-iconic\n" );
        (void) fprintf( stderr,
                "\t\tStart with the window in iconic state\n" );

        (void) fprintf( stderr, "%s\n", extra_message );

}       /* PrintUsageMessage */

/* end of file usage.c */
```

A PROGRAM TO CHECK FOR COMMAND-LINE PARAMETERS

We've put together a program, `chap11`, to check for command-line parameters and then set the window size and location, font name, and display name, or perhaps just print out a help message. All your X applications should check for at least these command-line parameters. We'll introduce more in the next chapter.

SOURCE CODE FOR CHAP11.C

```
/*
 *      chap11.c
 *      Example program for Chapter 11.
 *
 *      Written for X Window Applications
 *      Programming, 2nd Edition
 */

#include <stdio.h>
#include <X11/Xlib.h>
#include <X11/Xutil.h>

/*
 *      Globals for black and white colors
 */
unsigned long   black, white;

/*
 *      Font names.
 */
#define FONT_NAME           "variable"
#define FALLBACK_FONT_NAME  "fixed"

/*
 *      Event mask for our top-level window.
 */
#define EVENT_MASK (KeyPressMask       | \
                    ExposureMask)
```

```
/*
 *      Name of bitmap file we'll use for an icon.
 *      You can create this bitmap file with the
 *      standard X program named bitmap.
 */
#define ICON_FILENAME "icon.xbm"

main( argc, argv )

int     argc;
char    *argv[];

{       /* main */
        Display     *display;
        Display     *OpenDisplay();
        Window      rootwindow, window;
        Window      OpenWindow();
        int         screen;
        int         x, y, width, height;
        Visual      *visual = CopyFromParent;
        GC          gc;
        GC          CreateGC();
        char        font_name[200];
        XFontStruct *font_struct;
        XFontStruct *LoadFontName();
        XEvent      event;
        int         done;
        char        string[20];
        KeySym      keysym;

        /*
         * Check if user asked for "-help" option.
         */
        if ( CheckForHelp( argc, argv, "" ) == True )
              {
              exit( 0 );
              }

        /*
         * Connect to X server
         */
        display = OpenDisplay( argc, argv,
```

```
                &screen,
                &rootwindow );

        /*
         * Set up "colors" we'll use
         */
        black = BlackPixel( display, screen );
        white = WhitePixel( display, screen );

        /*
         * Load a font
         */
        (void) strcpy( font_name, FONT_NAME );

        font_struct = LoadFontName( display, argc, argv,
                font_name, FALLBACK_FONT_NAME );

        /*
         * Set up default window sizes
         */
        x      = 10;
        y      = 10;
        width  = 420;
        height = ( FontHeight( font_struct ) + 1 ) * 5;

        /*
         * Check to see if the user
         * asked for a particular
         * size for our window
         */
        CheckGeometry( argc, argv,
             DisplayWidth( display, screen ),
             DisplayHeight( display, screen ),
             &x, &y, &width, &height );

        /*
         * Create a window on the display
         */
        window = OpenWindow( display,
                rootwindow,
                x, y, width, height,
                black, white,
                EVENT_MASK,
                visual );
```

```
/*
 * Provide information to the window manager.
 */
SetStandardHints( display, window,
      argv[0], argv[0],
      x, y, width, height );

/*
 * Load up bitmap file and
 * turn it into an icon.
 */
LoadIcon( display, window,
      ICON_FILENAME, argv[0] );

/*
 * Create graphics context for drawing
 */
gc = CreateGC( display, window, black, white );

/*
 * Set the GC to draw with our font.
 */
XSetFont( display, gc,
      font_struct->fid );

/*
 * Make the window actually appear
 */
XMapRaised( display, window );
XFlush( display );

/*
 * Loop on events. Quit when the user types
 * a Meta-Q.
 */
done = False;

while( !done )
      {
      XNextEvent( display, &event );

      switch( event.type )
```

```
                {
                case Expose:
                   Redraw( display, window,
                      gc, font_struct );
                   break;
                case KeyPress:
                   done = DecodeKeyPress( &event,
                           &keysym, string );

                   if ( IsMetaQ( &event, string ) )
                      {
                      done = True;
                      }
                   break;
                case MappingNotify:
                   XRefreshKeyboardMapping( &event );
                   break;
                }
             }

        XCloseDisplay( display );

}       /* main */

Redraw( display, window, gc, font_struct )

Display      *display;
Window       window;
GC           gc;
XFontStruct  *font_struct;

{       /* Redraw */
        int   x, y, height;

        /*
         * Determine height of one line
         */
        height = FontHeight( font_struct ) + 1;

        y = 30;
        x = 30;

        DrawString( display, window, gc, x, y,
```

```
                "This text should be in your desired font," );

        y += height;
        DrawString( display, window, gc, x, y,
                "if you used the -font command-line" );

        y += height;
        DrawString( display, window, gc, x, y,
                "parameter. Press Meta-Q to quit." );

        /*
         * Send all our requests over the network,
         * so that the drawing is visible.
         */
        XFlush( display );

}       /* Redraw */

/* end of file chap11.c */
```

COMPILING AND LINKING THE CHAP11 PROGRAM

The `chap11` program requires the following files:

`args.c`	
`bitmap.c`	(Chapter 9)
`chap11.c`	
`classhnt.c`	(Chapter 2)
`connect.c`	(Chapter 1)
`display.c`	
`drawstr.c`	(Chapter 6)
`fontht.c`	(Chapter 5)
`fontname.c`	
`gc.c`	(Chapter 3)
`geometry.c`	
`icon.c`	(Chapter 9)

key.c	(Chapter 7)
loadfont.c	(Chapter 5)
pixmap.c	(Chapter 9)
sizehint.c	(Chapter 2)
usage.c	
window.c	(Chapter 2)
wmname.c	(Chapter 2)
wmhints.c	(Chapter 2)

You can compile and link the chap11 program with a command like:

```
cc -o chap11 -DX11R4 bitmap.c chap11.c classhnt.c connect.c gc.c \
       icon.c key.c pixmap.c sizehint.c window.c wmname.c \
       geometry.c args.c display.c usage.c fontname.c \
       loadfont.c wmhints.c -lX11
```

You can also use the Makefile in Appendix A and type:

```
make chap11
```

RUNNING THE CHAP11 PROGRAM

The chap11 program just puts up a window, in either a default size or a user-specified size, and then displays some text, again, in a default font or a user-specified font. You can connect to a local X server or a remote X server using the `-display` option. Press Alt-Q (or Meta-Q) to quit.

Here are some example command lines:

```
chap11 -display attila:0.0 -geometry 400x100+5+432
```

This tries to connect to the X server on the machine named attila and create a 400x100-pixel window, location at 5 (X) and 432 (Y).

```
chap11 -font 9x15
```

This uses the default display name (from the `DISPLAY` environment variable) and sets the font to a font named *9x15*.

The following command creates the display in Figure 11.1.

```
chap11 -font "-adobe-courier-bold-r-normal--18-180-75-75-m-
110-iso8859-1"
```

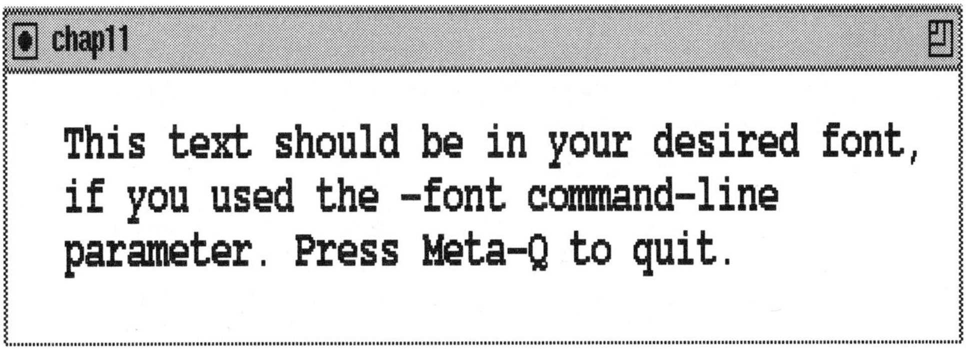

Figure 11.1. The chap11 Program.

CONNECTION HASSLES

X servers, by default, allow only local programs to establish a connection. If you try using the `chap11` program to connect to another X server, you may have problems.

X users a number of ways to control access. The simplest is the `xhost` mechanism. You need to log on to the remote machine and allow access to its X server via the `xhost` program. If you're on a machine named flame and type

```
xhost +attila
```

you are allowing X clients from machine attila to connect to the X server on flame.

To do this the other way around, log on to machine attila and then type:

```
xhost +flame
```

This allows X clients on machine flame to connect to the X server on attila.

There are other, more secure authentication schemes under X. If you're using one—and having problems—see your system administrator.

SUMMARY

When setting up your program's parameters, such as the color, font, and window size, you need to use a number of command-line arguments. These are prefixed by - (hyphen) and are listed earlier in the chapter.

Because X is designed to run on a number of different systems, you must include the display name.

Using X's geometry, you specify the size and location of an application's main window. X defines this geometry as:

```
[Width x Height][{+/-}XOffset{+/-}YOffset]
```

where `[Width x Height]` refers to the pixel dimensions of the display, and the x,y coordinates are computed from the top right of the screen. Negative x,y coordinates mean that the window's lower edge should be positioned relative to the lower edge of the screen.

Because of the wide variety of supported X hardware, your applications need to accept these command-line parameters, because otherwise your application may look nice on one machine and wretched on another.

XLIB FUNCTIONS AND MACROS INTRODUCED IN THIS CHAPTER

`XParseGeometry`

Chapter 12

SENDING MORE INFORMATION TO THE WINDOW MANAGER

Most X programs are expected to follow certain minimal standards, especially for placing the program's top-level windows. Window managers also require more information about your application's requests for screen real estate. It is a good idea to provide this information, because window managers essentially control the screen real estate and the placement of windows on the screen. This chapter covers some of these extended topics needed to round out your applications.

In X, the window manager is simply another client program, albeit a special client program. The basic idea of a window manager is that the window manager controls the screen. It can specify where applications place their windows and the sizes of those windows. Some window managers ensure that windows never overlap, creating a tiled window manager. Others—most, in fact—allow for overlapping windows.

Figure 12.1. Mwm Window Manager Title Bars.

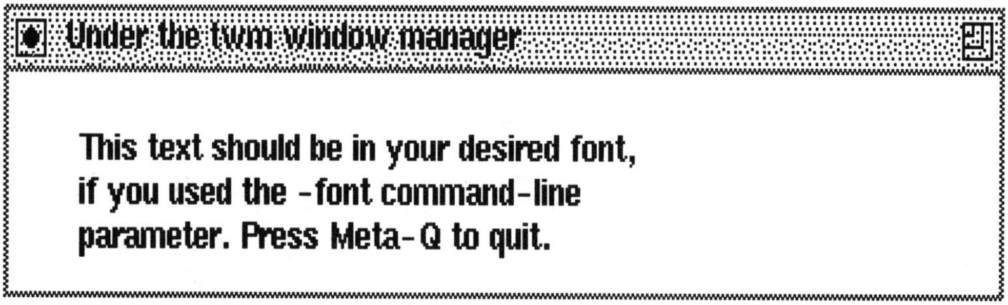

Figure 12.2. Twm Window Manager Title Bars.

Most window managers place title bars or other decorations on a window. Thus it is important to register a window's title with the window manager. Some window managers also provide the ability to collapse a window into an icon, so applications should register an icon name with the window manager, too. In all cases, since the window manager can mess with your application's windows, it is a good idea to tell the window manager what you want and hope for the best.

CHECKING FOR MORE COMMAND-LINE PARAMETERS

In this chapter, we extend the set of command-line parameters introduced last chapter:

Command Line	*Meaning*
`-iconic`	Begin in iconic state
`-name`	Set application name; default window title
`-title`	Use the text following as the window's title, rather than the default title.

STARTING OUT ICONIC

Standard X applications take an `-iconic` (or simply `-icon`) command-line parameter to specify that the application should start out iconic. Icons help clean a cluttered screen and your applications should, if at all possible, follow the dictates of the user.

The function `FindInitialState`, in `topwind.c`, below, checks the command-line parameters for `-iconic` and returns either `NormalState` or `IconicState`. This value is then passed to `SetWMHints` (which calls `XSetWMHints`) in `wmhints.c` (see Chapter 2).

`FindWindowName`, also in `topwind.c`, checks for the `-title` or `-name` options on the command line. If found, it calls `SetWindowName` with the window's name. The default window name is `argv[0]`, the program name. Officially, the `-name` option sets the application name as passed to `XSetClassHints`, which is used as a default title. The `-title` option sets the window's title explicitly.

SETTING THE COMMAND HINT

All X applications should register the command line that started them. This information may be used by the window manager or by a session manager, although few session managers exist as of this writing. Well-behaved X applications should call `XSetCommand` to set the command-line parameters:

```
Display      *display;
Window       window;
char         *argv[];
int          argc;

XSetCommand( display, window,
        argv, argc );
```

Note that `argv` comes first, even though your main function is called with `argc` after `argv`. This is a potential problem area.

SETTING THE STANDARD PROPERTIES

The rules for well-behaved X applications, contained in the *ICCCM*, demand that applications provide a lot of information for window managers and other programs. It's a good idea to follow these rules so your applications fit into the X world. There are some shortcuts, though.

`XSetStandardProperties` sets the most-asked-for information about your window. This information is stored in what are called *properties* on the window. (Knowledge of properties is not essential at this stage. We cover properties in depth in the companion to this work, *Advanced X Window Applications Programming*.)

```
Display      *display;
Window       window;
char         *window_name
char         *icon_name;
Pixmap       icon_pixmap;
char         *argv[];
int          argc;
XSizeHints   *sizehints;

XSetStandardProperties( display, window,
            window_name, icon_name, icon_pixmap,
            argv, argc, sizehints );
```

Unfortunately, `XSetStandardProperties` was obsoleted by `XSetWMProperties` in Release 4. But `XSetWMProperties` isn't available at all to R3 and older systems. So, again, you're stuck with the compatibility dilemma. We've chosen to ignore the short-cut routines and fill in all the proper values one at a time. This way, we have less problems with compatibility between releases of X.

`XSetWMProperties` replaces `XSetStandardProperties`. `XSetWMProperties` uses the `XTextProperty` structures introduced in R4 for storing the window and icon names:

```
Display             *display;
Window              window;
XTextProperty       *window_name;
XTextProperty       *icon_name;
char                *argv[];
int                 argc;
XSizeHints          *sizehints;
XWMHints            *wmhints;
XClassHint          *classhints;

XSetWMProperties ( display, window,
        window_name, icon_name,
        argv, argc,
        sizehints, wmhints, classhints );
```

SOURCE CODE FOR TOPWIND.C

The function `TopWindow` acts as a wrapper to `OpenWindow`, by checking the command-line parameters for a window's geometry (size and location), name, and initial state (iconic or normal). `TopWindow` also calls `XSetCommand` to set the `WM_COMMAND` property, as required by the *ICCCM*, as well as `SetSizeHints`, `SetClassHints` and `SetWMHints`, introduced in Chapter 2.

TopWindow returns a window ID, so you need to predeclare the function:

```
Window  TopWindow();
```

The file `topwind.c` contains utility functions to create an application's top-level window:

```
/*
 *      topwind.c
 *      Convenience routine to create a
 *      top-level window.
 */

#include  <stdio.h>
#include  <X11/Xlib.h>
#include  <X11/Xutil.h>
```

```
/*
 *      Define application class.
 */
#define APPL_CLASS          "Examples"

Window TopWindow( display, parent, argc, argv,
       x, y, width, height,
       bordercolor, backcolor, event_mask, visual )

Display          *display;         /* X server connection */
Window           parent;           /* parent window */
int              argc;
char             *argv[];          /* command-line parameters */
int              *x, *y;           /* default location */
int              *width, *height;  /* default size */
unsigned long    bordercolor;
unsigned long    backcolor;
unsigned long    event_mask;
Visual           *visual;          /* often CopyFromParent */

{       /* TopWindow */
        Window   OpenWindow();
        Window   window;
        int      screen;
        int      initial_state;

        /*
         * Check to see if the user
         * asked for a particular
         * size for our window
         */
        screen = DefaultScreen( display );

        CheckGeometry( argc, argv,
                DisplayWidth( display, screen ),
                DisplayHeight( display, screen ),
                x, y, width, height );

        /*
         * Create a window on the display
         */
        window = OpenWindow( display,
                    parent,
```

```
                *x, *y, *width, *height,
                bordercolor, backcolor,
                event_mask,
                visual );

        /*
         * Provide information to the window manager.
         */
        SetSizeHints( display, window,
                *x, *y, *width, *height );

        SetClassHints( display, window,
                argv[0],        /* res_name */
                APPL_CLASS );   /* res_class */

        /*
         * Set window name
         */
        FindWindowName( display, window, argc, argv );

        /*
         * Determine initial state based
         * on "-iconic" command-line
         * parameter.
         */
        initial_state = FindInitialState( argc, argv );

        SetWMHints( display, window,
              initial_state );

        /*
         * Set WM_COMMAND property,
         * as per the ICCCM.
         */
        XSetCommand( display, window,
              argv, argc );  /* note: argv comes first! */

        return( window );

}       /* TopWindow */

FindInitialState( argc, argv )
```

```
int     argc;
char    *argv[];

{       /* FindInitialState */
        char    *FindParameter();
        char    *ptr;

        ptr = FindParameter( argc, argv, "-icon" );

        if ( ptr != (char *) NULL )
             {
             return( IconicState );
             }
        else
             {
             return( NormalState );
             }

}       /* FindInitialState */

FindWindowName( display, window, argc, argv )

Display      *display;
Window       window;
int          argc;
char         *argv[];

{       /* FindWindowName */
        char    *FindParameter();
        char    *ptr;
        char    window_name[300];

        /*
         * Default name
         */
        (void) strcpy( window_name, argv[0] );

        ptr = FindParameter( argc, argv, "-name" );

        if ( ptr != (char *) NULL )
             {
             (void) strcpy( window_name, ptr );
             }
```

```
        else
              {
              ptr = FindParameter( argc, argv, "-title" );

              if ( ptr != (char *) NULL )
                  {
                  (void) strcpy( window_name, ptr );
                  }
              }

        SetWindowName( display, window, window_name );

}       /* FindWindowName */

/* end of file topwind.c */
```

SOURCE CODE FOR CHAP12.C

The `chap12` program extends our `chap11` program by checking for window titles and allowing applications to start in iconic state:

```
/*
 *      chap12.c
 *      Example program for Chapter 12.
 *
 *      Written for X Window Applications
 *      Programming, 2nd Edition
 */

#include <stdio.h>
#include <X11/Xlib.h>
#include <X11/Xutil.h>

/*
 *      Globals for black and white colors
 */
unsigned long   black, white;

/*
 *      Font names.
 */
```

```
#define FONT_NAME            "variable"
#define FALLBACK_FONT_NAME   "fixed"

/*
 *      Event mask for our top-level window.
 */
#define EVENT_MASK (KeyPressMask        | \
             ExposureMask)


/*
 *      Name of bitmap file we'll use for an icon.
 *      You can create this bitmap file with the
 *      standard X program named bitmap.
 */
#define ICON_FILENAME "icon.xbm"

main( argc, argv )

int     argc;
char    *argv[];

{       /* main */
        Display     *display;
        Display     *OpenDisplay();
        Window      rootwindow, window;
        Window      TopWindow();
        int         screen;
        int         x, y, width, height;
        Visual      *visual = CopyFromParent;
        GC          gc;
        GC          CreateGC();
        char        font_name[200];
        XFontStruct *font_struct;
        XFontStruct *LoadFontName();
        XEvent      event;
        int         done;
        char        string[20];
        KeySym      keysym;

        /*
         * Check if user asked for "-help" option.
         */
```

```
if ( CheckForHelp( argc, argv, "" ) == True )
      {
      exit( 0 );
      }

/*
 * Connect to X server
 */
display = OpenDisplay( argc, argv,
         &screen,
         &rootwindow );

/*
 * Set up "colors" we'll use
 */
black = BlackPixel( display, screen );
white = WhitePixel( display, screen );

/*
 * Load a font
 */
(void) strcpy( font_name, FONT_NAME );

font_struct = LoadFontName( display, argc, argv,
         font_name, FALLBACK_FONT_NAME );

/*
 * Set up default window sizes
 */
x      = 10;
y      = 10;
width  = 420;
height = ( FontHeight( font_struct ) + 1 ) * 5;

/*
 * Create a top-level window on the display
 */
window = TopWindow( display,
            rootwindow,
            argc, argv,
            &x, &y, &width, &height,
            black, white,
            EVENT_MASK,
            visual );
```

```
/*
 * Load up bitmap file and
 * turn it into an icon.
 */
LoadIcon( display, window,
      ICON_FILENAME, argv[0] );

/*
 * Create graphics context for drawing
 */
gc = CreateGC( display, window, black, white );

/*
 * Set the GC to draw with our font.
 */
XSetFont( display, gc,
      font_struct->fid );

/*
 * Make the window actually appear
 */
XMapRaised( display, window );
XFlush( display );

/*
 * Loop on events. Quit when the user types
 * a Meta-Q.
 */
done = False;

while( !done )
      {
      XNextEvent( display, &event );

      switch( event.type )
         {
         case Expose:
            Redraw( display, window,
               gc, font_struct );
            break;
         case KeyPress:
            done = DecodeKeyPress( &event,
                  &keysym, string );
```

```
                    break;
                case MappingNotify:
                    XRefreshKeyboardMapping( &event );
                    break;
                }
            }

        XCloseDisplay( display );

}       /* main */

Redraw( display, window, gc, font_struct )

Display       *display;
Window        window;
GC            gc;
XFontStruct   *font_struct;

{       /* Redraw */
        int   x, y, height;

        /*
         * Determine height of one line
         */
        height = FontHeight( font_struct ) + 1;

        y = 30;
        x = 30;
        DrawString( display, window, gc, x, y,
             "This text should be in your desired font," );

        y += height;
        DrawString( display, window, gc, x, y,
             "if you used the -font command-line" );

        y += height;
        DrawString( display, window, gc, x, y,
             "parameter. Press Meta-Q to quit." );

        /*
         * Send all our requests over the network,
         * so that the drawing is visible.
         */
        XFlush( display );
```

```
}        /* Redraw */

/* end of file chap12.c */
```

COMPILING AND LINKING THE CHAP12 PROGRAM

The `chap12` program requires the following files:

`args.c`	(Chapter 11)
`bitmap.c`	(Chapter 9)
`chap12.c`	
`classhnt.c`	(Chapter 2)
`connect.c`	(Chapter 1)
`display.c`	(Chapter 11)
`drawstr.c`	(Chapter 6)
`fontht.c`	(Chapter 5)
`fontname.c`	(Chapter 11)
`gc.c`	(Chapter 3)
`geometry.c`	(Chapter 11)
`icon.c`	(Chapter 9)
`key.c`	(Chapter 7)
`loadfont.c`	(Chapter 5)
`pixmap.c`	(Chapter 9)
`sizehint.c`	(Chapter 2)
`topwind.c`	
`usage.c`	(Chapter 11)
`window.c`	(Chapter 2)
`wmname.c`	(Chapter 2)
`wmhints.c`	(Chapter 2)

You can compile and link the `chap12` program with a command like:

```
cc -o chap12 -DX11R4 bitmap.c chap12.c classhnt.c connect.c gc.c \
       icon.c key.c pixmap.c sizehint.c window.c wmname.c \
       geometry.c args.c display.c usage.c fontname.c \
       loadfont.c topwind.c wmhints.c -lX11
```

You can also use the Makefile in Appendix A and type:

```
make chap12
```

RUNNING THE CHAP12 PROGRAM

Try using a variety of the command-line parameters to see what happens.

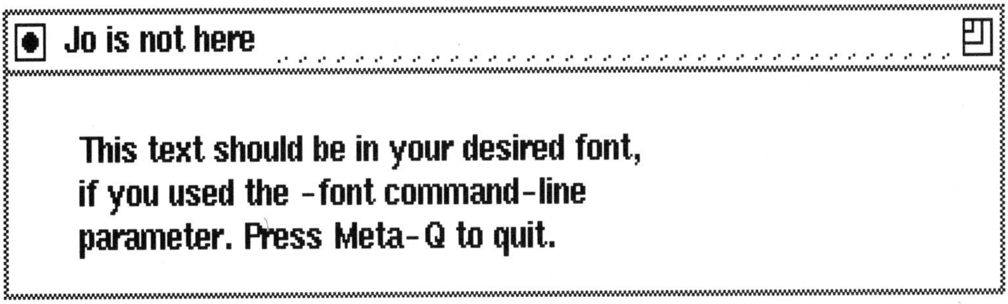

Figure 12.3. Chap12 with the Command Line: chap12 -title "Jo is not here" -font variable.

Figure 12.4. Chap12 with the Command Line: chap12 -iconic.

Press Alt-Q to quit.

DON'T KILL ME

Through most of this chapter, we've described what your applications need to do to be well-behaved in the X world. As we described above, well-behaved X applications adhere to rules set forth in the infamous *Inter-Client Communications Conventions Manual 1.1*, or *ICCCM*. We've tried to describe the minimum requirements on your applications, as the *ICCCM* is a thoroughly advanced topic (see our *Advanced X Window Applications Programming,* which has a very long section on the infamous *ICCCM*).

We highly recommend following what few rules there are for peaceful coexistence in the X world. We've shown most of what you need to do, but there's still one more thing: most X window managers provide a nasty utility to wipe out your applications.

Window managers, including the Motif window manager (`mwm`), the Open Look window manager (`olwm`) and the Tab (or Tom's) window manager (`twm`), allow you to wipe out X application windows through the use of a menu choice, usually named something like *kill*, *close*, *quit,* or *delete*. There's no standard on naming these choices and the same names often mean completely different things under different window managers. The *close* choice, for example, means *wipe out* to `mwm` and *iconify* to `olwm`, for example.

You probably don't want the window manager, however, to wipe out your application windows—especially if your application is used frequently by new users. This section shows how to prevent that from within your applications.

PREVENTING UNTIMELY DEATH

Here is a way to politely ask the window manager to let your application save its data and go through a proper shutdown procedure—rather than just trashing a window ID from underneath your application. To do this, we need to use one of the protocols described by the *ICCCM* for working with window managers. Your application tells the window manager which protocols it supports by writing that data into a `WM_PROTOCOLS` property.

The term *property* can mean many things. In X, *property* is a very technical term and is generally considered an advanced topic. But for now, treat a property as a named, typed collection of data bytes that the X server associates with a window ID. The data is stored in the X server and, in fact, most of the functions introduced in this and in the last chapter, such as `XSetWMProperties`, actually write data to specially formatted window properties under the hood.

THE WM_PROTOCOLS PROPERTY

The WM_PROTOCOLS property on an application's top-level window contains a list of X atoms. Each atom corresponds to a window-manager protocol that your application claims it supports. These protocols (and atoms) include WM_DELETE_WINDOW, WM_SAVE_YOURSELF, and WM_TAKE_FOCUS.

To ask the window manager not to arbitrarily wipe out windows, your application needs to support the WM_DELETE_WINDOW protocol. To do this, you need a two-step process. First, tell the window manager that your application supports the WM_DELETE_WINDOW protocol. Then, when the window manager wants your application to delete a window, it should send your application a message stating that fact.

The key word here is *should.* Remember that when dealing with a window manager, the window manager wins. Period. All your programs can do is ask that the window manager to act nicely. We should note that most window managers do support the WM_DELETE_WINDOW protocol, so you should have few problems.

To tell the window manager that your application supports the WM_DELETE_WINDOW protocol, you need to convert the string "WM_DELETE_WINDOW" to an atom. *Atoms* are 32-bit numbers used by X to speed string compares and avoid continuously sending long strings over the network. (The X server computes a form of hash number for the given string, returning that number to your application. Then, all future mentions of the string can use just the 32-bit number.) XInternAtom converts a string to an atom ID:

```
Atom      atom;
Display   *display;
char      *atom_name;
Bool      only_if_exists;

atom = XInternAtom( display,
          atom_name,
          only_if_exists );
```

If only_if_exists is False, the atom will be created if necessary. If only_if_exists is True, the atom will be returned only if it already existed. You almost always want to set only_if_exists to False. Here's how to convert the string "WM_DELETE_WINDOW" to an atom:

```
Display    *display;
Atom       wm_delete_window;

wm_delete_window = XInternAtom( display,
          "WM_DELETE_WINDOW",
          False );
```

Next, use the function XSetWMProtocols to register this information with the window manager. XSetWMProtocols writes out atom IDs to the WM_PROTOCOLS property on the given window:

```
Display    *display;
Window     window;
Atom       *protocol_list;
int        number_protocols;

status = XSetWMProtocols( display,
          window,
          protocol_list,
          number_protocols );
```

The status returned will be True or False.

Here's how we use XSetWMProtocols:

```
Display    *display;
Window     window;
Atom       wm_delete_window;
int        status;

wm_delete_window = XInternAtom( display,
               "WM_DELETE_WINDOW",
               False );

status = XSetWMProtocols( display,
          window,
          &wm_delete_window,
          1 );
```

4 Release

XSetWMProtocols is new in X11 Release 4. This may be a problem if you're using an older version of X. If so, you can emulate XSetWMProtocols by manually writing data to the WM_PROTOCOLS property on your application's top-level window. First, convert WM_PROTOCOLS to an atom:

```
Display   *display;
Atom      wm_protocols;

wm_protocols = XInternAtom( display,
               "WM_PROTOCOLS",
               False );
```

Use `XChangeProperty` to write out the atom for `WM_DELETE_WINDOW` into the property identified by the `WM_PROTOCOLS` atom.

Note that properties are not atoms and atoms are not properties. (It is very easy to confuse the two.) Atoms are used to name properties, but the property itself is a named, typed set of data associated with a window:

```
Display         *display;
Window          window;
Atom            property;
Atom            prop_type;
int             format; /* 32, 16 or 8 */
int             mode;
unsigned char   *data;
int             number_elements;

XChangeProperty( display, window,
     property,
     prop_type,
     format,
     mode,
     data,
     number_elements );
```

The mode can be `PropModeAppend`, `PropModePrepend` or `PropModeReplace`. We almost always use `PropModeAppend`. The format should be 32 for 32-bit items—and atoms are 32-bit items.

To set the `WM_DELETE_WINDOW` atom in the `WM_PROTOCOLS` property:

```
XChangeProperty( display, window,
     wm_protocols,
     XA_ATOM,
     32,
     PropModeAppend,
     &wm_delete_window,
     1 );
```

If the property doesn't exist, `XChangeProperty` will create the property.

USING THE WM_DELETE_WINDOW PROTOCOL

Whenever users ask the window manager to delete a window, the window manager should send your application a special `ClientMessage` event:

```
typedef struct {
     int              type;
     unsigned long    serial;
     Bool             send_event;
     Display          *display;
     Window           window;
     Atom             message_type;
     int              format;
     union {
          char         b[20];
          short        s[10];
          long         l[5];
          } data;
     } XClientMessageEvent;
```

With X, your application normally won't get events it does not specifically ask for. However, all X programs, no matter what, get sent `ClientMessage` events. The X server assumes that your application wants these events, and in this case, it does.

`ClientMessage` events are used in an arbitrary fashion for applications (including the window manager) to communicate with each other. There needs to be a way to distinguish the `ClientMessage` sent by the window manager indicating a `WM_DELETE_WINDOW` request from all other kinds of ClientMessage events.

To distinguish this message, examine the `XClientMessageEvent` structure:

- The type will be `ClientMessage`.
- The message_type (don't confuse this with the type) will be the atom for `WM_PROTOCOLS`.
- The format will be 32, for 32-bit data items.
- The first (long) data element will be the atom for `WM_DELETE_WINDOW`.

If all these conditions are met, then the user (through the intercession of the window manager) has asked to delete one of your application windows, namely, the one with the proper window ID in the—you guessed it—window field.

Here's a simple test, using the `wm_protocols` and `wm_delete_window` atoms interned above:

```
XClientMessageEvent      event;

if ( ( event.message_type == wm_protocols ) &&
     ( event.data.l[ 0 ] == wm_delete_window ) )
     {
     /*
      * Window manager is asking
      * our app to delete this
      * window.
      */
     }
```

When your application receives the `WM_DELETE_WINDOW` request, it needs to decide how to proceed. Assume the user asked for the window to be deleted. Your program can pop up a dialog and ask the user to confirm (or ask whether to save any changes made to a document), but if the user wants to go ahead, then your program should remove the offending window.

SUMMARY

Making sure your program interacts properly with an X window manager is important. This chapter covers the extended topics you need to make sure this interaction occurs properly.

When setting up your program's parameters (such as the color and font), you need to use a number of command-line arguments. These are prefixed by - (a hyphen) and are listed earlier in the chapter.

```
-iconic
-title
-name
```

Since the window manager controls the screen and sometimes needs information for title bars, it's important that you register a window's title with a window manager.

Also, to prevent your windows from being ungraciously destroyed, your application must set the `WM_DELETE_WINDOW` Atom in the `WM_PROTOCOLS` property.

The official rules for well-behaved X applications are called the *Inter-Client Communications Conventions Manual*, or *ICCCM*. We've covered the basic rules here and strongly suggest you read the *ICCCM*. If you haven't read the *ICCCM* yet, by all means do so. It should be part of your X documentation in a document titled *Inter-Client Communication Conventions Manual*, Version 1.1, MIT X Consortium Standard. The *ICCCM* also appears in an appendix of *X Window System: The Complete Reference to Xlib, X Protocol, ICCCM and XLFD* by Scheifler and Gettys (see Appendix F).

We cover even more of the rules for well-behaved applications in our next book, *Advanced X Window Applications Programming*.

XLIB FUNCTIONS AND MACROS INTRODUCED IN THIS CHAPTER

`XChangeProperty`

`XInternAtom`

`XSetCommand`

`XSetStandardProperties`

`XSetWMProperties`

`XSetWMProtocols`

Chapter 13

HANDLING CRITICAL ERRORS

One of the first steps in producing commercial-quality software is making sure the program doesn't crash. X programs will terminate on any X-related error, such as a bad window parameter—unless you install a critical error handler. An error handler will intercept the X error and allow your routine to process the error, rather than force a nasty program termination. To make any sort of commercial-quality software, you must set up functions to handle X errors, making this chapter's topic one of the most important in X programming.

DECODING THE ERROR MESSAGE

Most X errors present a message like the one below:

```
X Error of failed request: BadDrawable (invalid Pixmap or
Window parameter)
  Major opcode of failed request:  76 (X_ImageText8)
  Minor opcode of failed request:  0
  Resource id in failed request:  0x1
  Serial number of failed request:  12
  Current serial number in output stream:  13
```

The `BadDrawable` error tells us that the error involved a bad drawable ID: a bad window or pixmap. In addition, we can guess from the opcode of `76` (`X_ImageText8`) that the error had to do with a call to `XDrawImageString` or some similar function that outputs text. Finally, the resource ID of the failed request is `0x1`, which is normally a bad value. Later, when drawing to this nonexistent bad window (or pixmap), the application faulted. The serial numbers and minor opcodes don't do you a lot of good.

COMMON PROBLEMS

Common errors include:

- `BadFont`, an invalid font
- `BadName`, when the application attempts to load a nonexistent font
- `BadMatch`, usually involving attempts to copy data between drawables with different depths
- `BadAlloc`, the dreaded out-of-memory error

TRAPPING ERRORS IN PROGRAMS

The X library provides two error-trapping functions, `XSetErrorHandler` and `XSetIOErrorHandler`. `XSetErrorHandler` traps normal errors, such as out-of-memory and bad window ID errors. `XSetIOErrorHandler` traps fatal I/O errors, such as losing the network connection to the X server. Your application generally cannot recover from a fatal I/O error.

You pass `XSetErrorHandler` an error-handling function to be called back when error events arrive:

```
int     (*ErrorHandler)();

int     (*XSetErrorHandler(ErrorHandler))()
```

4 Release

With X11 Release 4 and later, `XSetErrorHandler` returns a pointer to the old error-handling function. Previous releases did not return the old error-handling function. Your `ErrorHandler` function will be passed the `Display` pointer and a pointer to the error event:

```
ErrorHandler( display, event )

Display       *display;
XErrorEvent   *event;

{       /* ErrorHandler */
        int   length = 120;
        char  string[ 130 ];

        XGetErrorText( display,
              event->error_code,
              string,
              length );

        (void) fprintf( stderr,
              "\n\nX Error:\n\t%s\n", string );

        (void) fprintf( stderr,
              "\tSerial number of request: %ld\n",
              event->serial );

        (void) fprintf( stderr,
              "\tOp Code: %d.%d %s\n\tError Code: %d\n",
              event->request_code,
              event->minor_code,
              ErrorCodes[event->request_code],
              event->error_code );

        (void) fprintf( stderr,
              "\tResource ID of failed request: %ld\n
              event->resourceid );

        (void) fprintf( "\ton display %s.\n",
              DisplayString( display ) );

}       /* ErrorHandler */
```

This error handler does nothing more than merely report the error to `stderr`.

Because X errors are typically generated by bad parameters passed to an Xlib function, and because X resources are usually used over and over again, one error will probably generate many errors. This is because the error-handler function

ErrorHandler does not deal with the error in any way except report it. In your code, you probably want to put in something to deal with the error.

The error-handling function can return if you judge the errors recoverable. Most of them are. The ErrorCodes array, set up in error.c, below, contains the names associated with the X protocol numbers.

X ERROR EVENTS

```
typedef struct {
    int             type;
    Display         *display;      /* Display the event was read from */
    unsigned long   serial;        /* serial number of failed request */
    unsigned char   error_code;    /* error code of failed request */
    unsigned char   request_code;  /* Major op-code of failed request */
    unsigned char   minor_code;    /* Minor op-code of failed request */
    XID             resourceid;    /* resource id */
    } XErrorEvent;
```

The X library delivers XErrorEvent structures to the error-handling function set up with XSetErrorHandler. If you set up an error handler with XSetErrorHandler and an X library error occurs, your error-handler will be called sometime after the error occurred. These error events arrive asynchronously, which makes it hard to associate the error with the offending routine. You can pull some useful information from the XErrorEvent structure, though.

The resourceid, an XID, is the ID of the offending resource, such as a window or pixmap. It is usually defined as an unsigned long (check the include file X.h to see how your system has it defined). The serial field is the serial number of the request, which usually isn't very helpful unless you are debugging an X server.

The request_code is the X protocol request number for the routine that actually caused the error. This can help when associating the error to the offending part of your code. The minor_code is, appropriately enough, the minor op-code of the failed X request.

The error_code tells what type of error happened. The XGetErrorText Xlib function returns the text message for a given error code.

XGetErrorText retrieves an error message associated with an error number and places that message in a character buffer:

```
Display       *display;
int           error_code;
char          buffer[ ARBITRARY_SIZE + 1 ];      /* RETURN */
int           max_bytes = ARBITRARY_SIZE;

XGetErrorText( display, error_code,
        buffer, max_bytes );
```

`XGetErrorText` pulls out a line of text that helps describe the error. It puts this text in a character-string buffer for which you must allocate space for. You also need to pass the maximum length for a buffer that your code can accept.

X ERROR NUMBERS

These error numbers are reported in the `error_code` field of the `XErrorEvent`:

Error Code	***Value***	***Meaning***
`Success`	0	No error
`BadRequest`	1	Bad request code
`BadValue`	2	Integer parameter out of range
`BadWindow`	3	Parameter not a valid Window
`BadPixmap`	4	Parameter not a valid Pixmap
`BadAtom`	5	Parameter not a valid Atom
`BadCursor`	6	Parameter not a valid Cursor
`BadFont`	7	Parameter not a valid Font
`BadMatch`	8	Parameter mismatch
`BadDrawable`	9	Parameter not a valid Pixmap or Window
`BadAccess`	10	Attempt to perform an illegal operation
`BadAlloc`	11	Insufficient resources or memory
`BadColor`	12	No such colormap
`BadGC`	13	Parameter not a valid GC
`BadIDChoice`	14	Choice not in range or already used
`BadName`	15	Font or color name doesn't exist
`BadLength`	16	Request length incorrect
`BadImplementation`	17	Server is defective

X PROTOCOL NUMBERS

The following are the standard X protocol request numbers. The XErrorEvent structure contains the protocol request that failed in the request_code field. X extensions may extend this set. These numbers reside in the file Xproto.h in whatever directory your X Window include files reside, which is normally /usr/include/X11. Near the end of Xproto.h, you'll see a listing of the X network protocol request numbers.

Request Name	*Number*
CreateWindow	1
ChangeWindowAttributes	2
GetWindowAttributes	3
DestroyWindow	4
DestroySubwindows	5
ChangeSaveSet	6
ReparentWindow	7
MapWindow	8
MapSubwindows	9
UnmapWindow	10
UnmapSubwindows	11
ConfigureWindow	12
CirculateWindow	13
GetGeometry	14
QueryTree	15
InternAtom	16
GetAtomName	17
ChangeProperty	18
DeleteProperty	19
GetProperty	20
ListProperties	21
SetSelectionOwner	22
GetSelectionOwner	23
ConvertSelection	24

Request Name	***Number (cont.)***
`SendEvent`	25
`GrabPointer`	26
`UngrabPointer`	27
`GrabButton`	28
`UngrabButton`	29
`ChangeActivePointerGrab`	30
`GrabKeyboard`	31
`UngrabKeyboard`	32
`GrabKey`	33
`UngrabKey`	34
`AllowEvents`	35
`GrabServer`	36
`UngrabServer`	37
`QueryPointer`	38
`GetMotionEvents`	39
`TranslateCoords`	40
`WarpPointer`	41
`SetInputFocus`	42
`GetInputFocus`	43
`QueryKeymap`	44
`OpenFont`	45
`CloseFont`	46
`QueryFont`	47
`QueryTextExtents`	48
`ListFonts`	49
`ListFontsWithInfo`	50
`SetFontPath`	51
`GetFontPath`	52
`CreatePixmap`	53
`FreePixmap`	54

Request Name	***Number (cont.)***
CreateGC	55
ChangeGC	56
CopyGC	57
SetDashes	58
SetClipRectangles	59
FreeGC	60
ClearArea	61
CopyArea	62
CopyPlane	63
PolyPoint	64
PolyLine	65
PolySegment	66
PolyRectangle	67
PolyArc	68
FillPoly	69
PolyFillRectangle	70
PolyFillArc	71
PutImage	72
GetImage	73
PolyText8	74
PolyText16	75
ImageText8	76
ImageText16	77
CreateColormap	78
FreeColormap	79
CopyColormapAndFree	80
InstallColormap	81
UninstallColormap	82
ListInstalledColormaps	83
AllocColor	84

Request Name	***Number (cont.)***
`AllocNamedColor`	85
`AllocColorCells`	86
`AllocColorPlanes`	87
`FreeColors`	88
`StoreColors`	89
`StoreNamedColor`	90
`QueryColors`	91
`LookupColor`	92
`CreateCursor`	93
`CreateGlyphCursor`	94
`FreeCursor`	95
`RecolorCursor`	96
`QueryBestSize`	97
`QueryExtension`	98
`ListExtensions`	99
`ChangeKeyboardMapping`	100
`GetKeyboardMapping`	101
`ChangeKeyboardControl`	102
`GetKeyboardControl`	103
`Bell`	104
`ChangePointerControl`	105
`GetPointerControl`	106
`SetScreenSaver`	107
`GetScreenSaver`	108
`ChangeHosts`	109
`ListHosts`	110
`SetAccessControl`	111
`SetCloseDownMode`	112
`KillClient`	113
`RotateProperties`	114

Request Name	***Number (cont.)***
`ForceScreenSaver`	115
`SetPointerMapping`	116
`GetPointerMapping`	117
`SetModifierMapping`	118
`GetModifierMapping`	119
`NoOperation`	127

HANDLING FATAL I/O ERRORS

`XSetErrorHandler` sets up a function called for any regular X error, such as when a bad window ID is passed to a drawing function. Other X errors, though, are fatal to an X program, especially errors involving loss of the server connection. This type of error could happen if the X server program itself tipped over, or if the network communication went down.

X calls these fatal errors *I/O errors*. If one occurs, Xlib will terminate your program whether you like it or not. You can, however, set up a fatal-error-handler function, much like the regular-error-handler function. This fatal-error handler, though, will be the last routine that your program executes. Therefore, it is a good idea to save files or generally clean up the system as much as possible in the little time remaining. (You can use the C routines `setjmp` and `longjmp` to jump out of the function and avoid the termination, if you wish.)

From a fatal-error handler you cannot use any Xlib routines that would generate a request of the X server (an I/O error means that the link to the X server is severed). You can register your fatal-error-handler function with X by calling the `XSetIOErrorHandler` function and passing the address of your fatal-error-handler routine.

`XSetIOErrorHandler` sets up a function to be called back on fatal I/O errors:

```
int          (*FatalErrorHandler)();

int (*XSetIOErrorHandler(FatalErrorHandler))()
```

Like `XSetErrorHandler`, `XSetIOErrorHandler` returns the old error-handling function starting with R4. Previous to R4, the old function was *not* returned. Your fatal-error-handler function is passed the (now bad) display pointer:

```
FatalErrorHandler( display )

Display        *display;

{       /* FatalErrorHandler */

        (void) fprintf( stderr,
              "X Error: Fatal IO error on display %s.\n",
              DisplayString( display ) );

        (void) fprintf( stderr,
              "Bailing out near line one.\n" );

        /*
         *    Put any clean-up code here.
         */

        /*
         *    Thus terminates another program
         */

        exit( 1 );

}       /* FatalErrorHandler */
```

Again, in this sample `FatalErrorHandler` function, not much is accomplished except reporting the error to the user. In the `Draw` application, to be presented in the following chapters, saving the file involves an Xlib call, as does most of the program. The `FatalErrorHandler` function cannot really do all that much. In a computer-aided design (CAD) program or an industrial process-control program, though, the story would probably be different. It seems rather arrogant for X to decide that it will terminate your program on a fatal I/O error, as it might be better if you could try to reopen a display connection at a later time, but that's what you have to live with.

In any case, most commercial-grade X applications will want to create error-handling routines like those described above.

SOURCE CODE FOR ERROR.C

The file `error.c` contains code for setting up error-handling functions and the error-handlers themselves. `SetErrorHandlers` sets up the regular-error and fatal-error handlers:

```
/*
 *      error.c
 *      X Window error-handling functions.
 *
 *      Written for X Window Applications
 *      Programming, 2nd Edition
 */

#include   <stdio.h>
#include   <X11/Xlib.h>
#include   <X11/Xutil.h>
#include   <X11/Xproto.h>

/*
 *      Global static table of X Protocol Code Ids
 */
static char  *ErrorCodes[]=
                {
                "",                          /* 0 */
                "CreateWindow",              /* 1 */
                "ChangeWindowAttributes",
                "GetWindowAttributes",
                "DestroyWindow",
                "DestroySubwindows",
                "ChangeSaveSet",
                "ReparentWindow",
                "MapWindow",
                "MapSubwindows",
                "UnmapWindow",               /* 10 */
                "UnmapSubwindows",
                "ConfigureWindow",
                "CirculateWindow",
                "GetGeometry",
                "QueryTree",
                "InternAtom",
                "GetAtomName",
```

```
"ChangeProperty",
"DeleteProperty",
"GetProperty",
"ListProperties",
"SetSelectionOwner",
"GetSelectionOwner",
"ConvertSelection",
"SendEvent",
"GrabPointer",
"UngrabPointer",
"GrabButton",
"UngrabButton",
"ChangeActivePointerGrab",
"GrabKeyboard",
"UngrabKeyboard",
"GrabKey",
"UngrabKey",
"AllowEvents",
"GrabServer",
"UngrabServer",
"QueryPointer",
"GetMotionEvents",
"TranslateCoords",
"WarpPointer",
"SetInputFocus",
"GetInputFocus",
"QueryKeymap",
"OpenFont",
"CloseFont",
"QueryFont",
"QueryTextExtents",
"ListFonts",
"ListFontsWithInfo",
"SetFontPath",
"GetFontPath",
"CreatePixmap",
"FreePixmap",
"CreateGC",
"ChangeGC",
"CopyGC",
"SetDashes",
"SetClipRectangles",
"FreeGC",
```

```
"ClearArea",
"CopyArea",
"CopyPlane",
"PolyPoint",
"PolyLine",
"PolySegment",
"PolyRectangle",
"PolyArc",
"FillPoly",
"PolyFillRectangle",
"PolyFillArc",
"PutImage",
"GetImage",
"PolyText8",
"PolyText16",
"ImageText8",
"ImageText16",
"CreateColormap",
"FreeColormap",
"CopyColormapAndFree",
"InstallColormap",
"UninstallColormap",
"ListInstalledColormaps",
"AllocColor",
"AllocNamedColor",
"AllocColorCells",
"AllocColorPlanes",
"FreeColors",
"StoreColors",
"StoreNamedColor",
"QueryColors",
"LookupColor",
"CreateCursor",
"CreateGlyphCursor",
"FreeCursor",
"RecolorCursor",
"QueryBestSize",
"QueryExtension",
"ListExtensions",
"ChangeKeyboardMapping",
"GetKeyboardMapping",
"ChangeKeyboardControl",
```

```
                "GetKeyboardControl",
                "Bell",
                "ChangePointerControl",
                "GetPointerControl",
                "SetScreenSaver",
                "GetScreenSaver",
                "ChangeHosts",
                "ListHosts",
                "SetAccessControl",
                "SetCloseDownMode",
                "KillClient",
                "RotateProperties",
                "ForceScreenSaver",
                "SetPointerMapping",
                "GetPointerMapping",
                "SetModifierMapping",
                "GetModifierMapping"
                };

SetErrorHandlers()

/*
 *      Sets up our Xlib error handlers.
 */

{       /* SetErrorHandlers */
        int   ErrorHandler();
        int   FatalErrorHandler();

        /*
         * Set up the normal error
         * handler, for things like
         * bad window IDs, etc.
         */
        XSetErrorHandler( ErrorHandler );

        /*
         * Set up the fatal error handler
         * for a broken connection with
         * the X server, and other nasties.
         */
        XSetIOErrorHandler( FatalErrorHandler );
```

```
}       /* SetErrorHandlers */

ErrorHandler( display, event )

Display      *display;
XErrorEvent  *event;

/*
 *      ErrorHandler handles non-fatal X errors.
 *      This routine basically just prints out
 *      the error message and returns. Thus, we
 *      can probaly expect many, many errors to be
 *      generated, since nothing stops the erroneous
 *      condition. This function mainly exists so
 *      that the program does not terminate on a minor
 *      error. No one seems to like unexpected program
 *      termination, at least in a production environment.
 *
 */
{       /* ErrorHandler */
        int  length = 120;
        char string[ 130 ];

        XGetErrorText( display,
             event->error_code,
             string,
             length );

        (void) fprintf( stderr,
             "\n\nX Error:\n\t%s\n", string );

        (void) fprintf( stderr,
             "\tSerial number of request: %ld\n",
             event->serial );

        (void) fprintf( stderr,
             "\tOp Code: %d.%d %s\n\tError Code: %d\n",
             event->request_code,
             event->minor_code,
             ErrorCodes[event->request_code],
             event->error_code );

        (void) fprintf( stderr,
```

```
                "\tResource ID of failed request: %ld\n",
                event->resourceid );

        (void) fprintf( stderr, "\ton display %s.\n",
                DisplayString( display ) );

        /* ErrorHandler */

FatalErrorHandler( display )

Display         *display;

/*
 *      FatalErrorHandler takes care of
 *      fatal X errors, like a broken
 *      connection to the X server.
 *      If this routine does not exit,
 *      and returns, the XLib will exit
 *      anyway. Thus, in this function
 *      you need to save all important
 *      data and get ready for a fatal
 *      termination. Note: Do not call
 *      Xlib routines from a fatal X
 *      error handler.
 *
 *      This function is registered
 *      with X by use of the
 *      XSetIOErrorHandler Xlib function.
 */

{       /* FatalErrorHandler */

        (void) fprintf( stderr,
                "X Error: Fatal IO error on display %s.\n",
                DisplayString( display ) );

        (void) fprintf( stderr,
                "Bailing out near line one.\n" );

        /*
         *    Put any clean-up code here.
         *
         */
```

```
        /*
         *    Thus terminates another program
         */

        exit( 1 );

}       /* FatalErrorHandler */

/* end of file error.c */
```

SOURCE CODE FOR STARTUPX.C

Now that we can handle errors, we've completed that last step in setting up an X application. The function `StartupX`, below, checks for user-requested help, opens up a connection to an X server, sets up error handlers, and then retrieves the default values for black and white, providing a handy utility for common start-up activity.

`StartupX` returns a pointer to a `Display` structure, so it must be predeclared:

```
Display *StartupX();

/*
 *      startupx.c
 *      Convenience routine to start up
 *      connection to X server.
 */

#include  <X11/Xlib.h>

Display *StartupX( argc, argv, screen, rootwindow,
        black, white, message )

int             argc;
char            *argv[];
int             *screen;
Window          *rootwindow;
unsigned long   *black, *white;
char            message[];  /* extra help message */

{       /* StartupX */
        Display     *OpenDisplay();
        Display     *display;
```

```
        /*
         * Check if user asked for "-help" option.
         */
        if ( CheckForHelp( argc, argv, message ) == True )
             {
             exit( 0 );
             }

        display = OpenDisplay( argc, argv,
                     screen, rootwindow );

        /*
         * Set up error handlers
         */
        SetErrorHandlers();

        /*
         * Set up "colors" we'll use.
         */
        *black = BlackPixel( display, *screen );
        *white = WhitePixel( display, *screen );

        return( display );

}       /* StartupX */

/* end of file startupx.c */
```

SOURCE CODE FOR CHAP13.C

Unlike most X programs, the `chap13` program is designed to create errors, rather than avoid them. We do this to show the actions of the Xlib error handlers at work:

```
/*
 *      chap13.c
 *      Example program for Chapter 13.
 *
 *      Contrary to most programming
 *      practice, this program tries to
 *      generate errors, rather than
 *      avoid them.
 *
```

```
 *      The whole purpose, of course,
 *      is to test X's error-trapping
 *      abilities.
 *
 *      Written for X Window Applications
 *      Programming, 2nd Edition
 */

#include <stdio.h>
#include <X11/Xlib.h>
#include <X11/Xutil.h>

main( argc, argv )

int     argc;
char    *argv[];

{       /* main */
        Display         *display;
        Display         *StartupX();  /* startupx.c */
        Window          rootwindow, window;
        Window          TopWindow();
        int             screen;
        GC              gc;
        GC              CreateGC();
        unsigned long   black = 1, white = 0;
        int             x, y, width, height;
        Visual          *visual = CopyFromParent;
        XEvent          event;

        /*
         * Connect to X server
         */
        display = StartupX( argc, argv,
                &screen, &rootwindow,
                &black, &white, "" );

        /*
         * Create a top-level window on the display
         */
        x = 0;
        y = 0;
        width = 100;
```

```
        height = 100;
        window = TopWindow( display,
                    rootwindow,
                    argc, argv,
                    &x, &y, &width, &height,
                    black, white,
                    ExposureMask,     /* event mask */
                    visual );

        /*
         * Create graphics context for drawing
         */
        gc = CreateGC( display, window, black, white );

        /*
         * Make the window actually appear
         */
        XMapRaised( display, window );
        XFlush( display );

        XNextEvent( display, &event );

        /*
         * Now, let's generate some errors:
         */
        window = (Window) 1L;
        XDrawImageString( display, window, gc,
             10, 10, "This is a bad string", 10 );

        XDrawLine( display, window, gc,
             100, 100, 200, 200 );

        XFlush( display );

        /*
         * Wait on the next event, then quit
         */
        XNextEvent( display, &event );

        XCloseDisplay( display );

}       /* main */

/* end of file chap13.c */
```

COMPILING AND LINKING THE CHAP13 PROGRAM

The chap13 program requires the following files:

args.c	(Chapter 11)
chap13.c	
classhnt.c	(Chapter 2)
connect.c	(Chapter 1)
display.c	(Chapter 11)
error.c	
gc.c	(Chapter 3)
geometry.c	(Chapter 11)
sizehint.c	(Chapter 2)
topwind.c	(Chapter 12)
usage.c	(Chapter 11)
window.c	(Chapter 2)
wmname.c	(Chapter 2)
wmhints.c	(Chapter 2)

You can compile and link the chap13 program with a command like:

```
cc -o chap13 -DX11R4 chap13.c classhnt.c connect.c gc.c \
       sizehint.c window.c wmname.c geometry.c args.c \
       display.c usage.c topwind.c wmhints.c -lX11
```

You can also use the Makefile in Appendix A and type:

```
make chap13
```

RUNNING THE CHAP13 PROGRAM

When you run the chap13 program, you'll see X errors like the ones below:

```
X Error:
        BadDrawable (invalid Pixmap or Window parameter)
        Serial number of request: 12
```

```
        Op Code: 76.0 ImageText8
        Error Code: 9
        Resource ID of failed request: 0
        on display unix:0.0.

X Error:
        BadDrawable (invalid Pixmap or Window parameter)
        Serial number of request: 13
        Op Code: 66.0 PolySegment
        Error Code: 9
        Resource ID of failed request: 0
        on display unix:0.0.
```

SUMMARY

This chapter introduces you to error handling in the X Window System. Unless a critical error handler is installed in your programs, you may never know exactly where the error occurred. In addition, you can set up fatal-error-handler functions that will clean up the system or save active files before the program terminates.

Every commercial-grade X application needs error-handling functions. Period.

XLIB FUNCTIONS AND MACROS INTRODUCED IN THIS CHAPTER

`XGetErrorText`

`XSetErrorHandler`

`XSetIOErrorHandler`

Section III

PUTTING IT ALL TOGETHER: BUILDING X WINDOW APPLICATIONS

In this section we pull together the work in all the previous chapters and build a working X Window application, a bitmap-editing program. We've updated this program with a new look and feel that fits in better with modern X applications.

To implement our Draw application, we'll build a small set of toolkit functions which will make our interface easier to program and to use. After building the toolkit in chapters 14 and 15 we provide a user's guide to the Draw application and then go over the Draw source code.

In Chapter 19, we cover areas where our simple application can be enhanced and extended, providing hints, ideas, and strategies to get you started enhancing the application. We think that you'll learn a lot about X if you stretch beyond this book and extend the Draw application.

Chapter 14

BUILDING A SMALL TOOLKIT FOR X APPLICATIONS

When building larger X applications, you'll soon discover that when creating multiple windows, you are faced with duplicating large sections of code for event handling and redrawing the window contents on `Expose` events.

You'll also soon discover that creating subwindows allows you to encapsulate tasks into windows. For example, a pushbutton could be based in a single window. `XNextEvent` reports events relating to that pushbutton window, so your code will be a lot smaller than trying to constantly determine if mouse clicks happened in a given pushbutton area.

In this chapter, we'll create a small toolkit that allows us to share code for many like-minded tasks. While there are full-fledged X Window toolkits (see Section IV), we intend to show the rationale for building these toolkits and some of the design decisions facing toolkit builders. This toolkit is based on the concept of toolkit windows.

TOOLKIT WINDOWS

Each toolkit component, usually called a *widget* in the vernacular, forms a self-contained unit inside a window. Each component has its own window. This means that each component is responsible for redrawing its window contents and reacting to keyboard and mouse events inside that window. Many other X toolkits provide this one-to-one window-to-component correspondence.

Our components will include pushbuttons, where a mouse click executes a function; text-entry areas, where the user can type an entry; and static text labels. Most of the code, though, is in the infrastructure to handle any sort of toolkit window. The actual code for pushbutton toolkit components, as you'll see in the file `pushb.c`, below, is rather small. With the proper toolkit, you can easily build and add functionality. Our example toolkit certainly isn't full-fledged, but we provide it as a means to see how toolkits are designed and what they should do.

Each window in the toolkit has an associated data structure:

```
typedef struct {
        Display     *display;
        Window      parent;
        Window      window;
        GC          gc;      /* usually shared */
        XFontStruct *font;
        int         width, height;
        int         state;   /* used for toggling */
        int         group;   /* used for toggling */
        int         id;
        char        name[ MAX_NAME_LEN + 1 ];
        void        (*drawfunc)();
        void        (*userfunc)();
        void        (*eventfunc)();
        } ToolWindow;
```

The `display`, `window`, `gc`, and `font` are for drawing into the window. The GC is usually shared with other components of the same type. For example, all pushbutton windows will share the same GC. The `state` and `group` allow a group of pushbuttons to act as *radio buttons*; that is, only one item in a group can have the active state. All other items must be inactive, much like the buttons on a car radio (you can only tune in one station at a time). The `id` identifies toolkit items, so that you can add and retrieve information.

The toolkit window's name is used as the text to display for pushbuttons and static labels. Then we have three function pointers. (You'll find most X toolkits make extensive use of function pointers.) The drawfunc redraws the window on Expose events and when the window's contents change. The eventfunc handles other events, such as keyboard and mouse events. The userfunc allows special user-written functions; for example, the pushbutton components execute the userfunc when "pushed" in.

CREATING TOOLKIT WINDOWS

The function CreateToolWindow, below, creates one of our toolkit windows and fills in the relevant ToolWindow structure. You'll note that we have a global array of these structures, called TWArray, and that we have a fixed number of toolkit windows we can create. Real toolkits would call malloc to allocate memory for ToolWindow structures and, therefore, have an unlimited supply of toolkit windows (as unlimited as available virtual memory, that is). CreateToolWindow returns the ID of the new toolkit window. That ID is then used to access values in the ToolWindow structure later. The actual code itself isn't that long:

```
CreateToolWindow( display, parent, x, y, width, height,
        bordercolor, backcolor, event_mask, visual )

Display         *display;
Window          parent;
int             x, y, width, height;
unsigned long   bordercolor;
unsigned long   backcolor;
unsigned long   event_mask;
Visual          *visual;

{       /* CreateToolWindow */
        int      id;
        Window   OpenWindow();
        void     NullDrawFunc();
        void     NullUserFunc();
        void     NullEventFunc();

        /*
         * Check for a free slot
         */
        if ( tool_max_id >= MAX_TOOL_WINDOWS )
              {
```

```
            return( -1 );
            }

        /*
         * Open a window
         */
        id = tool_max_id;

        TWArray[id].window = OpenWindow( display,
                        parent,
                        x, y, width, height,
                        bordercolor,
                        backcolor,
                        event_mask,
                        visual );

        /*
         * Fill in ToolWindow structure.
         */
        if ( TWArray[id].window != (Window) None )
            {
            TWArray[id].display   = display;
            TWArray[id].parent    = parent;
            TWArray[id].width     = width;
            TWArray[id].height    = height;
            TWArray[id].state     = False;     /* not on */
            TWArray[id].group     = 0;
            TWArray[id].drawfunc  = NullDrawFunc;
            TWArray[id].userfunc  = NullUserFunc;
            TWArray[id].eventfunc = NullEventFunc;

            TWArray[id].name[0]   = '\0';

            tool_max_id++;

            /*
             * Don't map window.
             */
            return( id );
            }

        return( -1 );

}       /* CreateToolWindow */
```

HANDLING EVENTS FOR TOOLKIT WINDOWS

The function `ToolEvent` determines in which toolkit window an event occurred. It then calls `DispatchEvent` to send that event to the proper toolkit window. If the event didn't happen in a toolkit window but instead happened in another application window, `ToolEvent` returns `False`. `ToolEvent` returns `True` if it handled the event.

```
ToolEvent( event )

XEvent  *event;

{       /* ToolEvent */
        int      id, i;

        /*
         * Determine which ToolWindow
         * the event occurred in.
         */
        id = (-1);
        for( i = 0; i < tool_max_id; i++ )
              {
              if ( TWArray[i].window ==
                 event->xany.window )
                 {
                 id = i;
                 }
              }

        /*
         * Dispatch event.
         */
        if ( id >= 0 )
              {
              DispatchEvent( id, event );

              /*
               * We handled the event
               */
              return( True );
              }
```

```
        return( False );

}       /* ToolEvent */
```

The function `DispatchEvent` dispatches an event to the proper toolkit window. It sends `Expose` events to the toolkit window's `drawfunc`. All other events go to the toolkit window's `eventfunc`, except for `MappingNotify` events, which are handled here. Keyboard events are converted into the `keysym` and `string`, which are then passed to the toolkit window's `eventfunc`:

```
DispatchEvent( id, event )

int     id;
XEvent  *event;

{       /* DispatchEvent */
        int      done = False;
        char     string[100];
        KeySym   keysym;

        /*
         * Initialize string and keysym
         * to known null values.
         */
        string[0] = '\0';
        keysym = 0x0;

        switch( event->type )
              {
              case Expose:
                  (*TWArray[id].drawfunc)( TWArray[id].display,
                     id, event );
                  break;
              case KeyPress:
                  done = DecodeKeyPress( event,
                        &keysym, string );

              if ( IsMetaQ( event, string ) )
                     {
                     done = True;
                     }
                  /* NOBREAK */
```

```
            case ButtonPress:
            case ButtonRelease:
            case MotionNotify:
               (*TWArray[id].eventfunc)(TWArray[id].display,
                  id, event, keysym, string );
               break;
            case MappingNotify:
               XRefreshKeyboardMapping( event );
               break;
            default:
               (*TWArray[id].eventfunc)(TWArray[id].display,
                  id, event, keysym, string );
            }

        return( done );

}       /* DispatchEvent */
```

CALLBACK FUNCTIONS

We need functions to set up the toolkit window callbacks: `drawfunc`, `eventfunc`, and `userfunc`. The code looks very similar to the code in the previous section. The function `ToolSetUserFunc` follows:

```
ToolSetUserFunc( id, userfunc )

int     id;
void    (*userfunc)();

{       /* ToolSetUserFunc */

        if ( ( id >= 0 ) && ( id < tool_max_id ) )
             {
             TWArray[id].userfunc   = userfunc;
             }

}       /* ToolSetUserFunc */
```

To execute a user callback, then, we use the function `ToolExec`. Each user function is passed just one parameter, the ID of the toolkit window for which the callback was called:

```
ToolExec( id )

int     id;

/*
 *      Executes a ToolWindow callback.
 */

{       /* ToolExec */

        if ( ( id >= 0 ) && ( id < tool_max_id ) )
                {
                (*TWArray[id].userfunc)( id );
                }

}       /* ToolExec */
```

DRAWING CENTERED TEXT IN A TOOLKIT WINDOW

Much of our toolkit deals with pushbuttons, text entry, and displaying static text labels—that is, drawing text. In fact, all these toolkit components need text centered inside the toolkit window. (*Need* is a rather strong word. Our chosen interface style is to center the text. You can, of course, choose any interface style you'd like.)

```
ToolCenterText( id, text )

int     id;
char    text[];

{       /* ToolCenterText */
        int   x, y, width, height;

        if ( ( id >= 0 ) && ( id < tool_max_id ) )
                {
                height = FontHeight( TWArray[id].font );

                width = XTextWidth( TWArray[id].font,
                        text,
                        strlen( text ) );
```

```
        x = ( TWArray[id].width - width ) / 2;
        y = ( TWArray[id].height - height ) / 2 +
           TWArray[id].font->ascent;

        XDrawImageString( TWArray[id].display,
           TWArray[id].window,
           TWArray[id].gc,
           x, y, text, strlen( text ) );
        }

}       /* ToolCenterText */
```

DRAWING 3D BEVELS

To look good, we draw most toolkit windows with a 3D bevel.

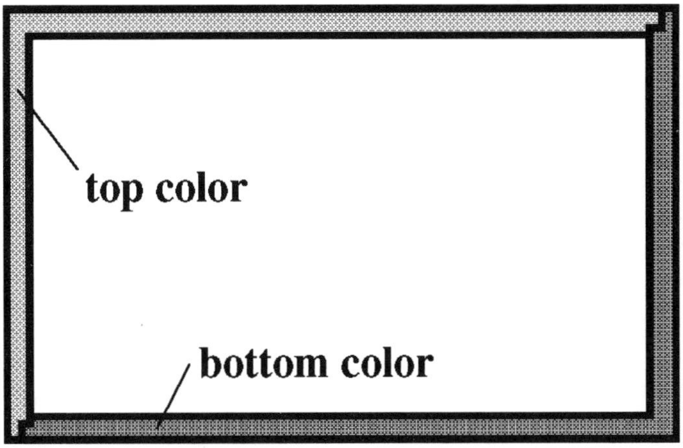

Figure 14.1. A 3D Bevel.

We implement this bevel by drawing two lines along each side of the rectangle. The inner lines are one pixel shorter than the outer lines. Using a top color of `white` and a bottom color of `dimgrey` (with an inside color of `lightgrey`) makes a toolkit window look like it sticks out of the window. Swapping the bevel colors, so that the top is in `dimgrey` and the bottom `white`, makes the toolkit window look like it's pushed in. The function `ToolHighlight` draws the 3D bevel to highlight a toolkit window:

```
ToolHighlight( id, top, bottom )

int             id;
unsigned long   top, bottom;

{       /* ToolHighlight */

        if ( ( id < 0 ) || ( id >= tool_max_id ) )
              {
              return;
              }

        /*
         * Draw Top bevel
         */
        ToolSetForeground( id, top );

        ToolDrawLine( id, 0, 0, TWArray[id].width, 0 );
        ToolDrawLine( id, 0, 1, TWArray[id].width-1, 1 );

        ToolDrawLine( id, 0, 0, 0, TWArray[id].height );
        ToolDrawLine( id, 1, 1, 1, TWArray[id].height-1 );

        /*
         * Draw Bottom Bevel
         */
        ToolSetForeground( id, bottom );

        ToolDrawLine( id, 0, TWArray[id].height,
              TWArray[id].width, TWArray[id].height );
        ToolDrawLine( id, 1, TWArray[id].height-1,
              TWArray[id].width-1, TWArray[id].height-1 );

        ToolDrawLine( id, TWArray[id].width,
              TWArray[id].height,
              TWArray[id].width, 0 );
        ToolDrawLine( id, TWArray[id].width-1,
              TWArray[id].height-1,
              TWArray[id].width-1, 1 );

}       /* ToolHighlight */
```

TOOLKIT ACCESS UTILITY FUNCTIONS

We provide the following utility functions in `toolkit.c`, below, for working with toolkit windows. These functions provide the infrastructure for a small toolkit, and other C files will add specific features, such as pushbutton support and text editing.

Function	***Purpose***
`ToolClear`	Calls XClearWindow on toolkit window.
`ToolDrawLine`	Draws a line in a toolkit window.
`ToolDrawName`	Draws the toolkit window's name, centered.
`ToolGetDisplay`	Gets display pointer for a toolkit window.
`ToolGetGroup`	Gets a toolkit window's group ID.
`ToolGetName`	Gets a toolkit window's name.
`ToolGetState`	Gets a toolkit window's state value.
`ToolGetWindow`	Gets a toolkit window's window ID.
`ToolHighlightGroup`	Draws 3D bevel on all items in a group.
`ToolRedraw`	Redraws toolkit window by called drawfunc.
`ToolSetBackground`	Sets background text color.
`ToolSetFont`	Sets the text font for a toolkit window.
`ToolSetForeground`	Sets foreground drawing color.
`ToolSetFunctions`	Sets the three callback functions.
`ToolSetGC`	Sets the graphics context for a toolkit window.
`ToolSetGroup`	Sets a toolkit window's group ID.
`ToolSetName`	Sets a toolkit window's name.
`ToolSetState`	Sets a toolkit window's state value.

RESIZING TOOLKIT WINDOWS

Sometimes you need to resize a window, and that's what `ToolResize`, below, does. `ToolResize` calls `XResizeWindow`:

```
Display         *display;
Window          window;
unsigned int    new_width, new_height;

XResizeWindow( display, window, new_width, new_height );
```

Note that window managers may intercept the call to resize a window and force that window to have a different size. Window managers will only do this on your application's top-level windows, so you needn't worry about subwindows. Here's `ToolResize`:

```
ToolResize( id, new_width, new_height )

int     id;
int     new_width, new_height;

/*
 *      Changes the size of a ToolWindow.
 */

{       /* ToolResize */

        if ( ( id >= 0 ) && ( id < tool_max_id ) )
             {
             if ( ( TWArray[id].width != new_width ) ||
                ( TWArray[id].height != new_height ) )
                {
                TWArray[id].width = new_width;
                TWArray[id].height = new_height;

                XResizeWindow( TWArray[id].display,
                   TWArray[id].window,
                   TWArray[id].width,
                   TWArray[id].height );
                }
             }

}       /* ToolResize */
```

SOURCE CODE FOR TOOLKIT.C

The file `toolkit.c` contains the infrastructure for our small toolkit:

```
/*
 *      toolkit.c
 *      Source code for a mini X toolkit.
 *
 *      Written for X Window Applications
 *      Programming, 2nd Edition
 */
```

```
#include <X11/Xlib.h>
#include <X11/Xutil.h>

#define MAX_NAME_LEN  80

/*
 *      Structure for our ToolWindow type.
 *      We are essentially building a very
 *      tiny X toolkit here.
 */

typedef struct
        {
        Display     *display;
        Window      parent;
        Window      window;
        GC          gc;          /* usually shared */
        XFontStruct *font;
        int         width, height;
        int         state;       /* used for toggling */
        int         group;       /* used for toggling */
        int         id;
        char        name[ MAX_NAME_LEN + 1 ];
        void        (*drawfunc)();
        void        (*userfunc)();
        void        (*eventfunc)();
        } ToolWindow;

/*
 *      Maximum number of global toolkit windows.
 */
#define MAX_TOOL_WINDOWS  40

/*
 *      Global toolkit windows
 */
static ToolWindow     TWArray[ MAX_TOOL_WINDOWS + 1 ];
static int            tool_max_id = 0;

CreateToolWindow( display, parent, x, y, width, height,
        bordercolor, backcolor, event_mask, visual )
```

```
Display          *display;
Window           parent;
int              x, y, width, height;
unsigned long    bordercolor;
unsigned long    backcolor;
unsigned long    event_mask;
Visual           *visual;

/*
 *      Creates a window and fills
 *      in a ToolWindow structure.
 *      Returns an ID on success,
 *      -1 otherwise.
 */

{       /* CreateToolWindow */
        int      id;
        Window   OpenWindow();
        void     NullDrawFunc();
        void     NullUserFunc();
        void     NullEventFunc();

        /*
         * Check for a free slot
         */
        if ( tool_max_id >= MAX_TOOL_WINDOWS )
              {
              return( -1 );
              }

        /*
         * Open a window
         */
        id = tool_max_id;

        TWArray[id].window = OpenWindow( display,
                                  parent,
                                  x, y, width, height,
                                  bordercolor,
                                  backcolor,
                                  event_mask,
                                  visual );
```

```
        /*
         * Fill in ToolWindow structure.
         */
        if ( TWArray[id].window != (Window) None )
              {
              TWArray[id].display   = display;
              TWArray[id].parent    = parent;
              TWArray[id].width     = width;
              TWArray[id].height    = height;
              TWArray[id].state     = False;     /* not on */
              TWArray[id].group     = 0;
              TWArray[id].drawfunc  = NullDrawFunc;
              TWArray[id].userfunc  = NullUserFunc;
              TWArray[id].eventfunc = NullEventFunc;

              TWArray[id].name[0]   = '\0';

              tool_max_id++;

              /*
               * Don't map window.
               */
              return( id );
              }

        return( -1 );

}       /* CreateToolWindow */

Display *ToolGetDisplay( id )

int     id;

{       /* ToolGetDisplay */

        if ( ( id >= 0 ) && ( id < tool_max_id ) )
              {
              return( TWArray[id].display );
              }
        else
              {
              return( TWArray[0].display );
              }
```

```
}       /* ToolGetDisplay */

Window  ToolGetWindow ( id )

int     id;

{       /* ToolGetWindow */

        if ( ( id >= 0 ) && ( id < tool_max_id ) )
              {
              return( TWArray[id].window );
              }
        else
              {
              return( TWArray[0].window );
              }

}       /* ToolGetWindow */

ToolSetBackground( id, color )

int               id;
unsigned long     color;

{       /* ToolSetBackground */

        if ( ( id >= 0 ) && ( id < tool_max_id ) )
              {
              XSetBackground( TWArray[id].display,
                 TWArray[id].gc,
                 color );
              }

}       /* ToolSetBackground */

ToolSetForeground( id, color )

int               id;
unsigned long     color;

{       /* ToolSetForeground */

        if ( ( id >= 0 ) && ( id < tool_max_id ) )
```

```
                {
                XSetForeground( TWArray[id].display,
                    TWArray[id].gc,
                    color );
                }

}       /* ToolSetForeground */

ToolSetGC( id, gc )

int     id;
GC      gc;

{       /* ToolSetGC */

        if ( ( id >= 0 ) && ( id < tool_max_id ) )
                {
                TWArray[id].gc = gc;
                }

}       /* ToolSetGC */

ToolSetFont( id, font_struct )

int             id;
XFontStruct     *font_struct;

/*
 *      MUST call ToolSetGC() first!
 */

{       /* ToolSetFont */

        if ( ( id >= 0 ) && ( id < tool_max_id ) )
                {
                TWArray[id].font = font_struct;

                XSetFont( TWArray[id].display,
                    TWArray[id].gc,
                    TWArray[id].font->fid );
                }

}       /* ToolSetFont */
```

```
ToolGetGroup( id )

int     id;

{       /* ToolGetGroup */

        if ( ( id >= 0 ) && ( id < tool_max_id ) )
              {
              return( TWArray[id].group );
              }

        return( -1 );

}       /* ToolGetGroup */

ToolSetGroup( id, group )

int     id;
int     group;

{       /* ToolSetGroup */

        if ( ( id >= 0 ) && ( id < tool_max_id ) )
              {
              TWArray[id].group = group;
              }

}       /* ToolSetGroup */

ToolGetState( id )

int     id;

{       /* ToolGetState */

        if ( ( id >= 0 ) && ( id < tool_max_id ) )
              {
              return( TWArray[id].state );
              }

        return( False );
}       /* ToolGetState */
```

```
ToolSetState( id, state )

int     id;
int     state;

{       /* ToolSetState */

        if ( ( id >= 0 ) && ( id < tool_max_id ) )
              {
              TWArray[id].state = state;
              }

}       /* ToolSetState */

ToolGetName( id, name )

int     id;
char    name[];

{       /* ToolGetName */

        if ( ( id >= 0 ) && ( id < tool_max_id ) )
              {
              (void) strcpy( name, TWArray[id].name );
              }
        else
              {
              name[0] = '\0';
              }

}       /* ToolGetName */

ToolSetName( id, name )

int     id;
char    name[];

{       /* ToolSetName */

        if ( ( id >= 0 ) && ( id < tool_max_id ) &&
              ( strlen(name) < MAX_NAME_LEN ) )
              {
              (void) strcpy( TWArray[id].name, name );
              }
```

```
}       /* ToolSetName */

ToolCenterText( id, text )

int     id;
char    text[];

{       /* ToolCenterText */
        int   x, y, width, height;

        if ( ( id >= 0 ) && ( id < tool_max_id ) )
              {
              height = FontHeight( TWArray[id].font );

              width = XTextWidth( TWArray[id].font,
                    text,
                    strlen( text ) );

              x = ( TWArray[id].width - width ) / 2;
              y = ( TWArray[id].height - height ) / 2 +
                 TWArray[id].font->ascent;

              XDrawImageString( TWArray[id].display,
                 TWArray[id].window,
                 TWArray[id].gc,
                 x, y, text, strlen( text ) );
              }

}       /* ToolCenterText */

ToolDrawName( id )

int     id;

/*
 * Draws the ToolWindow name in the
 * center of the window.
 */

{       /* ToolDrawName */
        char  name[ MAX_NAME_LEN + 1 ];

        ToolGetName( id, name );
```

```
        ToolCenterText( id, name );

}       /* ToolDrawName */

ToolSetFunctions( id, drawfunc, eventfunc, userfunc )

int     id;
void    (*drawfunc)();
void    (*eventfunc)();
void    (*userfunc)();

{       /* ToolSetFunctions */

        if ( ( id >= 0 ) && ( id < tool_max_id ) )
              {
              TWArray[id].drawfunc  = drawfunc;
              TWArray[id].eventfunc = eventfunc;
              TWArray[id].userfunc  = userfunc;
              }

}       /* ToolSetFunctions */

ToolSetUserFunc( id, userfunc )

int     id;
void    (*userfunc)();

{       /* ToolSetUserFunc */

        if ( ( id >= 0 ) && ( id < tool_max_id ) )
              {
              TWArray[id].userfunc  = userfunc;
              }

}       /* ToolSetUserFunc */

ToolExec( id )

int     id;

/*
 *      Executes a ToolWindow callback.
 */
```

```
{       /* ToolExec */

        if ( ( id >= 0 ) && ( id < tool_max_id ) )
              {
              (*TWArray[id].userfunc)( id );
              }

}       /* ToolExec */

/* ARGSUSED */
void NullDrawFunc( display, id, event, keysym, string )

Display      *display;
int          id;
XExposeEvent *event;
KeySym       keysym;
char         string[];

{       /* NullDrawFunc */
}       /* NullDrawFunc */

void NullUserFunc( id )

int          id;

{       /* NullUserFunc */
}       /* NullUserFunc */

void NullEventFunc( display, id, event )

Display      *display;
int          id;
XEvent       *event;

{       /* NullEventFunc */
}       /* NullEventFunc */

ToolHighlightGroup( static_id, group, top, bottom )

int             static_id;
int             group;
unsigned long   top, bottom;
```

```
/*
 *      Highlights or unhighlights all
 *      items of a particular group,
 *      EXCEPT for static_id.
 */

{       /* ToolHighlightGroup */
        int   id;

        for( id = 0; id < tool_max_id; id++ )
              {
              if ( ( ToolGetGroup( id ) == group ) &&
                 ( id != static_id ) )
                 {
                 ToolHighlight( id, top, bottom );
                 }
              }

}       /* ToolHighlightGroup */

ToolHighlight( id, top, bottom )

int             id;
unsigned long   top, bottom;

{       /* ToolHighlight */

        if ( ( id < 0 ) || ( id >= tool_max_id ) )
              {
              return;
              }

        /*
         * Draw Top bevel
         */
        ToolSetForeground( id, top );

        ToolDrawLine( id, 0, 0, TWArray[id].width, 0 );
        ToolDrawLine( id, 0, 1, TWArray[id].width-1, 1 );

        ToolDrawLine( id, 0, 0, 0, TWArray[id].height );
        ToolDrawLine( id, 1, 1, 1, TWArray[id].height-1 );
```

```
        /*
         * Draw Bottom Bevel
         */
        ToolSetForeground( id, bottom );

        ToolDrawLine( id, 0, TWArray[id].height,
              TWArray[id].width, TWArray[id].height );
        ToolDrawLine( id, 1, TWArray[id].height-1,
              TWArray[id].width-1, TWArray[id].height-1 );

        ToolDrawLine( id, TWArray[id].width,
              TWArray[id].height,
              TWArray[id].width, 0 );
        ToolDrawLine( id, TWArray[id].width-1,
              TWArray[id].height-1,
              TWArray[id].width-1, 1 );

}       /* ToolHighlight */

ToolDrawLine( id, x1, y1, x2, y2 )

int     id;
int     x1, y1, x2, y2;

{       /* ToolDrawLine */

        if ( ( id >= 0 ) && ( id < tool_max_id ) )
              {
              XDrawLine( TWArray[id].display,
                 TWArray[id].window,
                 TWArray[id].gc,
                 x1, y1, x2, y2 );
              }

}       /* ToolDrawLine */

ToolClear( id )

int     id;

/*
 *      Clears a ToolWindow
 */
```

```
{       /* ToolClear */

        if ( ( id >= 0 ) && ( id < tool_max_id ) )
              {
              XClearWindow( TWArray[id].display,
                 TWArray[id].window );
              }

}       /* ToolClear */

ToolRedraw( id )

int     id;

/*
 *      Redraws ToolWindow contents.
 */

{       /* ToolRedraw */
        XEvent      event;

        if ( ( id >= 0 ) && ( id < tool_max_id ) )
              {
              event.type = Expose;

              event.xexpose.x = 0;
              event.xexpose.y = 0;
              event.xexpose.width = TWArray[id].width;
              event.xexpose.height = TWArray[id].height;

              event.xexpose.count = 0;

              DispatchEvent( id, &event );
              }

}       /* ToolRedraw */

ToolResize( id, new_width, new_height )

int     id;
int     new_width, new_height;
```

```
/*
 *      Changes the size of a ToolWindow.
 */

{       /* ToolResize */

        if ( ( id >= 0 ) && ( id < tool_max_id ) )
              {
              if ( ( TWArray[id].width != new_width ) ||
                 ( TWArray[id].height != new_height ) )
                 {
                 TWArray[id].width = new_width;
                 TWArray[id].height = new_height;

                 XResizeWindow( TWArray[id].display,
                    TWArray[id].window,
                    TWArray[id].width,
                    TWArray[id].height );
                 }
              }

}       /* ToolResize */

ToolEvent( event )

XEvent  *event;

{       /* ToolEvent */
        int      id, i;

        /*
         * Determine which ToolWindow
         * the event occurred in.
         */
        id = (-1);
        for( i = 0; i < tool_max_id; i++ )
              {
              if ( TWArray[i].window ==
                 event->xany.window )
                 {
                 id = i;
                 }
              }
```

```
        /*
         * Dispatch event.
         */
        if ( id >= 0 )
              {
              DispatchEvent( id, event );

              /*
               * We handled the event
               */
              return( True );
              }

        return( False );

}       /* ToolEvent */

DispatchEvent( id, event )

int           id;
XEvent  *event;

{       /* DispatchEvent */
        int      done = False;
        char     string[100];
        KeySym   keysym;

        /*
         * Initialize string and keysym
         * to known null values.
         */
        string[0] = '\0';
        keysym = 0x0;

        switch( event->type )
              {
              case Expose:
                 (*TWArray[id].drawfunc)( TWArray[id].display,
                    id, event );
                 break;
              case KeyPress:
                 done = DecodeKeyPress( event,
                       &keysym, string );
```

```
                if ( IsMetaQ( event, string ) )
                    {
                    done = True;
                    }
                /* NOBREAK */
            case ButtonPress:
            case ButtonRelease:
            case MotionNotify:
                (*TWArray[id].eventfunc)(TWArray[id].display,
                    id, event, keysym, string );
                break;
            case MappingNotify:
                XRefreshKeyboardMapping( event );
                break;
            default:
                (*TWArray[id].eventfunc)(TWArray[id].display,
                    id, event, keysym, string );
            }

        return( done );

}       /* DispatchEvent */

/* end of file toolkit.c */
```

CREATING STATIC TEXT LABELS FROM TOOLKIT WINDOWS

The simplest component we'll add to our small toolkit is a static text label. This label just contains a text message, centered in the toolkit window. This message could be a file name, a prompt or some other text string. We store the text in the name field of the `ToolWindow` structure, above. That way, we can change the text message by calling `ToolSetName`. The only events the text labels handle are `Expose` events.

```
/*
 *      label.c
 *      Label windows for the mini toolkit.
 *
 *      Written for X Window Applications
```

```
 *      Programming, 2nd Edition
 */

#include <X11/Xlib.h>

#define LABEL_EV_MASK  ExposureMask

extern unsigned long  black, lightgrey;

CreateTextLabel( display, parent, x, y, width, height,
        gc, font_struct, label )

Display         *display;
Window          parent;
int             x, y, width, height;
GC              gc;
XFontStruct     *font_struct;
char            label[];

{       /* CreateTextLabel */
        Visual          *visual = CopyFromParent;
        void            LabelDraw();
        extern void     NullEventFunc();
        extern void     NullUserFunc();
        int             id;

        id = CreateToolWindow( display,
                parent,
                x, y, width, height,
                lightgrey, lightgrey,
                LABEL_EV_MASK, visual );

        if ( id >= 0 )
              {
              ToolSetName( id, label );

              ToolSetGC( id, gc );
              ToolSetForeground( id, black );
              ToolSetBackground( id, lightgrey );
              ToolSetFont( id, font_struct );

              ToolSetGroup( id, -999 );
```

```
                ToolSetFunctions( id,
                    LabelDraw,
                    NullEventFunc,
                    NullUserFunc );
                }

        return( id );

}       /* CreateTextLabel */

/* ARGSUSED */
void LabelDraw( display, id, event )

Display      *display;
int          id;
XExposeEvent *event;

{       /* LabelDraw */

        if ( event->count != 0 )
               {
               return;
               }

        /*
         * Draw text
         */
        ToolSetForeground( id, black );
        ToolDrawName( id );

}       /* LabelDraw */

/* end of file label.c */
```

CREATING PUSHBUTTON TOOLKIT WINDOWS

We can extend the idea of static text labels to create pushbuttons. Pushbuttons push *in* when the user clicks a mouse button in the toolkit window then execute a user function. When the user function is complete, the pushbutton pushes back *out*, to provide feedback to the user that the task is done. We'll use pushbuttons in the Draw application to provide Quit, Save, and Wipe Out pushbuttons.

We create a pushbutton with `CreatePushButton`, which looks a lot like `CreateTextLabel`, above.

When a `ButtonPress` event arrives, the 3D bevel on the pushbutton is reversed, to make a pushed-in effect. Then `ToolExec` executes the `userfunc` callback function, and, finally, the 3D bevel is restored so that the pushbutton looks pushed out, which is its normal state.

SOURCE CODE FOR PUSHB.C

The file `pushb.c` adds pushbuttons to our small toolkit:

```
/*
 *      pushb.c
 *      Routines for creating "PushButtons"
 *      Uses the features of the mini
 *      toolkit in toolkit.c.
 *
 *      Written for X Window Applications
 *      Programming, 2nd Edition
 */

#include  <X11/Xlib.h>

#define PUSH_EV_MASK   (ButtonPressMask | \
                        ExposureMask)

extern unsigned long  dimgrey, lightgrey, black, white;

CreatePushButton( display, parent, x, y, width, height,
        gc, font_struct, name, callback )

Display       *display;
Window        parent;
int           x, y, width, height;
GC            gc;
XFontStruct   *font_struct;
char          name[];
void          (*callback)();
```

```
{       /* CreatePushButton */
        Visual   *visual = CopyFromParent;
        void     PushButtonDraw();
        void     PushButtonEvent();
        int      id;

        id = CreateToolWindow( display, parent,
                 x, y, width, height,
                 lightgrey, lightgrey,
                 PUSH_EV_MASK, visual );

        if ( id >= 0 )
             {
             ToolSetName( id, name );

             ToolSetGC( id, gc );
             ToolSetForeground( id, black );
             ToolSetBackground( id, lightgrey );
             ToolSetFont( id, font_struct );

             ToolSetFunctions( id,
                PushButtonDraw,
                PushButtonEvent,
                callback );
             }

        return( id );

}       /* CreatePushButton */

/* ARGSUSED */
void PushButtonEvent( display, id, event, keysym, string )

Display      *display;
int          id;
XEvent       *event;
KeySym       keysym;
char         string[];

{       /* PushButtonEvent */

        /*
         * Unhighlight all members
```

```
         * of the group.
         */
        ToolHighlightGroup( id,
              ToolGetGroup( id ),
              white, dimgrey );

        /*
         * Highlight this item.
         */
        ToolSetState( id, True );

        ToolHighlight( id, dimgrey, white );
        XFlush( display );

        /*
         * Execute user callback
         */
        ToolExec( id );

}       /* PushButtonEvent */

/* ARGSUSED */
void PushButtonDraw( display, id, event )

Display      *display;
int          id;
XExposeEvent *event;

{       /* PushButtonDraw */

        if ( event->count != 0 )
              {
              return;
              }

        /*
         * Draw 3D border, based on state.
         */
        if ( ToolGetState( id ) == True )
              {
              ToolHighlight( id, dimgrey, white );
              }
        else
```

```
                {
                ToolHighlight( id, white, dimgrey );
                }

        /*
         * Draw text
         */
        ToolSetForeground( id, black );
        ToolDrawName( id );

}       /* PushButtonDraw */

UnhighlightPushButton( id )

int     id;

{       /* UnhighlightPushButton */

        ToolSetState( id, False );

        ToolHighlight( id, white, dimgrey );

}       /* UnhighlightPushButton */

/* end of file pushb.c */
```

EDITING TEXT IN TOOLKIT WINDOWS

A very common need for a toolkit is some sort of text-entry widget, allowing the user to type in a file name and handle prompted text input. We call such a widget in our small toolkit a *text-entry widget*. The function `TextEntryEvent`, below, handles the task of editing a string. The actual contents of the string are stored in the name field of the `ToolWindow` structure, through the utility functions `ToolGetName` and `ToolSetName`.

The simple editing function checks keyboard events to see if the returned `keysym` is a printable character and, if so, appends it onto the edited string. On delete and backspace events, the last character is removed. When the return key is pressed, the user callback is executed via `ToolExec`. In a real toolkit, the left and right arrows (`XK_Right` and `XK_Left`) would move an editing cursor and provide a much better text-editing interface. This callback function should handle the completed text entry:

```
void TextEntryEvent( display, id, event, keysym, string )

Display       *display;
int           id;
XEvent        *event;
KeySym        keysym;
char          string[];

{       /* TextEntryEvent */
        int   length;
        char  name[200];

        /*
         * Get current text
         */
        ToolGetName( id, name );

        if ( keysym < 255 )
              {
              if ( isprint( keysym ) )
                 {
                 (void) strcat( name, string );

                 ToolSetName( id, name );

                 ToolSetForeground( id, black );
                 ToolDrawName( id );
                 }
              }
        else
              {
              switch( keysym )
                 {
                 case XK_Return:
                    ToolExec( id );
                    break;
                 case XK_Delete:
                 case XK_BackSpace:
                    length = strlen( name );

                    if ( length > 0 )
                       {
                       length--;
                       name[length] = '\0';
```

```
                    ToolSetName( id, name );

                    ToolClear( id );

                    ToolHighlight( id,
                       dimgrey, white );

                    ToolSetForeground( id,
                       black );
                    ToolDrawName( id );
                    }
                 break;
              }
           }

}       /* TextEntryEvent */
```

BUILDING TEXT-ENTRY TOOLKIT WINDOWS

The function `CreateTextEntry`, in the file `entry.c`, below, creates a text-entry widget. `TextEntryDraw` redraws the current string, centering the string in the toolkit window. This code is fairly simple, as it just builds on the code in `toolkit.c`.

SOURCE CODE FOR ENTRY.C

```
/*
 *      entry.c
 *      Routines for creating Text Entry Fields
 *      Uses the features of the mini
 *      toolkit in toolkit.c.
 *
 *      Written for X Window Applications
 *      Programming, 2nd Edition
 */

#include  <stdio.h>
#include  <ctype.h>
```

```
#include  <X11/Xlib.h>
#include  <X11/keysym.h>
#include  <X11/keysymdef.h>

#define ENTRY_EV_MASK  (KeyPressMask | ExposureMask)

extern unsigned long  dimgrey, lightgrey, black, white;

CreateTextEntry( display, parent, x, y, width, height,
       gc, font_struct, name, callback )

Display         *display;
Window          parent;
int             x, y, width, height;
GC              gc;
XFontStruct     *font_struct;
char            name[];
void            (*callback)();

/*
 *      Creates a text entry field.
 */

{       /* CreateTextEntry */
        Visual   *visual = CopyFromParent;
        void     TextEntryDraw();
        void     TextEntryEvent();
        int      id;

        id = CreateToolWindow( display, parent,
                 x, y, width, height,
                 lightgrey, lightgrey,
                 ENTRY_EV_MASK, visual );

        if ( id >= 0 )
             {
             ToolSetName( id, name );

             ToolSetGC( id, gc );

             ToolSetForeground( id, black );
             ToolSetBackground( id, lightgrey );
```

```
            ToolSetFont( id, font_struct );

            ToolSetGroup( id, (-97) );

            ToolSetFunctions( id,
               TextEntryDraw,
               TextEntryEvent,
               callback );
            }

        return( id );

}       /* CreateTextEntry */

/* ARGSUSED */
void TextEntryEvent( display, id, event, keysym, string )

Display         *display;
int             id;
XEvent          *event;
KeySym          keysym;
char            string[];

{       /* TextEntryEvent */
        int   length;
        char  name[200];

        /*
         * Get current text
         */
        ToolGetName( id, name );

        if ( keysym < 255 )
             {
             if ( isprint( keysym ) )
                {
                (void) strcat( name, string );

                ToolSetName( id, name );

                ToolSetForeground( id, black );
                ToolDrawName( id );
                }
```

```
               }
        else
               {
               switch( keysym )
                  {
                  case XK_Return:
                     ToolExec( id );
                     break;
                  case XK_Delete:
                  case XK_BackSpace:
                     length = strlen( name );

                     if ( length > 0 )
                        {
                        length--;
                        name[length] = '\0';

                        ToolSetName( id, name );

                        ToolClear( id );

                        ToolHighlight( id,
                           dimgrey, white );

                        ToolSetForeground( id,
                           black );
                        ToolDrawName( id );
                        }
                     break;
                  }
               }

}       /* TextEntryEvent */

/* ARGSUSED */
void TextEntryDraw( display, id, event )

Display          *display;
int              id;
XExposeEvent     *event;

{       /* TextEntryDraw */
```

```
        if ( event->count != 0 )
              {
              return;
              }

        /*
         * Draw 3D border, based on state.
         */
        ToolHighlight( id, dimgrey, white );

        /*
         * Draw text
         */
        ToolSetForeground( id, black );
        ToolDrawName( id );

}       /* TextEntryDraw */

/* end of file entry.c */
```

ENHANCING OUR TOOLKIT

With our small toolkit, we're not trying to put the Open Software Foundation's Motif toolkit out of business. Instead, we're trying to show why toolkits are popular and how one could go about designing one. Obviously, a full-fledged toolkit would provide a lot more than our small example, including:

- Geometry managers to handle window resizes. One way to do this would be to resize all toolkit windows so that they still extend across an application's main window, whether the main window was shrunk or enlarged.
- Child toolkit windows. Our toolkit really doesn't handle the idea of child windows.
- The ability to create and destroy toolkit windows on the fly. We can create them any time, but there are no destroy functions.
- Allow an unlimited number of toolkit windows, instead of the fixed array of `ToolWindow` structures.
- Provide better text-handling capabilities.

MORE EFFICIENT TOOLKITS

This chapter outlines a very small toolkit for writing X applications. Most commercial X toolkits are much larger in size and scope. We'll cover two of these toolkits in Section IV.

Many commercial X toolkits are showing problems when creating a large number of toolkit windows, usually called *widgets* in the X vernacular. What toolkit designers found was that creating one window per widget resulted in a great many windows that tend to eat up memory in the X server. Because of this, commercial toolkits added lightweight widgets, much like operating systems are adding lightweight tasks (often called *threads*). The Motif toolkit's lightweight widgets are called *gadgets*. The Open Look toolkit's lightweight widgets are called *flat widgets*.

SUMMARY

In this chapter we created an admittedly limited X Window toolkit. While not posing any threat to the OSF's Motif toolkit, our toolkit accomplishes some modest goals, mostly related to text input.

XLIB FUNCTIONS AND MACROS INTRODUCED IN THIS CHAPTER

`XResizeWindow`

Chapter 15

POP-UP DIALOGS AND TRANSIENT WINDOWS

A pop-up window pops up for a short period of time and is used for menus, dialogs, warning messages, or requests for data from the user.

A dialog box typically handles a dialog with the user, where the application asks the user to enter in a piece of data. In this case, the Draw application asks the user to enter in the name of a bitmap file to load.

In the dialog box described here, the user types in the name of the file to be loaded and then presses a mouse button in either the `OK` or `Cancel` areas. A press in the `Cancel` cancels the operation, and no file will be loaded. A press in the `OK` area signals the application to load in the new file. Pressing the Return key or the Escape key also acts like the `OK` and `Cancel` buttons, respectively.

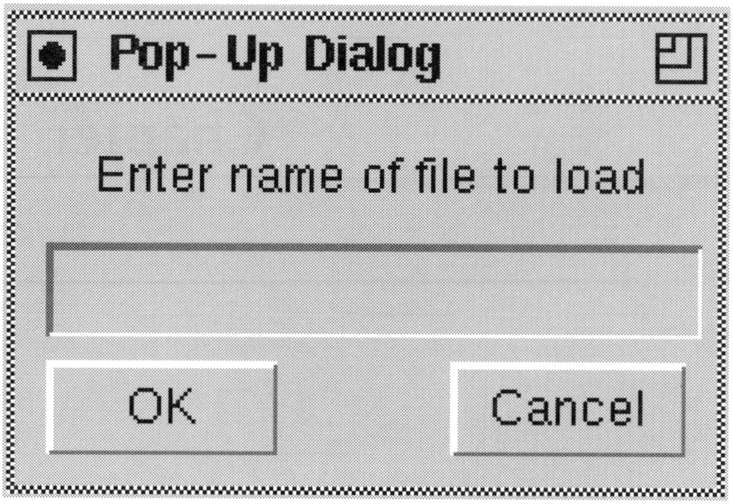

Figure 15.1. The File Dialog Box.

Pop-up windows are meant to appear as instantly as possible, as well as near as possible to the area of interest on the screen, even though the exact area of interest may be impossible to determine.

Pop-up windows should be small, because larger windows may take more time to appear and will certainly take more time to disappear, if you count the time to refresh the display. There are two main types of pop-up window in X: *transient* windows and *override-redirect* windows. We discussed override-redirect windows in Chapter 2. These windows should be used for quick pop-up menus. Pop-up dialog boxes, which normally remain on the screen for a longer time, should be transient windows.

Setting up a pop-up dialog in X is rather easy. You create the window just like any other window but tell the window manager that your new window is a transient window connected to your application's main window. This is done by calling `XSetTransientForHint`.

HINTING ABOUT TRANSIENT WINDOWS

X seems to like a lot of hinting, rather than requiring you to come right out and say something. In most cases, though, the hints are really *hints*, and the X server or the window manager has the option of taking the hint or not.

In X, you can set a property for a window that specifies the window is a transient window. A transient window is expected to remain only for a short time. Some window managers may treat transient windows differently than normal windows and supply different decorations around the window. For example, many window managers don't allow transient windows to be iconified—you iconify the main window instead, and all transients follow. The goal is to make all transient windows share the window manager's look and feel for transient windows. That way, the user is presented with a consistent look and feel across many applications. Of course, this lofty goal is easier said than done, especially with competing interface standards.

`XSetTransientForHint` tells an X window manager that the new window will be around only for a short time (we hope) and is a transient window for a given application. Window managers may decorate transient windows differently than normal application windows:

```
Display      *display;
Window       dialog_transient;
Window       application_top_level_window;

XSetTransientForHint( display, dialog_transient,
             application_top_level_window );
```

The `dialog_transient` is the dialog main window. The `application_top_level_window` is one of your application's top-level windows. `XSetTransientForHint` associates the transient window with your application's top-level window.

It's a good idea to set the `transient-for` hint for any larger dialog box or other pop-up window you use (pop-up selections, pop-up help, etc.). Menus, in particular, should appear instantly on the screen and don't really need title bars. In addition, some window managers may mandate that no top-level windows overlap. Pop-up menus wouldn't look good if they couldn't overlap the main application window—yet another reason to use `override_redirect` for pop-up menus.

SOURCE CODE FOR TRANWIND.C

The function `CreateTransientWindow`, in `tranwind.c`, below, creates a top-level transient window. Note that we don't set all the same hints for transient windows that we do for regular application top-level windows, but we do set most of them.

```
/*
 *      tranwind.c
 *      Pop-up Transient Windows for
 *      the Draw Application.
 *
 *      Written for X Window Applications
 *      Programming, 2nd Edition
 */

#include  <X11/Xlib.h>

Window CreateTransientWindow( display, parent, owner,
        x, y, width, height, border, backcolor,
        event_mask, visual, colormap, app_name, wind_name )

Display         *display;
Window          parent;  /* typically root window */
Window          owner;   /* main application window */
int             x, y, width, height;
unsigned long   border, backcolor;
unsigned long   event_mask;
Visual          *visual;
Colormap        colormap;
char            app_name[];
char            wind_name[];

/*
 *      Creates a transient window, used for pop-up dialogs.
 */

{       /* CreateTransientWindow */
        Window     window;
        Window     OpenWindow();

        window = OpenWindow( display, parent,
                x, y, width, height,
                border, backcolor,
                event_mask,
                visual );

        if ( window != (Window) None )
             {
```

```
                /*
                 * Set transient window properties.
                 */
                XSetTransientForHint( display,
                   window, owner );

                SetStandardHints( display, window,
                   app_name, wind_name,
                   x, y, width, height );

                /*
                 * Just in case the colormap is not
                 * associated with the new window
                 * or its parent.
                 */
                XSetWindowColormap( display, window,
                   colormap );

                XSetWindowBackground( display, window,
                   backcolor );
                }

        return( window );

}       /* CreateTransientWindow */

/* end of file tranwind.c */
```

FINDING THE MOUSE POINTER LOCATION

In the Draw application, the user can ask the program to load another bitmap file for editing. The user does this by pressing a mouse button over the load choice in the list of command pushbuttons. When that happens, the application pops up a dialog window to get the name of the file the user wants loaded. The program asks the X server where the mouse pointer is currently located and then pops up the dialog window so that the mouse pointer is within the dialog window. The assumption here is that the mouse pointer is located near the area in which the user is currently interested. (If the system isn't too slow, this area should be over the load pushbutton.)

The Draw application could pop up the window anywhere on the screen and move the mouse into the window (called *warping the mouse* in X vernacular), but in general it is a bad idea to warp the mouse anywhere. Warping the mouse is unexpected and tends to confuse the user.

There are certain times, though, when you might want to warp the mouse pointer. One such time could be in a program that allows users to zoom a window up to full-screen size and unzoom the window later on. In this case, it might be easier on the user to have the mouse automatically follow the window, and remain in the same relative location in the window as the mouse was before the window was zoomed or unzoomed.

To move, or warp, the mouse pointer on the screen, use the Xlib function `XWarpPointer`:

```
Display         *display;
Window          src_window, dest_window;
int             src_x, src_y;
unsigned int    src_width, src_height;
int             dest_x, dest_y;

XWarpPointer( display, src_window, dest_window,
        src_x, src_y, src_width, src_height,
        dest_x, dest_y );
```

Looking at all the parameters to XWarpPointer and knowing X like we all do, you would expect the parameters to take on a host of different meanings in different conditions, right? Right.

The simplest way to use `XWarpPointer` is to set `dest_window` to the root window. Then, `dest_x` and `dest_y` are global coordinates and specify the new mouse location. This is a lot easier than messing with all the options. Also set `src_window` to `None`, so that the source coordinates are ignored and the mouse is warped no matter what.

The `dest_window` is the destination window. It can be `None`. If `dest_window` is `None`, then the `dest_x` and `dest_y` are taken to mean move offsets relative to the current position of the pointer.

The `src_window` is the source window. If `src_window` is an actual window ID and not `None`, then `XWarpPointer` will work only if the mouse is within the rectangle starting at `src_x`, `src_y` and with size `src_width` and `src_height`. (`XWarpPointer` should actually be called `XMaybeWarpPointer`.) A `src_width` of `0` specifies that the whole width of the window is to be used (this is handy if you don't know how wide the window is). Similarly, a `src_height` of 0 specifies using the whole height of the window.

If `src_window` is `None`, then it doesn't matter where the mouse is—it will be moved to the new location.

If all this doesn't make any sense, it's probably meant to be that way, because the designers of X really don't want you to use `XWarpPointer`. Ever.

If you do warp the mouse, though, you should have a pretty good idea where the mouse coordinates are (the location you warped the mouse to). If you haven't just warped the mouse and need to find out where the mouse pointer is located, use `XQueryPointer`:

```
int             status, screen;
Window          rootwindow, childwindow;
int             rootx, rooty;
int             childx, childy;
unsigned int    button_state;

screen = DefaultScreen( display );

status = XQueryPointer( display,
             RootWindow( display, screen ),
             &rootwindow,       /* RETURN */
             &childwindow,      /* RETURN */
             &rootx, &rooty,    /* RETURN */
             &childx, &childy,  /* RETURN */
             &button_state );   /* RETURN */

if( status == True )
        {
        /* pointer is on screen */
        }
```

This returns information about the current pointer location. `rootwindow` is the root window the pointer is in; `childwindow` is the ID of any subwindow below the window that the pointer is in. `rootx, rooty` is the location relative to `rootwindow`; `childx, childy` is the location relative to the window. The `button_state` mask contains the state of the pointer buttons and any modifier keys, such as the Control, Shift, and Caps Lock keys. This is the same as the `state` field in an `XButtonPressEvent` structure.

XQueryPointer returns a status of True if the mouse pointer is on the same screen as the window we passed—in this case the root Window X. Otherwise, it returns False and most of the values will not be valid, except for rootwindow, rootx, and rooty.

If XQueryPointer returns True, the coordinates childx and childy contain the mouse pointer location with respect to the childwindow.

In the code below, the function QueryPointer finds the global mouse coordinates, relative to the root window for the display. QueryPointer doesn't worry about child windows or coordinates; it just concerns itself with the root window's coordinate space, which is the global coordinate space for a given screen.

SOURCE CODE FOR QUERY.C

The QueryPointer function is contained in query.c:

```
/*
 *      query.c
 *      Queries current mouse pointer location.
 *
 *      Written for X Window Applications
 *      Programming, 2nd Edition
 */

#include  <X11/Xlib.h>

QueryPointer( display, x, y )

Display *display;
int          *x, *y;     /* RETURN */

/*
 *      Convenience routine that sits over
 *      XQueryPointer. Returns the current
 *      location of the mouse pointer in
 *      global coordinates.
 */
```

```
{       /* QueryPointer */
        int             status, screen;
        Window          rootwindow, childwindow;
        int             rootx, rooty;
        int             childx, childy;
        unsigned int    button_state;

        screen = DefaultScreen( display );

        status = XQueryPointer( display,
                    RootWindow( display, screen ),
                    &rootwindow,            /* RETURN */
                    &childwindow,           /* RETURN */
                    &rootx, &rooty,         /* RETURN */
                    &childx, &childy,       /* RETURN */
                    &button_state );        /* RETURN */

        if( status == True )
              {
              *x = rootx;
              *y = rooty;
              }
        else
              {
              *x = 0;
              *y = 0;
              }

}       /* QueryPointer */

/* end of file query.c */
```

IMPLEMENTING THE DIALOG BOX

After determining the mouse coordinates, the Draw application pops up a dialog box window to ask the user to enter a filename. The function `CreateDialog` in `dialog.c`, below, creates a transient window for a dialog and then creates a number of toolkit windows. `CreateDialog` creates two pushbuttons (`OK` and `Cancel`), a text label (for the prompt), and a text entry toolkit window.

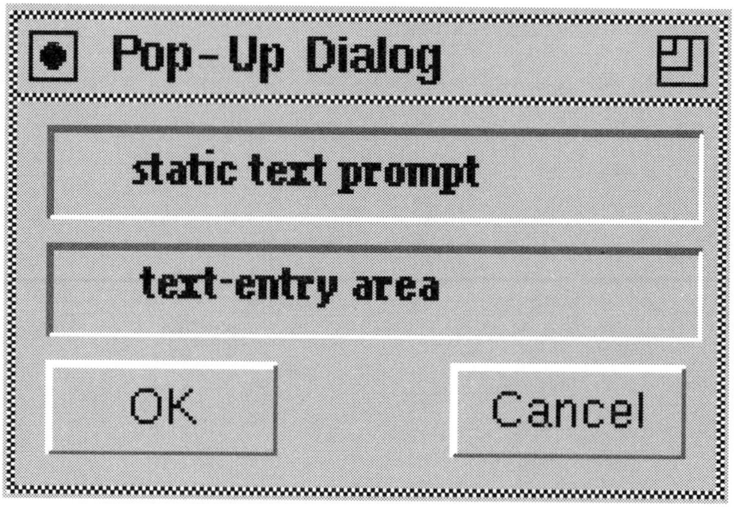

Figure 15.2. The Dialog Windows.

POPPING UP AND POPPING DOWN DIALOGS

We keep the top-level dialog transient window ID stored in a global variable, `dialog_window`. This means that we can only have one pop-up dialog on screen at a time in our application, but that's fine (at least for now). What we can do is pop up and pop down the dialog. We do this by mapping and unmapping the dialog's transient window, stored in the global `dialog_window`.

We can pop up the dialog with the following code after the dialog and its windows have been created:

```
void PopUpDialog()

{       /* PopUpDialog */
        Display  *display;
        Display  *ToolGetDisplay();
        int      x, y;

        if ( ( dialog_window != (Window) None ) &&
             ( dialog_up == False ) )
             {
             display = ToolGetDisplay( 0 );
```

```
            /*
             * Move window to current
             * pointer location.
             */
            QueryPointer( display, &x, &y );
            XMoveWindow( display, dialog_window, x, y );

            /*
             * Map window to screen.
             */
            XMapRaised( display, dialog_window );
            XMapSubwindows( display, dialog_window );

            XFlush( display );

            dialog_up = True;
            }

}       /* PopUpDialog */
```

We introduced two new functions inside `PopUpDialog`. `XMapSubwindows` maps all subwindows—or child windows—of a given window:

```
Display       *display;
Window        dialog_window;

XMapSubwindows( display, dialog_window );
```

`XMoveWindow` moves a window's location on the screen. Note that we move the window before it is mapped or visible to avoid any delay while a visible window is moved. Thus the window will just pop up on the screen in a new position:

```
Display       *display;
Window        dialog_window;
int           x, y;

XMoveWindow( display, dialog_window, x, y );
```

We can then pop down the dialog, after the user has entered a file name or canceled the operation, with the following code:

```
void PopDownDialog( id )

int     id;
```

```
/*
 *      id is ignored.
 */

{       /* PopDownDialog */
        Display     *display;
        Display     *ToolGetDisplay();

        if ( id >= 0 )
             {
             UnhighlightPushButton( id );
             }

        if ( ( dialog_window != (Window) None ) &&
             ( dialog_up == True ) )
             {
             display = ToolGetDisplay( id );

             XUnmapWindow( display, dialog_window );
             XFlush( display );

             dialog_up = False;
             }

}       /* PopDownDialog */
```

We don't destroy the dialog windows when we pop them down, as creating windows takes a (relatively) long time. If we pop up the dialog once, chances are we'll pop it up again, so we cache the dialog's windows. The next time the dialog appears, it may have a different prompt and purpose, but the actual look and feel of the dialog remains the same.

SOURCE CODE FOR DIALOG.C

The file `dialog.c` contains a number of functions for creating and managing pop-up dialogs:

```
/*
 *      dialog.c
 *      Pop-up dialogs for the Draw Application.
 *      Written for X Window Applications
```

```
 *      Programming, 2nd Edition
 */

#include  <X11/Xlib.h>

/*
 *      Dialog globals: window and ToolWindow IDs
 */
Window          dialog_window = (Window) None;
int             dial1_button = (-1), dial2_button = (-1);
int             dial_label = (-1);
int             dial_edit = (-1);
int             dialog_up = False;

/*
 *      external globals
 */
unsigned long   black, white, lightgrey;

#define BUTTON_WIDTH    60

Window CreateDialog( display, parent, owner, visual, colormap,
        font_struct, app_name, prompt, callback )

Display         *display;
Window          parent;
Window          owner;
Visual          *visual;
Colormap        colormap;
XFontStruct     *font_struct;
char            app_name[];
char            prompt[];
void            (*callback)();

/*
 *      Finds the mouse cursor and places the
 *      dialog window there.
 */

{       /* CreateDialog */
        int           x, y, width, height;
        Window        window;
        Window        CreateTransientWindow();
```

```
GC          gc;
GC          CreateGC();
void        PopDownDialog();
int         button_height;

/*
 * Determine location of pointer
 */
QueryPointer( display, &x, &y );

width = BUTTON_WIDTH * 3;
height = FontHeight( font_struct ) * 7;

/*
 * Create transient window
 * for dialog.
 */
window = CreateTransientWindow( display,
        parent, owner,
        x, y, width, height,
        black, lightgrey,
        KeyPressMask,       /* no event mask */
        visual, colormap,
        app_name, "Pop-Up Dialog" );

/*
 * Create a GC
 */
gc = CreateGC( display, window, black, white );

XSetFont( display, gc, font_struct->fid );

/*
 * Create label for prompt
 */
button_height = FontHeight( font_struct ) + 10;

dial_label = CreateTextLabel( display, window,
        6, 5,
        width - 12, button_height,
        gc, font_struct, prompt );

/*
 * Create edit area for
```

```
         * entering data.
         */
        dial_edit = CreateTextEntry( display, window,
                    6, button_height + 10,
                    width - 12, button_height,
                    gc, font_struct,
                    "", callback );

        /*
         * Create pushbuttons
         */
        dial1_button = CreatePushButton( display, window,
                    6,
                    height - button_height - 10,
                    BUTTON_WIDTH, button_height,
                    gc, font_struct,
                    "OK", callback );

        dial2_button = CreatePushButton( display, window,
                    width - BUTTON_WIDTH - 10,
                    height - button_height - 10,
                    BUTTON_WIDTH, button_height,
                    gc, font_struct,
                    "Cancel", PopDownDialog );

        dialog_window = window;

        return( window );

}       /* CreateDialog */

void PopDownDialog( id )

int     id;

/*
 *      id is ignored.
 */

{       /* PopDownDialog */
        Display     *display;
        Display     *ToolGetDisplay();
```

```
        if ( id >= 0 )
              {
              UnhighlightPushButton( id );
              }

        if ( ( dialog_window != (Window) None ) &&
              ( dialog_up == True ) )
              {
              display = ToolGetDisplay( id );

              XUnmapWindow( display, dialog_window );
              XFlush( display );

        dialog_up = False;
        }

}       /* PopDownDialog */

void PopUpDialog()

{       /* PopUpDialog */
        Display     *display;
        Display     *ToolGetDisplay();
        int         x, y;

        if ( ( dialog_window != (Window) None ) &&
              ( dialog_up == False ) )
              {
              display = ToolGetDisplay( 0 );

              /*
               * Move window to current
               * pointer location.
               */
              QueryPointer( display, &x, &y );
              XMoveWindow( display, dialog_window, x, y );

              /*
               * Map window to screen.
               */
              XMapRaised( display, dialog_window );
              XMapSubwindows( display, dialog_window );
```

```
                XFlush( display );

                dialog_up = True;
                }

}       /* PopUpDialog */

GetDialogData( data )

char            data[];

{       /* GetDialogData */

        if ( dial_edit >= 0 )
                {
                ToolGetName( dial_edit, data );
                }

}       /* GetDialogData */

SetDialogCallback( callback )

void    (*callback)();

{       /* SetDialogCallback */

        /*
         * Set up callback for both
         * "OK" pushbutton and
         * text entry field.
         */
        if ( dial1_button >= 0 )
                {
                ToolSetUserFunc( dial1_button, callback );
                }

        if ( dial_edit >= 0 )
                {
                ToolSetUserFunc( dial_edit, callback );
                }

}       /* SetDialogCallback */
```

```
SetDialogCancelCallback( callback )

void    (*callback)();

{       /* SetDialogCancelCallback */

        if ( dial2_button >= 0 )
              {
              ToolSetUserFunc( dial2_button, callback );
              }

}       /* SetDialogCancelCallback */

SetDialogData( new_data )

char          new_data[];

{       /* SetDialogData */

        if ( dial_edit >= 0 )
              {
              ToolSetName( dial_edit, new_data );

              ToolClear( dial_edit );
              ToolRedraw( dial_edit );
              }

}       /* SetDialogData */

SetDialogPrompt( prompt )

char          prompt[];

{       /* SetDialogPrompt */

        if ( dial_label >= 0 )
              {
              ToolSetName( dial_label, prompt );

              ToolClear( dial_label );
              ToolRedraw( dial_label );
              }
```

```
}       /* SetDialogPrompt */

/* end of file dialog.c */
```

MODAL AND NONMODAL DIALOGS

The dialog box presented here is called a *nonmodal* dialog; that is, the user can enter text into the dialog or continue drawing—the application doesn't care. Other types of dialogs, called *modal* dialogs, require the user to interact with the modal dialog before doing anything else. We find modal dialogs to be restrictive, but sometimes you really need one; most times, though, you really don't.

By using the callback method discussed in the last two chapters, you can generally avoid the need for modal dialogs. If you cannot do an operation until the user has answered a particular question, you can place that task in the OK callback of the dialog that answers the question. Until the user answers the question, that task will not be executed.

SUMMARY

In this chapter we described how to create pop-up windows and dialog boxes. A pop-up window is usually used for menus, dialogs, or warning messages. A dialog box typically asks the user for a piece of data, such as the name of a bitmap file to edit. In the Draw application, we used a dialog box to ask the user to enter a filename and to verify that choice with a mouse click.

It's easy to set up a pop-up window in X—you merely create a window and make it a transient window for your application's main window.

As mentioned, we created a pop-up window that allows users to call bitmap files. First the user must click a mouse button in the load pushbutton window for this purpose. After that, the pop-up dialog appears, asking for the filename.

In our case, we created the window under the current mouse location. The X designers include another option, called warping the mouse, which moves the mouse into the window. In most circumstances, we feel that warping the mouse only serves to confuse the user. There are situations, though, where warping the mouse might be acceptable.

After we've determined where to create the window, it pops up asking the user for a filename. (You don't need to use dialog boxes to just call up files—it can be any character string.)

XLIB FUNCTIONS AND MACROS INTRODUCED IN THIS CHAPTER

XMapSubwindows

XMoveWindow

XQueryPointer

XSetTransientForHint

XWarpPointer

Chapter 16

INTRODUCING THE DRAW APPLICATION

Now that we've covered building a small toolkit, we'll implement an application using the toolkit.

The simple Draw application introduced in this section will contain code to handle:

- Multiple windows in one application, including subwindows
- Pop-up dialog windows
- The ability to undo an operation
- Pixmap operations
- Critical error handling

It is precisely these attributes that will be needed to produce commercial-quality software that runs under the X Window System. The Draw application presented here is by no means a production piece of software—it does, however, present the major areas where X application developers must concentrate when creating commercial-grade software packages.

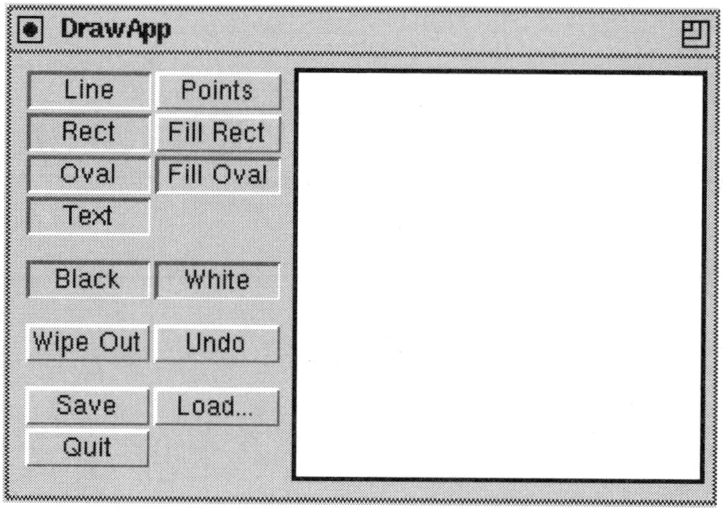

Figure 16.1. The Draw Application.

USER MANUAL FOR THE DRAW APPLICATION

It is usually a good idea to start out with a user manual in an often futile attempt to describe what is planned to be accomplished. This section presents a description of how the Draw application works.

The Draw application is a simple real-size bitmap editor. The X Window System normally comes with a magnified bitmap editor, a client program called *bitmap*. The bitmap program, though fun, suffers from a number of drawbacks. It cannot load in a new file once it has been run. It cannot undo a drawing operation. And, because it always edits in enlarged mode, it is very hard to edit really large bitmaps, such as the bitmaps that make up a screen background. It cannot draw text into a bitmap. The latest bitmap program, part of Release 5, solves most of these problems (except for drawing text), as does the Draw application. The Draw application, presented in this book, is designed to overcome some of those limitations while describing aspects of X application development.

The Draw application edits all bitmaps in real size—it does not enlarge the bitmap in any way—even though this would be a very nice additional feature.

THE PUSHBUTTON PALETTE

The Draw application uses a pushbutton palette to allow the user to choose what kind of item to draw, be it text, lines, points, or ovals.

This palette allows the user to:

- Save the current drawing file
- Draw in black or draw in white (bitmaps are monochrome)
- Draw points
- Draw lines
- Draw rectangles
- Fill rectangles in the current drawing color
- Draw ovals
- Fill ovals in the current drawing color
- Draw text in a user-specified font
- Undo the last drawing operation
- Load in a new bitmap file to edit
- Wipe out (clear) the current drawing area (to start over completely)
- Quit the program

Each item is selected when a cursor is positioned over the given area of the palette window and a button is pressed. To start drawing lines, for example, the user clicks the mouse over the line part of the palette. Then, to actually draw a line, the user moves the mouse pointer over the draw window. The line is started when a mouse button is held down. The line ends when the user lifts the mouse button. As the button is held down, the line will follow the cursor, like a rubber-band.

POINTS

Points are selected by pressing a mouse button over the point area of the palette. When drawing, points will appear wherever the mouse moves as a button is pressed down.

TEXT

To draw text, the user clicks in the text area of the palette. Then the mouse pointer is moved over the draw window. A simple click of a mouse button specifies where the text starts. Any KeyPress events that follow will be interpreted as text input, and the text will be drawn starting where the mouse pointer was when the mouse button was pressed. The back space or the delete key will remove the last character typed. Pressing the Return key will lock in the text, completing the text-drawing operation.

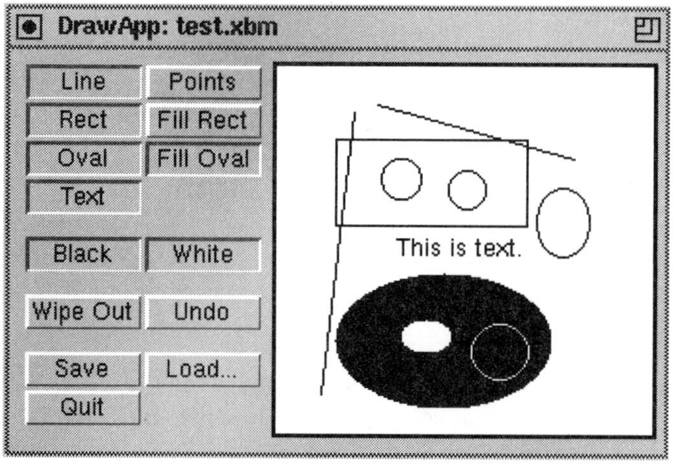

Figure 16.2. Drawing Text in a Bitmap

Other items are drawn in much the same way. This is a simple application, so it should be easy to pick up.

LOADING NEW FILES

A mouse-button press over the file area of the palette signals that the user wants to load a new file. A file dialog box appears. The user can enter the name of a bitmap-style file to load and then choose to cancel the dialog box (and skip loading any file) or accept the file name by pressing a mouse button over the OK box.

These files are in the same format as files created by the bitmap program. This format uses an ASCII-encoding for the bitmap data and is actual C source code. A sample bitmap file appears as follows:

```
#define fi_width 16
#define fi_height 16
static char fi_bits[] = {
  0xff, 0xff, 0xff, 0xff, 0x07, 0xff, 0x73, 0xfe, 0x73, 0xfe, 0x03, 0xfe,
  0xf3, 0xff, 0x73, 0xfe, 0x07, 0xff, 0xff, 0xff, 0xff, 0xff, 0xff, 0xff,
  0xff, 0xff, 0xff, 0xff, 0xff, 0xff, 0xff, 0xff};
```

You can include this file in a C program and compile in a bitmap definition, or you can use an X function (described in Chapter 9) to load in the file to an X client.

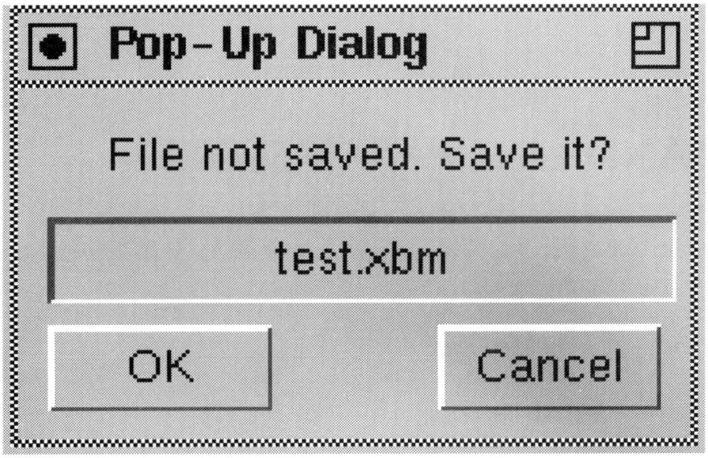

Figure 16.3. The File Dialog Box.

UNDOING DRAWING OPERATIONS

Any time the user presses a mouse button over the `Undo` palette choice (or presses Meta-U), the drawing area is filled with what was there before the last drawing took place. This means that you can undo any drawing operation, but you can undo only one level; you cannot undo all the way back to the beginning of a drawing operation, for example.

Undo is a very handy feature, especially for people who are not used to drawing with a mouse. Undo also allows for a less-worried user environment: the user doesn't have to worry about making a mistake, as any drawing can always be undone.

Other palette items include:

- `Save`, which saves the current file to disk. Frequent saves are encouraged. The default file name is `test.xbm`.
- `Black` and `White`, which toggles between drawing in black or drawing in white (bitmap files are monochrome). Whatever color name shows active (pushed in) is the color that is in use.
- Rectangles and filled rectangles.
- Ovals and filled ovals.
- `Wipe Out`, which wipes out the bitmap so that it appears as a clear white rectangle.
- Quit.

COMMAND-LINE PARAMETERS

Users on a UNIX machine may pass command-line parameters to an X program, as described in Chapter 11. The Draw application will accept a number of command-line parameters:

Command Line	*Meaning*
`-h`	
`-help`	Print help message
`-display`	Use the display name following for the X server
`-geom`	
`-geometry`	Accept user location and/or size for the window
`-fn`	
`-font`	Use the font name that follows, instead of the default
`-iconic`	Begin in iconic state
`-name`	
`-title`	Use the text following as the window's title, rather than the default
`-size`	Sets size of bitmap; use *WidthxHeight*
`-file`	Use given filename (following "`-file`")

POWER-USER META-KEY SHORTCUTS

Power users often like the ability to use shortcut commands on the keyboard, instead of moving the mouse over to the right section of the palette and clicking the mouse buttons.

The Draw application supports the use of the first Meta key (often the only Meta key on a keyboard) to provide keyboard shortcuts. The most common keyboard shortcut is Meta-Q (or Alt-Q), which quits the Draw application. The keyboard shortcuts used in the Draw application are summarized below:

Key	*Function*
Meta-F	Filled Rect
Meta-L	Line
Meta-O	Oval
Meta-P	Point
Meta-Q	Quit
Meta-R	Rect
Meta-S	Save
Meta-T	Text
Meta-U	Undo

SUMMARY

This chapter serves as a short introduction to the Draw application. A real-size bitmap editor, Draw improves on the X bitmap editor by allowing users to load in new files, undo drawing operations, draw text into a bitmap, and edit large bitmaps.

Draw is based on the small X Window toolkit built up in the last two chapters. The toolkit functions provide a foundation on which to build a whole application.

Draw is built around a pushbutton palette, a typical feature of window-based systems. By pressing mouse buttons when the cursor is positioned over different areas of the palette, the user can import existing files and draw lines, points, text, and other items.

The Draw application also supports Meta keys intended for use by power users. The Undo command found on the palette, for instance, can be called through the keyboard by the Meta-U combination.

In the next chapter we'll cover pixmap/bitmap editing in the Draw application. In Chapter 18, we'll provide the rest of the Draw application source code.

Chapter 17

EDITING PIXMAPS

This chapter covers some of the intricate parts of the Draw application concerning pixmaps. We describe our method for providing an undo function, as well as how we generally manage pixmap editing.

UNDO USING PIXMAPS

By using a backing pixmap, we can undo a previous operation by copying the contents of the backing (undo) pixmap into the current drawing pixmap, overwriting the current drawing pixmap's contents. This backing pixmap needs to be kept up-to-date, but needs to be at least one step behind the drawing pixmap, or we won't be able to undo anything.

OVERVIEW OF THE UNDO OPERATION

The following steps document how we intend to allow the user to undo drawing operations:

1. Maintain two pixmaps, the drawing pixmap and the undo pixmap, in addition to the main drawing window.
2. Draw all operations into the drawing pixmap and the drawing window.
3. Before drawing any new item into the drawing pixmap, copy the drawing pixmap into the undo pixmap. That way, the undo pixmap is always one drawing item (one step) behind the drawing pixmap.
4. If the user requests that a drawing operation be undone, copy the contents of the undo pixmap into the drawing pixmap and the drawing window. This provides only one level of undo, not multiple levels.

HANDLING UNDO

`CreateUndoPixmap`, below, creates our pixmap the size of the editing window and pixmap. `DestroyUndoPixmap` deletes the undo pixmap, so it can be created again (presumably at a different size).

The function `MaintainUndo` is called before each drawing operation to save the contents of the drawing pixmap before the new drawing operation writes over it. This way, we can undo the new drawing operation and restore the previous state by copying the contents of the undo pixmap onto the drawing pixmap. We do just that with the `Undo` function. `Undo` copies the undo pixmap to both the current drawing pixmap and the drawing window. We copy to the drawing window so the user sees the result of the undo right away.

All these functions are in the file `da_undo.c`:

```
/*
 *      da_undo.c
 *      Written for X Window Applications
 *      Programming, 2nd Edition.
 */

#include  <X11/Xlib.h>
#include  "drawapp.h"
```

```
/*
 *      Global undo pixmap
 */
Pixmap          undo_pixmap;
GC              undo_gc;

CreateUndoPixmap( display, parent, width, height )

Display         *display;
Window          parent;
int             width, height;

{       /* CreateUndoPixmap */
        GC    CreateGC();

        undo_pixmap = XCreatePixmap( display,
                    parent,
                    width, height,
                    1 );  /* depth */

        if ( undo_pixmap == (Pixmap) None )
              {
              return( False );
              }

        undo_gc = CreateGC( display,
                   undo_pixmap,
                   0L, 0L );

        /*
         * Clear pixmap
         */
        XFillRectangle( display,
              undo_pixmap, undo_gc,
              0, 0, width, height );

        /*
         * Set GC to draw.
         */
        XSetForeground( display, undo_gc, 1L );

        return( True );
```

```
}       /* CreateUndoPixmap */

DestroyUndoPixmap( display )

Display      *display;

/*
 *      Frees data for undo_pixmap and undo_gc.
 */

{       /* DestroyUndoPixmap */

        XFreePixmap( display, undo_pixmap );

        XFreeGC( display, undo_gc );

}       /* DestroyUndoPixmap */

MaintainUndo( display )

Display      *display;

/*
 *      Copies the contents of the current
 *      bitmap to the undo bitmap, so that
 *      the older contents can be restored.
 */

{       /* MaintainUndo */
        extern int     editing_width, editing_height;
        extern Pixmap  drawing_pixmap;

        CopyPlane( display,
              drawing_pixmap,    /* source */
              undo_pixmap,       /* dest */
              undo_gc,           /* dest gc */
              0, 0,
              editing_width, editing_height,
              editing_width, editing_height );

}       /* MaintainUndo */

void Undo( id )
```

```
int     id;

/*
 *      Copies contents of the undo bitmap to
 *      the current pixmap, and then to the screen.
 */

{       /* Undo */
        extern int     drawing_color;
        extern int     editing_width, editing_height;
        extern Pixmap  drawing_pixmap;
        extern GC      drawing_gc, pixmap_gc;
        extern Window  drawing_window;
        int            old_color;
        Display        *display;
        Display        *ToolGetDisplay();

        display = ToolGetDisplay( id );

        old_color = drawing_color;

        SetDrawAppColor( display, DRAWING_BLACK );

        CopyPlane( display,
              undo_pixmap,       /* source */
              drawing_pixmap,    /* dest */
              pixmap_gc,         /* dest gc */
              0, 0,
              editing_width, editing_height,
              editing_width, editing_height );

        CopyPlane( display,
              undo_pixmap,       /* source */
              drawing_window,    /* dest */
              drawing_gc,        /* dest gc */
              0, 0,
              editing_width, editing_height,
              editing_width, editing_height );

        SetDrawAppColor( display, old_color );

        UnhighlightPushButton( id );
        XFlush( display );
```

```
}       /* Undo */

/* end of file da_undo.c */
```

MANAGING THE DRAWING PIXMAP

`CreateDrawingPixmap`, below, creates a drawing pixmap. This single-plane pixmap acts as backing store for our drawing window and allows us to save its contents to a X bitmap file (in ASCII format, using `XWriteBitmapFile`). All drawing is done simultaneously to the drawing window and to the drawing pixmap (see `da_draw.c`, next chapter).

`DestroyDrawingPixmap` destroys the drawing pixmap, so it can be created again.

SOURCE CODE FOR DA_PIX.C

```
/*
 *      da_pix.c
 *      Draw Application editing pixmap functions.
 *
 *      Written for X Window Applications
 *      Programming, 2nd Edition.
 */

#include  <X11/Xlib.h>
#include  <X11/Xutil.h>

/*
 *      Global drawing pixmap and GC.
 */
Pixmap  drawing_pixmap;
GC              pixmap_gc;

/*
 *      External Globals
 */
extern XFontStruct *drawapp_font;

CreateDrawingPixmap( display, window, width, height )
```

```
Display       *display;
Window        window;
int           width, height;

{       /* CreateDrawingPixmap */
        GC    CreateGC();

        drawing_pixmap = XCreatePixmap( display, window,
                    width, height, 1 );

        pixmap_gc = CreateGC( display, drawing_pixmap,
                 0L, 0L );

        /*
         * Clear pixmap
         */
        XFillRectangle( display, drawing_pixmap,
              pixmap_gc,
              0, 0, width, height );

        XSetForeground( display, pixmap_gc, 1L );

        XSetFont( display, pixmap_gc, drawapp_font->fid );

        if ( ( drawing_pixmap != (Pixmap) None ) &&
              ( pixmap_gc != (GC) None ) )
              {
              return( True );
              }
        else
              {
              return( False );
              }

}       /* CreateDrawingPixmap */

DestroyDrawPixmap( display )

Display       *display;

/*
 *      Destroys our drawing pixmap and gc.
 */
```

```
{       /* DestroyDrawPixmap */

        XFreePixmap( display, drawing_pixmap );
        XFreeGC( display, pixmap_gc );

}       /* DestroyDrawPixmap */

/* end of file da_pix.c */
```

SUMMARY

By using a backing pixmap, we can undo a previous operation by copying the contents of the backing (undo) pixmap into the current drawing pixmap, overwriting the current drawing pixmap's contents.

Chapter 18

THE DRAW APPLICATION SOURCE CODE

This chapter contains all-new source files for the Draw application described in chapters 14-17. The application provides a real example of what you need to do to create a fully functional X Window application.

SOURCE FILES FOR THE DRAW APPLICATION

The source files presented in this long chapter include: `drawapp.h`, `drawapp.c`, `da_draw.c`, `da_file.c`, `da_edit.c`, and `da_meta.c`. These files make up the rest of the Draw application.

All in all, the Draw application requires the following files:

`args.c`	(Chapter 11)
`bitmap.c`	(Chapter 9)
`classhnt.c`	(Chapter 2)
`color.c`	(Chapter 4)
`connect.c`	(Chapter 1)
`da_draw.c`	
`da_edit.c`	
`da_file.c`	
`da_meta.c`	
`da_pix.c`	(Chapter 17)
`da_undo.c`	(Chapter 17)
`dialog.c`	(Chapter 15)
`display.c`	(Chapter 11)
`drawapp.h`	
`drawapp.c`	
`entry.c`	(Chapter 14)
`error.c`	(Chapter 13)
`fontht.c`	(Chapter 5)
`fontname.c`	(Chapter 11)
`gc.c`	(Chapter 3)
`geometry.c`	(Chapter 11)
`icon.c`	(Chapter 9)
`key.c`	(Chapter 7)
`label.c`	(Chapter 14)
`loadfont.c`	(Chapter 5)
`oval.c`	(Chapter 3)
`pixmap.c`	(Chapter 9)
`pushb.c`	(Chapter 14)
`query.c`	(Chapter 15)
`sizehint.c`	(Chapter 2)
`startupx.c`	(Chapter 13)

`toolkit.c`	(Chapter 14)
`topwind.c`	(Chapter 12)
`tranwind.c`	(Chapter 15)
`usage.c`	(Chapter 11)
`visual.c`	(Chapter 4)
`window.c`	(Chapter 2)
`wmhints.c`	(Chapter 2)
`wmname.c`	(Chapter 2)
`xor.c`	(Chapter 10)

You can compile the Draw application with a command like:

```
cc -o -DX11R4 drawapp toolkit.c pushb.c entry.c label.c dialog.c \
       drawapp.c da_edit.c da_file.c da_draw.c da_pix.c \
       tranwind.c da_undo.c fontht.c query.c da_meta.c \
       args.c display.c geometry.c usage.c color.c error.c \
       bitmap.c icon.c pixmap.c \
       fontname.c gc.c key.c loadfont.c startupx.c \
       oval.c topwind.c visual.c xor.c \
       classhnt.c connect.c sizehint.c window.c \
       wmhints.c wmname.c -lX11
```

Or you can use the Makefile in Appendix A and type:

```
make drawapp
```

There's a lot you can do to extend the Draw application, which we cover in the next chapter. For now, here's the source code.

The contents of the header file `drawapp.h` follows:

```
/*
 *      drawapp.h
 *      Header file for Draw Application
 *
 *      Written for X Window Applications
 *      Programming, 2nd Edition
 */


/*
 *      Editing/Drawing Window
```

```
 */
#define EDITING_WINDOW      0

/*
 *      Drawing shapes
 */
#define DRAW_LINE     1
#define DRAW_POINTS   2
#define DRAW_RECT     3
#define FILL_RECT     4
#define DRAW_OVAL     5
#define FILL_OVAL     6
#define DRAW_TEXT     7

/*
 *      Drawing Modes
 */
#define NOT_DRAWING       0
#define DRAWING           1

/*
 *      Drawing Colors
 */
#define DRAWING_BLACK     8
#define DRAWING_WHITE     9

/*
 *      Action windows
 */
#define WIPE_OUT      10
#define UNDO_LAST     11
#define SAVE_FILE     12
#define LOAD_FILE     13
#define QUIT_ID       14

/*
 *      Bitmap-saved flags
 */
#define BITMAP_SAVED      0
#define BITMAP_CHANGED    1

/* end of file drawapp.h */
```

SOURCE CODE FOR THE FILE DRAWAPP.C

```
/*
 *      drawapp.c
 *      Main functions for the Draw Application
 *
 *      Written for X Window Applications
 *      Programming, 2nd Edition
 */

#include <stdio.h>
#include <X11/Xlib.h>
#include <X11/Xutil.h>

/*
 *      Drawing shapes and Modes
 */
#include "drawapp.h"

/*
 *      Globals for black and white colors
 */
unsigned long   black, white, lightgrey, dimgrey;

/*
 *      Font names.
 */
/* #define FONT_NAME  "variable" */
#define FONT_NAME     "-adobe-helvetica-medium-r-normal—12-
120-75-75-p-67-iso8859-1"
#define FALLBACK_FONT_NAME  "fixed"

/*
 *      Event mask for all but
 *      our top-level window.
 */
#define EV_MASK ( ButtonPressMask | \
                ButtonReleaseMask | \
                ButtonMotionMask | \
                KeyPressMask | \
                ExposureMask )
```

```
#define MAX_WIDTH       48
#define MAX_4_WIDTH     192
#define BUTTON_WIDTH    60

/*
 *      Name of bitmap file we'll use for an icon.
 *      You can create this bitmap file with the
 *      standard X program named bitmap.
 */
#define ICON_FILENAME "drawapp.xbm"

/*
 *      Globals for drawing shape, mode
 *      and pen locations.
 */
int     drawing_shape = DRAW_LINE;
int     drawing_mode  = NOT_DRAWING;
int     drawing_color = DRAWING_BLACK;
int     changed_flag = BITMAP_SAVED;

/*
 *      Draw Application Globals
 */
XFontStruct  *drawapp_font;
Window       main_window;

main( argc, argv )

int     argc;
char    *argv[];

{       /* main */
        Display         *display;
        Display         *StartupX();
        Window          rootwindow;
        Window          TopWindow();
        int             screen;
        int             x, y, width, height;
        Visual          *visual = CopyFromParent;
        GC              gc;
        GC              CreateGC();
        char            string[200];
        XFontStruct     *LoadFontName();
```

```
int             depth, status;
Colormap        colormap;
unsigned long   AllocNamedColor();
Window          dialog;
Window          CreateDialog();
extern void     NullUserFunc(); /* TEMPORARY */
extern void     Quit();

/*
 * Connect to X server
 */
display = StartupX( argc, argv,
        &screen, &rootwindow,
        &black, &white, "" );

/*
 * Load a font
 */
(void) strcpy( string, FONT_NAME );

drawapp_font = LoadFontName( display, argc, argv,
        string, FALLBACK_FONT_NAME );

/*
 * Find a PseudoColor visual for our window
 */
status = SetUpVisual( display, screen,
        &visual,
        &depth );

/*
 * If we cannot find a
 * PseudoColor visual,
 * do everything in black
 * and white. YOUR apps
 * should be able to support
 * more than PseudoColor
 * visuals.
 */

/*
 * Set up default window sizes
 */
```

```
x      = 10;
y      = 10;
width  = (BUTTON_WIDTH * 2) + MAX_4_WIDTH + 24;
height = ( FontHeight( drawapp_font ) + 1 ) * 14;

/*
 * Are we supposed to load in a file?
 */

/*
 * Create a top-level window on the display
 */
main_window = TopWindow( display,
        rootwindow,
        argc, argv,
        &x, &y, &width, &height,
        black, white,
        KeyPressMask,
        visual );

/*
 * Set up a Colormap, AFTER we've created the window.
 */
status = SetUpColormap( display, screen, main_window,
        visual, &colormap );

if ( status < 1 )
     {
     /* do nothing on errors */
     }

/*
 * Allocate 3D colors,
 * even if we couldn't
 * get the right visual
 * and colormap.
 */
black   = AllocNamedColor( display, colormap,
        "black", BlackPixel( display, screen ) );

white   = AllocNamedColor( display, colormap,
        "white", WhitePixel( display, screen ) );
```

```
lightgrey = AllocNamedColor( display, colormap,
        "LightGrey", WhitePixel( display, screen ) );

dimgrey = AllocNamedColor( display, colormap,
        "DimGrey", BlackPixel( display, screen ) );

XSetWindowBackground( display, main_window,
        lightgrey );

/*
 * Load uup bitmap file and
 * turn it into an icon.
 */
LoadIcon (display, main_window,
     ICON_FILENAME, argv[0] );

/*
 * Create graphics context for drawing
 */
gc = CreateGC( display, main_window,
        black, lightgrey );

/*
 * Set the GCs to draw with our font.
 */
XSetFont( display, gc, drawapp_font->fid );

/*
 * Create drawing window,
 * BEFORE creating pushbuttons.
 */
CreateEditingWindow( display, main_window, argc, argv,
     136, 6, MAX_4_WIDTH, MAX_4_WIDTH,
     EV_MASK, visual );

/*
 * Create Pushbuttons
 */
CreateButtons( display, main_window,
     gc, drawapp_font );

/*
 * Create dialog, set up for
```

```
 * File load.
 */
dialog = CreateDialog( display, rootwindow,
         main_window, visual,
         colormap, drawapp_font,
         argv[0],
         "Enter name of file to load",
         NullUserFunc );

/*
 * Set "test.xbm" as the
 * default file name.
 */
SetFileName( display, main_window,
      "test.xbm" );

/*
 * Now, check if the user asked
 * to load in a different file.
 */
CheckForFileLoad( display, main_window, argc, argv );

/*
 * Make the window and its
 * subwindows actually appear
 */
XMapRaised( display, main_window );
XMapSubwindows( display, main_window );
XFlush( display );

/*
 * Mark that we haven't changed
 * the bitmap yet.
 */
changed_flag = BITMAP_SAVED;

/*
 * Loop on events. Quit when the user types
 * a Meta-Q.
 */
EventLoop( display );
```

```
        /*
         * Prompt to save if data
         * is changed, then quit.
         */
        Quit( QUIT_ID );

}       /* main */

EventLoop( display )

Display       *display;

{       /* EventLoop */
        XEvent   event;
        int      done = False;
        int      handled;
        KeySym   keysym;
        char     string[100];

        while( !done )
              {
              XNextEvent( display, &event );

              handled = ToolEvent( &event );

              /*
               * Decode key event.
               */
              if ( event.type == KeyPress )
                 {
                 done = DecodeKeyPress( &event,
                       &keysym,
                        string );

                 if ( IsMetaKey( &event ) == True )
                    {
                    HandleMetaKey( string );
                    }
                 }
              }

}       /* EventLoop */
```

```
CreateButtons( display, window, gc, font_struct )

Display       *display;
Window        window;
GC            gc;
XFontStruct   *font_struct;

{       /* CreateButtons */
        int   y, height;
        int   id;
        void  SetDrawingShape();
        void  SetDrawingColor();
        void  WipeOut();
        void  Undo();
        void  SaveFile();
        void  PopUpLoadFile();
        void  Quit();

        height = FontHeight( font_struct ) + 4;
        y = 6;

        id = CreatePushButton( display, window,
              6, y, BUTTON_WIDTH, height,
                 gc, font_struct,
                 "Line", SetDrawingShape );
        ToolSetGroup( id, 1 );
        ToolSetState( id, True );

        id = CreatePushButton( display, window,
              68, y, BUTTON_WIDTH, height,
              gc, font_struct,
              "Points", SetDrawingShape );
        ToolSetGroup( id, 1 );

        y += height + 2;

        id = CreatePushButton( display, window,
              6, y, BUTTON_WIDTH, height,
                 gc, font_struct,
                 "Rect", SetDrawingShape );
        ToolSetGroup( id, 1 );

        id = CreatePushButton( display, window,
```

```
        68, y, BUTTON_WIDTH, height,
           gc, font_struct,
           "Fill Rect", SetDrawingShape );
ToolSetGroup( id, 1 );

y += height + 2;

id = CreatePushButton( display, window,
        6, y, BUTTON_WIDTH, height,
           gc, font_struct,
           "Oval", SetDrawingShape );
ToolSetGroup( id, 1 );

id = CreatePushButton( display, window,
        68, y, BUTTON_WIDTH, height,
           gc, font_struct,
           "Fill Oval", SetDrawingShape );
ToolSetGroup( id, 1 );

y += height + 2;

id = CreatePushButton( display, window,
        6, y, BUTTON_WIDTH, height,
           gc, font_struct,
           "Text", SetDrawingShape );
ToolSetGroup( id, 1 );

y += height + 12;

id = CreatePushButton( display, window,
        6, y, BUTTON_WIDTH, height,
           gc, font_struct,
           "Black", SetDrawingColor );
ToolSetGroup( id, 2 );
ToolSetState( id, True );

id = CreatePushButton( display, window,
        68, y, BUTTON_WIDTH, height,
           gc, font_struct,
           "White", SetDrawingColor );
ToolSetGroup( id, 2 );

y += height + 12;
```

```
        id = CreatePushButton( display, window,
              6, y, BUTTON_WIDTH, height,
                 gc, font_struct,
              "  Wipe Out", WipeOut );

        id = CreatePushButton( display, window,
              68, y, BUTTON_WIDTH, height,
                 gc, font_struct,
                 "Undo", Undo );

        y += height + 12;

        id = CreatePushButton( display, window,
              6, y, BUTTON_WIDTH, height,
                 gc, font_struct,
                 "Save", SaveFile );

        id = CreatePushButton( display, window,
              68, y, BUTTON_WIDTH, height,
                 gc, font_struct,
                 "Load...", PopUpLoadFile );

        y += height + 2;

        id = CreatePushButton( display, window,
              6, y, BUTTON_WIDTH, height,
                 gc, font_struct,
                 "Quit", Quit );

}       /* CreateButtons */

void SetDrawingShape( id )

int     id;

{       /* SetDrawingShape */

        drawing_mode  = NOT_DRAWING;
        drawing_shape = id;

}       /* SetDrawingShape */

/* end of file drawapp.c */
```

SOURCE CODE FOR THE BITMAP FILE DRAWAPP.XBM

```
#define drawapp.xbm_width 32
#define drawapp.xbm_height 32
static char drawapp.xbm_bits[] = {
   0x00, 0x00, 0x00, 0x00, 0x00, 0x00, 0x00, 0x00, 0xc0, 0x01, 0xc0, 0x01,
   0xe0, 0x03, 0x80, 0x01, 0x10, 0x03, 0x80, 0x01, 0x00, 0xbb, 0xf1, 0x01,
   0x00, 0x73, 0x9b, 0x01, 0x80, 0x31, 0x9b, 0x01, 0xc0, 0x30, 0x9b, 0x01,
   0x20, 0x30, 0x9b, 0x01, 0xf0, 0x33, 0x9b, 0x01, 0xf0, 0x3b, 0x77, 0x03,
   0x00, 0x00, 0x00, 0x00, 0x00, 0x00, 0x00, 0x00, 0x00, 0x00, 0x00, 0x00,
   0xe0, 0x1f, 0x0e, 0x00, 0xc0, 0x10, 0x0c, 0x00, 0xc0, 0x10, 0x0c, 0x00,
   0xc0, 0x84, 0x0f, 0x00, 0xc0, 0xc7, 0x0c, 0x00, 0xc0, 0xc4, 0x0c, 0x00,
   0xc0, 0xd0, 0x0c, 0x00, 0xc0, 0xd0, 0x0c, 0x00, 0xc0, 0xd8, 0xcc, 0x00,
   0xe0, 0x9f, 0xdb, 0x00, 0x00, 0x00, 0x00, 0x00, 0x00, 0x00, 0x00, 0x00,
   0x00, 0x00, 0x00, 0x00, 0x00, 0x00, 0x00, 0x00, 0x00, 0x00, 0x00, 0x00,
   0x00, 0x00, 0x00, 0x00, 0x00, 0x00, 0x00, 0x00};
```

SOURCE CODE FOR THE FILE DA_DRAW.C

```
/*
 *      da_draw.c
 *      Shape-Drawing Functions for
 *      the Draw Application.
 *
 *      Written for X Window Applications
 *      Programming, 2nd Edition
 */

#include  <stdio.h>
#include  <ctype.h>
#include  <X11/Xlib.h>

/*
 *       Drawing shapes and Modes
 */
#include "drawapp.h"
```

```
/*
 *      Globals for the editing window.
 */
char            drawing_string[ 400 ];

/*
 *      External drawing modes
 */
extern int      drawing_mode;
extern int      drawing_color;

/*
 *      Pixmaps for actually storing the bitmap
 */
Window          drawing_window;
Pixmap          drawing_pixmap;
GC              pixmap_gc;
GC              drawing_gc;

/*
 *      External colors
 */
extern unsigned long  black, white;

DrawItem( display, shape, x1, y1, x2, y2 )

Display         *display;
int             shape;
int             x1, y1, x2, y2;

/*
 *      Draws given shape into
 *      the window and the pixmap,
 *      first making sure the old
 *      pixmap contents are saved for
 *      undo-ing.
 */

{       /* DrawItem */
        extern int  changed_flag;

        MaintainUndo( display );
```

```
        /*
         * Draw item into window
         */
        DrawShape( display,
              drawing_window, drawing_gc,
              shape,
              x1, y1, x2, y2 );

        /*
         * Draw item into pixmap
         */
        DrawShape( display,
              drawing_pixmap, pixmap_gc,
              shape,
              x1, y1, x2, y2 );

        /*
         * We have changed the
         * picture.
         */
        changed_flag = BITMAP_CHANGED;

}       /* DrawItem */

DrawShape( display, drawable, gc, shape, x1, y1, x2, y2 )

Display       *display;
Drawable      drawable;
GC            gc;
int           shape;
int           x1, y1, x2, y2;

{       /* DrawShape */
        int   width, height;

        height = y2 - y1;
        width  = x2 - x1;

        switch( shape )
              {
              case DRAW_LINE:
                 XDrawLine( display, drawable, gc,
                    x1, y1, x2, y2 );
```

```
        break;
    case DRAW_POINTS:
        XDrawPoint( display, drawable, gc,
            x2, y2 );
        break;
    case DRAW_RECT:
        if ( ( height > 1 ) && ( width > 1 ) )
            {
            XDrawRectangle( display, drawable, gc,
                x1, y1, width, height );
            }
        break;
    case FILL_RECT:
        if ( ( height > 1 ) && ( width > 1 ) )
            {
            XFillRectangle( display, drawable, gc,
                x1, y1, width, height );
            }
        break;
    case DRAW_OVAL:
        if ( ( height > 1 ) && ( width > 1 ) )
            {
            DrawOval( display, drawable, gc,
                x1, y1, width, height );
            }
        break;
    case FILL_OVAL:
        if ( ( height > 1 ) && ( width > 1 ) )
            {
            FillOval( display, drawable, gc,
                x1, y1, width, height );
            }
        break;
    case DRAW_TEXT:
        if ( strlen( drawing_string ) > 0 )
            {
            XDrawImageString( display,
                drawable, gc,
                x1, y1,
                drawing_string,
                strlen( drawing_string ) );
            }
    }
```

```
}       /* DrawShape */

SetDrawAppColor( display, color )

Display         *display;
int             color;

{       /* SetDrawAppColor */

        drawing_mode  = NOT_DRAWING;
        drawing_color = color;

        if ( drawing_color == DRAWING_BLACK )
              {
              XSetForeground( display,
                 drawing_gc,
                 black );

              XSetBackground( display,
                 drawing_gc,
                 white );

              XSetForeground( display,
                 pixmap_gc,
                 1L );

              XSetBackground( display,
                 pixmap_gc,
                 0L );
              }
        else
              {
              XSetForeground( display,
                 drawing_gc,
                 white );

              XSetBackground( display,
                 drawing_gc,
                 black );

              XSetForeground( display,
                 pixmap_gc,
                 0L );
```

```
            XSetBackground( display,
               pixmap_gc,
                 1L );
            }

}       /* SetDrawAppColor */

/* end of file da_draw.c */
```

SOURCE CODE FOR THE FILE DA_EDIT.C

```
/*
 *      da_edit.c
 *      Functions for editing a bitmap,
 *      drawing into windows and
 *      pixmaps.
 *
 *      Written for X Window Applications
 *      Programming, 2nd Edition
 */

#include  <stdio.h>
#include  <ctype.h>

#include  <X11/Xlib.h>
#include  <X11/keysym.h>
#include  <X11/keysymdef.h>

/*
 *      Drawing shapes and Modes
 */
#include "drawapp.h"

/*
 *      Globals for the editing window.
 */
int           drawing_last_x = 0;
int           drawing_last_y = 0;
int           drawing_x = 0;
int           drawing_y = 0;
```

```
char           drawing_string[ 400 ];

/*
 *      External drawing modes
 */
extern int    drawing_shape;
extern int    drawing_mode;
extern int    drawing_color;

/*
 *      Globals
 */
Window  drawing_window;
GC      update_gc;
GC      drawing_gc;
GC      xor_gc;

/*
 *      External Globals
 */
extern Pixmap          drawing_pixmap;
extern GC              pixmap_gc;
extern XFontStruct     *drawapp_font;

int            editing_width  = 0;
int            editing_height = 0;

/*
 *      External colors
 */
extern unsigned long  black, white;

CreateEditingGCs( display, window )

Display        *display;
Window         window;

{       /* CreateEditingGCs */
        GC    CreateGC();
        GC    CreateXorGC();

        xor_gc      =  CreateXorGC( display, window,
                       black, white );
```

```
        drawing_gc =  CreateGC( display, window,
                      black, white );
        update_gc  =  CreateGC( display, window,
                      black, white );

        XSetFont( display, drawing_gc, drawapp_font->fid );
        XSetFont( display, xor_gc, drawapp_font->fid );

}       /* CreateEditingGCs */

CreateEditingWindow( display, parent, argc, argv,
        x, y, width, height, eventmask, visual )

Display         *display;
Window          parent;
int             argc;
char            *argv[];
int             x, y, width, height;
unsigned long   eventmask;
Visual          *visual;

{       /* CreateEditingWindow */
        void        EditingDrawFunc();
        extern void NullUserFunc();
        void        EditingEventFunc();
        int         id, status;
        Window      ToolGetWindow();
        char        *parameter, *FindParameter();
        int         i;

        /*
         * Did the user set an initial size,
         * with the -size WidthxHeight option?
         */
        parameter = FindParameter( argc, argv, "-size" );

        if ( parameter != (char *) NULL )
                {
                /*
                 * The proper format is WidthxHeight
                 */
                i = sscanf( parameter, "%dx%d",
                        &editing_width, &editing_height );
```

```
            if ( i < 1 )
               {
               editing_width = width;
               }

            if ( editing_width < 16 )
               {
               editing_width = 16;
               }

            if ( i < 2 )
               {
               editing_height = height;
               }

            if ( editing_height < 16 )
               {
               editing_height = 16;
               }
            }
      else
            {
            editing_width = width;
            editing_height = height;
            }

      id = CreateToolWindow( display, parent,
            x, y, editing_width, editing_height,
            black, white,
            eventmask, visual );

      ToolSetGroup( id, (-99) );

      ToolSetFunctions( id, EditingDrawFunc,
            EditingEventFunc, NullUserFunc );

      drawing_window = ToolGetWindow( id );

      /*
       * Set up graphic contexts for drawing.
       */
      CreateEditingGCs( display, drawing_window );
```

```
        /*
         * Create pixmaps for drawing into and
         * undoing drawings we don't want.
         */
        status = CreateDrawingPixmap( display, parent,
                editing_width, editing_height );

        if ( status == True )
             {
             status = CreateUndoPixmap( display, parent,
                  editing_width, editing_height );
             }

        /*
         * Check for errors
         */
        if ( status == False )
             {
             (void) fprintf( stderr,
                "Error creating pixmaps.\n" );
             XCloseDisplay( display );
             exit( 1 );
             }

        /*
         * Initial global text string.
         */
        drawing_string[0] = '\0';

}       /* CreateEditingWindow */

ResizeEditingWindow( width, height )

int             width, height;

{       /* ResizeEditingWindow */

        if ( ( editing_width != width ) ||
             ( editing_height != height ) )
             {
             ToolResize( EDITING_WINDOW, width, height );
             }
```

```
        editing_width = width;
        editing_height = height;

}       /* ResizeEditingWindow */

/* ARGSUSED */
void EditingDrawFunc( display, id, event )

Display         *display;
int             id;
XExposeEvent    *event;

{       /* EditingDrawFunc */

        UpdateWindowFromBitmap( display,
              drawing_window,
              update_gc,
              drawing_pixmap,
              event,
              editing_width,
              editing_height );

}       /* EditingDrawFunc */

/* ARGSUSED */
void EditingUserFunc( id )

int             id;

/* does nothing */

{       /* EditingUserFunc */
}       /* EditingUserFunc */

void EditingEventFunc( display, id, event, keysym, string )

Display         *display;
int             id;
XEvent          *event;
KeySym          keysym;
char            string[];

{       /* EditingEventFunc */
```

```
/*
 * Undraw Xor item
 */
if ( drawing_mode == DRAWING )
     {
     DrawShape( display,
        drawing_window,
        xor_gc,
        drawing_shape,
        drawing_last_x,
        drawing_last_y,
        drawing_x,
        drawing_y );
     }

switch( event->type )
     {
     case MotionNotify:
        if ( drawing_mode == DRAWING )
              {
              /*
               * Update coords
               */
              drawing_x = event->xbutton.x;
              drawing_y = event->xbutton.y;
              }
        break;
     case ButtonPress:
        /*
         * Turn on drawing mode,
         * and store pen location.
         */
        if ( drawing_mode != DRAWING )
              {
              drawing_mode = DRAWING;

              drawing_last_x = event->xbutton.x;
              drawing_last_y = event->xbutton.y;
              drawing_x = event->xbutton.x;
              drawing_y = event->xbutton.y;

              /*
               * Re-initialize drawing_string
```

```
                */
               drawing_string[0] = '\0';
               }
         break;
      case ButtonRelease:
         /*
          * Turn off drawing mode,
          * draw real item into
          * pixmap.
          */
         if ( drawing_mode == DRAWING )
            {
            drawing_mode = NOT_DRAWING;

            drawing_x = event->xbutton.x;
            drawing_y = event->xbutton.y;

            /*
             * Draw item into
             * window and pixmap.
             */
            DrawItem( display,
               drawing_shape,
               drawing_last_x,
               drawing_last_y,
               drawing_x,
               drawing_y );
            }
         break;
      case KeyPress:
         /*
          * Are we in text-drawing mode?
          */
         if ( drawing_shape == DRAW_TEXT )
            {
            /*
             * Note that we won't be in
             * the proper drawing_mode,
             * because of ButtonRelease events.
             */
            drawing_mode = DRAWING;

            EditText( display, id, keysym, string );
```

```
                    }
                break;
            }

        /*
         * Redraw Xor item
         */
        if ( drawing_mode == DRAWING )
            {
            DrawShape( display,
                drawing_window,
                xor_gc,
                drawing_shape,
                drawing_last_x,
                drawing_last_y,
                drawing_x,
                drawing_y );
            }

        XFlush( display );

}       /* EditingEventFunc */

void SetDrawingColor( id )

int     id;

{       /* SetDrawingColor */
        Display     *display;
        Display     *ToolGetDisplay();

        display = ToolGetDisplay( id );

        SetDrawAppColor( display, id );

}       /* SetDrawingColor */

void WipeOut( id )

int             id;

{       /* WipeOut */
        int       old_color;
```

```
        Display  *display;
        Display  *ToolGetDisplay();

        display = ToolGetDisplay( id );

        /*
         * Save old drawing color
         */
        old_color = drawing_color;

        SetDrawAppColor( display, DRAWING_WHITE );

        DrawItem( display,
              FILL_RECT,
              0, 0,
              editing_width,
              editing_height );

        /*
         * Restore old color
         */
        SetDrawAppColor( display, old_color );

        UnhighlightPushButton( id );
        XFlush( display );

}       /* WipeOut */

EditText( display, id, keysym, string )

Display       *display;
int           id;
KeySym        keysym;
char          string[];

{       /* EditText */
        int      length;

        if ( keysym < 255 )
              {
              if ( isprint( keysym ) )
                  {
                  (void) strcat( drawing_string,
```

```
                string );
            }
        }
    else
        {
        switch( keysym )
            {
            case XK_Return:
                /*
                 * Draw item into
                 * window and pixmap.
                 */
                DrawItem( display,
                    drawing_shape,
                    drawing_last_x,
                    drawing_last_y,
                    drawing_x,
                    drawing_y );

                /*
                 * Re-initialize
                 * modes and string
                 */
                drawing_mode = NOT_DRAWING;
                drawing_string[0] = '\0';
                break;

            case XK_Delete:
            case XK_BackSpace:
                length = strlen( drawing_string );

                if ( length > 0 )
                    {
                    /*
                     * Re-draw window contents.
                     */
                    ToolRedraw( id );

                    /*
                     * Shorten string.
                     */
                    length--;
                    drawing_string[length] = '\0';
```

```
                    /*
                     * Redraw to make new
                     * shape visible.
                     */
                    if ( length > 0 )
                      {
                      DrawShape( display,
                        drawing_window,
                        xor_gc,
                        drawing_shape,
                        drawing_last_x,
                        drawing_last_y,
                        drawing_x,
                        drawing_y );
                      }
                    }
                  break;
              }
          }

}       /* EditText */

/* end of file da_edit.c */
```

SOURCE CODE FOR THE FILE DA_FILE.C

```
/*
 *      da_file.c
 *      Draw Application Load and Save functions
 *
 *      Written for X Window Applications
 *      Programming, 2nd Edition
 */

#include <stdio.h>
#include "drawapp.h"

#include <X11/Xlib.h>
#include <X11/Xutil.h>
```

```
/*
 *      Global file name.
 */
#define MAX_CHARS  400

char            da_filename[MAX_CHARS + 1];

void PopUpLoadFile( id )

int     id;

{       /* PopUpLoadFile */
        void        LoadFile();
        extern void PopUpDialog();

        /*
         * Set up dialog values for
         * loading files.
         */
        SetDialogData( "" );
        SetDialogPrompt( "Enter name of file to load" );
        SetDialogCallback( LoadFile );

        /*
         * Make load file dialog appear
         */
        PopUpDialog();

        UnhighlightPushButton( id );

}       /* PopUpLoadFile */

void LoadFile( id )

int     id;

/*
 *      Actually loads up a given file.
 */

{       /* LoadFile */
        char            filename[200];
        extern void     PopDownDialog();
```

```
        extern Window  main_window;
        Display        *ToolGetDisplay();

        UnhighlightPushButton( id );

        PopDownDialog( -1 );

        GetDialogData( filename );

        LoadDrawappFile( ToolGetDisplay( id ),
             main_window, filename );

        /* LoadFile */

LoadDrawappFile( display, window, filename )

Display      *display;
Window       window;
char         filename[];

{       /* LoadDrawappFile */
        int            width, height;
        Pixmap         new_bitmap;
        Pixmap         LoadBitmap();
        extern Pixmap  drawing_pixmap;
        extern GC      pixmap_gc;
        extern int     editing_width, editing_height;

        /*
         * Load up new bitmap
         */
        new_bitmap = LoadBitmap( display, window,
                filename,
                &width, &height );

        if ( new_bitmap == (Pixmap) None )
             {
             (void) fprintf( stderr,
                "Error loading bitmap file [%s]\n",
                filename );
             return;
             }
```

```
/*
 * If we have a different size, then
 * we need to re-create the pixmaps.
 */
if ( ( editing_width != width ) ||
     ( editing_height != height ))
     {
     /*
      * Destroy old bitmap
      * and undo bitmap.
      */
     DestroyUndoPixmap( display );
     DestroyDrawPixmap( display );

     /*
      * Re-create pixmaps
      */
     CreateUndoPixmap( display, window,
        width, height );
     CreateDrawingPixmap( display, window,
        width, height );

     /*
      * Change edit window size
      * to new bitmap size.
      */
     ResizeEditingWindow( width, height );
     }

/*
 * Copy new bitmap to
 * editing window and to
 * backing pixmaps.
 */
CopyPlane( display,
     new_bitmap,     /* source */
     drawing_pixmap,/* dest */
     pixmap_gc,      /* dest gc */
     0, 0,
     width, height,
     width, height );

XFlush( display );
```

```
        /*
         * Free up storage.
         */
        XFreePixmap( display, new_bitmap );

        /*
         * Refresh window
         */
        ToolRedraw( EDITING_WINDOW );

        /*
         * Store new file name.
         */
        SetFileName( display, window, filename );

        /*
         * Send output to X server.
         */
        XFlush( display );

}       /* LoadDrawappFile */

CheckForFileLoad( display, window, argc, argv )

Display         *display;
Window          window;
int             argc;
char            *argv[];

/*
 *      Looks for both "-file" and "-load"
 *      command-line arguments.
 */

{       /* CheckForFileLoad */

char            *filename, *FindParameter();

        filename = FindParameter( argc, argv, "-file" );

        if ( filename == (char *) NULL )
              {
              filename = FindParameter( argc, argv, "-load" );
              }
```

```
        if ( filename != (char *) NULL )
              {
              LoadDrawappFile( display, window, filename );
              }

}       /* CheckForFileLoad */

void SaveFile( id )

int     id;

{       /* SaveFile */
        extern int     editing_width, editing_height;
        extern Pixmap  drawing_pixmap;
        extern int     changed_flag;
        int            status;
        Display        *display;
        Display        *ToolGetDisplay();

        display = ToolGetDisplay( id );

        /*
         * Save current file
         */
        GetDialogData( da_filename );

        status = SaveBitmap( display,
                 da_filename,
                 drawing_pixmap,
                 editing_width, editing_height );

        if ( status != BitmapSuccess )
              {
              (void) fprintf( stderr,
                 "Error in saving to [%s]\n",
                 da_filename );
              }
        else
              {
              /*
               * Set global that file is saved.
               */
              changed_flag = BITMAP_SAVED;
              }
```

```
        UnhighlightPushButton( id );

}       /* SaveFile */

SetFileName( display, window, filename )

Display       *display;
Window        window;
char          filename[];

{       /* SetFileName */
        char          window_name[400];
        extern int    changed_flag;

        (void) strncpy( da_filename, filename,
                MAX_CHARS );

        da_filename[ MAX_CHARS ] = '\0';

        SetDialogData( da_filename );

        (void) sprintf( window_name,
                "DrawApp: %s", da_filename );

        SetWindowName( display, window, window_name );

        /*
         * Since we changed the file
         * name, we haven't yet saved.
         */
        changed_flag = BITMAP_CHANGED;

}       /* SetFileName */

void Quit( id )

int     id;

{       /* Quit */
        extern int      changed_flag;
        extern void     PopUpDialog();
        void            ReallyQuit();
        static int      quit_flag = 0;
```

```
        if ( quit_flag > 0 )
              {
              SaveFile( id );
              }

        /*
         * Prompt to save changes, if necessary
         */
        if ( changed_flag == BITMAP_CHANGED )
              {
              /*
               * Set up dialog values for
               * loading files.
               */
              SetDialogData( da_filename );
              SetDialogPrompt( "File not saved. Save it?" );

              SetDialogCallback( Quit );
              SetDialogCancelCallback( ReallyQuit );

              quit_flag = 1;

              PopUpDialog();
              }
        else
              {
              exit( 0 );
              }

}       /* Quit */

void ReallyQuit( id )

int     id;

{       /* ReallyQuit */

        exit( 0 );

}       /* ReallyQuit */

/* end of file da_file.c */
```

SOURCE CODE FOR THE FILE DA_META.C

```
/*
 *      da_meta.c
 *      Meta-Key handling in the Draw Application.
 *
 *      Written for X Window Applications
 *      Programming, 2nd Edition
 */

#include <X11/Xlib.h>
#include "drawapp.h"

HandleMetaKey( string )

char    string[];

{       /* HandleMetaKey */
        XEvent      event;
        KeySym      keysym;
        int         id = -1;
        void        PushButtonEvent();
        Display     *ToolGetDisplay();

        switch( string[0] )
              {
              case 'F':
              case 'f': id = FILL_RECT; break;
              case 'L':
              case 'l': id = DRAW_LINE; break;
              case 'O':
              case 'o': id = DRAW_OVAL; break;
              case 'P':
              case 'p': id = DRAW_POINTS; break;
              case 'Q':
              case 'q': id = QUIT_ID; break;
              case 'R':
              case 'r': id = DRAW_RECT; break;
              case 'S':
              case 's': id = SAVE_FILE; break;
              case 'T':
```

```
            case 't': id = DRAW_TEXT; break;
            case 'U':
            case 'u': id = UNDO_LAST; break;
            }

        if ( id >= 0 )
            {
            keysym = 0x0;
            event.type = ButtonPress;

            PushButtonEvent( ToolGetDisplay( id ), id,
               &event, keysym, string );
            }

}       /* HandleMetaKey */

/* end of file da_meta.c */
```

Chapter 19

ENHANCING THE DRAW APPLICATION

The Draw application, as presented in Section III of this book, is certainly not the be-all, end-all of X application programming. The Draw application does, however, cover most of the areas of X programming that you will need for creating your own application software.

This short chapter details some enhancements that you might want to make to the Draw application to better the program and learn more about X. Our intention is to provide ideas for both the Draw application and your own software, as well as give you some pointers as to how the ideas could be implemented. We outline a number of strategies and we suggest you pick at least one area and extend the Draw application. The best way to learn X programming is to do it, and building on a working foundation will make your extensions easier to program.

MULTIPLE LEVELS OF UNDO

Users tend to love undo functions, because they don't need to worry about making a bad mistake: the work can always be undone. Our Draw application provides undo, but only one level of undo. Implementing an undo that allows work to be undone back to the beginning would be a very useful, if hard to implement, feature.

HANDLING EXPOSE EVENTS

When dealing with really large bitmap files, the single most important enhancement to the Draw application would be to handle `Expose` events better. There are a number of choices for handling `Expose` events. We chose to redraw the exposed rectangle on each `Expose` event. For large bitmaps, this probably won't be very efficient. It may be better to wait until all of a given batch of `Expose` events arrive (when the count field equals zero), and then redraw the total area of the `Expose` events. The Draw application could keep a running count of the total area (bounding rectangle) for all the `Expose` events. Calling `XCopyPlane` once for a larger area may prove faster than calling it multiple times for many small areas.

ENLARGEMENTS AND FAT BITS

In comparing the Draw application with the standard X client called *bitmap*, you will notice that the bitmap program enlarges the display of the bitmaps it edits.

The Draw application draws everything at real, normal size. For small bitmap files, though, editing at real size is next to impossible. Conversely, the bitmap program doesn't work too well on bitmaps greater than 32 x 32 pixels. Even with a large bitmap, though, it is nice to enlarge an area (an area of the user's choice) so that you can edit it better. For instance, there are CAD or electronic-design applications where editing at the bitmap level is essential.

How would you enlarge an area? To enlarge an area, you need to know about every pixel in the area—whether the pixel is on or off. One way to get the pixels in an area is to use the function `XGetImage` to grab an area of the pixmap (remember that the entire contents of the bitmap are stored in a pixmap in the X server). Once the image is captured (into an `XImage` format image) you can use

`XGetPixel` to pull out individual pixels and then draw each pixel four or more times larger (depending on how large you want to make the enlargement):

```
Display          *display;
XImage           *ximage;
Drawable         drawable;
int              x, y;
unsigned int     width, height;
unsigned long    planemask;
int              format;

ximage = XGetImage( display,
                 drawable,    /* the pixmap in our case */
                 x, y,
                 width, height,
                 planemask,
                 format );
```

The format can be either `XYPixmap` or `ZPixmap`. Normally, you will want to use `XYPixmap`, since it only gets those planes that were asked for (and we are using a one-plane pixmap image). The planemask value we have been using is `0x01` in all our calls to `XCopyPlane`.

Once you have successfully grabbed the full image from the pixmap, you would then want to parse out each pixel in the image and display the pixel enlarged somehow. The enlarging is up to you (try using rectangles to start with), but to get out a single pixel value from an `XImage` structure, use `XGetPixel`:

```
XImage           *ximage;
int              x, y;
unsigned long    pixel;

pixel = XGetPixel( ximage, x, y );
```

(Notice that this is one of the few X routines that does not take a `Display` pointer as a parameter.)

The pixel can then be compared with `1` or `0` for monochrome bitmaps. Since the Draw application is monochrome, if the pixel is `0` then the bit isn't drawn; if it's `1`, then the bit is drawn.

When the user draws in the enlarged area, you need to also draw those pixels into the main pixmap and window, too, to keep the bitmap up-to-date.

SCROLLING

How do you edit a bitmap image larger than your available screen real estate? Many programs use some form of scroll bars—vertical and horizontal bars that allow users to move a small image over a large area, much like moving a magnifying glass over a page of text. The *xterm* client program, for example, can be set up with scroll bars that allow you to view text that has scrolled by (and off) the window's displaying area. Adding scroll bars to the Draw application would certainly improve the program, especially if there is a fat bits area showing part of the image enlarged, and allowing the user to scroll over the whole picture, enlarging any part of it.

CURSOR EDITING

X cursors can be made from bitmaps (see Chapter 13) using `XCreatePixmapCursor`. The only missing item in the Draw application is the lack of hot spots required by all cursors at an x, y location. All our calls to `XReadBitmapFile` ignore any hot spots identified in a bitmap file. Similarly, all our calls to XWriteBitmapFile sends `-1` as each hot-spot coordinate (for no hot spot). To be able to edit cursor shapes with the Draw application, you would need to add code to save the hot spots read in, write the hot spots back to disk, and allow the user to move and set hot spots in the drawing window. You'd probably also want to add a try-out cursor function that would change the Draw application window's cursor to the cursor being edited.

CUTTING AND PASTING/MOVING AND COPYING AREAS

One of the most handy features of any editor is the ability to cut out areas and paste them somewhere else. Most Windows and Macintosh programs, for example, allow the user to cut out areas into a clipboard and to paste the clipboard back in at any time to any position. As another example, the bitmap client program allows the user to move areas of pixels and to copy areas as well. Whatever method you prefer, the ability to cut and paste is a handy, well-liked feature. In the Draw application, using `XCopyPlane` to copy pixels onto an extra pixmap (and back) would be a start for providing cut and paste functions.

Users ought to be able to select areas in the picture and then move, copy or clear those areas.

CROPPING

Cropping an image allows you to capture an arbitrary part of the image, leaving out the rest of the picture. With a giant screen-sized Godzilla picture, you might want to use cropping to trim out all the picture except for Godzilla's head or his foot.

Again, the Xlib function `XCopyPlane` could provide a start.

FLIPPING, REVERSING AND ROTATING

Other operations that are fun to do on bitmap images include flipping the image upside down, rotating the image by 90 degrees (or 45 degrees or whatever) and reversing the image (turning all the white bits black and vice versa—which is available in the bitmap program).

HANDLING RESIZE EVENTS ON THE MAIN WINDOW

Currently, our Draw application doesn't do much when the user changes the size of the main application window. Users ought to be able to resize the main window and have the draw application react accordingly. If the user sizes the window too small, then perhaps scroll bars are appropriate. If the user sizes the window larger, then either there is more space or the user wants to edit a larger bitmap. Another option would be to scale the image up or down to fit the new size. This is up to the interface designer, but the program should be very clear and inform the user what is happening.

SUMMARY

We realize that the Draw application is not the great shining path to complete X Window System programming. In this chapter we provide some ways that Draw can be improved—improvements that could be implemented into any X application.

XLIB FUNCTIONS AND MACROS INTRODUCED IN THIS CHAPTER

`XGetImage`

`XGetPixel`

Section IV

X TOOLKITS

So far we have been discussing programming with low-level Xlib tools. In this next abbreviated section, we examine X Toolkits.

A great deal of X's future lies within these toolkits. Essentially toolkits are prewritten graphics routines that make a programmer's life simpler. By learning how to use X Toolkits well, you can create X applications in less time than in other programming environments.

Chapter 20

AN INTRODUCTION TO X TOOLKITS

To this point we've concentrated on Xlib, the X programming library interface. However, it's a good idea to be aware of the many X toolkits. If Xlib is a low-level library, the X toolkits comprise the highest level of the X Window System architecture.

Essentially, X toolkits are preprogrammed graphics routines written in C. A toolkit is like an erector set; you can put together different parts to form a program. These parts are basic data types called *widgets*. (If you're familiar with object-oriented programming, a widget is akin to an object.)

Most of these toolkits (see Figure 20.1) sit on top of the X Toolkit Intrinsics, or Xt. This X toolkit layer consists of support routines for menus, window frames, scroll bars, panels, and other graphical tools that can be assembled into a graphical user interface. The Xt Intrinsics (a standard part of X) sit on top of the Xlib library.

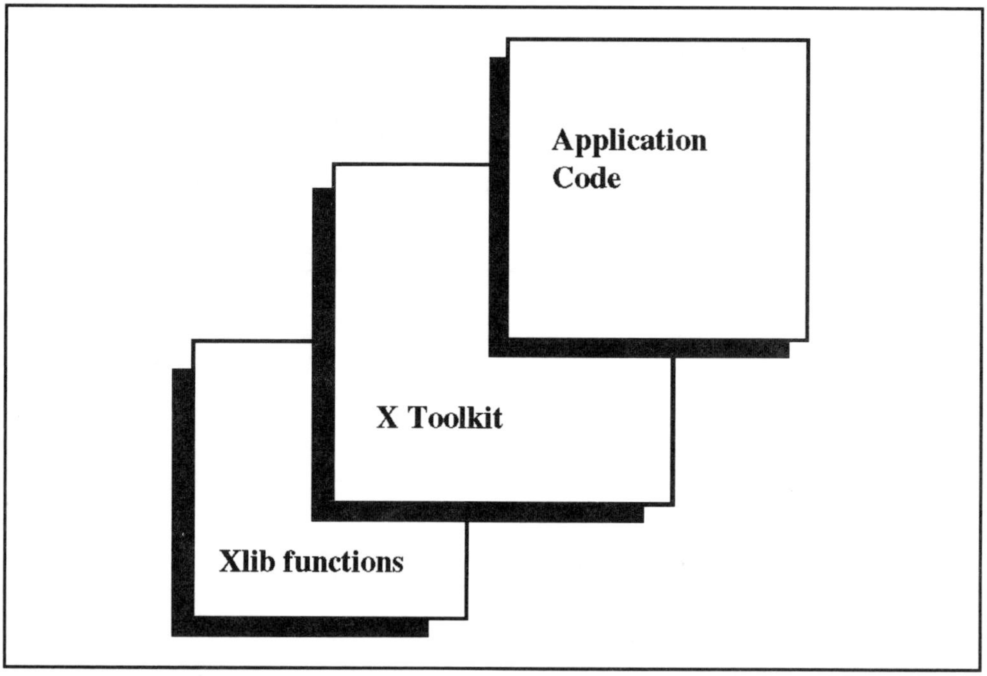

Figure 20.1. X Toolkit Layers.

The Xt Intrinsics provide a foundation for another layer's look and feel. Again, the designers of X pushed for mechanism, not policy. The Xt Intrinsics are part of the mechanism, and toolkits like the Athena widget set and Motif are the policy. Motif, for example, is paired with the Xt Intrinsics. Most X toolkits, in fact, build on top of the Xt Intrinsics. (Notable exceptions include Sun's XView toolkit, the Solbourne OI C++ toolkit and the InterViews C++ toolkit.)

Why toolkits?

- X designers worked hard to ensure software portability, so it shouldn't be surprising that they included guidelines for prewritten graphical user interfaces—why should software designers reinvent the wheel?
- The toolkit is the easiest way to provide consistent user interfaces from system to system and from implementation to implementation.
- Writing a complete application using Xlib forms is a significant task. Xlib isn't known for brevity. You can save a lot of coding time by using a toolkit.

In this chapter, we'll briefly introduce two popular widget-based toolkits, the Athena and Motif toolkits. It is beyond the scope of this book to cover the X toolkits in depth, but a small sample program will give you a flavor of both the good and the bad in these toolkits.

WIDGETS

Widgets form the basic building block for X toolkit-based applications. *Widgets* can be considered opaque data types that abstract user-interface components in an application. Widgets are used for scrollbars, pushbuttons, pop-up menus, and the like. Sound too dry and academic for you? Well, a widget is just a data structure—a *very* complicated data structure—that you create and manipulate. These widgets hide most of the messy details for managing the low-level interface, such as the task of scrolling a scrollbar. Unfortunately, while widgets take care of many low-level details in a graphical application, they also add their own complexity and force you to write applications in a certain convoluted style, whether you like it or not. All in all, X toolkits provide a handy means for creating applications more quickly than with just the X Library.

With Xt-based applications, you create widgets for your interface and set up all the desired options; after that, the Xt event-handling mechanism takes over, dispatching events to the proper widgets. The widgets then execute code in callback functions, much like our small toolkit built up in Section 3.

At its base level, a widget is simply a rectangle—a rectangle with a given means for input and output. In the sample below, we've chosen a simple class of widgets—the command or pushbutton class. For now, we need to create a widget-based program.

CREATING WIDGET-BASED PROGRAMS

There are five steps in creating a simple widget-based program:

1. Include the proper files.
2. Initialize the Xt Intrinsics and create a top-level widget.
3. Create your subwidgets.
4. Realize the widgets, mapping them to the screen.
5. Execute the Xt event loop—forever.

INCLUDING THE PROPER FILES

Almost every Xt-based C file needs to include the following files, `Intrinsic.h` and `StringDefs.h`:

```
#include <X11/Intrinsic.h>
#include <X11/StringDefs.h>
```

Also, you will probably need to include a header file for each widget class you use. Usually this file is named like the class, such as `Command.h` for the Athena command widget class:

```
#include  <X11/Xaw/Command.h>
```

There will also be a file containing the private parts of the widget class, with a P at the end of the name: `CommandP.h`.

Motif also requires an `include` file for each widget class, but these are different files than the Athena widget files. Motif `include` files are normally stored in `/usr/include/Xm`. Motif adds an extra file, `Xm.h`, which we'll cover below.

In the code below, we'll start with the Athena toolkit and then cover the same code structure using the Motif toolkit. Most X installations have either Motif or the Athena widgets; some have both. The concepts and the code for both are very similar, as you'll see. In fact, we'll use Xt functions exclusively and won't introduce any Athena or Motif-specific functions, because they simply aren't necessary for a short toolkit program like the one we'll develop. Both, for example, use the same code for initializing the Xt Intrinsics.

INITIALIZING THE INTRINSICS

For most Xt-based programs, the first step is initializing the Xt library with `XtInitialize`:

```
Widget              parent;
String              shell_name;
String              application_class;
XrmOptionDescRec    xrm_options[];
Cardinal            number_options;
Cardinal            argc;
String              argv[];
```

```
parent = XtInitialize( shell_name,
             application_class;
             xrm_options,
             number_options,
             &argc, argv );
```

The Xt Intrinsics function `XtInitialize` performs a number of functions:

- It sets up a display connection to the X server.
- It automatically handles all command-line parameters, as there is a mechanism to include your own special parameters with the standard X command-line parameters.
- It creates a top-level widget, which becomes the parent for all your other widgets.

Notice that there is no need for a `Display` pointer here. Also notice that the number of command-line parameters, `argc`, is sent as a pointer to an integer. `XtInitialize` may remove the options that it handles, modifying `argc` and `argv` in the process. Had we wanted to add in some of our own command-line parameters, they would be in the `XrmOptionDescRec` structure and the number of options passed would be in the variable `number_options`. In the code below, and in most cases, we have none.

4 Release

Starting with Release 4, `XtAppInitialize` replaces `XtInitialize`. Newer applications are supposed to use `XtAppInitialize`, but of course, older systems won't have this function available. In the code below, we again use the compile-time `define X11R4` to signify that you're compiling under an R4 or R5 system. With X11R4 defined, we use `XtAppInitialize`. Otherwise we use `XtInitialize`.

```
Widget                parent;
XtAppContext          app_context;
String                class_name;
XrmOptionDescList     xrm_options;
Cardinal              number_options;
cardinal              argc;
String                *argv;
String                *fallback_resources;
ArgList               args;
Cardinal              number_args;
```

```
parent = XtAppInitialize( app_context,
            class_name,
            xrm_options,
            number_options,
            &argc, argv,
            fallback_resources,
            args, number_args );
```

THE ATHENA COMMAND WIDGET

Both `XtAppInitialize` and `XtInitialize` return a top-level parent widget. This widget is a lot like the top-level application window we created for the Draw application in Section 3. You'll use this widget as the parent when creating child widgets, as we used the top-level window and a parent for child windows.

The first child widget we'll create is the Athena command widget. The command widget provides a mouse-activated pushbutton; that is, you move the mouse pointer into the window and click a mouse button. This activates the pushbutton and executes some code you've set up. You'll need to configure what code to execute, using a callback function.

The command widget requires the include file `Command.h`. Most widgets require a special include file.

ATHENA WIDGET INCLUDE FILES

4 Release

The standard place for the Athena widget include files are `/usr/include/X11/Xaw`. Prior to Release 4, these files were in `/usr/include/X11`, with all the other Xt and Xlib include files.

In the code below, we use the symbol `X11R4`, as we did starting in Chapter 2, to determine whether we want the files in `/usr/include/X11/Xaw` or `/usr/include/X11`. Note that your system may have the X `include` files in a different place; we're using the default locations.

Define `X11R4` if your system is at Release 4 of X11 or higher:

```
#ifdef X11R4
#include  <X11/Xaw/Command.h>
```

```
#else   /* older than Release 4 */

#include  <X11/Command.h>
#endif
```

CREATING WIDGETS

The next step is creating a command widget. The Xt Intrinsics function `XtCreateWidget` creates a widget of a given widget class.

Each widget has a unique name, a parent (in this case, the top-level widget returned by `XtInitialize`), a class (in this case the `commandWidgetClass`), and some values, stored in an array of `Arg` structures:

```
Widget          new_widget;
char            *widget_name;
Widget          parent_widget;
WidgetClass     widget_class = commandWidgetClass;
Arg             args[20];    /* arbitrary size */
Cardinal        number_args;

new_widget = XtCreateWidget( widget_name,
                widget_class,
                parent_widget,
                args, number_args );
```

MANAGING WIDGETS

Once widgets are created, they need to be managed. Managed widgets appear on the screen and are controlled by their parents. For example, the top-level parent widget will control the size of our command pushbutton widget. When the parent widget grows or shrinks, our command widget will grow or shrink accordingly. Call `XtManageChild` to manage a child widget:

```
Widget  widget;

XtManageChild( widget );
```

CREATING AND MANAGING WIDGETS

You can create and manage a widget with XtCreateManagedWidget:

```
Widget          new_widget;
char            *widget_name;
Widget          parent_widget;
WidgetClass     widget_class = commandWidgetClass;
Arg             args[20];    /* arbitrary size */
Cardinal        number_args;

new_widget = XtCreateManagedWidget( widget_name,
                widget_class,
                parent_widget,
                args, number_args );
```

We can create our widgets with the code below (written for R4 and higher):

```
#include  <stdio.h>
#include  <X11/Intrinsic.h>
#include  <X11/StringDefs.h>
#include  <X11/Xaw/Command.h>

main( argc, argv )

int     argc;
char    *argv[];

{       /* main */
        Widget          parent;
        Arg             args[20];
        int             n;
        Widget          quit_widget;
        XtAppContext    app_context;

        /*
         * Set up top-level shell widget
         */
        n = 0;
        parent = XtAppInitialize( &app_context,
                "Examples",
                (XrmOptionDescList ) NULL, 0,
                &argc, argv,
```

```
                (char *) NULL,
                args, n );

        /*
         * Set up command widget to
         * act as a push button
         */
        n = 0;
        quit_widget = XtCreateManagedWidget( "Quit-Program",
                commandWidgetClass,
                parent, args, n );

        ...
```

Note that we pass a widget name of Quit-Program and a widget class of `commandWidgetClass` (defined through `Command.h`). We pass no options in the `Arg` array.

Most widget names start with a lowercase letter, and the words are separated by capital letters. The name Quit-Program isn't a good name for a widget, but we're cheating here, since the widget's name is the default text to display in the window. We could also set up the text to display separately, but this is easier.

WIDGET CALLBACK FUNCTIONS

When the command widget is activated, it executes whatever C functions were set up as that widget's callback functions. You can set up a callback function with `XtAddCallback`. In our case, we want the command widget to call our `quit_callback` function (see below). `XtAddCallback` takes the following parameters:

```
Widget          widget;
String          which_callback;
XtPointer       client_data;
XtCallbackProc  (*callback_function)();

XtAddCallback( widget,
        which_callback,
        callback_function,
        client_data );
```

If your callback function doesn't need any extra data passed to it, you can pass NULL for the client_data:

```
client_data  = (caddr_t) NULL;
```

XtAddCallback requires the name of the callback. This sounds confusing, but each widget may support a number of callback functions for different things. A text widget, for example, may support a callback function for whenever the return key is pressed, as well as another callback function to handle each alphanumeric key that is pressed. In our case, the command widget's callback for when the pushbutton is activated is the "callback" callback. The constant XtNcallback is the string "callback":

```
which_callback = XtNcallback;
```

The actual callback function is passed the following parameters:

```
void callback_function( widget, client_data, call_data )

Widget       widget;
caddr_t      client_data;
caddr_t      call_data;

{       /* callback_function */
}       /* callback_function */
```

The widget is the widget for which this function is called back. The client_data is any extra data you chose to pass along. The call_data is any data passed from the widget. A list widget, for example, could pass the name of the selected item as the call_data. Usually, the call_data points to a structure specific to the widget. In our case, we really don't need to pay any attention to the call_data. You'll find this a lot when writing Xt-based programs.

Since each widget has a parent (except for the top-level widget), we end up with a hierarchy of widgets. These widgets still don't appear on the screen until you realize the hierarchy of widgets.

REALIZING WIDGETS

After a widget is created and managed in a hierarchy, it needs to be realized. Realizing a top-level widget will also realize all child widgets. XtRealizeWidget realizes a hierarchy of widgets and then maps these widgets to the screen with its default set up:

```
Widget  parent_widget;

XtRealizeWidget( parent );
```

`XtRealizeWidget` actually creates all the windows that underlie the widgets. Until you call `XtRealizeWidget`, no window IDs are created. (This is important if you mix Xlib and Xt programming.)

THE WIDGET EVENT LOOP

Once we've realized our widget hierarchy, we need to let the Xt Intrinsics take over with the toolkit's event loop.

In our Xlib source-code examples so far, the event-handling loop takes up a good portion of the source code. Using the Xt Intrinsics, however, you can handle events with one line of code, by calling the function `XtMainLoop`. `XtMainLoop` checks for X events and then dispatches these events to the proper widgets.

`XtMainLoop` loops until your program quits. You may not like this fact, but this is one of the conventions your code needs to follow when using the Xt Intrinsics.

4 Release

Starting with the development of application contexts in Release 4, `XtAppMainLoop` replaces `XtMainLoop`. `XtMainLoop` is now considered obsolete, and, of course, `XtAppMainLoop` doesn't exist prior to R4.

```
XtAppContext app_context;

XtAppMainLoop( app_context );
```

SOURCE CODE FOR THE ATHENA WIDGET PROGRAM

With one look at the source code below, you will see the most powerful aspect of the toolkits—the ability to deal with X in a high-level fashion. This program is tiny—about 2K on disk. But the functions it calls are powerful and large: the executable program took up 690K on disk using X11 R4 on a Data General Aviion.

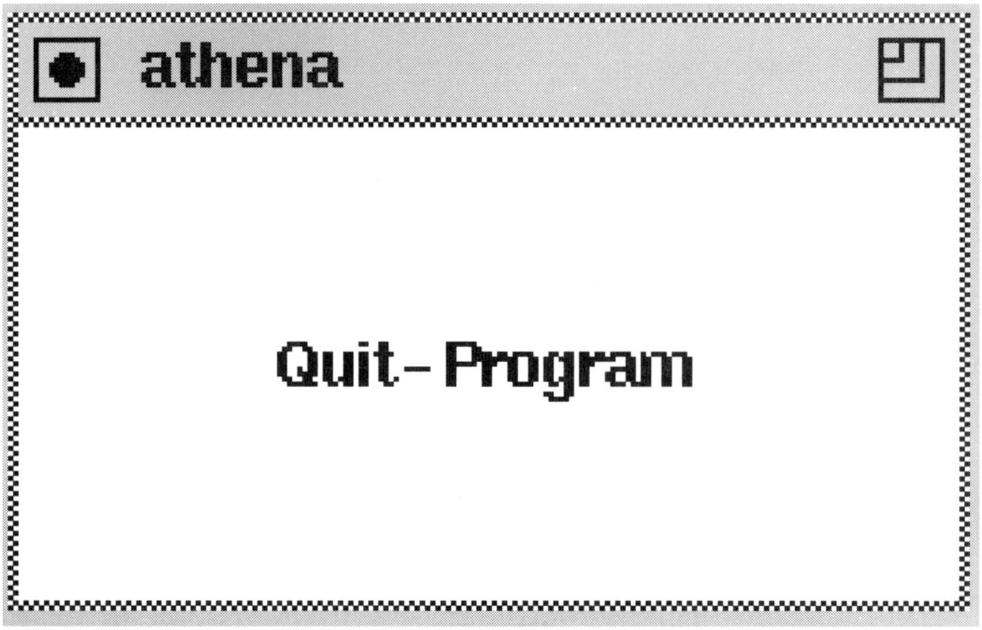

Figure 20.2. The Athena Program.

This program will create a window on the display with the string "Quit-Program" inside the window. The program will handle all events associated with the window, including redrawing exposed areas. Clicking the left mouse button inside the window will cause the program to quit.

The Athena widget sample program is in the file `athena.c`:

```
/*
 *      athena.c
 *      Simple Athena Widget Program
 *
 *      NOTE: If you are compiling under Release 4
 *      of X, or higher, be sure to define X11R4.
 *
 *      Written for X Window Applications
 *      Programming, 2nd Edition
 */

#include  <stdio.h>
#include  <X11/Intrinsic.h>
#include  <X11/StringDefs.h>
```

```
/*
 *      Release 4 has Athena include
 *      files in new places.
 */
#ifdef X11R4
#include  <X11/Xaw/Command.h>

#else   /* older than Release 4 */

#include  <X11/Command.h>
#endif

/* ARGSUSED */
void quit_callback( widget, client_data, call_data )

Widget        widget;
caddr_t       client_data;
caddr_t       call_data;

/*
 *      Callback function to quit program.
 *      We could close the connection to
 *      the X server here, or just call exit.
 */

{       /* quit_callback */

        exit( 0 );

}       /* quit_callback */

main( argc, argv )

int     argc;
char    *argv[];

{       /* main */
        Widget   parent;
        Arg      args[20];
        int      n;
        Widget   quit_widget;

#ifdef X11R4 /* Release 4 and newer */
```

```
        XtAppContext   app_context;

        /*
         * Set up top-level shell widget
         */
        n = 0;
        parent = XtAppInitialize( &app_context,
                  "Examples",
                  (XrmOptionDescList ) NULL, 0,
                  &argc, argv,
                  (char *) NULL,
                  args, n );

#else         /* Release 3 and older */

        parent = XtInitialize( argv[0],
                  "Examples",
                  NULL, 0,
                  &argc, argv );

#endif  /* X11R4 */

        /*
         * Set up command widget to
         * act as a push button
         */
        n = 0;
        quit_widget = XtCreateManagedWidget( "Quit-Program",
                     commandWidgetClass,
                     parent, args, n );

        /*
         * Set up a callback function
         * to be called whenever
         * the command push button is
         * "activated".
         */
        XtAddCallback( quit_widget, XtNcallback,
              quit_callback, (caddr_t) NULL );

        /*
         * Map widgets and handle events
         */
```

```
        XtRealizeWidget( parent );
#ifdef X11R4 /* Release 4 and newer */

        XtAppMainLoop( app_context );

#else         /* Release 3 and older */

        XtMainLoop();

#endif  /* X11R4 */

}       /* main */

/*      end of file athena.c */
```

COMPILING AND LINKING ATHENA WIDGET PROGRAMS

With Release 4 and higher, the Athena program requires the following libraries:

- The Athena widget library, `libXaw.a`, which provides the look and feel
- The (X Miscellaneous Utilities) library, `libXmu.a`
- The Xt Intrinsics library, `libXt.a`
- The X Extension library (for the SHAPE extension's rounded windows), `libXext.a`
- The low-level X library, `libX11.a`

These libraries should be stored in `/usr/lib`. Note that shared libraries may have a different name or (more likely) end with a different extension, such as `libXaw.so.4.0` for a shared version of the Athena widget library.

You can compile the Athena program with a command like:

```
cc -o athena -DX11R4 athena.c -lXaw -lXmu -lXt -lXext -lX11
```

You can use the Makefile in Appendix A and type:

```
make athena
```

First, though, you must configure the `Makefile` for the proper libraries and compile options necessary to create Athena widget programs.

Release 3 added the `Xmu` (X Miscellaneous Utilities) library, so you'll need to compile the Athena program with a command like:

```
cc -o athena athena.c -lXaw -lXmu -lXt -lX11
```

Prior to R3, you'll need a command like:

```
cc -o athena athena.c -lXaw -lXt -lX11
```

THE MOTIF TOOLKIT

Like the Athena widget set, the Motif toolkit provides a look and feel layer on top of the Xt Intrinsics. Motif includes a number of its own functions, but we don't need any for the short example program below. You'll find that Motif programs look a lot like Athena widget programs, which makes porting easier.

Like all Xt-based programs, the first step in writing a Motif program is to include the proper files. All Motif programs should include the following files:

```
#include <X11/Intrinsic.h>
#include <X11/StringDefs.h>
#include <Xm/Xm.h>
```

The `Xm.h` file contains standard Motif definitions and is usually stored in `/usr/include/Xm`. Your installations may vary. In addition to `Xm.h`, you'll also need to include a file for each type of widget you use, such as the Motif pushbutton widget.

THE MOTIF PUSHBUTTON WIDGET

The pushbutton widget (or `XmPushButton` in Motif terminology) is the Motif widget that most closely corresponds to the Athena command widget. Both widgets act much the same, but the Motif widget provides a 3D look and feel.

The pushbutton widget requires the include file `PushB.h`:

```
#include  <Xm/PushB.h>
```

We again use `XtCreateManagedWidget` to create the pushbutton widget, but note that the widget class is `xmPushButtonWidgetClass`:

```
Widget        new_widget;
char          *widget_name;
Widget        parent;
Arg           args[20];    /* arbitrary size */
Cardinal      number_args;

number_args = 0;
new_widget = XtCreateManagedWidget( "Quit-Program",
                  xmPushButtonWidgetClass,
                  parent, args, number_args );
```

The proper callback for the Motif pushbutton widget is the `activateCallback`, instead of the Athena name `callback`. Other than the different callback name, we use `XtAddCallback` in our Motif program the same way as we do in the Athena program:

```
XtAddCallback( new_widget,
             XmNactivateCallback,
             callback_function, (caddr_t) NULL );
```

SOURCE CODE FOR THE MOTIF PROGRAM

The sample Motif program acts exactly like the Athena program, above, except that the window shows the Motif 3D look.

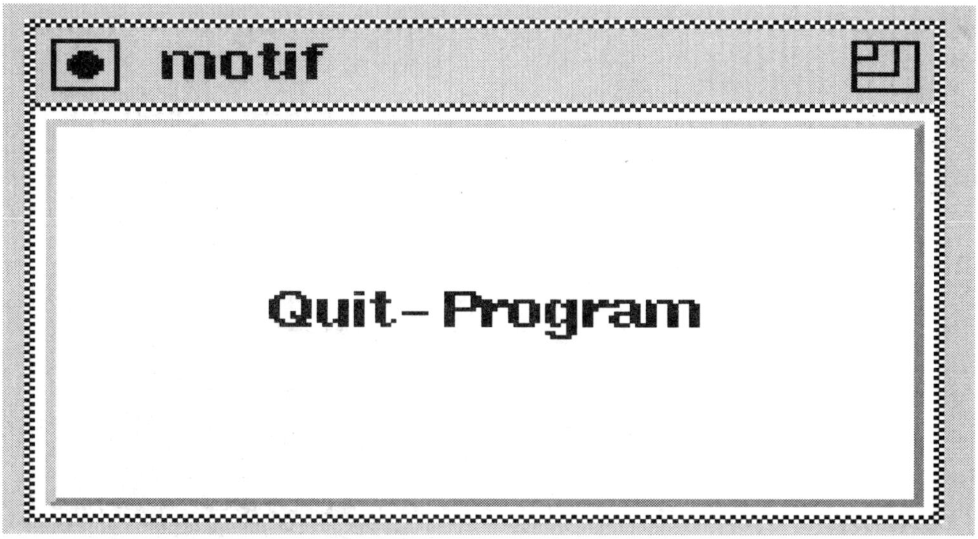

Figure 20.3. The Motif Program.

The sample Motif program is in the file `motif.c`:

```
/*
 *      motif.c
 *      Sample Motif widget program.
 *
 *      Written for X Window Applications
 *      Programming, 2nd Edition
 */

#include <stdio.h>

/*
 *      X Toolkit include files
 */
#include  <X11/Intrinsic.h>
#include  <X11/StringDefs.h>

/*
 *      Motif include files
 */
#include  <Xm/Xm.h>
#include  <Xm/PushB.h>

void quit_callback( widget, client_data, call_data )

Widget  widget;
caddr_t client_data;
caddr_t call_data;

/*
 *      Callback function to quit program.
 *      We could close the connection to
 *      the X server here, or just call exit.
 *
 *      Note that this callback is the same as
 *      the Athena widget callback.
 */

{        /* quit_callback */

        exit( 0 );
```

```
}       /* quit_callback */

main( argc, argv )

int     argc;
char    *argv[];

{       /* main */
        Widget   parent;
        Arg      args[10];
        int      n;
        Widget   quit_widget;

#ifdef X11R4 /* Release 4 and newer */
        XtAppContext   app_context;

        /*
         * Set up top-level shell widget
         */
        n = 0;
        parent = XtAppInitialize( &app_context,
                 "Examples",
                 (XrmOptionDescList ) NULL, 0,
                 &argc, argv,
                 (char *) NULL,
                 args, n );

#else          /* Release 3 and older */

        parent = XtInitialize( argv[0],
                 "Examples",
                 NULL, 0,
                 &argc, argv );

#endif  /* X11R4 */

        /*
         * Create a push button widget
         * to quit the program.
         */
        n = 0;
        quit_widget = XtCreateManagedWidget( "Quit-Program",
```

```
                xmPushButtonWidgetClass,
                parent, args, n );

             /*
              * Set up a callback function
              * to be called whenever
              * the push button is
              * "activated".
              */
             XtAddCallback( quit_widget,
                XmNactivateCallback,
                quit_callback, (caddr_t) NULL );

        XtRealizeWidget( parent );

#ifdef X11R4 /* Release 4 and newer */

        XtAppMainLoop( app_context );

#else        /* Release 3 and older */

#endif  /* X11R4 */

        XtMainLoop();

}       /* main */

/*      end of file motif.c */
```

COMPILING AND LINKING MOTIF PROGRAMS

Motif programs require the Motif library, `libXm.a`; the Xt Intrinsics library, `libXt.a`; and the X library, `libX11.a`. You can compile the sample program with a command like:

```
cc -o motif -DX11R4 motif.c -lXm -lXt -lX11
```

Or, you can use the Makefile in Appendix A. Be sure to configure the proper Motif libraries first:

```
make motif
```

FINDING OUT MORE ABOUT THE X TOOLKITS

This chapter only provides the barest glimpse at the advantages and disadvantages of X toolkits. Our book *Power Programming Motif* teaches Motif programming in far greater depth than this chapter ever could. (Look in *Power Programming Motif* Appendix H for a listing of more Motif and X toolkit books.) Many vendors provide Motif and Motif documentation with their version of the X Window System. The MIT X Consortium version of X includes the Athena widget set with documentation.

SUMMARY

X toolkits provide a means to shorten the development process by using a set of prewritten graphical routines.

If toolkits are so good, though, why use Xlib at all? Many people, in fact, hold this opinion. We've found, though, that not only do all significant X toolkit-based applications require the use of Xlib at various points, an understanding of the X Library is essential for building commercial-grade X applications.

We discuss two popular widget-based toolkits, the Athena and Motif toolkits. Widgets form the basic building block for X toolkit-based applications. A widget is just a data structure—a *very* complicated data structure—that you create and manipulate. These widgets hide most of the messy details for managing the low-level interface, such as the task of scrolling a scrollbar.

There are five steps in creating a simple-widget-based program:

1. Include the proper files.
2. Initialize the Xt Intrinsics and create a top-level widget.
3. Create your subwidgets.
4. Realize the widgets, mapping them to the screen.
5. Execute the Xt event loop—forever.

XT FUNCTIONS AND MACROS INTRODUCED IN THIS CHAPTER

XtAddCallback

XtAppInitialize

XtAppMainLoop

XtCreateManagedWidget

XtCreateWidget

XtInitialize

XtMainLoop

XtManageChild

XtRealizeWidget

Appendix A

A MAKEFILE FOR THE SAMPLE PROGRAMS

You can use the UNIX make utility to compile and link all the sample programs. You must first configure the Makefile below for your system, however. We find that configuring the Makefile once for your system avoids typing in the very complex commands to compile and link X programs.

Follow the steps 1 to 4 listed in comments in the Makefile to set everything up for your system.

The contents of the Makefile follow:

```
#
#       Makefile for X Window Applications
#       Programming, 2nd Edition
#
#       To compile all the example sources,
#       follow STEPS 1 to 4 below to customize this
#       Makefile for your system. Then, type
#
#            make all
#
#       and away you go.
#
```

```
#-----------------------------------------------------------
#
#       STEP 1: CC is the C compiler command you need to
#       invoke, plus whatever flags are necessary. Some
#       samples are below.
#
#       If you are using X11 Release 4 or higher (or the
#       equivalent thereof), define the symbol X11R4.
#
#       Some common defines for the C compiler:
#       cc       Standard Unix C compiler
#       gcc      GNU C compiler (standard cc on DG Aviions)
#       -O       Optimize
#       -g       Include debugging information (usually
#                precludes optimizing)
#       sysv     Unix System V or equivalent.
#       SYSV     Unix System V or equivalent.
#       SVR4_0   Unix System V Release 4
#       LAI_TCP  Lachman TCP definition for 386 UNIX
#       i386     386-based processor (Intel byte ordering)
#       X_WCHAR  May be needed for Release 5 pre-ANSI C
#
#       Generic X11 R4/R5    cc -g -DX11R4
#       Generic X11 R3       cc -g
#
#       HP-UX 7.0, HP 9000/800  cc -g
#       SCO ODT 1.0, 1.1     -DLAI_TCP -Di386 -DSYSV
#       Esix SVR4            -DX11R4 -DSYSV -DSVR4_0 -Di386
#       Aviion DG-UX 4.3     -DX11R4
#
#       Put the flags necessary for your system below:
CC=     cc -g -DX11R4
#
#-----------------------------------------------------------
#
#       STEP 2: LIBS are the libraries needed to link
#       an X program. You may need to specify where
#       the linker should look for the X
#       libraries, using the -L option.
#
#       If your X Window libraries are in a non-standard
#       place, like /usr/opt/X11, use something like the
#       following:  -L/usr/opt/X11/lib -lX11
```

```
#
#       Generic X11    -lX11
#
#       SCO Open Desktop  -lX11 -ltlisock -lsocket -lnsl_s
#       Esix SVR4         -lX11 -lsocket -lnsl -lns
#       Interactive  2.2  -lX11 -linet
#
#       Put the library flags below:
LIBS = -lX11
#
#---------------------------------------------------------
#
#       STEP 3: Toolkit Libraries
#       ATHENA_LIBS are the libraries needed to compile
#       an Athena widget (Xaw) program.
#
#       -lXaw Athena widget library, libXaw.a
#       -lXmu X Misc. Utilities library, libXmu.a
#       -lXt     Xt Intrinsics library, libXt.a
#       -lXext   X extension library, libXext.a
#       -lX11 good 'ol X library, libX11.a
#
#       X11R4/R5
#       -lXaw -lXmu -lXt -lXext -lX11
#       X11R3
#       -lXaw -lXt -lX11
#
ATHENA_LIBS= -lXaw -lXmu -lXt -lXext -lX11
#
#       MOTIF_LIBS are the libraries needed to compile
#       a Motif widget (Xm) program.
#
#       -lXm     Motif widget library, libXm.a
#
MOTIF_LIBS=  -lXm -lXt -lX11
#
#       Your system may not have both the Motif and Athena
#       libraries. TOOLKIT_APPS specify which toolkit
#       programs to build: motif and/or athena
#
#       TOOLKIT_APPS=  motif
#       TOOLKIT_APPS=  athena
#       TOOLKIT_APPS=  athena motif
```

```
#
TOOLKIT_APPS=   athena motif
#
#----------------------------------------------------------
#
#       STEP 4: Release 5 Application. If you have X11 R5
#       or higher, set R5_APPS to chap4cms.
#
#       Otherwise, comment out the R5_APPS definition.
#
#       Pre-R5:
#            R5_APPS=
#       R5:
#            R5_APPS= chap4cms
#
R5_APPS= chap4cms
#
#----------------------------------------------------------
#
#       Compile all the sample programs with make all.
#

all:    chap1 chap2 chap3 chap4 chap5 chap6 chap7 chap8 \
        chap9 chap10 chap11 chap12 chap13 drawapp \
        $(TOOLKIT_APPS) $(R5_APPS)

#
#       Chapter 1 Building a First X Program
#
connect.o:   connect.c
        $(CC) -c connect.c

chap1.o:     chap1.c
        $(CC) -c chap1.c

chap1:  chap1.o connect.o
        $(CC) -o chap1 chap1.o connect.o $(LIBS)

#
#       Chapter 2 Creating Windows
#
classhnt.o:  classhnt.c
        $(CC) -c classhnt.c
```

```
sizehint.o:  sizehint.c
        $(CC) -c sizehint.c

window.o:    window.c
        $(CC) -c window.c

wmhints.o:   wmhints.c
        $(CC) -c wmhints.c

wmname.o:    wmname.c
        $(CC) -c wmname.c

chap2.o:     chap2.c
        $(CC) -c chap2.c

chap2:       chap2.o classhnt.o connect.o sizehint.o window.o \
             wmhints.o wmname.o
        $(CC) -o chap2 chap2.o wmhints.o wmname.o \
             classhnt.o connect.o sizehint.o \
             window.o $(LIBS)

#
#       Chapter 3 Drawing With X
#
gc.o:   gc.c
        $(CC) -c gc.c

oval.o: oval.c
        $(CC) -c oval.c

chap3.o:     chap3.c
        $(CC) -c chap3.c

chap3:       chap3.o gc.o oval.o classhnt.o connect.o \
             sizehint.o window.o wmhints.o wmname.o
        $(CC) -o chap3 chap3.o gc.o oval.o wmhints.o wmname.o \
             classhnt.o connect.o sizehint.o window.o $(LIBS)

#
#       Chapter 4 Color
#
color.o:     color.c
        $(CC) -c color.c
```

```
colormap.o:  colormap.c
        $(CC) -c colormap.c

visual.o:    visual.c
        $(CC) -c visual.c

chap4.o:     chap4.c
        $(CC) -c chap4.c

chap4:       chap4.o color.o colormap.o gc.o oval.o \
             visual.o wmhints.o wmname.o classhnt.o \
             connect.o sizehint.o window.o
        $(CC) -o chap4 chap4.o color.o colormap.o gc.o oval.o \
             visual.o classhnt.o connect.o sizehint.o \
             window.o wmhints.o wmname.o $(LIBS)

#
#       Chapter 4 Release 5's Device-Independent Color
#
colorcms.o:  colorcms.c
        $(CC) -c colorcms.c

chap4cms:    chap4cms.o colorcms.o colormap.o gc.o oval.o \
             visual.o wmhints.o wmname.o \
             classhnt.o connect.o sizehint.o window.o
        $(CC) -o chap4cms chap4cms.o colorcms.o colormap.o \
             gc.o visual.o classhnt.o connect.o \
             sizehint.o window.o oval.o wmhints.o \
             wmname.o $(LIBS)

#
#       Chapter 5 Text and Fonts
#
chap5.o:     chap5.c
        $(CC) -c chap5.c

loadfont.o:  loadfont.c
        $(CC) -c loadfont.c

fontht.o:    fontht.c
        $(CC) -c fontht.c
```

```
chap5:        chap5.o fontht.o gc.o loadfont.o wmhints.o wmname.o \
              classhnt.o connect.o sizehint.o window.o
       $(CC) -o chap5 chap5.o fontht.o gc.o loadfont.o \
              classhnt.o connect.o sizehint.o window.o \
              wmhints.o wmname.o $(LIBS)


#
#
#      Chapter 6 Events
#
chap6.o:      chap6.c
       $(CC) -c chap6.c

append.o:     append.c
       $(CC) -c append.c

drawstr.o:    drawstr.c
       $(CC) -c drawstr.c

chap6: chap6.o append.o drawstr.o gc.o loadfont.o \
              classhnt.o connect.o sizehint.o window.o \
              wmhints.o wmname.o
       $(CC) -o chap6 chap6.o append.o drawstr.o \
              gc.o loadfont.o classhnt.o connect.o \
              sizehint.o window.o \
              wmhints.o wmname.o $(LIBS)


#
#      Chapter 7 Keyboard and Mouse Events
#
chap7.o:      chap7.c
       $(CC) -c chap7.c

key.o: key.c
       $(CC) -c key.c

chap7:        chap7.o append.o drawstr.o gc.o key.o loadfont.o \
              classhnt.o connect.o sizehint.o window.o \
              wmhints.o wmname.o
       $(CC) -o chap7 chap7.o append.o drawstr.o gc.o \
              key.o loadfont.o wmhints.o wmname.o \
              classhnt.o connect.o sizehint.o window.o $(LIBS)
```

```
#
#       Chapter 8 Cursors
#
chap8.o:        chap8.c
        $(CC) -c chap8.c

chap8:          chap8.o drawstr.o fontht.o gc.o key.o loadfont.o \
                classhnt.o connect.o sizehint.o window.o \
                wmhints.o wmname.o
        $(CC) -o chap8 chap8.o drawstr.o fontht.o gc.o key.o \
                loadfont.o wmhints.o wmname.o \
                classhnt.o connect.o sizehint.o window.o $(LIBS)

#
#       Chapter 9 Bitmaps and Icons: Off-Screen
#       Drawing with Pixmaps
#
bitmap.o:       bitmap.c
        $(CC) -c bitmap.c

icon.o: icon.c
        $(CC) -c icon.c

pixmap.o:       pixmap.c
        $(CC) -c pixmap.c

chap9.o:        chap9.c
        $(CC) -c chap9.c

chap9:          chap9.o gc.o key.o bitmap.o icon.o pixmap.o \
                classhnt.o connect.o sizehint.o window.o \
                wmhints.o wmname.o
        $(CC) -o chap9 chap9.o gc.o key.o \
                bitmap.o icon.o pixmap.o \
                classhnt.o connect.o sizehint.o window.o \
                wmhints.o wmname.o $(LIBS)

#
#       Chapter 10 Rubber-Band Lines and Shapes
#
chap10.o:       chap10.c
        $(CC) -c chap10.c
```

```
xor.o:  xor.c
        $(CC) -c xor.c

chap10:         chap10.o gc.o key.o oval.o xor.o bitmap.o \
                icon.o pixmap.o classhnt.o connect.o \
                sizehint.o window.o wmhints.o wmname.o
        $(CC) -o chap10 chap10.o gc.o key.o oval.o xor.o \
                bitmap.o icon.o pixmap.o wmhints.o wmname.o \
                classhnt.o connect.o sizehint.o window.o $(LIBS)


#
#       Chapter 11 Common Command-Line Parameters
#
args.o:         args.c
        $(CC) -c args.c

display.o:      display.c
        $(CC) -c display.c

fontname.o:     fontname.c
        $(CC) -c fontname.c

geometry.o:     geometry.c
        $(CC) -c geometry.c

usage.o:        usage.c
        $(CC) -c usage.c

chap11.o:       chap11.c
        $(CC) -c chap11.c

chap11:         chap11.o fontht.o fontname.o key.o bitmap.o \
                icon.o pixmap.o drawstr.o gc.o loadfont.o \
                wmhints.o wmname.o classhnt.o connect.o \
                sizehint.o window.o args.o display.o \
                geometry.o usage.o
        $(CC) -o chap11 chap11.o key.o fontht.o fontname.o \
                args.o display.o geometry.o usage.o \
                bitmap.o icon.o pixmap.o \
                drawstr.o gc.o loadfont.o wmhints.o wmname.o \
                classhnt.o connect.o sizehint.o window.o $(LIBS)
```

```
#
#       Chapter 12 Sending More Information to the
#       Window Manager.
#
topwind.o:   topwind.c
        $(CC) -c topwind.c

chap12.o:    chap12.c
        $(CC) -c chap12.c

chap12:      chap12.o fontht.o fontname.o key.o topwind.o \
             bitmap.o icon.o pixmap.o \
             drawstr.o gc.o loadfont.o wmhints.o wmname.o \
             classhnt.o connect.o sizehint.o window.o \
             args.o display.o geometry.o usage.o
        $(CC) -o chap12 chap12.o key.o fontht.o fontname.o \
             topwind.o bitmap.o icon.o pixmap.o \
             args.o display.o geometry.o usage.o \
             drawstr.o gc.o loadfont.o wmhints.o wmname.o \
             classhnt.o connect.o sizehint.o window.o $(LIBS)

#
#       Chapter 13 Handling X Errors
#
error.o:     error.c
        $(CC) -c error.c

startupx.o:  startupx.c
        $(CC) -c startupx.c

chap13.o:    chap13.c
        $(CC) -c chap13.c

chap13:      chap13.o error.o gc.o topwind.o startupx.o \
             args.o display.o geometry.o usage.o \
             classhnt.o connect.o sizehint.o window.o \
             wmhints.o wmname.o
        $(CC) -o chap13 chap13.o error.o gc.o topwind.o \
             args.o display.o geometry.o usage.o \
             startupx.o wmhints.o wmname.o \
             classhnt.o connect.o sizehint.o window.o $(LIBS)
```

```
#
#       Chapter 14 Building a Small Toolkit
#
toolkit.o:      toolkit.c
                $(CC) -c toolkit.c

pushb.o:        pushb.c
                $(CC) -c pushb.c

entry.o:        entry.c
                $(CC) -c entry.c

label.o:        label.c
                $(CC) -c label.c

#
#       Chapter 15 Pop-up Dialogs and Transient Windows
#
dialog.o:       dialog.c
                $(CC) -c dialog.c

query.o:        query.c
                $(CC) -c query.c

tranwind.o:     tranwind.c
                $(CC) -c tranwind.c

#
#       Chapter 17 Editing Pixmaps
#
da_undo.o:      da_undo.c drawapp.h
                $(CC) -c da_undo.c

#
#       Chapter 18 The Drawapp Application Source Code
#
da_file.o:      da_file.c drawapp.h
        $(CC) -c da_file.c

drawapp.o:      drawapp.c drawapp.h
                $(CC) -c drawapp.c
```

```
da_draw.o:     da_draw.c drawapp.h
               $(CC) -c da_draw.c

da_edit.o:     da_edit.c drawapp.h
               $(CC) -c da_edit.c

da_meta.o:     da_meta.c drawapp.h
               $(CC) -c da_meta.c

da_pix.o:      da_pix.c
               $(CC) -c da_pix.c

drawapp:       toolkit.o pushb.o entry.o label.o dialog.o \
               drawapp.o da_edit.o da_file.o da_draw.o da_pix.o \
               tranwind.o da_undo.o fontht.o query.o da_meta.o \
               args.o display.o geometry.o usage.o color.o \
               error.o colormap.o bitmap.o icon.o pixmap.o \
               fontname.o gc.o key.o loadfont.o startupx.o \
               oval.o topwind.o visual.o xor.o \
               classhnt.o connect.o sizehint.o window.o \
               wmhints.o wmname.o
               $(CC) -o drawapp toolkit.o pushb.o entry.o \
               label.o dialog.o drawapp.o da_edit.o \
               da_file.o da_draw.o da_pix.o tranwind.o \
               da_undo.o fontht.o query.o args.o display.o \
               geometry.o usage.o color.o error.o \
               colormap.o bitmap.o icon.o pixmap.o da_meta.o \
               fontname.o gc.o key.o loadfont.o startupx.o \
               oval.o topwind.o visual.o xor.o \
               classhnt.o connect.o sizehint.o window.o \
               wmhints.o wmname.o $(LIBS)

#
#       Chapter 20 Introducing X Toolkits
#
athena: athena.c
        $(CC) -o athena athena.c $(ATHENA_LIBS)

motif:  motif.c
        $(CC) -o motif motif.c $(MOTIF_LIBS)

#
#       end of file
#
```

Appendix B

EVENTS

The XEvent type returned by the event-checking routines is a union of many structures overlaid on top of each other. When an event is received, the key aspects are: 1) determining the event type, and 2) pulling out the relevant data from the event structure. The XEvent union is defined as:

```
typdef union _XEvent {
      int                              type;
      XAnyEvent                        xany;
      XKeyEvent                        xkey;
      XButtonEvent                     xbutton;
      XMotionEvent                     xmotion;
      XCrossingEvent                   xcrossing;
      XFocusChangeEvent                xfocus;
      XExposeEvent                     xexpose;
      XGraphicsExposeEvent             xgraphicsexpose;
      XNoExposeEvent                   xnoexpose;
      XVisibilityEvent                 xvisibility;
      XCreateWindowEvent               xcreatewindow;
      XDestroyWindowEvent              xdestroywindow;
      XUnmapEvent                      xunmap;
      XMapEvent                        xmap;
```

```
        XMapRequestEvent              xmaprequest;
        XReparentEvent                xreparent;
        XConfigureEvent               xconfigure;
        XGravityEvent                 xgravity;
        XResizeRequestEvent           xresizerequest;
        XConfigureRequestEvent        xconfigurerequest;
        XCirculateEvent               xcirculate;
        XCirculateRequestEvent        xcirculaterequest;
        XPropertyEvent                xproperty;
        XSelectionClearEvent          xselectionclear;
        XSelectionRequestEvent        xselectionrequest;
        XSelectionEvent               xselection;
        XColormapEvent                xcolormap;
        XClientMessageEvent           xclient;
        XMappingEvent                 xmapping;
        XErrorEvent                   xerror;
        XKeymapEvent                  xkeymap;
        long                          pad[24];
        } XEvent;
```

Using the information in the following, you can decode almost any event that comes in. First check the type, as:

```
int         type;

XEvent  event;

type = event.type;
```

Then, if the event is, say, a `ButtonPress` event, you can access the information associated with the event by using:

```
int         x, y;
XEvent  event;

x = event.xbutton.x;
y = event.xbutton.y;
```

And so on.

Each type of event is listed in the following section, with the event types (returned in the `XEvent` union), the event mask (to ask for in an `XSelectInput` or `XCreateWindow` call) and the event structure. They are listed in alphabetical order.

There are event masks to ask for just about every event type, and a few types arrive whether you want them or not.

Mask Defined	***Asks for Event Type***
`Button1MotionMask`	`MotionNotify`
`Button2MotionMask`	`MotionNotify`
`Button3MotionMask`	`MotionNotify`
`Button4MotionMask`	`MotionNotify`
`Button5MotionMask`	`MotionNotify`
`ButtonMotionMask`	`MotionNotify` (any button)
`ButtonPressMask`	`ButtonPress`
`ButtonReleaseMask`	`ButtonRelease`
`ColormapChangeMask`	`ColormapNotify`
`EnterWindowMask`	`EnterNotify`
`ExposureMask`	`Expose`
`FocusChangeMask`	`FocusIn, FocusOut`
`KeymapStateMask`	`KeymapNotify`
`KeyPressMask`	`KeyPress`
`KeyReleaseMask`	`KeyRelease`
`LeaveWindowMask`	`LeaveNotify`
`NoEventMask`	`None`
`OwnerGrabButtonMask`	`None`
`PointerMotionHintMask`	`None`
`PointerMotionMask`	`MotionNotify`
`PropertyChangeMask`	`PropertyNotify`
`ResizeRedirectMask`	`ResizeRequest`
`StructureNotifyMask`	`CirculateNotify, ConfigureNotify, DestroyNotify, GravityNotify, MapNotify, ReparentNotify, UnmapNotify`

Mask Defined	***Asks for Event Type (cont.)***
SubstructureNotifyMask	CirculateNotify, ConfigureNotify, CreateNotify, DestroyNotify, GravityNotify, MapNotify, ReparentNotify, UnmapNotify
SubstructureRedirectMask	CirculateRequest, ConfigureRequest, MapRequest
VisibilityChangeMask	VisibilityNotify

ButtonPress, ButtonRelease

Description: These are the pointer button events.

Event Mask: ButtonPressMask, ButtonReleaseMask

Event Structure Name: XButtonPressEvent, XButtonReleasedEvent

```
typedef struct {
    int          type;        /* of event */
    unsigned long serial;     /* # of last request processed by server */
    Bool         send_event;/* true if this came from SendEvent request*/
    Display      *display;    /* display the event was read from */
    Window       window;      /* event window it is reported relative to */
    Window       root;        /* root window that the event occurred on */
    Window       subwindow;   /* child window */
    Time         time;        /* milliseconds */
    int          x, y;        /* pointer coords relative to receiving window */
    int          x_root, y_root; /* coordinates relative to root */
    unsigned int state        /* key or button mask */
    unsigned int button;      /* detail */
    Bool         same_screen/* same screen flag */
 } XButtonEvent;

typedef XButtonEvent   XButtonPressedEvent;
typedef XButtonEvent   XButtonReleasedEvent;
```

CirculateNotify

Description: `CirculateNotify` events report a call to change the stacking order of a window configuration, including the final order of the window.

Event Mask: `StructureNotifyMask`

Event Structure Name: `XCirculateEvent`

```
typedef struct {
     int           type;
     unsigned long serial;     /* # of last request processed by server */
     Bool          send_event;/* true if this came from SendEvent request */
     Display       *display;  /* display the event was read from */
     Window        event;
     Window        window;
     int place;               /* PlaceOnTop, PlaceOnBottom */
     } XCirculateEvent;
```

CirculateRequest

Description: When the stacking order of a window is selected and changed, `CirculateRequest` events report when `XCirculateSubwindows`, `XCirculateSubwindowsUp`, or `XCirculateSubwindowsDown` is called.

Event Mask: `SubstructureRedirectMask`

Event Structure Name: `XCirculateRequestEvent`

```
typedef struct {
     int           type;
     unsigned long serial;     /* # of last request processed by server */
     Bool          send_event;/* true if this came from SendEvent request */
     Display       *display;  /* display the event was read from */
     Window        event;
     Window        window;
     int           place;     /* PlaceOnTop, PlaceOnBottom */
     } XCirculateRequestEvent;
```

ClientMessage

Description: These events occur when the function `XSendEvent` is called by a client.

Event Mask: Always selected.

Event Structure Name: `XClientMessageEvent`

```
typedef struct {
     int           type;
     unsigned long serial;     /* # of last request processed by server */
     Bool          send_event;/* true if this came from SendEvent request */
     Display       *display;  /* display the event was read from */
     Window        window;
     Atom          message_type;
     int           format;
     union {
        char       b[20];
        short      s[10];
        long       l[5];
        } data;
     } XClientMessageEvent;
```

ColormapNotify

Description: This event charts changes in the colormap attribute or to the attribute itself in a particular window.

Event Mask: `ColormapChangeMask`

Event Structure Name: `XColormapEvent`

```
typedef struct {
     int           type;
     unsigned long serial;     /* # of last request processed by server */
     Bool          send_event;/* true if this came from SendEvent request */
     Display       *display;  /* display the event was read from */
     Window        window;
     Colormap      colormap;  /* Colormap or None */
     Bool          new;
     int           state;     /* ColormapInstalled, ColormapUninstalled */
     } XColormapEvent;
```

ConfigureNotify

Description: This event highlights changes to a window's configuration.

Event Mask: StructureNotifyMask

Event Structure Name: XConfigureEvent

```
typedef struct {
    int           type;
    unsigned long serial;     /* # of last request processed by server */
    Bool          send_event;/* true if this came from SendEvent request*/
    Display       *display;  /* display the event was read from */
    Window        event;
    Window        window;
    int           x, y;
    int           width, height;
    int           border_width;
    Window        above;
    Bool          override_redirect;
    } XConfigureEvent;
```

ConfigureRequest

Description: This events reports when another client requests to change its window configuration.

Event Mask: SubstructureRedirectMask

Event Structure Name: XConfigureRequestEvent

```
typedef struct {
    int           type;
    unsigned long serial;     /* # of last request processed by server */
    Bool          send_event;/* true if this came from SendEvent request*/
    Display       *display;  /* display the event was read from */
    Window        parent;
    Window        window;
    int           x, y;
    int           width, height;
    int           border_width;
    Window        above;
    int           detail;     /* Above, Below, Topif, BottomIf, Opposite */
    unsigned long  value_mask;
    } XConfigureRequestEvent;
```

CreateNotify

Description: When windows are created, this event is reported to the client by the X server.

Event Mask: `SubstructureNotifyMask`

Event Structure Name: `XCreateWindowEvent`

```
typedef struct {
     int           type;
     unsigned long serial;     /* # of last request processed by server */
     Bool          send_event;/* true if this came from SendEvent request*/
     Display       *display;  /* display the event was read from */
     Window        parent;    /* parent of the window */
     Window        window;    /* window ID of window created */
     int           x, y;      /* window location */
     int           width, height;     /* size of window */
     int           border_width;      /* border width */
     Bool          override_redirect; /* creation should be overridden */
     } XCreateWindowEvent;
```

DestroyNotify

Description: As might be expected, `DestroyNotify` events report that a window has been destroyed.

Event Mask: `SubstructureNotifyMask`

Event Structure Name: `XDestroyWindowEvent`

```
typedef struct {
     int           type;
     unsigned long serial;     /* # of last request processed by server */
     Bool          send_event;/* true if this came from SendEvent request*/
     Display       display;   /* display the event was read from */
     Window        event;
     Window        window;
     } XDestroyWindowEvent;
```

EnterNotify, LeaveNotify

Description: These events occur when a pointer enters and leaves a window.

Event Mask: `EnterWindowMask, LeaveWindowMask`

Event Structure Name: `XCrossingEvent`

```
typedef struct {
     int          type;          /* EnterNotify or LeaveNotify */
unsigned long     serial;        /* # last request processed by server */
     Bool         send_event;    /* true if from XSendEvent */
     Display      *display;
     Window       window;               /* window event occurred on */
     Window       root;                 /* root window the event occurred on */
     Window       subwindow;            /* child window */
     Time         time;                 /* milliseconds */
     int          x, y;                 /* pointer x, y coordinates in window */
     int          x_root, y_root;       /* coordinates relative to root */
     int          mode;
     int          detail;
     Bool         same_screen;          /* same screen flag */
     Bool         focus;                /* boolean focus */
     unsigned int state;                /* key or button mask */
     } XCrossingEvent;

typedef XCrossingEvent     XEnterWindowEvent;
typedef XCrossingEvent     XLeaveWindowEvent;
```

Expose

Description: These events are generated when a window or a previously covered part of a window becomes visible.

Event Mask: `ExposureMask`

Event Structure Name: `XExposeEvent`

```
typedef struct {
     int          type;
     unsigned long serial;     /* # of last request processed by server */
     Bool         send_event;/* true if this came from SendEvent request*/
     Display      *display;  /* display the event was read from */
     Window       window;
     int          x, y;
     int          width, height;
     int          count;     /* if nonzero, at least this many more */
     } XExposeEvent;
```

FocusIn, FocusOut

Description: These events are generated when a focus window changes.

Event Mask: `FocusChangeMask`

Event Structure Name: `XFocusChangeEvent`

```
typedef struct {
     int          type;      /* FocusIn or FocusOut */
     unsigned long serial;     /* # of last request processed by server */
     Bool         send_event;/* true if this came from SendEvent request*/
     Display      *display;  /* display the event was read from */
     Window       window;    /* window of event */
     int          mode;      /* NotifyNormal, NotifyGrab, NotifyUngrab */
     int          detail;    /* NotifyAncestor, NotifyVirtual,
                              * NotifyInferior, NotifyNonLinear,
                              * NotifyNonLinearVirtual, NotifyPointer,
                              * NotifyPointerRoot, NotifyDetailNone */
     } XFocusChangeEvent;

typedef XFocusChangeEvent     XFocusInEvent;
typedef XFocusChangeEvent     XFocusOutEvent;
```

GraphicsExpose, NoExpose

Description: When `GraphicsExpose` events occur, it means that the source area for an `XCopyPlane` or `XCopyArea` was not available. When `NoExpose` events occur, it means that the source area was completety available.

Event Mask: Selected in GC by `graphics_expose` member.

Event Structure Name: `XGraphicsExposeEvent`, `XNoExposeEvent`

```
typedef struct {
    int           type;
    unsigned long serial;     /* # of last request processed by server */
    Bool          send_event;/* true if this came from SendEvent request*/
    Display       *display;  /* display the event was read from */
    Drawable      drawable;
    int           x, y;
    int           width, height;
    int           count;     /* if nonzero, at least this many more */
    int           major_code;/* core is CopyArea or CopyPlane */
    int           minor_code;/* not defined in the core      */
    } XGraphicsExposeEvent;

typedef struct {
    int           type;
    unsigned long serial;     /* # of last request processed by server */
    Bool          send_event;/* true if this came from SendEvent request*/
    Display       *display;  /* display the event was read from */
    Drawable      drawable;
    int           count;     /* if nonzero, at least this many more */
    int           major_code;/* core is CopyArea or CopyPlane */
    int           minor_code;/* not defined in the core      */
    } XNoExposeEvent;
```

GravityNotify

Description: When a parent window's size was changed, thus necessitating the movement of a child window, `GravityNotify` events occur.

Event Mask: `StructureNotifyMask`

Event Structure Name: `XGravityEvent`

```
ypedef struct {
     int           type;
     unsigned long serial;     /* # of last request processed by server */
     Bool          send_event;/* true if this came from SendEvent request*/
     Display       *display;  /* display the event was read from */
     Window        event;
     Window        window;
     int           x, y;
     } XGravityEvent;
```

KeymapNotify

Description: An application is awakened through these events when a keyboard or pointer focus enters a window.

Event Mask: `KeymapStateMask`

Event Structure Name: `XKeymapEvent`

```
typedef struct {
     int           type;
     unsigned long serial;     /* # of last request processed by server */
     Bool          send_event;/* true if this came from SendEvent request*/
     Display       *display;  /* display the event was read from */
     Window        window;
     char          key_vector[32];
     } XKeymapEvent;
```

KeyPress, KeyRelease

Description: Another self-explanatory set of events. These are generated for all keys, including those generated through Meta-key combinations.

Event Mask: KeyPressMask, KeyPressRelease

Event Structure Name: XKeyEvent

```
typedef struct {
    int          type;       /* of event */
    unsigned long serial;    /* # of last request processed by server */
    Bool         send_event /* true if this came from SendEvent request*/
    Display      *display;  /* display the event was read from */
    Window       window;     /* event window it is reported relative to */
    Window       root;       /* root window that the event occurred on */
    Window       subwindow; /* child window */
    Time         time;       /* milliseconds */
    int          x, y;       /* pointer x, y coordinates in receiving window */
    int          x_root, y_root;/* coordinates relative to root */
    unsigned int state;      /* modifier key and button mask */
    unsigned int keycode;    /* server-dependent code for key */
    Bool         same_screen;   /* same screen flag*/
    } XKeyEvent;

typedef XKeyEvent   XKeyPressedEvent;
typedef XKeyEvent   XKeyReleasedEvent;
```

MapNotify, UnmapNotify

Description: When a window changes from mapped to unmapped (or vice versa), these events occur.

Event Mask: StructureNotifyMask

Event Structure Name: XMapEvent, XUnmapEvent

```
typedef struct {
    int          type;
    unsigned long serial;     /* # of last request processed by server */
    Bool         send_event;/* true if this came from SendEvent request*/
    Display      *display;   /* display the event was read from */
    Window       event;
    Window       window;
    Bool         override_redirect; /* Boolean, is override set */
    } XMapEvent;
```

```
typedef struct {
     int           type;
     unsigned long serial;     /* # of last request processed by server */
     Bool          send_event;/* true if this came from SendEvent request*/
     Display       *display;  /* display the event was read from */
     Window        event;
     Window        window;
     Bool          from_configure;
     } XUnmapEvent;
```

MappingNotify

Description: `MappingNotify` events are generated when another client makes changes in mapping functions.

Event Mask: Always selected.

Event Structure Name: `XMappingEvent`

```
typedef struct {
     int           type;
     unsigned long serial;     /* # of last request processed by server */
     Bool          send_event;/* true if this came from SendEvent request*/
     Display       *display;  /* display the event was read from */
     Window        event;     /* unused */
     int           request;   /* one of the MappingModifier,
                               * MappingKeyboard, MappingPointer */
     int           first_keycode;     /* first keycode */
     int           count;     /* range of change with first_keyboard */
     } XMappingEvent;
```

MapRequest

Description: These events occur when `XMapWindows` or `XMapSubwindows` is commanded to map a window.

Event Mask: `SubstructureRedirectMask`

Event Structure Name: `XMapRequestEvent`

```
typedef struct {
    int           type;
    unsigned long serial;     /* # of last request processed by server */
    Bool          send_event;/* true if this came from SendEvent request*/
    Display       *display;  /* display the event was read from */
    Window        parent;
    Window        window;
    } XMapRequestEvent;
```

MotionNotify

Description: Any change in a pointer is traced through these events.

Event Mask: PointerMotionMask, PointerMotionHintMask, ButtonMotionMask, Button1MotionMask, Button2MotionMask, Button3MotionMask, Button4MotionMask, Button5MotionMask

Event Structure Name: XPointerMovedEvent

```
typedef struct {
    int           type;       /* of event */
    unsigned long serial;     /* # of last request processed by server */
    Bool          send_event;/* true if this came from SendEvent request*/
    Display       *display;  /* display the event was read from */
    Window        window;     /* event window it is reported relative to */
    Window        root;       /* root window that the event occurred on */
    Window        subwindow; /* child window */
    Time          time;       /* milliseconds */
    int           x, y;       /* pointer coords in receiving window */
    int           x_root, y_root;/* coordinates relative to root */
    unsigned int  state;      /* button and modifier key mask */
    char          is_hint;    /* is this a motion hint */
    Bool          same_screen;/* same screen flag*/
    } XMotionEvent;

typedef XMotionEvent   XPointerMovedEvent;
```

PropertyNotify

Description: When any property on a window changes, these events are generated.

Event Mask: `PropertyChangeMask`

Event Structure Name: `XPropertyEvent`

```
typedef struct {
     int           type;
     unsigned long serial;     /* # of last request processed by server */
     Bool          send_event;/* true if this came from SendEvent request*/
     Display       *display;  /* display the event was read from */
     Window        window;
     Atom          atom;
     Time          time;
     int           state;      /* NewValue, Deleted */
     } XPropertyEvent
```

ReparentNotify

Description: Changes in a window's parent is tracked through these events.

Event Mask: `StructureNotifyMask`, `SubstructureNotifyMask`

Event Structure Name: `XReparentEvent`

```
typedef struct {
     int           type;
     unsigned long serial;     /* # of last request processed by server */
     Bool          send_event;/* true if this came from SendEvent request*/
     Display       *display;  /* display the event was read from */
     Window        event;
     Window        window;
     Window        parent;
     int           x, y;
     Bool          override_redirect;
     } XReparentEvent;
```

ResizeRequest

Description: These events occur when another client attempts to resize a window.

Event Mask: `ResizeRedirectMask`

Event Structure Name: `XResizeRequestEvent`

```
typedef struct {
    int           type;
    unsigned long serial;     /* # of last request processed by server */
    Bool          send_event;/* true if this came from SendEvent request*/
    Display       *display;  /* display the event was read from */
    Window        window;
    int           width, height;
    } XReparentEvent;
```

SelectionClear

Description: These events tell the owner of a selection that the ownership was lost.

Event Mask: Always selected.

Event Structure Name: `XSelectionClearEvent`

```
typedef struct {
    int           type;
    unsigned long serial;     /* # of last request processed by server */
    Bool          send_event;/* true if this came from SendEvent request*/
    Display       *display;  /* display the event was read from */
    Window        window;
    Atom          selection;
    Time          time;
    } XSelectionClearEvent;
```

SelectionNotify

Description: A client sends these events to another client that requested a selection's data, signifying whether or not the selection data on version was made.

Event Mask: Always selected.

Event Structure Name: XSelectionEvent

```
typedef struct {
    int           type;
    unsigned long serial;     /* # of last request processed by server */
    Bool          send_event;/* true if this came from SendEvent request*/
    Display       *display;  /* display the event was read from */
    Window        requester; /* must be next after type */
    Atom          selection;
    Atom          target;
    Atom          property;  /* Atom or none */
    Time          time;
    } XSelectionEvent;
```

SelectionRequest

Description: These events notify the owner of a selection that another X client program requests the selection data.

Event Mask: Always selected.

Event Structure Name: XSelectionRequestEvent

```
typedef struct {
    int           type;
    unsigned long serial;     /* # of last request processed by server */
    Bool          send_event;/* true if this came from SendEvent request*/
    Display       *display;  /* display the event was read from */
    Window        owner;      /* must be next after type */
    Window        requester;
    Atom          selection;
    Atom          target;
    Atom          property;
    Time          time;
    } XSelectionRequestEvent;
```

VisibilityNotify

Description: These events are generated when a window's visibility is changed. This does not include changes in any subwindows.

Event Mask: `VisibilityChangeMask`

Event Structure Name: `XVisibilityEvent`

```
typedef struct {
    int           type;
    unsigned long serial;     /* # of last request processed by server */
    Bool          send_event;/* true if this came from SendEvent request*/
    Display       *display;  /* display the event was read from */
    Window        window;
    int           state;      /* either Obscured or UnObscured */
    } XVisibilityEvent;
```

Appendix C

SOME SAMPLE X CLIENT PROGRAMS

The X release from the MIT X Consortium comes with literally megabytes of X software. Much of the material was contributed by X users around the world. It's a good idea to take a look at some of the programs, especially if you have the source code. Looking at actual working examples of X code can obviously help improve your code and show how to avoid some of the traps and pitfalls inherent in X.

In addition to the contributed code, the base, or core, release contains a number of handy X utilities. Below, a few of these X utility programs are introduced. Feel free to experiment and play with these programs. The utilities mentioned here have proven to be very helpful to the authors for programming X and doing things like getting printouts of X window graphics. These are not the most glamorous X programs, merely among the most useful.

NOTE: If your system has been set up properly (and you are running under the UNIX operating system) these programs should be explained in the online manual pages. At the command prompt (%), try typing:

```
% man bitmap
```

or:

```
% man xwd
```

and see if the manual "pages" are loaded on your system.

BITMAP

The bitmap editor edits ASCII bitmap files, just like the Draw application introduced in Section 2. `bitmap` enlarges the pictures it edits, so that you can better draw the small, detailed parts of small bitmap files. The R5 bitmap program stands head and shoulders above all previous incarnations.

XDPYINFO

`xdpyinfo` stands for X Display Information. This program provides information about the display, screen, and X server you are using, much like the `chap1` program. `xdpyinfo` can give you information about whether the server supports color, what kind of byte-ordering is in use (normally Intel or Motorola ordering, although usually called something else), and so on. `xdpyinfo` displays its output to `stdout` (or an xterm window for the rest of us).

XEV

`xev` is a program that puts a window on the screen and then prints out (to an xterm window, for example) information about each event the window receives from the X server. This program is useful for showing the way events are sent to an application and for testing new keyboards to see what the X server thinks the keys you press really are. Try out the program and start typing keys (see if you can find the Help key, for example). `xev` is a real help when you first start working with events in X, especially when dealing with numeric keypads.

Some (edited) sample output of xev appears below.

```
PropertyNotify event, serial 4, synthetic NO, window 0x700001,
 atom 0x27 (WM_NAME), time 660526368, state PropertyNewValue

CreateNotify event, serial 7, synthetic NO, window 0x700001,
 parent 0x700001, window 0x700002, (10,10), width 50, height 50
 border_width 4, override NO

MapNotify event, serial 8, synthetic NO, window 0x700001,
 event 0x700001, window 0x700002, override NO

EnterNotify event, serial 9, synthetic NO, window 0x700001,
 root 0x8006b, subw 0x0, time 660526368, (0,60), root:(102,162),
 mode NotifyNormal, detail NotifyNonlinear, same_screen YES,
 focus NO, state 0

Expose event, serial 9, synthetic NO, window 0x700001,
 (0,0), width 178, height 10, count 3

MotionNotify event, serial 12, synthetic NO, window 0x700001,
 root 0x8006b, subw 0x0, time 660529456, (0,59), root:(102,161),
 state 0x0, is_hint 1, same_screen YES

LeaveNotify event, serial 12, synthetic NO, window 0x700001,
 root 0x8006b, subw 0x700002, time 660529632, (15,60), root:(117,162),
 mode NotifyNormal, detail NotifyInferior, same_screen YES,
 focus YES, state 0

ButtonPress event, serial 12, synthetic NO, window 0x700001,
 root 0x8006b, subw 0x0, time 660530112, (80,67), root:(182,169),
 state 0x0, button 1, same_screen YES

ButtonRelease event, serial 12, synthetic NO, window 0x700001,
 root 0x8006b, subw 0x0, time 660530272, (80,67), root:(182,169),
 state 0x100, button 1, same_screen YES

KeyPress event, serial 14, synthetic NO, window 0x700001,
 root 0x8006b, subw 0x0, time 660567968, (90,49), root:(202,354),
 state 0x1, keycode 8 (keysym 0x41, A), same_screen YES,
 XLookupString gives 1 characters: "A"
```

```
KeyRelease event, serial 14, synthetic NO, window 0x700001,
 root 0x8006b, subw 0x0, time 660568144, (90,49), root:(202,354),
 state 0x1, keycode 8 (keysym 0x41, A), same_screen YES,
 XLookupString gives 1 characters: "A"
```

Even though this output was highly edited to reduce space, notice also how KeyPress events are usually followed by KeyRelease events.

XFD

The output of the X Font Display program, `xfd`, has been discussed previously in the section on cursors. `xfd` puts up a window and displays the characters in font, with each character in a box in the `xfd` window. It is normally useful for digging through the font files in your system, especially for deciding what font would look best for an application program to use. The X utility `xlsfonts` (X List Fonts) will display a list of the font names available to your server. The Release 5 font server provides a slew of new fonts to play with.

XWD

`xwd` is the X Window Dumper. It dumps the pixels in a window to disk in a special, weird `XImage` format. `xwd` is next to useless by itself, but it comes with a few other programs that also understand the `xwd XImage` format. `xwud`, for example, will redraw the dumped window back onto the screen. This is not always particularly useful, but `xwud` can be used to verify the contents of the file.

`xpr`, though, is much better. `xpr` will print out a `xwd`-format file (made by dumping the contents of a window to disk, by `xwd`). Unfortunately, though, `xpr` only supports a few printer types.

PBM

`PBM`, the portable bitmap library, comes with a set of programs to convert graphic image files to and from the `PBM` canonical format. The basic `PBM` format is an ASCII format for monochrome bitmap images (there are color and gray-scale formats as well). An ASCII-based format takes up a lot more disk space than conventional image formats, but ASCII has proved to be the only truly portable format for file exchange between diverse systems (for example, this book was written using UNIX workstations, Macintoshes, and IBM PCs).

The program `xwdtopbm` converts an `xwd` file to a `PBM` file. Once in the `PBM` format, we could convert the file to a number of other image formats, including MacPaint files, Sun raster files, and much more.

XWININFO

`xwininfo`, X Window Information, provides information about a given window. It is normally run from the command line in an xterm window (like `xdpyinfo`). `xwininfo` will change the mouse cursor to a crosshair and then ask you to click a mouse button in any window on the display. `xwininfo` then gives information about the window you selected. Because `xwininfo` provides the coordinate location and size for windows, the program is a handy tool to help you place windows, especially the windows that you want to appear when you start up the X server.

Appendix D

WHAT YOU NEED TO RUN X

A common question comes from people who want to run X, but don't know the proper hardware or software setups.

Unfortunately, there are no shrink-wrap X packages on the market, where you simply throw a diskette in the drive and—voila!—X appears on your screen. The most common way that people acquire X is by purchasing a UNIX system of some sort that comes bundled with X. In these cases, it's simply not a matter of learning X—it's a matter of learning UNIX at the same time. This isn't an insurmountable task by any stretch—but be warned that an inexperienced computer user will put in a lot of work before ever reaching the X level.

For those of us without a Cray or a DEC VAX in our office, it's a matter of obtaining a workstation or PC with the firepower to run X. There are three basic paths to an X system: buy a UNIX workstation, an X terminal, or software to turn a personal computer (Macintosh or PC) into an X terminal. If you go the X terminal route, you'll also need another computer on a network that can run X applications (X terminals just provide the X server—not the most interesting of applications. You'll also need a host computer from which to run X client applications.)

If your budget allows, purchasing a workstation is the most simple solution. (Our personal budgets, alas, don't allow this, but our employers' budgets do.) Workstations from Data General, Hewlett-Packard, Motorola, DEC, IBM, Sun, and others all come bundled with X. Such a workstation (equipped with hard disk and tape or CD-ROM to load in software) will set you back about $10,000 at the low end, but it's an invaluable tool if you're a professional software developer, analyst, or designer. As versions of UNIX mature for the 386/486 market, a personal UNIX workstation is coming closer and closer to reality. SCO, Interactive, Everex, and Mt. Xinu all offer X and UNIX (or Mach, in the case of Mt. Xinu) for 386/486 IBM-compatibles.

Our experience shows that a workstation is still beyond the reach of a good portion of potential users. A lower-priced (and a lower-performing, alas) alternative is to configure a PC to run X by turning it into an X terminal or running X under UNIX. This can be a simple solution, but not every PC is equipped to run X.

First of all, you'll want to configure a PC as an X server. In theory, say some vendors and magazines, you can use an 80286, 80386, or 80486 system equipped with 640K of RAM, a monochrome display, a networking card, and X software.

Theory, though, falls short when it comes to performance. Reality dictates at least an 80386 or 80486 with eight megabytess of RAM, a very large hard drive (at least 200MB is good, 200+MB is better)—if you're running UNIX—and a large-screen color display. When running graphics-intensive programs on top of UNIX, the more power the better. With hardware prices (particularly in the RAM and 80386 fields) dropping rapidly, you're looking at a speed demon for under $6,000.

SOFTWARE

The software you choose dictates your ultimate hardware configuration. For PC, there are two software routes: X server software running under DOS or UNIX configurations that support X.

DOS and Windows X servers, like PC Xview from Spectagraphics, Desqview/X from Quarterdeck, Locus's PC Xsight, or Hummingbird's eXceed/plus essentially turns your DOS PC into an X terminal. Unless you have a fairly high-end PC with a fast graphics card and lots of memory, performance will not be very good. Note that X feels very confining with a monitor under 14 inches in size or 800x600 pixels in resolution. And, you'll still need another computer on the network to run X applications.

On PCs, our experience has been with versions of UNIX from Interactive Systems, Everex, SCO, Mt. Xinu, and Apple, as well as Hummingbird's DOS X terminal software. In addition, IBM supports X under AIX. Since X draws some features (in part) from the operating system underneath it, it seems like a good idea to use the power of UNIX if it's available.

If you're an Apple fan, A/UX will run Macintosh applications and X applications (via MacX)—a big, big bonus. You'll need a high-end Macintosh to run it (the IIfx is a perfect, if disgustingly expensive, choice). In addition, White Pine Systems offers eXodus, which allows you to open X windows within the Macintosh operating system.

CPUs

We're experienced with PCs, workstations, and Macintoshes. Again, more is better—more megahertz and more RAM. The amount of RAM needed will depend on the software—some PC versions of UNIX require a minimum of four megabytes, while others (like AIX) require eight. If you can afford it, don't buy the minimum—buy as much RAM as your checkbook allows. Eight megabytes is a realistic minimum for a system that runs UNIX and X. Sixteen megs is a lot better. Release 4 of the X Window System requires less RAM and provides much better performance than R3. R5, though, adds new complexity but better support for shared libraries. Unfortunately, few vendors have upgraded their X offerings to Release 4 as of this writing—never mind Release 5.

Using a 386 or a 486 as an X server also allows the users to run DOS applications. While we're not huge fans of DOS, there are some applications in DOS that don't have counterparts in the X world.

In addition, there's a version of X that runs under AmigaDOS from GfxBase. We can neither recommend it nor argue against it, but it's worth checking out.

MONITORS/GRAPHICS CARDS

Since X is a graphic windowing product, your monitor's resolution is important. Again, the more power the better.

You'll need a minimum of 640x480 resolution (VGA). This is probably the minimum usable for X—in other words, you'll hate it. Better yet is Super VGA (800x600 or 1024x768) or 8514/A (1024x768). High-end monitors cost more—

you'll need to pay extra for both the monitor and graphics card—but they can increase performance because part of the X server can be loaded onto the card's limited memory. Your CPU doesn't have to work as hard, thus speeding up your system.

When putting together your system, make sure that your software supports your particular graphics card. UNIX systems tend to be fussy about hard drives, graphics cards, and tape drives. Always write for a compatibility list from your UNIX vendor before putting together a system.

HARD DRIVES

There's only one rule to remember about hard drives: the bigger the better. A 200MB drive is the minimum—especially with UNIX—while 330MB is better. If you can afford a high-performance Wren drive, go for it.

NETWORKING CARD

Most DOS X implementations won't work without a networking card of some sort. The software you choose will ultimately depend on your networking needs and software compatibility.

X TERMINALS

If you already have a networked workstation in your business, you may want to look at dedicated X terminals. Several vendors, such as DEC, Hewlett-Packard, IBM, NCD, Tektronix, and Princeton Graphics, sell X terminals. These terminals are usually built around a Motorola 680X0 and come equipped with one and two megabytes of RAM and the necessarily networking equipment. Lately, RISC chips have become all the rage. The actual processor doesn't matter, as long as the X terminal provides a snappy performance.

Because X is graphics-intensive, you'll want as much RAM as you can afford on an X terminal. These terminals aren't cheap—between $1,500 and $6,000 (and beyond)—but can be a bargain when compared to X workstations. One benefit of X terminals over workstations is that X terminals are easier to administer. One drawback of X terminals is the increased load you place on a few hosts, because X terminals run just the X server software, you always need other computers to run the X applications. The recent trend in X terminals, though, is for the X terminals to offer some local applications, especially window managers. We predict that X terminals will grow to look more like diskless workstations and that workstations will grow to look more like X terminals.

Appendix E

OBTAINING X

The good folks at MIT and Project Athena make it amazingly easy to obtain the X Window System. They also put very few strings on it—you don't need to license X or pay royalties, and developers are encouraged to use X as a development tool.

There are three ways to obtain the X Window System: directly from MIT, through Internet and UUCP, or from commercial consulting firms and vendors.

MIT SOFTWARE DISTRIBUTION CENTER

MIT sells X, along with printed manuals and X Window System: *The Complete Reference to Xlib, X Protocol, ICCCM, XLFD*, Second Edition, (see Appendix F). X comes on a set of 1600bpi or QIC-24 tapes in UNIX tar format. You can write:

> **MIT Software Distribution Center**
> **Technology Licensing Office**
> **Room E32-300**
> **77 Massachusetts Ave.**
> **Cambridge, MA 02139**
> **or call 617/258-8330 (the X Ordering Hotline)**

You can also pick up the latest X11 release from a number of archive sites on the Internet or via UUCP from UUNET. It is generally easier on everybody concerned if you pick up X from the closest Internet archive site.

There are many, many commercial firms offering X in one form or another; a quick glance through the ads in *UNIX Review* or another UNIX magazine will yield many possibilities.

In addition, the following workstation and software vendors include the X Window System in their products: AT&T, Apple, Bull, DEC, Data General, Everex, Hewlett-Packard, IBM, Interactive Systems, Motorola, Mt. Xinu, NCR, SCO, Solbourne, Sony, Sun Microsystems, and many more every day.

Appendix F

FOR MORE INFORMATION

This book is an introductory look at the X Window System for people unfamiliar with X, and, as such, it does not include more advanced and in-depth discussions of some of X's capabilities. After reading this book, you should be ready to program X applications. If you're looking for more advanced material, you could check one of the X references listed below or in our advanced book.

Advanced X Window Applications Programming. Eric F. Johnson and Kevin Reichard. MIS: Press, 1990.

Our advanced book carries on where the book you have in your hands leaves off. We've included long sections on following the rules for well-behaved X applications, opening connections to multiple displays, and inter-process communication using selections.

X Window System: The Complete Reference to Xlib, X Protocol, ICCCM, XLFD, Second Edition. Robert Scheifler and Jim Gettys, with Jim Flowers, Ron Newman, and David Rosenthal. Digital Press, 1990.

The definitive reference work regarding the Xlib functions and protocol spec from some of the principal creators of X. This is essentially an enhanced version of the Xlib manual from Release 4. You won't find any real introductory information here about X, and some of it is written over most users' heads, which makes it ideal for advanced X programmers. The X11 Release 5 distribution contains much of this book online (updated to R5).

Xlib Programming Manual, volume 1. Adrian Nye. O'Reilly and Associates, 1990.

Xlib Programming Manual, volume 2. O'Reilly and Associates, 1990.

X Window System User's Guide. Tim O'Reilly, Valerie Quercia, Linda Lamb. O'Reilly and Associates, 1990.

These three volumes are based directly on the MIT documentation, and as a result some of the prose is lifted directly from the official manuals. Volume Two, a reference for all X calls, is probably the best of the lot.

Introduction to the X Window System. Oliver Jones. Prentice-Hall, 1989.

This is another introductory book to Xlib programming by a veteran X programmer. After an excellent introduction, Jones jumps in quickly with some complex programs and examples. Like any good X programming instructor, Jones includes a major Hello World program as his beginning application.

Developing Software for the User Interface. Len Bass and Joelle Coutaz. Addison-Wesley, 1991.

Designing the User Interface. Ben Shneiderman. Addison-Wesley, 1987.

User Interface Design. Harold Thimbleby. Addison-Wesley, 1990.

These three books are good examples of a burgeoning field of user interface design books. All provide good ideas on how to make your programs better interact with the user.

Computer Graphics: Principles and Practice, Second Edition. James D. Foley, Andries van Dam, Steven K. Feiner and John F. Hughes, Addison-Wesley, 1990.

This book forms an excellent introduction to the computer graphics and has a long section on advanced color, including the CIE color space.

MIT Project Athena: A Model for Distributed Campus Computing. George A. Champne, Digital Press, 1991.

The X Window System grew out of work done at MIT for Project Athena.

Inter-Client Communications Conventions Manual 1.1. David Rosenthal, 1991.

This document describes in cryptic detail how well-behaved X applications should act. Every X application developer should read this document, which should be available with the documentation provided by your X vendor.

Finally, your X System installation comes with some select articles; look in the doc directory for them. Also, for further programming tips check out the clients directory and look at sample programs like *xbiff* and *oclock*. Examining other peoples' code will help you out.

Appendix G

COMPANION SOURCE CODE DISKETTE FOR X WINDOW APPLICATIONS PROGRAMMING

We've put together a companion source-code diskette for *X Window Applications Programming* containing all the example programs in the book. This diskette is an MS-DOS-formatted disk containing the C sources in ASCII files.

All files on the source-code diskette should be straight ASCII files. When you transfer these files to a UNIX machine, you probably want to convert the filenames to lower case (except for the Makefile). There are no special subdirectories, so all files should be in the root directory.

To use the source-code diskette, you will need some way to transfer these files from the DOS-formatted diskette to your X development system. You can look at kermit, Ethernet FTP, or NFS or read the DOS diskette directly on your UNIX box. (Many UNIX workstations, such as the Sun SPARCStation-2, come with a disk drive and software that can read DOS-formatted diskettes.) Use the ad in the back of this book to order.

Index

Products are listed under manufacturers.

D

— E —

H

I

—Q—

—R—

S

Z